The Politics of Belonging in India

D1744563

Since the 1990s, the Indigenous movement worldwide has become increasingly relevant to research in India, re-shaping the terms of engagement with Adivasi (Indigenous/tribal) peoples and their pasts. This book responds to the growing need for an inter-disciplinary re-assessment of Tribal studies in postcolonial India and defines a new agenda for Adivasi studies. It considers the existing conceptual and historical parameters of Tribal studies, as a means of addressing new approaches to histories of de-colonisation and patterns of identity-formation that have become visible since national independence.

Contributors address a number of important concerns, including the meaning of Indigenous studies in the context of globalised academic and political imaginaries, and the possibilities and pitfalls of constructions of indigeneity as both a foundational and a relational concept. A series of short editorial essays provide theoretical clarity to issues of representation, resistance, agency, recognition and marginality. The book is an essential read for students and scholars of Indian Sociology, Anthropology, History, Cultural Studies and Indigenous studies.

Daniel J. Rycroft is Lecturer in South Asian Arts and Cultures at the School of World Art Studies and Museology, University of East Anglia, UK.

Sangeeta Dasgupta is Assistant Professor at the Centre for Historical Studies, Jawaharlal Nehru University, India.

Routledge contemporary South Asia series

The Politics of Belonging in India

Becoming Adivasi

Edited by Daniel J. Rycroft and
Sangeeta Dasgupta

Routledge
Taylor & Francis Group

LONDON AND NEW YORK

First published 2011
by Routledge
2 Park Square, Milton Park, Abingdon, Oxon OX14 4RN

Simultaneously published in the USA and Canada
by Routledge
711 Third Avenue, New York, NY 10017

Routledge is an imprint of the Taylor & Francis Group, an informa business

British Library Cataloguing in Publication Data
A catalogue record for this book is available from the British Library

Library of Congress Cataloging-in-Publication Data
The politics of belonging in India : becoming Adivasi / edited by Daniel J. Rycroft and Sangeeta Dasgupta.
  p. cm. – (Routledge contemporary South Asia series)
  Includes bibliographical references and index.
  1. Adivasis–Ethnic identity. 2. Adivasis–Social conditions. 3. Group identity–India. 4. India–Ethnic relations. 5. India–Social conditions, I. Rycroft, Daniel J. II. Dasgupta, Sangeeta.
  DS432.A2P65 2011
  305.800954–dc22
  2010040882
ISBN: 978-0-415-74868-1 (pbk)
ISBN: 978-0-415-60082-8 (hbk)
ISBN: 978-0-203-82601-0 (ebk)
Typeset in Times
by Wearset Ltd, Boldon, Tyne and Wear

First issued in paperback in 2013

To our families

Contents

Maps

Contributors

Roma Chatterji is Professor at the Department of Sociology, Delhi School of Economics, Delhi University. Apart from an abiding interest in folklore and narrative traditions, she has also worked on medical anthropology and collective violence. She is the author of *Writing identities: Folklore and the Performative Traditions of Purulia* and co-author of *Living with Violence: An Anthropology of Events and Everyday Life*. She has recently completed a project entitled 'Speaking Pictures: Folk art and the narrative tradition', funded by the India Foundation of the Arts.

Vinita Damodaran is the Director of the Centre for World Environmental History at the University of Sussex where she also teaches. She is a historian of modern India whose interests range from social and political history to environmental history. She has published numerous articles and books, and is engaged in enhancing the profile of South Asian studies and Environmental History at the University of Sussex.

Sangeeta Dasgupta is Assistant Professor at the Centre for Historical Studies, Jawaharlal Nehru University, New Delhi. Her research interests include Adivasi history, colonial ethnography, missionary studies and visual representations, and she is presently exploring issues of ethnicity through cross-cultural studies of India and Africa. She has published several articles in journals and edited books.

Abhijit Guha is Reader in Anthropology at Vidyasagar University, West Bengal. He has published many articles, book reviews, comments and book chapters. He has also written a book on land acquisition. He was a Visiting Fellow at the Department of Sociology, Delhi School of Economics.

Bengt G. Karlsson is Associate Professor in Social Anthropology at Stockholm University. He is the author of *Contested Belonging: An Indigenous People's Struggle for Forest and Identity in Sub-Himalayan Bengal* and *Unruly Hills: Nature and Nation in India's Northeast*. He has also edited two books, *Indigeneity in India* and *Human Rights: An Anthropological Enquiry*.

Darley Jose Kjosavik is Associate Professor at the Department of International Environment and Development Studies, Norwegian University of Life Sciences. She has an interdisciplinary academic background and her research interests include political economy of development with special reference to marginalised social groups, gender and development, conflict and development, climate change and development. She is currently involved in development research in South Asia, Africa and Latin America.

David Mosse is Professor of Social Anthropology at the School of Oriental and African Studies, University of London. He researches the anthropology of development, environmental history and natural resources management, and South Asian society and popular religion. He specialises in the ethnography of aid, international development and global governance, and has recently published *The Aid Effect* and *Brokers and Translators*. These works are a continuation of his studies of DfID policy and practice and his analyses of rural livelihoods development in western India, which have been published as *Cultivating Development*.

Amit Prakash is Associate Professor at the Centre for the Study of Law and Governance, Jawaharlal Nehru University, New Delhi. He has also served as Assistant Research Professor at the Centre for Policy Research, New Delhi. He has published in areas of politics of development; dynamics of socio-political and ethnic identity mobilization and its inter-linkages with the processes of public policy; Indian politics; governance and development; and global governance.

Daniel J. Rycroft is Lecturer in South Asian Arts and Cultures at the School of World Art Studies and Museology, University of East Anglia, Norwich. In 2006, he published *Representing Rebellion: Visual Aspects of Counter-insurgency in Colonial India*. He is currently joint editor of *World Art* (Routledge journals), and is also researching a monograph on anthropological flows pertaining to Adivasis in pre-independence India.

Tanika Sarkar is Professor at the Centre for Historical Studies, Jawaharlal Nehru University, New Delhi. She has published widely on gender, religion and society. Her latest books include *Hindu Wife, Hindu Nation* and *Rebels, Wives, Saints*. She has also edited *Women and Social Reform in Modern India*.

Asoka Kumar Sen is retired Professor of History and is presently an independent researcher in tribal history. His publications include *The Educated Middle Class and Indian Nationalism*; *Bengali Intelligentsia and Popular Uprisings 1855–73; Wilkinson's Rules, Context, Content and Ramifications* (as editor) and *Representing Tribe: The Ho of Singhbhum during Colonial Rule*.

Alpa Shah is Senior Lecturer in Anthropology at Goldsmiths College, University of London. She is the author of *In the Shadows of the State: Indigenous Politics, Environmentalism and Insurgency in Jharkhand, India*.

Willem van Schendel is Professor of Modern Asian History at the University of Amsterdam and heads the Asia Department of the International Institute of Social History. His most recent book is *A History of Bangladesh*.

Preface

This volume was conceptualised in 2006–7 as a response to the need for an inter-disciplinary re-assessment of Tribal studies in modern India. The volume engages in this process by defining a new field of Adivasi studies. As such, it prompts a review of the political and sociological categories of 'tribe' and 'Indigenous peoples'. This reconsideration is driven by the relevance of the Indigenous movement worldwide to current research in India. With the United Nations Declaration of the International Decade of the World's Indigenous Peoples in 1994, the Indigenous movement has influenced Adivasi self-perception and self-representation. Literally meaning original (*adi*) inhabitants (*vasi*), Adivasi self-identification as Indigenous peoples, or as 'Indigenous/tribal', has wide-ranging conceptual and ideological ramifications.

The move for Adivasi studies is also informed by the need to work beyond a critical impasse that has emerged in Tribal studies. In this largely nation-centric anthropological, historical and developmental discourse, identities and histories are often re-cast in essentialist ways, bypassing important facets of Adivasi subjectivity. In global terms, Indigenous studies has facilitated a particular type of anti-colonialist critique that brings together strands of radical and community-oriented scholarship, with movements for socio-political transformation, anti-racism, Indigenous knowledge and de-centralised governance. Also, since the 1980s, shifts in historiographic practice in India have ushered in new disciplinary formations and new analytical concepts that can be applied to more purposeful assessments. Recognising the multiplicity of events, sites and representations that infuse the discourses through which Indigenous or Adivasi subjectivity is, and has been, constructed and negotiated, as editors we intend to suggest various possibilities for Adivasi studies.

Our contributors discern the disciplinary implications of Adivasi studies, both in terms of its methods and approaches and its relations with other existing fields, such as Tribal studies, Subaltern studies and Indigenous studies. Such themes became evident at the symposia that we organised in 2005–6. As Research Fellow at the University of Sussex, Daniel Rycroft hosted an international conference on 'Re-interpreting Adivasi Movements in South Asia' (March 2005, Centre for World Environmental History). As Visiting Fellow at St Antony's College, University of Oxford, Sangeeta Dasgupta co-organised an international conference on

'Contesting Identities: Tribes, Indigenous Peoples and Adivasis in India' (November 2005, Department of History, Visva Bharati). Contributors to these conferences – which marked the 150th anniversary of the Hul or 'Santal rebellion' of 1855–6, a critical event in studies of Adivasi pasts – addressed the following concerns: the meaning of Indigenous studies in the context of globalised academic and political imaginaries; the possibilities and pitfalls of constructions of indigeneity as both a foundational and a relational concept; new approaches to Adivasi historiography; the politics of historical representation and collective memory; the interface between Adivasi activism and academic discourse; and the environmental aspects of Adivasi protest and identity.

These conferences formed part of the wider 'Santal Hul 150 Forum', which Daniel Rycroft had convened in association with Dr D. Mardi (Secretary General, Indian Confederation of Indigenous and Tribal Peoples – ICITP) on the occasion of the 150th anniversary of the Hul. The forum, lasting from March 2005 to June 2006, also encompassed the production and screening of a documentary film on the Hul (in association with ICITP); a mass *padayatra* (foot march) from Dumka to Bhognadih in the Santal Parganas area of Jharkhand state involving diasporic Santals (a large Adivasi community); numerous Adivasi assemblies organised by affiliate groups of the ICITP network; various other academic seminars; and popular/media publications and broadcasts. The forum aimed to reinstate forms of testimonial historiography, commemoration and justice that correspond with other social movements in India and other Indigenous movements worldwide.

By bringing together the work of contributors to the study of Adivasi-related history, anthropology and activism, this volume is evidence of our shared commitment to creating new kinds of intellectual enquiry. In our introductory essays we elaborate a range of analytical threads for our readers to consider the depth, complexity and vitality of the field of Adivasi studies. As editors, we anticipate that *The Politics of Belonging in India: Becoming Adivasi* will cultivate critical interest in wide-ranging readerships: from subaltern historians to cultural anthropologists; environmentalists to development planners; research students to political activists. Through this volume we propose that it is necessary for members of related disciplines to re-engage in critical dialogue and learn anew from each other, to take stock of the various trends that have defined Adivasi-oriented studies in recent years, and to further enhance the field of Adivasi studies.

Daniel Rycroft, UEA, Norwich
Sangeeta Dasgupta, JNU, New Delhi
August 2010

Hul Johar/Acknowledgements

In editing this book, we have journeyed through a difficult and yet rewarding terrain. A combined total of two new jobs, four house moves and five young children have in equal measure tested and enriched our intellectual and organisational skills. We are therefore enormously grateful to the authors who have remained committed to the 'Becoming Adivasi' project since their participation in the series of conferences that we organised in 2005 with a view to re-thinking the field of Tribal studies. Their vibrant approaches have enabled this book to exist. The unstinting support of colleagues at the Department of Art History and the Centre for World Environmental History (University of Sussex) and the faculty and students of the Department of History (Visva Bharati), where these conferences were held, deserve our warm thanks, as do the participants who made the conferences so memorable. We also recognise the urgency of the Adivasi movement in India, and the Indigenous movement internationally, in opening up new questions which demand ongoing and widespread recognition, hence our 'Hul Johar'.

In writing our editorial essays, we have benefited from the insightful comments of Padmanabh Samarendra, Rohan D'Souza, Elizabeth Prevost, Radhika Singha and M.S.S. Pandian. We would like to express our sincere appreciation to Mary Rycroft for proofreading the essays included in this volume, and to Neeladri Bhattacharya for his advice on several matters. In finalising our manuscript, we have built upon the valuable suggestions made by the anonymous readers from Routledge. We have found in our team of publishers an innovative and dynamic approach to Asian studies, and a capacity for organisational excellence.

It has been a delight to work amidst vibrant discussions with colleagues at the School of World Art Studies and Museology (University of East Anglia), and the Centre for Historical Studies (Jawaharlal Nehru University). The students on our courses – such as 'Indigenous Arts and Indigenous Peoples' and ' "Tribes" and History: Categories, Communities and Practices' – have helped us to rethink many of the ideas that we have explored in the volume. Daniel Rycroft would like to thank the respondents at various symposia, such as 'Seeking Bridges between Anthropology and Indigenous Studies' (Oxford Brookes University), who have helped him conceptualize interdisciplinary themes. Sangeeta Dasgupta would like to thank the Ministry for Human Resource Development and St Antony's College, Oxford, for the Agatha Harrison Memorial Fellowship, which made a break from teaching possible, to work on our editorial collaborations.

To our families, a huge 'thank you': Nicki, Lily, Juna and Bay (Rycroft), and Baba, Ma, Padmanabh, Ishan and Ayan (Dasgupta) have, despite their difficulties with our long absences, given us the greatest of support.

Most importantly, we are of course indebted to you, the unknown reader, for considering the book worthy of your time. We hope that through your engagement with the ideas put forward, the proposed field of Adivasi studies will gain a critical standing in the future.

1 Indigenous pasts and the politics of belonging

Daniel J. Rycroft and Sangeeta Dasgupta

Concept of Adivasi

Subjectivity is a central and commonplace analytical theme in the humanities and the social sciences (see Werbner 2002). Studies of subjectivity enable the grounds upon which collective identities are constructed to be revisited, affirmed or contested. Such journeys prompt a re-engagement with the dynamics of, and interface between, political, cultural and academic representations. The idea of Adivasi subjectivity is one that sustains the research that many of the contributors to this book have engaged in. This concept both corresponds with and disrupts the more recognisable 'tribal' identity that often appears in academic and activist writings, and is also enshrined in the constitution of independent India. Whilst tribal identity does have a bearing on 'being Adivasi', it does not chart an accurate or a particularly credible trajectory. The concept of Adivasi, in contrast, implies a range of historically defined, contested and mediated indigeneities, which cannot be apprehended through the reified notion of 'tribe'. The notion of Adivasi brings together two political genealogies: that of the mobilisation of Adivasis within the context of de-colonisation in India, and of the presence of Adivasis as indigenous peoples within the contemporary global arena (Xaxa 1999). Given the heterogeneity of Adivasi experiences of imperialism and modernity, one may accurately broach these issues by introducing the idea of multiple Adivasi subjectivities. This notion refers to Richard Werbner's discussion of plural 'inter-subjectivities' (Werbner 2002: 1).

The word Adivasi is a Hindi term that literally means (descendents of the) 'original inhabitants' of a given place (Xaxa 1999: 3590; Karlsson and Subba 2006). The term is uneven, having different connotations in terms of the people-place relationships, referring to wide-ranging topographies and inhabitations. As noted by S. Bosu Mullick (2003: iv–xvii), it was first used in a political context in the Jharkhand region of eastern India, with the formation of the Adivasi Mahasabha (the Great Council of Adivasis) in 1938. Colonial administrators and non-tribal nationalists also mobilised the term in the 1940s, but most debates at that time relied on existing categories of tribe and aboriginal (see Hardiman 1987: 13; Banerjee 2006).[1] The term is now often translated as 'Indigenous and Tribal Peoples' to resonate with the inclusive agenda of the transnational

Indigenous movement, which situates tribal specificity and local autochthony in directly political relationships to statehood, globalisation, sub-nationalism, etc. As such, it becomes embroiled in a host of historical and representational contests and controversies, which being both India-specific and more universal, merit close analysis.

Being a relatively new concept, the idea of 'Adivasi' can be unpacked to reveal political and representational tensions that can be re-read and re-articulated in wide-ranging activist and academic contexts. The ideas of racial difference and cultural distinctiveness, which have come to underscore Adivasi ethnicity, previously gained legibility through both ethnographic representations of India's 'aboriginal tribes and castes', and official responses to anti-colonial movements led by, and including, these communities (Bates 1995). Subaltern societies subsequently gained some visibility as tribal peoples, and certain customary laws were inscribed within post-insurgency administrative milieus (Singh 1993). Exponents of radical historiography and Indigenous studies have since reinterpreted these conflicts within identity movements, thereby enhancing Adivasi articulations of community consciousness and related 'recognition' claims.[2] Memories of these movements provided opportunities to fashion political foundations as Adivasi, and through these the means to negotiate the political realities of the imminent nation. Adivasi subjectivity engages the earlier colonial-era and the post-independence phases and therefore brings multiple historical and ideological coordinates into dialogue.

As indigeneity is asserted via the Adivasi concept and encountered in varied contexts, the concept of the 'tribe', with essentialist notions of difference, becomes somewhat less visible. Whilst critics of the indigeneity/Adivasi concepts may contend that these terms are also prone to essentialisation, as terms that can relate to national and global communities they are open to re-interpretation (and instrumentalisation) in ways that primordial categories, such as tribe, are not. Whereas the 'tribal' political and cultural formations may continue to operate locally, it is indigeneity that assumes a more politicised content (Karlsson and Subba 2006: 3). As the terms of indigeneity are more discursive, operating in relation to wider (including 'non-tribal') cultural codes and practices, indigeneity thus transgresses the boundaries of its own 'indigenousness', traverses multiple routes and assumes diverse forms.[3]

Indigeneity thus becomes a relevant concept for Adivasis and Adivasi studies. In India, it transforms into a site where related collective identities – such as those of Scheduled Tribes, or *janjatis* ('ethnic' peoples) – can be re-positioned and re-articulated.[4] Thus, claims to cultural and political belonging, or what Floya Anthias calls 'narratives of location', 'narratives of dislocation' and 'narratives of translocation', are consciously constructed through the interplay with seemingly unrelated discourses: such as nationality, and/or global indigeneity. These narratives and interactions may '... lead to more complex, contradictory and at times dialogical positionalities than others.' (Anthias 2001: 633–4) Numerous engaging issues are therefore raised through the study of the histories and patterning of Adivasi subjectivity. These may include the formation of community consciousness in anti-colonial movements; the legacy of counter-insurgencies in collective memory; the social performativity of memory-work; the internalisation and deployment of administrative categories; the negotiation of anthropological and development practices; the contestation of nationalist histories of de-colonisation; the intercultural construction of indigeneity, etc. Many of these issues assume urgency in the context of a liberalised political economy in India, which has given rise to new kinds of social exclusion and new forms of collectivisation and resistance (Baviskar 2005). In consideration of the papers collated for this volume, as editors we would argue that these translations and sites of identification proffer new sets of political and cultural matrices, which can be better grasped if the histories of 'becoming Adivasi' are themselves reconsidered.[5]

Beyond Tribal studies

Too often the ideas of 'tribe' and 'Adivasi' are conflated and confused, resulting in an impasse in Tribal studies. Exponents of Tribal studies, for example Dube (1977), may be aware of and at times sympathetic to the political dimensions of being Adivasi, but generally do not advocate a critical engagement with the hegemonic terms upon which Tribal studies stands. In such works, authors can obliquely employ the term 'tribe' and use its academic and public legibility to empty out the politics of 'becoming Adivasi'.[6] From their vantage points, adivasis (often written with a lower-case 'A'), 'aborigines' and 'tribes' can come to mean one and the same thing, creating an intellectual space where a more nuanced consideration of the term Adivasi and phrase 'becoming Adivasi' can be ignored (see Rath 2006). One needs then to historicise the concept of 'tribe', a subject of recent debate in the Indian context (Sundar 1997; Skaria 1999; Guha 1999).

In 1901, in the Census of India, H.H. Risley attempted to provide a definition of 'tribe' that would be applicable across India:

> A tribe as we find in India is a collection of families or groups of families bearing a common name which as a rule does not denote any specific occupation; generally claiming common descent from a mythical or historical ancestor and occasionally from an animal, but in some parts of the country held together by the obligations of blood-feud than by the tradition of kinship; usually speaking the same language and occupying, professing, or claiming to occupy a definite tract of country. A tribe is not necessarily endogamous ...
>
> (Risley 1903: 514)

The tribe, for the colonial state, by the end of the nineteenth century, had become a definable 'object' with clearly demarcated characteristics, an entity that was seemingly concrete and identifiable. It was now distinguished from the institution of 'caste', and from organised religions like Hinduism, Islam and

Christianity, as it came to be quantified in administrative reports. Yet, ethnographic texts and documents that would also become part of bureaucratic or official memory tell another story. As the concept of the tribe traversed many a winding road in the course of the nineteenth century, it became intertwined with terms like *mlechha* (ritually impure)[7], *chuar* and *dakait* (thieves and robbers) and *jangli* (wild), 'village community', 'hill and forest people', 'aboriginal races', etc., to move from an open descriptive entity to one of fixity and definition (Dasgupta 2007). Yet, even as the category became officially recognised/inscribed, regional variations and linguistic nuances could not necessarily be resolved.

These shifts within the understanding of the tribe were inevitably linked with wider administrative and academic developments in Europe. But it is important to note that they also operated within a colonial context comprising official interactions and dialogues with 'native' (non-tribal) elites, personal observations and group surveys of community practices, and the imperatives of rule as related to the resolution of local grievances or the suppression of protest movements (Rycroft 2006). Western and local 'non-tribal' categories were thus drawn upon, splintered and recast as colonial knowledge of 'the tribe'. Indeed one needs to understand the workings of the representation of 'the tribe' not through fixed frames of reference, but as refracting reality through multiple lenses: from departmental agenda, scientific concerns, military requirements, economic imperatives and the personal outlook/stance of individual researchers.

Describing their world in many different ways, imperial officers identified themselves with newly emerging disciplines of ethnology and anthropology and presented themselves as men of science, academia and civilisation. Ethnographic reports were thus more in dialogue with disciplinary boundaries that structured categories, cutting across regions and local specificities, and related to pan-Indian understandings. Local officers, as nineteenth-century reports indicate, did not necessarily negotiate with representations that were grounded in academic concerns and theoretical debates: segregating 'caste' and 'tribe' as defining categories was beyond the scope of revenue surveys that aimed to codify customary rights over land. Trans-local and local representations interacted with one another, and inevitably clashed, as colonial ethnography and colonial policy became interdependent (Dasgupta 2007). The category of tribe was thus born and continually improvised as authors responded to changing situations. Emerging disciplines intersected with personal experiences and structured interpretations. What is significant, however, is that 'the tribe' was inevitably understood within the vocabularies of contrast. The nature of 'otherness' varied according to changing binaries: hill- and forest-dwellers versus plains-people; *mlechhas* versus *suds* (ritually purified); aboriginals versus Hindus; animists versus polytheists; tribes versus castes. Unlike the close interface between Hindu society and colonial modernity, the 'tribe' typified geographical, cultural and economic separateness, and hence resonated with notions of 'the primitive'.

These ideas were frequently re-articulated in anthropological, travel and administrative discourses. From the visual agenda of Watson and Kaye's *The People of India* to Marguerite Milward's *Artist in Unknown India*, and from the classificatory principles of Risley's *Census of India*, to Ananthakrishna Iyer's *Mysore Tribes and Castes*, the aura of scientific legitimacy continued to inform twentieth century ethnographies. Such works, intentionally sustaining high imperialist views of racial difference, were not left uncritiqued by contemporary anthropologists. Yet, although they aimed to depart from the racial typological concerns of their intellectual forebears and undo civilisational prejudices of both Europeans and Indians against the so-called 'tribes', late-colonial writers such as Verrier Elwin (1939), William Archer (1947) and Christoph von Fürer-Haimendorf (1948) perpetuated primitivist tendencies whilst seeking to challenge the representational codes of a colonial legacy.

Modernist Indian thinkers also internalised and transformed the concept of primitivism that, following the demands of anti-colonial nationalism, would be recast within a new Indian anthropology of the 'tribe'. Influential writers, notably Sarat Chandra Roy (1937, 1938), bridged the domains of physical anthropology and cultural anthropology and brought an alternative analytical framework to the fore, which asserted the legitimacy of Hindu civilisational concepts in the reassessment of minority/tribal peoples and their movements. Observers such as Roy (1925) also presented 'tribal' culture as distant from the hierarchical caste society – as undifferentiated, homogeneous, and non-modern – and as embodied by remnants of pre-colonial and at times pre-political entities. When intra-tribal differences were perceived, they were subsumed within a romantic image of egalitarianism. On account of their production within a new 'universal anthropology', these shifts in approach raise interesting problems of interpretation for anthropologists and historians engaged in the re-evaluation of Indian anthropology (Vidyarthi 1979). Whilst Uberoi *et al.* (2007) have generated exciting ideas, further analysis is needed to generate wider understandings around publications such as *The Modern Review*, *Man in India* and their vernacular counterparts (see Dasgupta 2004; Rycroft forthcoming).

As previously suggested, Tribal studies initially became the disciplinary loci for anthropology (as distinct from sociology).[8] Once it moved away from British to American theoretical frames, and towards micro-studies of culture change, the concept of 'tribe' was re-evaluated. In the synchronic studies of the colonial phase, 'the tribe' was accepted as a universal category, structurally distinct from caste/peasant societies, and to be understood primarily through kinship and lineage structures. These studies emphasised 'tribal' isolation. Although they perpetuated the myth of a caste/tribe duality, both F.G. Bailey's model of a caste-tribe continuum (1960), and Surajit Sinha's modified version of 'tribe-caste' (in the framework of extended kinship) and 'tribe-peasant' (in the framework of territorial systems) continua (1965), exposed the limits of the isolationist model. N.K. Bose went further by questioning the supposed 'difference in economic life between them (the tribe) and their neighbouring peasant-and-artisan communities' (1971: 4). S.C. Dube argued against tribes 'living in isolation' and pointed to their patterns of migrations (1977: 2–3). André Béteille, emphasising the uniqueness of the Indian context and therefore the need to move away from established 'text-book definitions of the tribe' (1974: 68), suggested the need for recognising 'the co-existence of the tribal and other types of social organization within the same social and historical context' since 'tribes have for centuries and millennia continued to exist in the lap of state and civilization, and be marked by their impress' (1980: 826).

Such methods have become embedded in post-independence anthropological enquiries in India, often ignoring the relevance of post-structuralist thought that questions the typological tendencies of the nation-state and the social construction of ethnographic authority (Asad 1973; Stocking 1983; Fabian 1983; Clifford and Marcus 1986; Comaroff and Comaroff 1992). It is worth noting that in the context of independent India, some imperial tendencies and ideologies remain in place, with exponents of physical anthropology, such as S.S. Sarkar (1954), ushering into their enquiries racial elements that directly correspond with the work of Nazi 'scientists', notably Eugen Fischer. In contemporary genetic research (see Bhasin 2006), colonialists such as Risley and more recent Indian collaborators such as S.S. Sarkar are still quoted freely as founders of relevant scientific knowledge.

Departing from such somatic-centric debates, Susan Devalle (1992) was one of the first to argue in the Indian context that the 'tribe' was a groundless colonial category. Ajay Skaria and Sumit Guha have extended this argument. Skaria finds the distinction between tribe and caste, as it evolved in India in the nineteenth and twentieth centuries, to be 'a product of colonial theories and practices' rather than a 'continuation' of 'Indian practices' (1999: 730). Guha suggests that 'the equivalence of tribal and aboriginal originates in ... nineteenth-century racial theory' (1999: 6). Yet, how might one interested in the contemporary articulation of an Adivasi identity be able to engage meaningfully with such problematic terms as 'tribe' and 'aboriginal'?

As editors, we advocate an Adivasi studies approach that departs from the Tribal studies paradigms in its ability to draw upon the related fields of Indigenous studies and Subaltern studies. In some ways it is too simplistic to organise exponents of Indigenous, Subaltern and Tribal studies into distinct academic camps, more so when some recent writers have all but made a case for an Adivasi studies approach (for example Xaxa 1999; Skaria 1999; Sundar 1997). Their efforts require a collective reflection, and we anticipate that this volume may provide some starting points for such a conceptual exercise.

If this is to become meaningful in terms of Adivasi empowerment and intellectual enrichment, our reflections can work towards and indeed elaborate the conditions of 'de-coloniality' (Mignolo 2007). The concept of de-coloniality is an analytical term that has emerged from contemporary sociologies of the global south that have been inspired by Subaltern and Indigenous studies. Exponents of de-coloniality aim to recognise, negotiate and move beyond the political and intellectual limits of a colonial/post-colonial patterning. De-coloniality therefore offers pathways towards a reflexive and transformative method. If realised, these pathways could annotate the distance between de-colonisation, as an ongoing process of political and intellectual radicalism, and post-coloniality. Post-coloniality refers both to conditions of politico-cultural transformation in the global south and beyond (especially as these are organised through statist power), and to the variegated processes, experiences and memories of subordination and resistance in former colonial states. The issue of *de-coloniality* arises whenever and wherever the political, ethical and intellectual integrity of post-colonialism – as an academic field – is called into question (perhaps on account of perceived collusions with dominant interests). Theorists of de-coloniality use the concept to 'de-link' spheres of radicalism from the constraints of both national culturalism and global multiculturalism, thereby promoting new outlooks and possibilities for exponents of insurgent and radical knowledge, especially those positioning themselves *after* the post-colonial turn (Mignolo 2007: 452–3).

Politics of belonging

What potential meanings do the phrases 'indigenous pasts' and 'the politics of belonging' carry (see Castles and Davidson 2000; Ellemor 2005) and to whom are they relevant (see Karlsson 2000)? The idea of an indigenous collectivity is central to this line of inquiry, and although this loose epithet is somewhat problematic in the context of Indian society and civilisation, it has gained a ubiquitous presence in the global arena leading to stimulating anthropological debates (Béteille 1998; Bowen 2000; Kuper 2003). This ubiquity has been fostered by the emergence of a transnational Indigenous movement, whose exponents aim to reassert in educational, legal, cultural and political milieus the values and institutions that they claim have historically been marginalised and suppressed. Such notions have shaped how international instruments, such as the United Nations' Indigenous forums and pro-Indigenous UNESCO recommendations, have recognised and attempted to implement these objectives (Barsh 1986). Through discourses of Indigenous studies and indigenous advocacy, and the divergent rhetoric of indigeneity, as political condition, and indigenousness, as representational ideology (see Weaver 2000), these values and institutions have increasingly gained recognition and international support.

The Adivasi concept has gained widespread resonance and currency in contemporary India, but it has yet to supersede the concept of the 'tribe' in national arenas. Although it was first used in the pre-independence phase, and even though the government of India eventually came to support minority agendas as part of a secular constitution after independence, the indigeneity/Adivasi concept has not been widely inscribed within the Constitution of India. However, this constitution does readily redeploy categories like Scheduled Tribe and Scheduled Area that echo British administrative approaches to India's tribes and 'partially excluded areas' (Oraon 1996). This uneven situation results partly because of the national relevance and secularist longevity of the minority paradigm that has framed Adivasis as 'tribals', and Dalits as Scheduled Castes (Sheth and Mahajan 1999: 3–4). In a useful but nation-centric article on Adivasi encounters with social research, Shalina Mehta elaborates: 'The tribal situation in India cannot be perceived in isolation. It has to be studied, reviewed and planned keeping in view the structural and functional limitations of the nation.' (1996: 64) In theory, the hegemonic framework upholds notions of tribal customary law through the Fifth and Sixth schedules of India's constitution. These are the official instruments that generate some provision for 'tribal' representation through Scheduled Areas Advisory Committee and Tribes Advisory Councils (Savyasaachi 1998). Yet they deny Adivasi autochthony, as contrary to the ideals of shared citizenship and sovereign national territoriality. The Adivasi subjectivity therefore gains visibility in ways that are legible through the idea of 'tribe' and can be woven into the dominant social, cultural and political fabric of a liberal nation. Yet, and this is a crucial concern for contemporary exponents of Adivasi identity, a significant disavowal occurs in such processes: of folding the narratives of Adivasi dislocation and Indigenous translocation into a more singular narrative of 'tribal' belonging. Some representatives of the Adivasi constituency, for example Jaipal Singh (2003: 5) have thus consistently rejected this paternalistic enframing.

This disavowal concerns the imbalance of the dual tenets of Adivasi subjectivity: that is the privileging of the 'tribal' over the 'indigenous'. Whilst tribe-oriented tenets are largely upheld in administrative and popular spheres, making terms like 'tribal', Scheduled Tribe, and Scheduled Area normative, the idea of Adivasi indigeneity remains marginalised by dominant interests. This has become an increasingly vexed issue in recent decades, especially in view of the self-representation of Adivasis (within the United Nations and other pro-Indigenous networks) that has shown how the internalisation of concepts pertaining to global Indigenous rights may occur (Rycroft 2011). This marginality has meant that Adivasi peoples' claims to indigeneity have resulted in a new set of discursive formations, which require careful documentation and analysis. The field of Adivasi studies can therefore be addressed, as related to, but somewhat distinct from, both Tribal studies (in India) and Indigenous studies (globally). Although Indigenous studies have currency and resonance in the context of post-settler de-colonisations (see Smith 1999), Tribal studies pertains more to the Indian context of 'tribal heritage' and Scheduled Tribes/Scheduled Areas (Dube 1977; Singh 1993; Mann 1993).

On account of the status afforded to the Adivasi constituency as Scheduled Tribes, the notion of indigeneity has not assumed a widespread presence even within the Adivasi movement. In response to the transnational Indigenous movement, and in moves towards a global civil society, Adivasi activists are today increasingly recasting these Indigenous pasts in more counter-ideological terms. This process pertains more to the political instrumentalisation of indigeneity than to any real or imagined autochthony in a plural and syncretic civilization, such as India (Béteille 1998). This shift has made the minority paradigm a site of contest in itself (Gupta 1999), between those Adivasis advocating hegemonic and 'democratic' (or state-oriented) processes, and those implementing 'counter-hegemonic' pathways (see Mittleman and Chin 2005) towards alternative conditions of de-coloniality.

As configured in Adivasi discourse, therefore, a 'politics of belonging' assumes multiple orientations, towards regional or state-level recognition as well as global citizenship. It is at times difficult to grasp this multiplicity, especially when studying localised ethnographies or pre-modern pasts. Yet studies of Adivasi society and anti-colonial pasts are more often than not mediated through regimes of representation that, whilst purporting to objectivity, implicate authors within dominant political fabrics (see Pels 1997). It is these representational histories that can also be addressed in order to recover sites of Adivasi articulation, even if those sites were inscribed before the emergence of an international Indigenous Peoples' discourse. And it is a critical awareness of these representational practices that clarifies 'the politics of belonging' as a live issue. By addressing colonial-era pasts and post-colonial frameworks in this way, it may be possible to discern the intellectual and political spaces that an Adivasi studies traverses.

Approaching Adivasi studies

All of the papers in the volume attest in some way to the conceptual ground that an Adivasi studies trajectory assumes. Their choice of case studies reflects the diversity of Adivasi subjects in wide ranging spatial and historical contexts. As editors, we have developed five conceptual themes that will assist interdisciplinary approaches to the topics of Adivasi pasts and the politics of belonging. These are addressed in our further editorial introductions to the five parts that make up the volume: (i) Contesting categories, blurring boundaries, (ii) Revisiting resistance, (iii) Landscape and Adivasi agency, (iv) Politics, participation and recognition, and (v) Mainstreams and margins. We are aware that in focusing on these areas other important themes have been afforded less emphasis. We have already noted how the political, cultural and intellectual terrains of Adivasi subjectivity are continually in flux. As research moves between and beyond the boundaries of communities and nations, away from exceptionalism and towards global and intercultural comparative frames, Adivasi subjectivity gains new significance. Adivasi pasts become relevant to narratives of de-colonisation and imaginaries of belonging in new and engaging ways that do not depend upon state power. Yet these imaginaries may also become embroiled within interconnected patterns of imperialism and anti-imperialism, colonisation and decoloniality, global capitalism and de-centralised development. These present conceptual challenges to historians, anthropologists and sociologists in an era of global indigeneity. Whilst the volume is India-specific, the contributors to *The Politics of Belonging in India: Becoming Adivasi* address wider inter-disciplinary concerns and raise issues that, we hope, will generate new and shared understandings of place, experience, agency, resistance, governance, heritage and identity.

Notes

1 See W.G. Archer Papers, Document Number 208C, Letter to Mr Thakkar, dated 28.10.40, MSS Eur F 236, Asian and African Collections (British Library).

2 Early Adivasi exponents of the Adivasi concept based in Jharkhand (formerly southern Bihar State), such as Jaipal Singh (2003, reprinted from 1948), sought to subvert and transcend colonial categories of being.
3 For a recent anthropological consideration of the Indigenous movement, see Merlan (2009).
4 Positionality is a crucial analytical theme explored by Anthias (2001); see also Baviskar 2005: 5110. Identisation is a sociological process theorised by Mueller (2003).
5 Werbner advocates a nuanced historicisation of the interface between inter-subjectivity and subjectivity, which he considers to be a neglected theme in postcolonial studies (Werbner 2002: 2). Skaria (1999: 277–81) has coined the phrase 'becoming Adivasi', to denote the relationship between the concepts of tribe/*adivasi*/Indigenous Peoples.
6 On the varied usage of the concept of 'tribe' in anthropological and sociological debates and policies see Sinha (2004) and Baviskar (2005: 5106).
7 On the idea of the *mlechha*, see Thapar (1971); Parasher-Sen (2004).
8 For the difficulties of institutionally separating the anthropology and sociology in the Indian context, see Uberoi *et al.* (2007).

References

Anthias, F. (2001) 'New Hybridities, Old Concepts: The Limits of "Culture"', *Ethnic and Racial Studies*, 24(4): 619–41.
Archer, W.G. (1947) *The Vertical Man: A Study in Primitive Indian Sculpture*, London: George Allen and Unwin.
Asad, T. (ed.) (1973) *Anthropology and the Colonial Encounter*, Amherst: Humanities Books.
Bailey, F.G. (1960) 'Tribe and Caste in India', *Contributions to Indian Sociology*, 5(1): 13–14.
Banerjee, P. (2006) 'Culture/Politics: The Irresolvable Double-Bind of the Indian Adivasi', *The Indian Historical Review*, 33(1): 99–126.
Barsh, R.L. (1986) 'Indigenous Peoples: An Emerging Object of International Law', *The American Journal of International Law*, 80(2): 369–85.
Bates, C. (1995) ' "Lost Innocents and the Loss of Innocence": Interpreting *Adivasi* Movements in South Asia', in R.H. Barnes, A. Gray and B. Kingsbury (eds) *Indigenous Peoples of Asia*, Ann Arbor: Association for Asian Studies, 103–99.
Baviskar, A. (2005) 'Adivasi Encounters with Hindu Nationalism in MP [Madhya Pradesh]', *Economic and Political Weekly*, November 26, 5105–13.
Béteille, A. (1974) *Six Essays in Comparative Sociology*, New Delhi: Oxford University Press.
—— (1980) 'On the Concept of Tribe', *International Social Science Journal*, 32(4): 826.
—— (1998) 'The Idea of Indigenous People', *Current Anthropology*, 39(2): 187–91.
Bhasin, M.K. (2006) 'Genetics of Castes and Tribes of India: Indian Population Milieu', *International Journal of Human Genetics*, 6(3): 233–74.
Bose, N.K. (1971) *Tribal Life in India*, New Delhi: National Book Trust.
Bosu Mullick, S. (2003) 'Introduction', in R.D. Munda and S. Bosu Mullick (eds) *The Jharkhand Movement: Indigenous Peoples' Struggle for Autonomy in India*, Copenhagen: International Work Group for Indigenous Affairs, iv–xvii.
Bowen, J.R. (2000), 'Should We Have a Universal Concept of "Indigenous Peoples' Rights"? Ethnicity and Essentialism in the Twenty-first Century', *Anthropology Today*, 16(4): 12–16.

Castles, S. and Davidson, A. (2000) *Citizenship and Migration: Globalization and the Politics of Belonging*, New York: Routledge.

Clifford, J. and Marcus, G. (eds) (1986) *Writing Culture: The Poetics and Politics of Ethnography*, Berkeley: University of California Press.

Comaroff, J. and Comaroff, J. (1992) *Ethnography and the Historical Imagination*, Colorado and Oxford: Westview Press.

Dasgupta, S. (2004) 'The Journey of an Anthropologist in Chotanagpur', *Indian Economic and Social History Review*, 41(2): 165–98.

—— (2007) 'From Description to Definition: Locating the Oraon Tribe in Nineteenth Century Chotanagpur', South Asian History Seminar, St Antony's College, University of Oxford, May 2007.

Devalle, S. (1992) *Discourses of Ethnicity: Culture and Protest in Jharkhand*, New Delhi: Sage Publications.

Dube, S.C. (ed.) (1977) *Tribal Heritage of India*, New Delhi: Vikas Publishing House.

Ellemor, H. (2005) 'White Skins, Black Heart? The Politics of Belonging and Native Title in Australia', *Social and Cultural Geography*, 38(1): 43–57.

Elwin, V. (1939) *The Baiga*, New Delhi: Gyan Publishing House, republished in 2007.

Fabian, J. (1983), *Time and the Other: How Anthropology Makes its Object*, New York: Columbia University Press.

Fürer-Haimendorf, C. von (1948) 'Culture Strata in the Deccan', *Man*, 48: 87–90.

Guha, S. (1999) *Environment and Ethnicity, 1200–1901*, Cambridge: Cambridge University Press.

Gupta, D. (1999) 'Secularization and Minoritization: The Limits of Heroic Thought', in D.L. Sheth and G. Mahajan (eds) *Minority Identities and the Nation State*, New Delhi: Oxford University Press, 38–58.

Hardiman, D. (1987) *The Coming of the Devi: Adivasi Assertion in Western India*, New Delhi: Oxford University Press.

Karlsson, B. (2000) *Contested Belonging: An Indigenous Peoples' Struggle for Forest and Identity in Sub-Himalayan Bengal*, Richmond: Curzon.

Karlsson, B. and Subba, T.B. (2006) 'Introduction', in B. Karlsson and T.B. Subba (eds) *Indigeneity in India*, London: Kegan Paul, 1–19.

Kuper, A. (2003) 'The Return of the Native', *Current Anthropology*, 43(3): 389–402.

Mann, R.S. (1993) *Culture and Integration of Indian Tribes*, New Delhi: M.D. Publications.

Mehta, S. (1996) 'Tribal Situation in India: Encounters with Empiricism', in R.S. Mann (ed.) *Tribes of India: Ongoing Challenges*, New Delhi: M.D. Publications, 55–66.

Merlan, F. (2009) 'Indigeneity: Global and Local', *Current Anthropology*, 50(3): 303–33.

Mignolo, W. (2007) 'De-linking', *Cultural Studies*, 21(2): 449–514.

Mittleman, J. and Chin, C. (2005) 'Conceptualizing Resistance to Globalization', in L. Amoore (ed.) *The Global Resistance Reader*, Abingdon: Routledge, 17–27.

Mueller, C. (2003) ' "Recognition Struggles" and Process Theories of Social Movements', in B. Hobson (ed.) *Recognition Struggles and Social Movements: Contested Identities, Agency and Power*, Cambridge: Cambridge University Press, 274–91.

Oraon, P.C. (1996) 'Tribal Cultural Identity', in K.K. Chakravarty (ed.) *Tribal Identity in India: Extinction or Adaptation*, Bhopal: IGRMS, 88–95.

Parasher-Sen, A. (2004) *Subordinate and Marginal Groups in Early India*, New Delhi: Oxford University Press.

Pels, P. (1997) 'The Anthropology of Colonialism: Culture, History and the Emergence of Western Governmentality', *Annual Review of Anthropology*, 26: 163–83.

Rath, G.C. (2006) 'Introduction', in G.C. Rath (ed.) *Tribal Development in India: The Contemporary Debate*, New Delhi: Sage Publications, 15–62.

Risley, H.H. (1903) *Census of India, 1901*, Vol. 1, Part 1, Calcutta: Office of the Superintendent of Government Printing.

Roy, S.C. (1925) *The Birhors: A Little Known Jungle Tribe of Chota Nagpur*, Ranchi: K.E.M. Mission Press.

—— (1937) 'The Study of Anthropology from the Indian View-point', *Journal of the Benares Hindu University*, 10 August, 243–56.

—— (1938) 'An Indian Outlook on anthropology', *Man*, 38: 146–50.

Rycroft, D.J. (2006) *Representing Rebellion: Visual Aspects of Counter-insurgency in Colonial India*, New Delhi: Oxford University Press.

—— (2011) 'Beyond Resistance: Idioms and Memories of Insurgency in the Adivasi Movement, Jharkhand State, India', in S. Dasgupta and R.S. Basu (eds), *Narratives from the Margins: Aspects of Adivasi History in India*, New Delhi: Pluto Press, 257–76.

—— (forthcoming) 'Indian anthropology and the Construction of 'Tribal Ethnicity' Before Independence', in S. Gupta (ed.), *Nationhood and Identity Movements in Asia: Colonial and Postcolonial Times*, New Delhi: Manohar Publishers.

Sarkar, S.S. (1954) *The Aboriginals of India*, Calcutta: Bookland.

Savyasaachi (1998) *Tribal Forest Dwellers and Self-Rule: Constituent Assembly Debates on the Fifth and Sixth Schedules*, New Delhi: Indian Social Institute.

Sheth, D.L. and G. Mahajan (eds) (1999) *Minority Identities and the Nation State*, New Delhi: Oxford University Press.

Singh, J. (2003) 'Jai Jharkhand! Jai Adibasi! Jai Hind' (1948), reprinted in R.D. Munda and S. Bosu Mullick (eds) *The Jharkhand Movement: Indigenous Peoples' Struggle for Autonomy in India*, Copenhagen: International Work Group for Indigenous Affairs, 2–14.

Singh, K.S. (1993) 'Introduction', in K.S. Singh (ed.), *Tribal Ethnography, Customary Law and Change*, New Delhi: Concept Publishing, 13–20.

Sinha, A.C. (2004) 'Colonial Anthropology vs. Indological Sociology: Elwin and Ghurye on Tribal Policy in India', in T.B. Subba and S. Som (eds), *Between Ethnography and Fiction: Verrier Elwin and the Tribal Question in India*, Hyderabad: Orient Longman, 86–109.

Sinha, S. (1965) 'Tribe-Caste and Tribe-Peasant Continua in Central India', *Man in India*, 45(1): 57–83.

Skaria, A. (1999) *Hybrid Histories: Forests, Frontiers and Wildness in Western India*, New Delhi: Oxford University Press.

Smith, L.T. (1999) *Decolonizing Methodologies: Research and Indigenous Peoples*, London: Zed Books.

Stocking, G.W. (ed.) (1983) *Observers Observed: Essays on Ethnographic Fieldwork*, Madison: University of Wisconsin Press.

Sundar, N. (1997) *Subalterns and Sovereigns: An Anthropological History of Bastar, 1854–1996*, New Delhi: Oxford University Press.

Thapar, R. (1971) 'The Image of the Barbarian in Early India', *Comparative Studies in Society and History*, 13(4): 408–36.

Uberoi, P., Sundar, N., and Deshpande, S., eds, (2007), *Anthropology in the East: Founders of Indian Sociology and Anthropology*, New Delhi: Permanent Black.

Vidyarthi, L.P. (1979) *Rise of World Anthropology, as Reflected Through the International Congresses: 1934–1978*, Delhi: Concept Publishing.

Weaver, J. (2000) 'Indigenousness and Indigeneity', in H. Schwarz and S. Ray (eds) *A Companion to Postcolonial Studies*, London: Blackwell, 221–35.

Werbner, R. (2002) 'Introduction – Postcolonial Subjectivities: The Personal, the Political and the Moral', in R. Werbner (ed.) *Postcolonial Subjectivities in Africa*, London: Zed Books, 1–22.

Xaxa, V. (1999) 'Tribes as Indigenous People of India', *Economic and Political Weekly*, 34(51): 3589–95.

Part I

Contesting categories, blurring boundaries

Introduction to Part I

Part I sets out a terrain of opposition that is political and academic, and characterised by the discursive construction, representation and negotiation of Adivasi subjectivity. Here, we present contributions from anthropo-historical and folklorist perspectives in order to draw attention to the contested nature of the categories of Adivasi, Indigenous Peoples and 'tribe'. Contributors to this section demonstrate the fluidity and malleability of these concepts, their regional as well as temporal variability. But how might these variations signal wider questions for Adivasi studies?

In his theorisation of geographies of resistance, Steve Pile (1997: 9–14) conceptualises the 'terrain of opposition' as the spatial and discursive sites at which radical group identities are realised vis-à-vis dominant states. These sites enable the constitution of alternative subjectivities and experiences that disrupt the authority and fixity of social identities. These processes foster a blurring of political identities and boundaries, giving rise to multiple and fragmented discourses and narratives of dislocation. Peter Pels takes the debate further within the context of anthropology:

> We are in need of ethnographies of decolonization, focusing on the continuity between past and present practices of development, welfare and good governance, and the way these were constituted by anthropology. ... If we are ever going to be capable of disengaging anthropology from colonialism, we first need to reflexively blur the boundaries between colonialism and our present anthropology.
>
> (Pels 1997: 178)

Pels' assessment can be redrawn in the context of an emerging Adivasi studies trajectory because it prompts researchers to re-assess their own positioning vis-à-vis colonialism, de-colonisation and de-coloniality. Virginius Xaxa is an influential figure in this re-assessment, providing a pertinent response to exponents of anti-Adivasi and anti-Indigenous agenda: 'It is only with the internationalisation of the rights and privileges associated with it that the term indigenous has come to be critically challenged in the Indian context.' (Xaxa 1999: 3590) Invoking Xaxa's thesis on Adivasi consciousness and belonging, an Adivasi studies trajectory may crystallise a new geography of resistance that blurs the boundaries between, on the one hand, scholarly researchers and advocates of indigeneity and, on the other, the matrices of power operating in Tribal studies.

Whilst the notion of Adivasi purports to aboriginality, unlike the concept of 'tribe', it does so not to re-inscribe the 'rule of difference', but to contest it through a re-engagement with histories of subordination and resistance. As noted by Prathama Banerjee, the Adivasi concept is '... a political statement of distinctiveness and autonomy and a defiance of the colonial anthropological categories like 'tribe' and 'aborigine'.' (2006a: 105) Banerjee therefore highlights the role of the Adivasi concept in providing the conceptual apparatus for negotiations of national and global processes.[1] But we also need to question how writers such as Banerjee position themselves in order to grasp the challenges raised by an Adivasi studies approach. In a move that is clearly distinct from Xaxa's affirmative action, Banerjee interrogates the concept of Adivasi as '... an emphatically historicist category ...' (2006a: 105). In this context, Banerjee apprehends those Adivasi elites who advocate the concept as a means to perpetuate culturalist mythologies and critiques their legitimation of (inter)national representations of 'tribal' peoples as marginal entities. Unlike Xaxa, Banerjee is wary of ideological representations, and attempts to position her own political and intellectual self somewhat external to the Adivasi discourse. An understanding of this kind of alternative intellectual positioning is crucial to the success of Adivasi studies as an open discourse. This is because it allows the reflexive blurring of the boundaries between the subject and objects of political and academic representation, in ways that are, on the one hand, left unacknowledged in Tribal studies and, on the other, subsumed within the rhetoric of Adivasi assertiveness. In this discursive space, the Adivasi studies researcher might – as Van Schendel and Chatterji do – address issues in Adivasi studies to further an intercultural understanding of indigenous pasts and subjectivities.

Van Schendel critically discusses the replacement of 'tribe' by 'adivasi' and 'indigenous peoples' in South Asian public and academic discourses. The usage of these terms, he argues, has real consequences: they affect the structure, dynamics and futures of South Asian societies and may influence the 'everyday practices' of a very large population in South Asia. The anchoring of the term 'tribe' in the legal frameworks of India, Pakistan, Bangladesh and Nepal has ossified a colonial term into a postcolonial reality. For Van Schendel, the new Adivasi discourse continues to incorporate the notion of 'tribal' distinctiveness, of people far removed from the 'civilised' and 'modern' state and the attendant political economies that Adivasis now claim for themselves. 'Indigenous peoples', the most compelling of terms in his opinion, is also a temporary conceptual refuge: adherents of the 'indigenous people' approach tend towards a romantic and non-critical celebration of the indigenous. This approach is linked with the dangerous exclusionary 'politics of belonging' and is constructed upon an outdated concept of place. Taking up the Northeast as his focus of study, Van Schendel argues that 'place' needs to be re-imagined as more open and hybrid allowing for coexistence and power sharing.

Roma Chatterji, on the other hand, addresses the question of identity through an analysis of performative genres – the *chho* (gestural, often masked) dance, the *jhumur* (group) song and the ritual complex around the folk goddess Bhadu. These performative genres are seen as prisms to understand representations of community and folkloric culture in the region of Purulia, a 'border zone' between West Bengal and the 'tribal' milieu of Jharkhand. Chatterji sees boundaries as discursive spaces, and as cultural fields. The concept of boundary, she argues, is a shifting frame that gives a temporary coherence to a set of heterogeneous themes and practices. In the process of demarcating autonomous spaces, boundaries thus produce transitional zones or 'crossings' where different identities meet and sometimes clash. Purulia, as one such border zone, accordingly lends itself to a variety of representations, some of which contradict each other. It is sometimes seen as a living museum from which Bengal's ancient pre-Hindu, or rather pre-Vedic or non-Brahmanical, pasts could be re-constituted. At other times, it is seen as an extension of Jharkhand and thus of a distinctive and authentic Adivasi/tribal culture. Chatterji analyses locally situated terms that signify particular representations of sociality. The substitutions and interplay between these terms, often by the same author in a single text, point to the fact that these terms are part of an open-ended series. 'Culture' then, as it is constituted in the discourse of folklore, is mobile and configured through the circulation of cultural artefacts, signs and contested meanings.

Note

1 Banerjee (2006b: 239) writes: 'We must move ... beyond the realization that the ordering concepts of our world – progress or modernity or development – can never be found as pure, originary concepts, that they necessarily function as contested moments both within and outside Europe.'

References

Banerjee, P. (2006a) 'Culture/Politics: The Irresolvable Double-Bind of the Indian Adivasi', *The Indian Historical Review*, 33(1): 99–126.

—— (2006b), *Politics of Time: Primitives and History Writing in a Colonial Society*, New Delhi: Oxford University Press.

Pels, P. (1997) 'The Anthropology of Colonialism: Culture, History and the Emergence of Western Governmentality', *Annual Review of Anthropology*, 26: 163–83.

Pile, S. (1997) 'Introduction: Opposition, Political Identities and the Spaces of Resistance', in S. Pile and M. Keith (eds) *Geographies of Resistance*, London: Routledge, 1–32.

Xaxa, V. (1999) 'Tribes as Indigenous People of India', *Economic and Political Weekly*, 34(51): 3589–3595.

2 The dangers of belonging

Tribes, indigenous peoples and homelands in South Asia

Willem van Schendel[1]

Introduction

In South Asian public and academic discourses, the term 'tribe' is used freely. In many other parts of the world this is not the case, and the term is considered problematic. It has been replaced by other terms such as 'indigenous people', 'first nation' or 'autochthon'. In this chapter, I examine the implications of the terms; we need to reflect upon them because they have real consequences. They influence everyday practices: tens of millions of people in South Asia believe themselves (or others) to be tribal, and others identify themselves as indigenous people. How anthropologists, politicians and policy makers engage with these terms affects the structure, dynamics and futures of South Asian societies.

The first part of this chapter outlines the historical background and contemporary implications of the use of 'tribe' and 'indigenous people' in South Asia. The second part critiques the way in which demands for 'indigenous' power are routinely translated into claims for ethnic homelands. Taking the case of Northeast India, I show how this practice has led to territorial fragmentation as well as to enormous suffering and disempowerment, especially among 'indigenous' groups. Finally, I propose a new way of imagining place – one that goes beyond territorial exclusivity and allows for coexistence and power sharing.

The 'tribe' in South Asia

The term 'tribe' has a long and chequered history. In ancient Rome, *tribus* referred to the original divisions of Roman citizens and ever since it has been in use in Mediterranean and European languages to denote groups of people having a common character, occupation or interest. In South Asia, the term was introduced many centuries later by Europeans trying to make sense of the social complexities that they encountered. For a long time they used it more or less interchangeably with 'race', 'people', 'caste', 'class', 'clan' and other words denoting groups of human beings. These words had slightly different meanings in different European languages – notably Portuguese, Dutch, English and French – but here we are concerned only with English because this became the language of rule in South Asia.

In the colonial context the term 'tribe' became part of a vocabulary of power that distinguished not only between European rulers and South Asian subjects but also between categories of subjects in South Asia. As David Arnold writes:

> By the eighteen-thirties, as the interior of India became more accessible to Europeans, an increasingly explicit 'racial' contrast was being drawn between the Indians of the plains, who were seen broadly to conform to the Caucasian 'type' and whose ancestors were thought centuries earlier to have brought the Aryan or Indo-European languages into South Asia, and the 'aboriginal' or 'tribal' peoples of India who inhabited hills and forests, especially across central India. In this evolving representation of India's 'aboriginals' several sets of antithetical ideas were brought together – the almost naked versus the fully clothed, hunting and shifting cultivation as against settled agriculture as the primary mode of subsistence, and the jungle-dweller as opposed to the denizen of the plains.
>
> (Arnold 2004: 266)

Gradually, however, the concept of 'tribe' took on a more specific meaning as it became differentiated from 'race' and 'caste'. By the late nineteenth century British colonialists had developed a style of thinking that Ajay Skaria refers to as *anachronism*:

> Anachronistic thought ranked ... societies in relation to each other, situating them ... in relation to the modern time that was now epitomized by Europe. Different societies were thus ranked according to how much behind the time of Europe they were. The specific time that societies occupied – the question of how "advanced" they were – was measured by various criteria.
>
> (Skaria 1997: 727)

For the first time, 'tribe' became part of a comparative taxonomy: contemporary societies that Europeans considered to be farthest behind in time were designated as 'tribes', 'primitives', 'aborigines' or 'savages'. Therefore colonial constructions of 'tribe' differed from previous ones. First, in colonial South Asia, the term 'tribe' came to refer to groups that were given a low rank in a hierarchical system based upon civilization and modernity. They were *uncivilized* (hence wild, primitive and savage) and *unmodern* (hence backward and ruled by custom). Second, those South Asians who came to be defined as 'tribal' were seen as members of a universal category: in the nineteenth century Europeans were discovering 'tribes' all over the world. In South Asia, therefore, 'tribe' was diametrically opposed to 'caste': the former pointed to global comparisons, the latter to the essence of South Asia.

These ideas were closely linked to influential academic theories of the time, notably unilinear evolutionist anthropology or social evolutionism, a scientific theory that offered an ordered explanation for human difference. This theory posited that all human beings shared the same potential for progress and that different groups of mankind advanced along a single line of progress, from one stage to the next. Study of the social arrangements of contemporary people using primitive technology could therefore yield information about the social arrangements of distant ancestors of Europeans who had reached the same point along the single path to civilization much earlier. These contemporary ancestors were classified according to the stage of technological and human development that they had reached, e.g. savagery, barbarism or civilization (for a notably influential scheme, see Morgan 1878). Social evolutionism also inspired an ideology known as social Darwinism, which held that the most civilized were destined to dominate the others. Applying the biological idea of the 'survival of the fittest' to human beings, this ideology served imperial interests. By casting Europeans in the role of the fittest and all others as less fit, it sought to provide legitimacy to European rule over non-European populations.

This is what made 'tribe' such a useful administrative category in South Asian colonial circumstances. It defined groups of South Asians as especially unfit to rule themselves and as natural wards of European colonial officers. It fell to these officials to define which criteria made a group a 'tribe'. Whereas anthropologists were debating schemes of human evolution based on levels of technology, colonial officials in South Asia had no time for methodological niceties – they had to administer a vast population. Taking the general idea of evolutionism, they applied a mishmash of graded characteristics to identify groups as 'tribal'. These characteristics included modes of subsistence (e.g. hunting and pastoralism), understandings of race (e.g. 'Aryan' and 'Dravidian'), levels of technology (e.g. non-plough agriculture), 'wild' and 'remote' territories (e.g. hills and forests), an absence of written script or codified law, and being isolated and self-contained as a social formation. These European ideas were not thrust upon an unwilling society. On the contrary, they meshed well with South Asian elites' hierarchical attitude towards people living in forests. The common term *jongoli* (jungly) summed up this attitude. It means both 'living in the jungle' and 'uncivilized, wild, uncouth'. By the late nineteenth century, as Ajay Skaria points out,

> seizing upon and magnifying some differences [and] imagining differences, an exhaustive list of the 'tribes' of India had been prepared. Needless to say, the list was fundamentally arbitrary ... in almost all cases, the so-called tribes shared more cultural, social and economic practices with their caste neighbours in the region than with other 'tribes' all over India with whom British officials clubbed them. It is in this sense that one can really describe the colonial list of tribes as a process of primitivization, or of the invention of primitive societies.
>
> (Skaria 1997: 731–2)

Thus, 'tribe' became not so much a container of specific cultural traits – it was hard to imagine what Pashtuns might have in common with Nagas and Todas – but rather a term fixing a relationship of very unequal power. To be tribal meant to be subordinated to a superior power with a civilizing mission.

The term 'tribe' came to represent a particular relationship between British rulers and selected South Asian populations, a relationship in which paternalistic protection and violent correction went hand in hand. Arguably the rulers' perception that they needed a specific policy to deal with these groups of 'savages' was what created 'tribes' as a political reality. Important elements in colonial tribal policy were spatial and administrative separation of 'tribals' from 'non-tribal' South Asians (who were often thought to have a corrupting influence upon 'tribals'), incentives to abandon shifting cultivation, and the propagation of Christianity. Equally important was the fact that officials felt entitled to unleash violent punishment upon 'tribals' who resisted their assigned position at the lowest rung of the political ladder. Brutal punitive expeditions were justified in the name of protecting intransigent 'tribals' against themselves and helping them find the road to civilization and modernity (Robb 1997). This political context determined the strategic options open to South Asian 'tribals' in their dealings with rulers. It is in the range of their tactical relationships with power holders, not in their cultural traits, that Pashtuns, Nagas, Todas and other 'tribals' in South Asia may be fruitfully compared.

The strategic options open to groups classified as 'tribes' and 'castes' began to diverge as colonial policy transformed the relationship between them. Anti-colonial, nationalist politicians had to take this divergence seriously if they were to mobilize both 'castes' and 'tribes' for the cause of a unified independent nation. This concern was reflected in the political neologisms of the late-colonial period. Nationalists invented a non-insulting word for the lowest, untouchable 'caste' groups – *harijan* (children of God) – and this was mirrored by the introduction of a similarly non-derogatory word for 'tribals' – *adivasi* (inhabitants from the earliest time, aboriginals, autochthons). Unlike *harijan*, the term *adivasi* became popular and it is currently the politically correct word for 'tribals' in India – but not in other countries of South Asia, e.g. Pakistan (where *qaum* is common) or Bangladesh (where *upojati* is widely used).

Despite inventing a new term, dominant nationalist politicians (overwhelmingly upper-caste men) were quite similar to British officials in perceiving 'tribals' as 'savages' or 'primitives', people far removed from the civilized and modern state that these men claimed for themselves. Their civilizing mission was, if anything, more urgent because the Indian nation could not become truly modern until the backwardness of 'tribals' was removed. *Adivasis* had to be 'developed', they had to join the 'mainstream', they were to assimilate. The inclusion of a list, or schedule, of 'tribes' in the Indian Constitution was seen as a significant instrument to fast-track the benefits of civilization and modernity to wild, backward communities. Those registered as 'scheduled tribes' could now claim special protection and largesse from the postcolonial state. Once again it fell to state officials to decide what criteria would define a community as a 'tribe'. The Constitution of India did not spell it out but a series of official committees arrived at a list including indications of primitive traits, distinctive culture, geographical isolation, shyness of contact with the community at large, and social and economic backwardness. By the early twenty-first century the administrative view of 'tribes' remained strongly 'anachronistic' and wedded to ideas of backwardness and failed modernity. In the words of India's 10th Five-Year Plan (2002–2007):

> Tribal communities continue to be vulnerable even today, not because they are poor, asset-less and illiterate compared to the general population; but often their distinct vulnerability arises from their inability to negotiate and cope with the consequences of their integration with the mainstream economy, society, cultural and political systems, from all of which they were historically protected by their relative isolation.
>
> (Government of India 2001: 451)

Among anthropologists …

Nineteenth-century colonial officials who elaborated the category of 'tribe' in South Asia took their cue from contemporary anthropological theorizing. Once 'tribe' had become part of the administrative structure and the vocabulary of rule, however, they no longer needed the input of anthropology. As a result, the growing scepticism among anthropological professionals about the analytical usefulness of the term 'tribe' did not communicate itself to official thinking. From the turn of the twentieth century, evolutionary schemes rapidly lost ground among anthropologists as they turned to other models of social analysis. Spurred on by more systematic field studies and functionalist understandings of societies they progressively rejected as untenable the idea of a single trajectory to civilization and distinct stages of human evolution. Anthropologists no longer assumed that they could study contemporary groups with simple technology as if these were surviving ancestors caught in a time warp. It took functionalist anthropologists time to expose the notion of 'tribe' as a red herring in social analysis; they did so decisively only after postcolonial elites in the South began to accuse anthropologists of 'primitivizing' their societies. By the 1970s most anthropologists around the world had abandoned the term 'tribe' and today it is no longer used much in professional discourse on comparative social analysis (Southall 1970; Fried 1975).

Two dimensions of this dissolution of an anthropological category are of importance here. First, the decline in the use of 'tribe' differs markedly between world regions. Africanists have generally rejected it as misleading, inaccurate and unhelpful in understanding African realities (Lowe *et al.* 1997). The same is true for Oceania and the Americas. But in the study of South Asia, Central Asia and the Middle East, many persist in using the term as an analytical tool. In South Asia, the problematic connotations of 'tribe' certainly have been discussed among social scientists. Historians have insisted that groups now known as 'tribes' or 'adivasis' should be understood not as primitives without history who are in need of catching up with modernity, but as groups whose present powerlessness is the outcome of long, variegated histories. As Crispin Bates writes:

> In the case of the so-called 'adivasis', a description of who they were and where they came from ought not to begin by plucking them as specimens from the colonial era, but by examining their resistance to colonialism, and the previous history of the rise and fall of tribal kingdoms in a period when they were much more largely masters of their own fate.
>
> (Bates 1995: 257)

There is abundant historical evidence to demonstrate that 'tribes' and non-'tribes' in South Asia have a sustained experience of cultural and social inter-connectedness and exchange, and that neither racial nor territorial, technological, linguistic, or religious measures can be used as effective markers of 'tribal' identities.

Despite these conceptual misgivings, the administrative category remains hegemonic and there is a huge anthropological literature in South Asia that continues to take 'tribe' very much as a given term, applying it more or less unself-consciously to populations around the subcontinent.[2] As André Béteille puts it: 'anthropologists in India, both before and after independence, have been concerned more with the practical problem of designation than with the theoretical one of definition' (Béteille 1998: 188). This has problematic implications if we use South Asian findings comparatively. For example, one aspect that is sometimes overlooked in general pronouncements about 'tribes' in South Asia is the enormous variety of relationships between these 'tribes' and their rulers today. The 'adivasis' of central India – themselves a very diverse category – provide the dominant model. So far anthropologists have not bothered much to compare them systematically with 'tribals' living under other South Asian states, in which quite different tribal-ruler relationships have developed. Even the situation in Northeast India diverges sharply from that in central India. Here the proportion of 'tribals' goes up to over 80 per cent in some states (Mizoram topping the charts with 95 per cent) and these groups have never adopted the term 'adivasi' as a self-identifying label, reserving it for 'tribals' from central India. Another contrast is that government presence did not commence in some parts of Northeast India till the 1940s and that non-tribals have long been barred from huge tracts of 'tribal' territory (Blackburn 2003). In view of such disparities, it is regrettable that generalizations about 'tribes' in India, let alone South Asia, rarely take these into account.[3] As a result, there is no 'tribal' anthropology of South Asia to speak of. Instead, there are several clusters of 'tribal' studies, each of which remains remarkably parochial and (sub)national in scope. They have contributed little to comparative understandings, even on a South Asian scale.

The anchoring of the term 'tribe' in the legal frameworks of India, Pakistan, Bangladesh and Nepal has ossified it by turning a colonial term into a postcolonial identity marker for selected groups whose rights claims *must* be made in the idiom of 'tribe' versus rulers.[4] Reluctantly or enthusiastically, political activists have appropriated the imposed label 'tribal'/'adivasi' as a group tag in their communications with the state to claim group rights. And many now think of themselves as 'tribals'. In South Asia the category of 'tribe' is an undeniably important tool of identity politics. This may be one reason why many anthropologists of the region continue to feel comfortable using it at a time when their colleagues working on, say, Africa have firmly discarded it.

Turning tribes on their heads: 'indigenous people'

Since the 1980s the main contender of the term 'tribe' has been that of 'indigenous people' (Minde 1996; Niezen 2000). This category makes less of a claim to internal consistency – indigenous peoples are not thought to share a particular set of cultural, social or technological characteristics – but highlights two relational aspects. One is a relationship of belonging to a particular territory because of a long association with it. In this sense being indigenous (or autochthonous or native) is a claim to a particular part of the earth's surface on the basis of history. The other aspect is being oppressed by later arrivals in the territory, or being exploited by postcolonial states that treat indigenous territories as internal colonies. In this sense being indigenous is a claim to rights that have been denied and it may involve claims to reparation or compensation. In a way, 'indigenous people' turns 'tribe' upside down. There is no sense of backwardness, wildness, or isolation from the mainstream. On the contrary, the idea of indigeneity marginalizes the 'mainstream' and unsettles the hierarchical assumptions of civilization vs. wildness. It implies a radical switch of perspective but it shares with the idea of 'tribe' two characteristics: simplification and boundary making (Li 2000).

Not surprisingly, the idea of 'indigenous people' has rapidly gained popularity among marginalized groups around the world wishing to politicize their identity and among outsiders eager to make 'indigenous' voices heard. It has brought immense material and immaterial gains to the elites (and sometimes all members) of these groups. The United Nations system embraced the term (United Nations 2007), states from Norway to Brazil to Australia to the Philippines passed legislation on the rights of 'indigenous peoples', and innumerable non-governmental organizations mobilized funds for the rights and development of 'indigenous peoples'. Notice how carefully, indeed unctuously, the World Bank frames its policies in terms of partnership, a far cry from the paternalistic tone associated with the discourse on 'tribes':

> Indigenous Peoples are a significant and important portion of humanity. Their heritage, their ways of life, their stewardship of this planet, and their cosmological insights are an invaluable treasure house for us all. The World Bank is honored to be working worldwide with Indigenous Peoples in global dialogue and in development projects. The World Bank aims to promote Indigenous Peoples' development in a manner which ensures that the development process fosters full respect for the dignity, human rights, and uniqueness of Indigenous Peoples.
>
> (World Bank 2010)

The idea of 'indigenous people' works better in the Americas and Australia – where in recent centuries large numbers of Europeans and Africans settled, outstripping and marginalizing local populations of much longer residence – than in South Asia, where this was not the case (Béteille 1998; Bowen 2000; Kingsbury 1998). Here issues of earlier and later settlement are often much harder to establish, partly because of an extremely long (pre)history of mobility and intermingling, partly because theories of historical population movements are contested, and partly because many groups identifying themselves as 'indigenous' are relatively recent social formations.

This has led to a discussion on the applicability of the term to South Asia that boils down to the acceptability of the perspectives informing the terms 'tribe' and 'indigenous people'. Is it possible to shear 'tribe' from its connotations of primitivity, unmodernity, and colonialist and nationalist guardianship? Is it possible to re-imagine it as part of an emancipatory perspective? Does a rejection of the term 'indigenous people' imply a rejection of the dignity, citizens' rights and agency of the groups concerned? Should anthropologists and historians be drawn into 'claims research' – research commissioned by 'indigenous' groups to present new interpretations of history that support their claims?[5] Should historians take issue with the often unverifiable histories of origins and homelands on which 'indigenous' claims are based? These are vexed questions, made more complicated by the fact that they are bound up with future access to resources.

The discussion has produced an interesting line-up. In the 'tribe' corner we have, roughly, the governments of South Asia and 'tribal' leaders/ideologues with a stake in state largesse. In the 'indigenous people' corner we have international bodies like the UN and the World Bank, non-governmental organizations, and 'indigenous' leaders/ideologues with a stake in international or NGO largesse. And what about anthropologists, expert knowledge producers in this field? They show an interesting spread, with those working on central India and Pakistan's Northwest Frontier Province tending to favour 'tribe'/'adivasi' and those working on Northeast India and Bangladesh appearing to have moved a considerable distance in the direction of 'indigenous people'. There may also be a generational difference, with the crowd in the 'tribe' corner generally being a bit older than those rooting for 'indigenous people'.

Could it be that identity politics resulting from state policy towards 'tribals' determine how anthropologists conceptualize their subject? India and Pakistan have well established policies that are particularly suited to the interests of 'tribal' elites in central India and the Northwest Frontier Province. By contrast, Bangladesh has no 'tribal' policies to speak of, and the Indian scheduled-tribe policy has run into serious legitimacy problems in the Northeast.[6] In both these latter cases, the state has sought to control 'tribal' dissatisfaction by widespread and long-term military violence, justified, as during colonial times, in the name of protecting 'tribals' against themselves and helping them find the road to civilization and modernity.[7] It remains to be seen if this state practice will be effective in the long run. The affected populations have responded by leapfrogging their states, not just by claiming global citizenship and seeking refuge in the transnational category of 'indigenous people' – Nagas from Northeast India and Jummas from Bangladesh were early members of various international indigenous organizations[8] – but also in some cases by rejecting the state and claiming the legal status of an independent people with the full right to self-determination.

It is interesting to note that, in India, the word 'adivasi' is now used widely in contemporary academic writings in English. The reason for this may be that it allows authors to sidestep the conceptual minefield of choosing between the English words 'tribe' and 'indigenous people'. 'Adivasi' was introduced as a translation of 'tribe' and is still commonly used as its formal equivalent – but its literal meaning happened to foreshadow the term 'indigenous people'. It also shares with the latter term an emphasis on distinct identities that are separate from the discourse of the Indian nation. This slippage may have made it easier to retain the term 'adivasi' in the 1980s when the 'indigenous people' discourse came up, rendering the use of the English term 'tribe' more awkward.[9]

Worldwide, the term 'tribe' is being abandoned for the term 'indigenous people'. South Asia is a world region where this change is slow. Three important reasons are that: 1) South Asian governments are adverse to buying into the idea of some groups being more indigenous than others; 2) many groups have a stake in self-identification as 'tribal' and others are uncomfortable with some connotations of 'indigenous'[10]; and 3) some of South Asia's most influential anthropologists have challenged the appropriateness of the term 'indigenous people' in the South Asian context (Roy Burman 1998; Béteille 2006). As a result, in the public sphere the 'tribes' remain modernity's opposites. Over time, the public emphasis upon backwardness and the need to 'join the national mainstream' has lessened somewhat – in India, the writings of Mahasweta Devi played a significant role – and there is an increasing acceptance of 'tribal' cultural practices, provided these are supportive of the nation's self-image as modern. This translates into media images of innocuous, harmonious and decorative practices such as dance, ceremonies and dress, feeding middle-class fantasies that distant hills and forests are inhabited by contented and colourful tribal rustics whom the state assists in developing into modern citizens (Geschiere and Nyamnjoh 2000: 423).[11] As a result, the public tends to ignore reports about violent clashes between 'the mainstream' and 'tribes' in military, economic, cultural and development terms, or to dismiss them as inexplicable ungratefulness on the part of misguided anti-socials or traditionalists. With growing public access to independent flows of information, however, it is likely that the term 'indigenous people' will become more current among the middle classes in South Asia.

An alternative modernity?

Even though the 'indigenous people' approach has established itself worldwide, it cannot be more than a temporary and shaky conceptual refuge. First, adherents of the 'indigenous people' approach tend towards a romantic celebration of the indigenous. Second, there are worrisome links between this approach and an exclusionary 'politics of belonging'. And third, the notion of 'indigenous people' is constructed upon an outdated concept of place.

The discourse on 'indigenous peoples' frequently presumes them to be bearers of an alternate modernity because of the environmental sustainability imputed to 'indigenous' lifestyles. In the face of discredited models of development, 'indigenous people' are held up as benevolent guardians of nature graced with special wisdom and foresight, united in supportive communities, who can lead the world out of the quagmire of technological shortsightedness and consumerism by providing 'strong antisystemic resistance against global capitalism' (Hall and Fenelon 2004). According to this view, they are alternative modern subjects who are in touch with age-old traditions that may yet save the planet. They are credited with special wisdom regarding stewardship of environmental resources and they are held up as paragons of more sustainable ways of life. Unlike those who live alienated (post-)industrial lives, 'indigenous peoples' are thought still to be able to provide cultural resistance against mindless consumerism. They alone seem capable of bridging the gap between the modern and a past that has almost slipped away; they represent the biodiversity of modernity. As the World Bank quote above attests, such essentialist ideas are not restricted to romantic environmental activists but have become acceptable in the world's bastions of hard-nosed technocracy.

Miraculously, the very groups that were seen only yesterday as the opposite of modern are now presented as harbingers of an alternate modernity. Now they escape the opprobrium of being primitive but they remain the object of an externally-imposed cultural scheme in which the 'indigenous' is essentialized and set apart as the Other of hegemonic modernity. There is of course much evidence to show that 'indigenous' politics – 'indigenism' (Niezen 2000) – is in fact a recent product of modernity. The romantic celebration of the 'indigenous' tells us more about the celebrator than about the celebrated – 'indigenous' politics can have very dark sides as well.

The dangers of belonging

A romantic celebration of indigeneity (or autochthony) may lead to disturbing and paradoxical results. It may produce an intensification of the 'politics of belonging':

> fierce debates on who belongs where, violent exclusion of 'strangers' (even if this refers to people with the same nationality who have lived for generations in the area), and a general affirmation of roots and origins as the basic criteria of citizenship and belonging.
>
> (Geschiere and Nyamnjoh 2000: 423)

South Asian societies have strong traditions of social inclusiveness and many institutional mechanisms for including people (e.g. classificatory kinship terminologies). At the same time, social distinctions between locals and non-locals were always important, but the implications were different from today. For example, in the past, rulers often emphasized their origin from elsewhere, and yet they had privileged access to political positions. From the late colonial period and particularly since the violent partition of 1947, however, autochthony has increasingly been used as a powerful slogan to exclude the stranger – from the vote, from land and from jobs – and in recent years this decidedly non-liberal tendency towards exclusion, homogenization and purification has intensified (Geschiere and Nyamnjoh 2000: 423). The Assam Movement of the 1980s (which sought to expel Bangladeshi immigrants) and the campaign against Sonia Gandhi from 1998 (an attempt to discredit her as a candidate for high office in India because of her foreign birth) are well-known South Asian examples of this new spatial imagination that is preoccupied with boundaries and exclusion.

The concept of 'indigenous people' can play into this tendency. Unlike the more clearly defined notion of ethnicity (where people identify with groups on the basis of a shared language and history), notions of indigeneity/autochthony are less specific.

They are equally capable of arousing strong emotions regarding the defence of home and of ancestral lands, but since their substance is not named they are both more elusive and more easily subject to political manipulation.

(Geschiere and Nyamnjoh 2000: 424)

In the complex social world of South Asia almost any group can present itself as indigenous and as threatened by invading Others. For example, the creation of Jharkhand state in India, the expulsion of Nepalis from Bhutan, and confrontations between locals and the Pakistan army in South Waziristan all play upon notions of defending the Homeland against the Other. 'Indigenous' is anything but a registered trademark. Indeed, it can be claimed by dominant groups to eliminate aliens. Anti-foreigner movements in Europe, Hutus killing Tutsis in Rwanda, and Hindu nationalist campaigns against Muslims and Christians have all used the beleaguered-indigenous versus threatening-outsider dichotomy to their political advantage. In fact, Hindu nationalists in India reject the category of 'tribals'/'adivasis' altogether – they aver that Hindus rather than 'adivasis' are India's indigenous inhabitants.[12] In other words, the 'indigenous' label can be used to many ends, from demanding basic rights for dispossessed communities to mobilizing support for majoritarian racist and fascist projects (Ceuppens and Geschiere 2005). In addition, these movements, whatever their political content, may develop into movements for defensible places, exclusionary territories or geographical apartheid.

Is this a traditionalist defence against modernity? Or is it better understood as part of the process of accelerating flows of people, information, goods and capital around the world that is usually described as 'globalization'? Many people have stressed that globalization is not just a process of increasing cosmopolitanism and openness. On the contrary, it triggers strong urges towards localization and exclusion. The politics of belonging, grounded in notions of autochthony, are best understood as an integral element of globalization.

In the current global conjuncture, progressive ideas about 'indigenous people' may therefore fuse with xenophobic ideologies of belonging. When political entrepreneurs elevate to an unassailable principle the 'natural' rights that arise from rootedness in a place of birth, whip up emotions about the urgency to defend the community's identity because time has run out, and turn the community into a fetish at the expense of individual members' opinions, they create ideologies and practices of belonging that point to claims of *exclusive* rights and to strategies of purification that may result in ethnic cleansing. Beneath the surface of South Asian polities we can hear the rumblings of a counter-politics of indigenous assertion that raises fundamental questions about national citizenship and the territorial jurisdiction of the liberal modernist state (Comaroff and Comaroff 2003). These rumblings can be heard in debates swirling around demands for 'tribal'-dominated states, autonomous regions and 'indigenous' land councils, as in the cases of Jharkhand, Bodoland, the Chittagong Hill Tracts or the Northwest Frontier Province. They are equally noticeable in the resolve to (re)impose colonial 'Inner Line' permits upon domestic tourists wanting to visit Northeast Indian states, in the annihilation of non-indigenous co-citizens (e.g. Bihari labourers in Assam), and in human rights abuses perpetrated by one indigenous group upon another (e.g. the fate of Chakmas in Arunachal Pradesh, Santals in Assam or Brus in Mizoram).

The sovereignty of the state is at stake, challenged by an alternative authority sanctioning different forms of justice, force, entitlements and taxation. When 'indigenous people' decide that full citizenship is unattainable for them, or at least irreconcilable with 'indigenous' identities, the national citizen of legal and much mass-mediated discourse can find him/herself at loggerheads with the indigenous subject with exclusive jurisdiction over indigenous affairs. Under these circumstances, 'the received notion of polities based upon cultural homogeneity and a sense of horizontal fraternity … is rapidly giving way to imagined communities of difference,' and political personhood becomes fractured, unstable and easily manipulated (Comaroff and Comaroff 2003: 454).

To counter this tendency, the transformation of the state has to go well beyond multiculturalism – the national majority recognizing and appreciating the customs and cuisine of minorities – or state policies dealing with 'indigenous' entitlements and human rights by offering modernity-by-development or legal pluralism. Today it seems that in parts of South Asia the politics of belonging has developed to a point where it is not satisfied with recognition. On the contrary, it is questioning the very possibility of a coexistence of indigenous rights (now underwritten by powerful global institutions) and national citizens' rights.

State elites in South Asia are slowly waking up to the fact that threats to their sovereignty are perhaps not so much the external ones with which they were so preoccupied in the twentieth century but may stem from a new internal politics of belonging that has abandoned the dream of full liberal citizenship and a future national commonwealth. This unexpected global agency of communities that only yesterday seemed to be of little weight in state affairs provides a huge challenge for those who are still caught up in the paternalistic 'tribal' discourse. But it also dares those who propound the 'indigenous peoples' discourse to consider its less-than-emancipatory connotations. And it should alert all of us to the fact that we are not ready to face the unfamiliar and ominous landscape of the new politics of belonging.

Homelands

The core question before us is how to square notions of 'indigenous' self-determination with notions of territorial and political inclusiveness (Karlsson 2003: 423). Obviously, this is a question that concerns the whole world, not just South Asia. Social scientists working on these issues in South Asia are, however, well placed to contribute to solutions. In South Asia, claims to indigenous rights have focused strongly upon place. 'Indigenous' groups have struggled for 'differential geographies: that is, the right to make their own places, rather than have them made for them' (Castree 2004: 136). The argument is straightforward: in colonial times a process commenced in which groups that now identify themselves as indigenous were dispossessed without compensation for their land, its biodiversity and mineral resources, and their knowledge about these. The process continues today. Non-indigenous groups took control, either by declaring land and resources to be public property, or by non-indigenous individuals acquiring private property rights in land previously held by 'indigenous' groups. In each country of South Asia, enormous tracts of forests were (and continue to be) exploited by the Forest Department, a colonial institution. Inhabitants were driven out and their descendents are barred from settling there (Van Schendel *et al.* 2000: 131–48, 204). Currently, biodiversity prospecting and patenting of genetic material form new threats to which 'indigenous' groups point to underline the urgency of rapid action (Castree 2004: 161–2).

Because dispossession and dislocation have created 'indigenous' communities in South Asia, it is no surprise that imagined solutions take the form of claims to specific territories with a view to re-appropriating them. Making a place for yourself is, however, dependent upon how you think about place. If you see place as a coherent location occupied by a particular group until it is ousted by another group, you will see reclamation as a process of driving out intruders to restore the status quo ante. There are all kinds of problems with this view, from obliterating histories of human mobility and coexistence to the impossibility ever to restore an earlier status quo. On the other hand, there are good reasons for 'indigenous' groups to reject another view of places: as entirely open to flows of people and commodities, and as integrated in a global economy over which they have no power whatsoever. Finding solutions that are in between these two extremes is very important. The costs of the 'borderless world' approach for 'indigenous' communities are well known, the costs of the 'exclusive location' approach less so. And this is exactly where South Asian experiences are significant.

South Asia has ample – and bitter – experience of the realities of exclusive homelands. The decolonization of British India took the form of the creation of two homelands, one for South Asia's Muslims and another for non-Muslims. For those who found themselves in the wrong homeland, the consequences could vary from being seen as fifth-columnists and becoming second-class citizens to being driven into exile or losing one's life. Countless South Asian lives were – and continue to be – troubled by the experience (Ray 2000–1; Van Schendel 2002, 2005). Not only were the economic, social, political and psychological costs of the homeland approach enormous, but what many had not anticipated: they continue to this day. There are many who have argued that the remedy of Partition – as the creation of the two homelands in 1947 came to be known – has been worse than the disease it sought to cure (Krishna 1999: 239).

And yet, despite these serious misgivings, the model of partition as a solution to political discord has struck deep roots in South Asia. To many, creating a homeland and casting out others appears to be a feasible answer to current griev-ances. In South Asia the ideology of separation has been flourishing ever since 1947. It powered important movements for separate homelands in the territories of India (e.g. Khalistan, Nagaland), Pakistan (e.g. Bangladesh, Sindh) and Sri Lanka (Tamil Eelam). The most successful to date was the movement for Bang-ladesh, leading to the establishment of a separate state in 1971. Over the years there have been many other movements fighting for autonomous homelands within the framework of the existing states, some of them quite successful. India's Jharkhand and Uttarakhand are good examples; Bangladesh's Chittagong Hill Tracts are a less fortunate case. One area in which the idea of separate homelands has come to dominate regional politics is Northeast India, where dozens of 'homeland-bound' movements have been operating with varying success.

Homelands in Northeast India

Northeast India is itself a creation of partition; it has experienced all the quandaries of territorial separation. The partition of 1947 ripped it from its neighbour East Pakistan (later to become Bangladesh). Its economy was torn asunder and its communications through East Pakistan/Bangladesh were severed. Its Muslim inhabitants faced discrimination and violent expulsion and it received large numbers of similarly expelled non-Muslim refugees from East Pakistan/Bangladesh. Last but not least, it was saddled with an unlikely territorial shape, linked to the rest of India only by a narrow corridor between Nepal and East Pakistan/Bangladesh. The idea of an exclusive homeland for South Asia's Muslims had created this isolated territory just as much as it had created neighbouring East Pakistan/Bangladesh (see Map 1).

And yet, despite this unsettling experience, the model of the exclusive home-land became ever more popular *within* Northeast India, both as a political project of aspiring regional elites and as an administrative solution to law and order problems. The splitting up of the state of Assam shows this clearly. In response

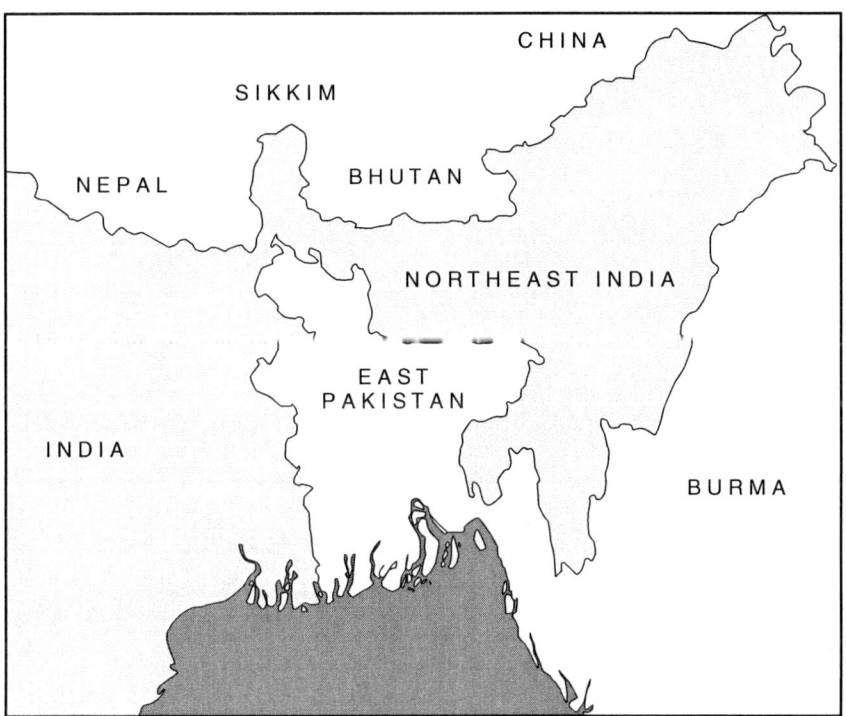

Map 1 The shape of Northeast India, 1947.

to political campaigns after independence in 1947, the Indian government gradually detached the mountainous parts of this state from the plains. The eventual result was the creation of several separate states that were conceived of as ethnic homelands: Nagaland, Meghalaya, Arunachal Pradesh and Mizoram (Maps 2 and 3).

The logic of homelands did not stop here. It continues to lead to further subdivision. Take Mizoram, which became a state after a 20-year war of secession was concluded with a treaty in 1986. Henceforth, Mizoram was to be the homeland of the Mizo community. It was detached from Assam (where this region had previously been known as the Lushai Hills) and became a separate state within the union of India. But other communities now became minorities in this new state and demanded their own homelands. Three were partly successful: Mara, Lai and Chakma won separate autonomous districts for themselves in southern Mizoram (Map 4).

They continue to feel threatened by Mizo politicians, however, and some local leaders are trying to detach their districts from Mizoram state altogether and turn them into a 'union territory,' i.e. administered directly from Delhi. They also have homeland claims beyond the Indian state. For example, the Mara claim 'East Maraland', a region now administered by Burma/Myanmar.[13] The

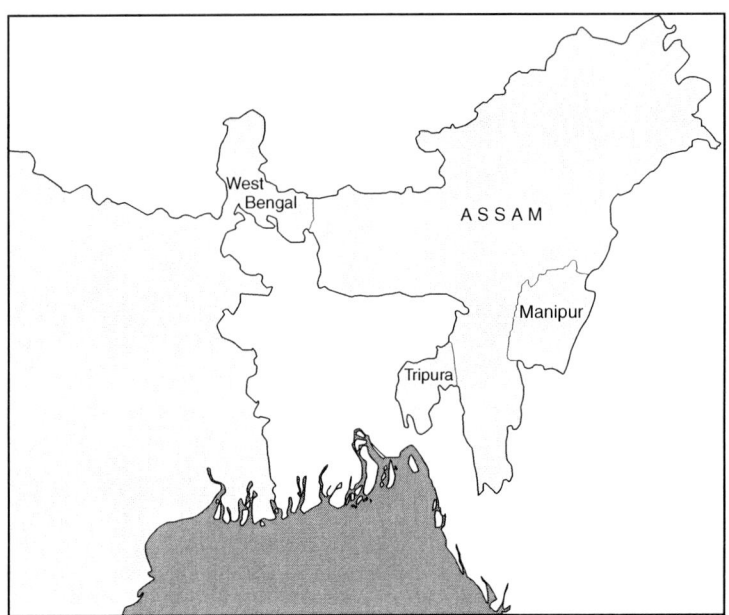

Map 2 States of Northeast India, 1947.

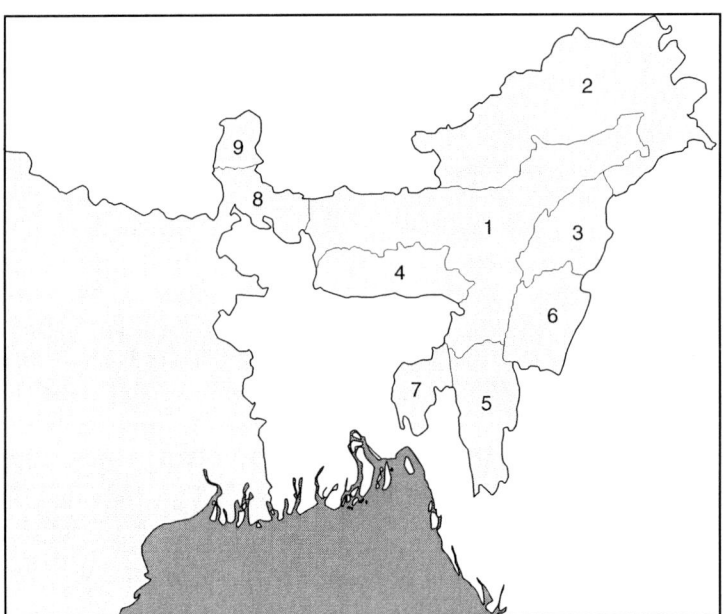

Map 3 States of Northeast India, 1987.

Notes

1 Assam (became a state in India in 1947);
2 Arunachal Pradesh (formerly North Eastern Frontier Agency, or NEFA; 1987);
3 Nagaland (1963);
4 Meghalaya (1972);
5 Mizoram (1987);
6 Manipur (1972);
7 Tripura (1972);
8 West Bengal (1947);
9 Sikkim (1975).

Map 4 Homelands in Mizoram and Tripura.

Notes
1 Chakma;
2 Lai;
3 Mara;
4 'Tribal'.

homeland logic did not work out so well for other minorities in Mizoram, however, notably the Bru in northern Mizoram whose drive for an autonomous district led to armed clashes, the formation of the Bru National Liberation Front, the expulsion of tens of thousands of Bru from Mizoram to Tripura, and abductions and killings.

The Mizoram story exemplifies a trend all over Northeast India: the homeland logic creates further subdivisions within states. Assam now has no less than nine autonomous districts (the most recent created in 2005), Manipur has six, Meghalaya three and Arunachal Pradesh is planning two. Only Nagaland is without autonomous districts. Thus Assam, the sole state of Northeast India in 1947, was joined by two more (Tripura and Manipur) in 1949; by 1987 there were seven states in Northeast India and today these contain 22 autonomous districts. And in each state there are movements afoot to create more homelands.[14] Clearly, over the years many people in Northeast India have been captivated by the homeland logic. The general pattern is for 'indigenous' organizations to claim an exclusive homeland and for the state to grant – often reluctantly and after violent confrontations – an 'autonomous district'. Further claims may lead to the status of a 'territorial areas district', an 'autonomous state within a state', a 'union territory' or even a full-fledged (federated) state.[15] This march toward the exclusive homeland is supported by specific legislation for the region. The Constitution of India contains a Sixth Schedule comprising 'Provisions as to the Administration of Tribal Areas in the States of Assam, Meghalaya, Tripura and Mizoram' and spelling out the regulations governing autonomous districts and regions.[16] These districts and regions are far more autonomous than similar areas in the rest of India. The latter are under a different part of the Constitution, the Fifth Schedule, which deals with the administration of 'scheduled areas' and 'scheduled tribes'.[17] In other words, the legal tools for achieving territorial autonomy are more robust in Northeast India than in other parts of India.

The march toward the exclusive homeland is hazardous and often excruciating, and it is by no means simply a case of 'indigenous' people battling a 'non-indigenous' state. For example, despite the fact that in 1982 most of Tripura became a 'tribal areas autonomous district' (see Map 4), this did nothing to lessen the internecine warfare that dominates life here. Violent confrontations between Meitheis and Nagas in Manipur revolve around a possible inclusion of Manipur's hill districts into Nagaland. The Arunachal Pradesh government seeks to deport Hajongs and Chakmas from its territory despite the Delhi High Court's ruling that they are Indian citizens. In Assam, which now boasts nine autonomous districts, Bodo attacks have driven Santals into refugee camps.[18] Inhabitants of the Meghalaya-Assam borderland have become victims of fighting because Meghalaya has staked a claim on chunks of Assamese territory. And so on … the indigenous versus indigenous casualty list is much longer. The main cause of so much violence is that the idea of the exclusive homeland does not fit with the reality of settlement patterns that are anything but exclusive. The assumption underlying homelands – that 'tribes' or 'indigenous people' live in clearly demarcated contiguous territories in which they are the first and only, or at least the prior and still predominant, group – cannot be applied to a demographic reality of ethnic dispersion and overlap without inviting violent expulsion and displacement.

None of these conflicts pitches 'indigenous' people against 'non-indigenous people' (although there are plenty of such examples in Northeast India as well). This means that the making of exclusive places has terrible side effects for the very people who should stand to benefit. But the situation is even more peculiar. Today a homeland can also be won by a group that the state has not classified as 'tribal'. In 2005 the Assam Assembly passed a bill to create an autonomous district for the Thengal Kacharis who had never previously been recognized as a 'tribal' community (Prabhakara 2005). Even more extreme is the demand for the Assamese (the dominant ethnic group in the state of Assam and never considered a 'tribe') to be included in the category of 'indigenous people' and to deny other Indian citizens the right to contest elections in the state (Baruah 2005: 204). Thus, what Baruah calls Northeast India's 'protective discrimination regime' has had unintended consequences. Here, as in many other parts of the world, an exclusionary politics of belonging has developed, based on roots and origins. And 'the geographical imaginations that local actors and institutions have deployed to command their home "turf" have often been chauvinistic, essentialist, and exclusive, as opposed to ecumenical, open and inclusive' (Castree 2004: 141; Ceuppens and Geschiere 2005). What is urgently needed, then, is a geographical imagination that is less destructive in its consequences.

Levels of 'indigenous' power

The rationale for claiming territory is that it provides a dependable basis for absolute control of resources, which in turn makes it possible to redress extremely skewed power relations. Place is a means to power and an insurance against continued powerlessness. If exclusive homelands do not provide the expected solution – in Northeast India or elsewhere – the answer may lie in pragmatically exploring other ways of attaining power. Places may have to be reimagined as more open and hybrid, nodes in a flexible mixture of power relations that allow for coexistence and power sharing.

How are we to imagine such places? One way would be to create 'indigenous' places that are graduated. For example, think of different levels of 'indigenous' control. Level 1 consists of *indigenous places*. These places have a high level of exclusivity and autonomy in terms of access to material and immaterial resources. They resemble autonomous regions and homelands in terms of the bundles of 'indigenous' rights that they provide but without fetishizing geography: they are not necessarily contiguous. In spatial terms they form archipelagos and this makes it easier – but by no means simple – to accommodate the problem of overlapping homeland claims.[19]

Level 2 comprises *joint indigenous places*. Here a system of equal power sharing is negotiated between two or more 'indigenous' communities laying claim to the same territory and its resources, and not willing to relinquish their claims. Again these places need not be contiguous. There is some experience with this in the region but building stable arrangements of this type will require much effort and experimentation.

Level 3 are *co-managed places*, resources and sites that 'indigenous' groups share with non-'indigenous' groups and institutions such as local and state governments, or non-governmental organizations. These co-managed places are essential for two reasons. First, they act as a counterweight to the perceived loss of the solidity of an 'exclusive homeland.' Second, they allow 'indigenous' groups to exercise rights beyond their territories and so assert their rights as Indian (Bangladeshi, Pakistani, etc.) citizens. These co-managed places consist of both places *in* the homeland as it is currently imagined – e.g. roads, dams, airfields, power stations, forests, water bodies, mines, plantations, nature parks, educational and health institutions, heritage sites – and places *beyond* it – e.g. industries processing timber, bamboo, oil, coal and other resources from 'indigenous' areas as well as media, educational and tourism institutions engaged in shaping images of 'indigenous'/non-'indigenous' relations.

It makes sense to think of these co-managed places more in terms of shared 'bundles of powers' than of exclusive 'bundles of rights' (Ribot and Peluso 2003) – they may involve a redistribution of economically valuable resources and assets without co-ownership. Powerful non-'indigenous' (state) institutions will take part in co-management, not out of some altruistic urge but because of well-considered self-interest. Without building local/trans-local relationships based upon 'indigenous'/non-'indigenous' trust, the politics of belonging are set to become more intensely chauvinistic, essentialist, exclusive, and separatist.

Clearly, opposition against these arrangements will be intense at all three levels because for most people identity is so closely bundled with spatial exclusivity. Opposition is likely to be especially intense at Level 3, however, because here the arrangements outlined above confront dominant political and economic powers at the regional, national and transnational scale. To these powers the right to make their own places, rather than have them made for them, appears as a birthright. Their conceptions of place are usually as exclusive and proprietary as those underpinning the idea of the homeland – indeed, this is exactly why 'indigenous' claims take the form of exclusive homelands – and retooling them to allow co-management will be an arduous struggle. And yet, these older notions of place have become obsolete because they are non-sustainable. This awareness has led to experiments with co-managed places in different parts of the world. Although these tend to be restricted to places within 'indigenous' homelands – e.g. social forestry (Clay *et al.* 2000: 26) – they reveal the possibilities and difficulties involved (Wily 1999; Appiah 2001; Hughes 2001; Mehta and Heinen 2001; cf. Fernández-Giménez 2002; Kellert *et al.* 2000).[20] Co-managed places beyond the confines of 'indigenous' homelands do not exist anywhere in Northeast India; in fact, they are still extremely rare worldwide (Biolsi 2005).

As we have seen, the social groups that, in South Asian discourses, are commonly talked about as 'tribes' or 'indigenous peoples' acquired these designations during two different periods – about 150 years apart – in which political and academic discourses globalized rapidly. Both terms became domesticated in South Asia where they are now essential – and at times competing – rhetorical elements in struggles over rights, power, place, authenticity and self-definition. Their relationship with a verifiable past may at times be tenuous – e.g. the Thengal Kacharis' tribal status, or the Mizo claim to an exclusive homeland where Bru do not belong – and their referential substance ill defined. This has led some social scientists to cross swords over the credentials of these terms in academic communication (Karlsson and Subba 2006). Others focus on the emergence of 'indigenous' claims and their often unintended consequences. In this chapter I have looked at the dangers inherent in 'indigenous' claims to exclusive homelands and at the victimization of outsiders that almost inescapably accompanies these claims. Re-imagining places as more inclusive and hybrid, allowing for coexistence and power sharing, may be a necessary first step in preventing such politics of belonging from turning into a 'politics of geographical hate' (Castree 2004: 163), played out not just in faraway corners of South Asia but increasingly in its centres of political and economic power.

Notes

1 I thank Peter Geschiere, the participants of the conference in Santiniketan, India (November 2005) and an anonymous reader for comments on an earlier version.

2 This style of social analysis could be called 'tribalist discourse' because it presumes that all 'tribes' share characteristics that are fundamentally different from, even opposite to, those of 'civilised' people (Van Schendel 1992: 103 fn. 34; Bal 2007).

3 One of the connotations of 'adivasi' is its opposition to dominant upper-caste Hindu groups and their discourse of social hierarchy and the nation. In parts of South Asia where the dominant group is different (e.g. Muslims in Pakistan or Bangladesh, Buddhists in Bhutan, Christians in Mizoram), where 'tribals' form the vast majority of the population (Meghalaya, Mizoram, Arunachal Pradesh), or where the discourse of the nation has always been much less hegemonic (Northeast India), the term is more a tool in dialogues with the state than an enthusiastically adopted self-identification – here 'indigenous people' evokes the stronger emotions. Also, comparison of the different vocabularies to denote 'tribals' in India, Pakistan and Bangladesh could be useful in analysing the very different nationalisms that now dominate erstwhile British India.

4 The Constitutions of India (e.g. Fifth and Sixth Schedules), Pakistan and Nepal mention 'tribe' or 'tribal area'. The Bangladesh Constitution does not, but other legal instruments do, e.g. the 1997 Chittagong Hill Tracts Treaty which describes the region as a 'Tribal Populated Region'.

5 On claims research since the arrival of the 'modern claims era' in North America and Australia, see Ray (2005).

6 On Pakistan, see Ali and Rehman (2001); on Bangladesh, see Bal (2007); on Northeast India, see Baruah (2005).

7 On Bangladesh's policy, see Chittagong Hill Tracts Commission (1991, 1994, 1997, 2000). On India's policy, see Hazarika (1994); Baruah (1999).

8 For example. the International Work Group on Indigenous Affairs (IWGIA), Survival International, the Unrepresented Nations and Peoples Organisation (UNPO) and the United Nations Working Group on Indigenous Populations; see Karlsson (2003).

9 For a detailed discussion of conceptual complexities and regional variation within India, see Karlsson and Subba (2006).

10 Mainly because it makes the struggle to be accepted as 'regular' national citizens more difficult. In this, they resemble the Peruvians described by Frank Salomon:

> In Huarochirí Province (Department of Lima), as throughout modern highland Peru, campesinos find the rhetoric of 'ethnicity' and the 'indigenous' highly problematic because they perceive these as marked terms that distance their bearers from normal standing as citizens. Far from connoting healthy pluralism, as they do in international academic discourse, terms such as 'indigenous' seem to peasant ears (*c.*1970–2000) to be freighted with unacceptable racial connotations and unpleasant memories of *de haut en bas* indigenism.
>
> Salomon (2002: 475)

11 For a description of the complexities of one such performance in Nagaland, see Kikon (2005).

12 On the political use of *vanavasi*, see Rycroft (2009).

13 See www.maraland.net/maraland/east-maraland.html (accessed 1 June 2010).

14 For the movement for 'Ahomland', see Saikia (2004).

15 Under article 244A of the Indian constitution, Meghalaya briefly was an 'autonomous state within Assam' before it became a separate state; this intermediate position is now demanded by the movement for a homeland in Karbi Anglong and the North Cachar Hills (currently autonomous districts). The Bodoland movement in Assam was able to upgrade the Bodoland Autonomous District (created in 1993) to the Bodoland Territorial Areas District in 2003.

16 For information on the implementation of the Sixth Schedule, see Baruah (2005: 188–193).

17 For distinctions between the Fifth and Sixth Schedules, see Sonntag (1999; 2006).

18 The character of these autonomous bodies varies but in all cases falls far short of the territorial autonomy demanded by the organisations concerned. Between 1993 and 2005 autonomous (territorial) councils were created for the Bodo, the Mising, the Karbi Anglong district, the North Cachar Hills, the Rabha, the Tiwa, the Sonowal Kachari, the Deori and the Thengal Kachari. For details, see the Sixth Schedule of the Constitution of India ('Provisions as to the Administration of Tribal Areas in the States of Assam, Meghalaya, Tripura and Mizoram').

19 In some cases such 'indigenous places' might develop from movements to reinstate old systems of governance that were less focused on territorial sovereignty, for example because they were based on controlling people rather than land; see Karlsson (2005).

20 For introductions to the Indian joint forestry programme, see Sundar (2000); Prasad and Kant (2003); Gupte (2004).

References

Ali, S.S. and Rehman, J. (2001) *Indigenous Peoples and Ethnic Minorities of Pakistan Constitutional and Legal Perspectives,* Richmond: NIAS/Curzon Press.

Appiah, M. (2001) 'Co-Partnership in Forest Management: The Gwira-Banso Joint Forest Management Project in Ghana', *Environment, Development and Sustainability,* 3: 343–60.

Arnold, D. (2004) 'Race, Place and Bodily Difference in Early Nineteenth-Century India', *Historical Research,* 77: 254–73.

Bal, E. (2007) *They Ask If We Eat Frogs: Garo Ethnicity in Bangladesh,* Singapore: Institute of Southeast Asian Studies.

Baruah, S. (1999) *India Against Itself: Assam and the Politics of Nationality,* Philadelphia: University of Pennsylvania Press.

—— (2005) *Durable Disorder: Understanding the Politics of Northeast India,* New Delhi: Oxford University Press.

Bates, C. (1995) 'Race, Caste, and Tribe in Central India: The Early Origins of Indian Anthropometry', in P. Robb (ed.), *The Concept of Race in South Asia,* New Delhi: Oxford University Press, 219–57.

Béteille, A. (1998) 'The Idea of Indigenous People', *Current Anthropology,* 39: 187–91.

—— (2006) 'What Should We Mean By "Indigenous People"?' in B.G. Karlsson and T.B. Subba (eds), *Indigeneity in India,* London: Kegan Paul, 19–31.

Biolsi, T. (2005) 'Imagined Geographies: Sovereignty, Indigenous Space, and American Indian Struggle', *American Ethnologist,* 32: 239–59.

Blackburn, S. (2003) 'Colonial Contact in the "Hidden Land": Oral History Among the Apatanis of Arunachal Pradesh', *The Indian Economic and Social History Review,* 40: 335–65.

Bowen, J.R. (2000) 'Should We Have a Universal Concept of "Indigenous Peoples' Rights"? Ethnicity and Essentialism in the Twenty-First Century', *Anthropology Today,* 16: 12–6.

Castree, N. (2004) 'Differential Geographies: Place, Indigenous Rights, and Local Resources', *Political Geography,* 23: 133–67.

Ceuppens, B. and Geschiere, P. (2005) 'Autochthony: Local or Global? New Modes in the Struggle over Citizenship and Belonging in Africa and Europe', *Annual Review of Anthropology,* 34: 385–407.

Chittagong Hill Tracts Commission (1991) *Life Is Not Ours: Land and Human Rights in the Chittagong Hill Tracts, Bangladesh, Report,* Copenhagen/Amsterdam: IWGIA/OCCHTC.

—— (1992) *Life Is Not Ours: Land and Human Rights in the Chittagong Hill Tracts, Bangladesh, Update 1,* Copenhagen/Amsterdam: IWGIA/OCCHTC.

—— (1994) *Life Is Not Ours: Land and Human Rights in the Chittagong Hill Tracts, Bangladesh, Update 2,* Copenhagen/Amsterdam: IWGIA/OCCHTC.

—— (1997) *Life Is Not Ours: Land and Human Rights in the Chittagong Hill Tracts, Bangladesh, Update 3,* Copenhagen/Amsterdam: IWGIA/OCCHTC.

—— (2000) *Life Is Not Ours: Land and Human Rights in the Chittagong Hill Tracts, Bangladesh, Update 4,* Copenhagen/Amsterdam: IWGIA/OCCHTC..

Clay, J.W., Alcorn, J. and Butler, J. (2000) *Indigenous Peoples, Forestry Management and Biodiversity Conservation: An Analytical Study for the World Bank's Forestry Policy Implementation Review and Strategic Development Framework,* Washington DC: The World Bank.

Comaroff, J. and Comaroff, J. (2003) 'Reflections on Liberalism, Policulturalism, and Ideology. Citizenship and Difference in South Africa', *Social Identities,* 9: 445–73.

Fernández-Giménez, M.E. (2002), 'Spatial and Social Boundaries and the Paradox of Pastural Land Tenure: A Case Study from Postsocialist Mongolia', *Human Ecology,* 30: 49–78.

Fried, M.H. (1975) *The Notion of Tribe,* Menlo Park: Cumming Publishing Company.

Geschiere, P. and Nyamnjoh, F. (2000) 'Capitalism and Autochthony: The Seesaw of Mobility and Belonging', *Public Culture,* 12: 423–52.

Government of India (2001) *10th Five-Year Plan (2002–2007),* Delhi: Planning Commission.

Gupte, M. (2004) 'Participation in a Gendered Environment: The Case of Community Forestry in India', *Human Ecology,* 32: 365–82.

Hall, T.D. and Fenelon, J.V. (2004) 'The Futures of Indigenous Peoples: 9–11 and the Trajectory of Indigenous Survival and Resistance', *Journal of World-Systems Research,* 10: 153–97.

Hazarika, S. (1994) *Strangers of the Mist: Tales of War & Peace from India's Northeast,* Delhi: Viking.

Hughes, D.M. (2001) 'Cadastral Politics: The Making of Community-Based Resource Management in Zimbabwe and Mozambique', *Development and Change,* 32: 741–68.

Karlsson, B.G. (2003) 'Anthropology and the "Indigenous Slot": Claims to and Debates about Indigenous Peoples' Status in India', *Critique of Anthropology,* 23: 403–23.

—— (2005) 'Sovereignty through Indigenous Governance: Reviving "Traditional Political Institutions" in Northeast India', *The NEHU Journal,* 3: 1–15.

Karlsson, B.G. and Subba, T.B. (eds) (2006) *Indigeneity in India,* London: Kegan Paul.

Kellert, S.R., Mehta, J.N., Ebbin, S.A. and Lichtenfeld, L.L. (2000) 'Community Natural Resource Management: Promise, Rhetoric and Reality', *Society & Natural Resources,* 13: 705–15.

Kikon, D. (2005) 'Operation Hornbill Festival 2004', *Seminar,* 550. www.india-seminar. com/2005/.../550%20dolly%20kikon.htm (Accessed 3 January 2006)

Kingsbury, B. (1998) ' "Indigenous Peoples" in International Law: A Constructivist Approach to the Asian Controversy', *American Journal of International Law,* 92: 414–57.

Krishna, S. (1999) *Postcolonial Insecurities: India, Sri Lanka and the Question of Nationhood,* Minneapolis: University of Minnesota Press.

Li, T.M. (2000) 'Articulating Indigenous Identity in Indonesia: Resource Politics and the Tribal Slot', *Comparative Studies in Society and History,* 42: 149–79.

Lowe, C., Brimah, T., Marsh, P-A., Minter, W. and Muyangwa, M. (1997) 'Talking about

"Tribe": Moving from Stereotypes to Analysis', *Africa Policy E-Journal*. http://apic. igc.org/bp/ethall.htm (accessed 3 January 2006)

Mehta, J.N. and Heinen, J.T. (2001) 'Does Community-Based Conservation Shape Favorable Attitudes Among Locals? An Empirical Study From Nepal', *Environmental Management*, 28: 165–77.

Minde, H. (1996) 'The Making of an International Movement of Indigenous Peoples', *Scandinavian Journal of History*, 21: 221–46.

Morgan, L.H. (1878) *Ancient Society, or Researches in the Line of Human Progress from Savagery through Barbarism to Civilization*, New York: Holt.

Niezen, R. (2000) 'Recognizing Indigenism: Canadian Unity and the International Movement of Indigenous Peoples', *Comparative Studies in Society and History*, 42: 119–48.

Prabhakara, M.S. (2005) 'Manufacturing Identities?' *Frontline*, 22, 24 September–7 October.

Prasad, R. and Kant, S. (2003) 'Institutions, Forest Management, and Sustainable Human Development – Experiences from India', *Environment, Development and Sustainability*, 5: 353–67.

Ray, A.J. (2005) 'Constructing and Reconstructing Native History: A Comparative Look at the Impact of Aboriginal and Treaty Rights Claims in North America and Australia', *Native Studies Review*, 16: 15–39.

Ray, M. (2000–1) 'Growing Up Refugee: On Memory and Locality', *Hindi: Language, Discourse, Writing*, 1: 148–98.

Ribot, J.C. and Peluso, N.L. (2003) 'A Theory of Access', *Rural Sociology*, 68: 153–81.

Robb, P. (1997) 'The Colonial State and Constructions of Indian Identity: An Example on the Northeast Frontier in the 1880s', *Modern Asian Studies*, 31: 245–83.

Roy Burman, B.K. (1998) 'Tribal and Indigenous Rights and Wrongs' in B.K. Roy Burman and B.G. Verghese (eds), *Aspiring to Be: Tribal/Indigenous Condition*, Delhi: Konark Publishers.

Rycroft, D.J., 2009, 'Revisioning Birsa Munda: visual constructions of the "*vanavasi*" in Jharkhand', in N.K. Das and V.R. Rao (eds), *Identity, Cultural Pluralism and the State: South Asia in Perspective*, Delhi: Macmillan Publishers, 261–80.

Saikia, Y. (2004) *Fragmented Memories: Struggling to be Tai-Ahom in India*, Durham and London: Duke University Press.

Salomon, F. (2002) 'Unethnic Ethnohistory: On Peruvian Peasant Historiography and Ideas of Autochthony', *Ethnohistory*, 49: 475–506.

Skaria, A. (1997) 'Shades of Wildness: Tribe, Caste, and Gender in Western India', *The Journal of Asian Studies*, 56: 726–45.

Sonntag, S.K. (1999) 'Autonomous Councils in India: Contesting the Nation-State', *Alternatives*, 24: 415–34.

—— (2006) 'Self-Government, Indigeneity and Cultural Authenticity: A Comparative Study of India and the United States', in B.G. Karlsson and T.B. Subba (eds), *Indigeneity in India,* London: Kegan Paul, 187–208.

Southall, A. (1970) 'The Illusion of Tribe' in P. Gutkind (ed.), *The Passing of Tribal Man in Africa* Leiden: Brill, 28–51.

Sundar, N. (2000) 'Unpacking the "Joint" in Joint Forest Management', *Development and Change*, 31: 255–79.

United Nations (2007) 'United Nations adopts Declaration on Rights of Indigenous Peoples', www.un.org/apps/news/story.asp?NewsID=23794&Cr=indigenous&Cr1 (accessed 1 June 2010).

Van Schendel, W. (1992) 'The Invention of the "Jummas": State Formation and Ethnicity in Southeastern Bangladesh', *Modern Asian Studies*, 26: 95–128.

—— (2002) 'Stateless in South Asia: The Making of the India-Bangladesh Enclaves', *The Journal of Asian Studies*, 61: 115–47.

—— (2005) *The Bengal Borderland: Beyond State and Nation in South Asia*, London: Anthem Press.

Van Schendel, W., Mey, W. and Dewan, A.K. (2000) *The Chittagong Hill Tracts: Living in a Borderland*, Bangkok: White Lotus.

Wily, L. (1999) 'Moving Forward in African Community Forestry: Trading Power, Not Use Rights', *Society & Natural Resources*, 12: 4961.

World Bank (2010) 'Indigenous Peoples', http://web.worldbank.org/WBSITE/EXTER-NAL/TOPICS/EXTSOCIALDEVELOPMENT/EXTINDPEOPLE/0,,menuPK: 407808~pagePK: 149018~piPK: 149093~theSitePK: 407802,00.html (accessed 1 June 2010).

3 Performative genres as boundary markers

Folklore and the creation of Purulia as a border zone

Roma Chatterji

Introduction

'*Adivasi* is a word invented by Gandhiji!' This statement was made by an elderly Brahmin man – a descendent of the priestly family that had been brought to Purulia District in West Bengal by the *rajas* (princes) of Baghmundi and settled in the village of Chorida, where I was doing fieldwork in the early 1980s.[1] The context was a discussion on the term *Adivasi* brought about by the fact that the Chorida dance troupe was trying to choreograph a new *chho* dance item (*pala*) on the theme 'The Origin of the Adivasis' (*Adibashir Uttpotti*). Gambhir Singh Mura, one of the leading exponents of the masked *chho* dance genre and the leader of the troupe, was insistent that the story to be enacted had to be authenticated by a sacred text.[2] The dancers were in a quandary because they could not locate a sacred text within which to embed the story. Finally, they used a story from the *Sharaboli* – a collection of stories about the god Krishna taken largely from the *Harivamsa*.[3] The story describes the origin of an earth born *jati* (caste) called *Pashana* (stone).[4] This name was taken to symbolize the Bhumij for the purpose of the dance story as they are the dominant *Adivasi* group in the village. As one of the dancers explained to me, '*Bhumij* means 'born of the earth' (*bhui theke hoenche*) and the stone (*pashana*) symbolizes their *jaat* (*jati* or group)'.[5]

Purulia as a border zone

As this incident shows, *Adivasi* as a term for self-designation had still not stabilized in the Baghmundi region (Purulia district) in the 1980s. My informants in Chorida were conscious that it was a constructed term, which was used largely in political contexts such as the rallies that were being held in Baghmundi village to mobilize support for the Jharkhand Party during the assembly elections and so on. But knowledge about the Jharkhand movement, and about tribal identity-formation, was at a nascent stage. The situation in Baghmundi is now radically different as Rycroft's recent work shows (Rycroft 2009), though the term *Adivasi* continues to have political connotations.[6] I use this anecdote to mark out the terrain that I hope to cover in this chapter, notably the discourse of folklore and its role in the articulation of Bengali sub-nationalism.

In this discourse, terms such as *adivasi/odhibashi*, *bhumiputra*, *tribe*, *jana-pada*, *janagushti*, *jati*, *loka/folk* are used as signifiers suggesting particular repre-sentations of culture, sociality and sometimes territory.[7] The substitutions and interplay between these terms (often by the same author in a single text), com-bined with the fact that these terms are part of an open-ended series, indicate that 'culture', as it is constituted in the discourse of folklore, is thought of as mobile, configured through the circulation of cultural artifacts. Sites of original produc-tion or location of cultural artifacts are not necessarily the places where they are finally consumed, re-articulated or replicated. This holds true for canonical folk-lore objects like oral narratives, as it does for mass-produced forms of popular culture (Evans 2005). At first sight, this stance seems to contradict the basic assumption of the ideology of ethnic nationalism that insists on an originary and fundamental relationship between territory, habitation and culture. Terms such as *Adivasi* or *bhumiputra* or even the more generic 'tribe' occur along a fault line, suggesting certain border zones between established spaces.

In this chapter I will discuss Purulia as a border zone between West Bengal and the so-called 'tribal' state of Jharkhand. This is of critical importance in con-temporary constructions of Bengali identity since identity-formation is always constituted in opposition to an 'other'. Typically, folk culture is seen as the archetypal other and as a source for the reconstruction of tradition. As far as Bengal is concerned, Bangla (Bengali language) folklore is used to establish its distinctive position within Indian civilization and is an important source for nationalist historiography (Chatterji 2003). Bengal's culture is supposed to have emerged from the intermixing of Aryan, Brahmanic and pre-Aryan, folk or rural influences (Chatterji 2005). Until the partition of the Indian subcontinent, East Bengal was the privileged space of the other, and most studies of Bangla folk-lore were located in this region. Since then, after the re-organization of states in the 1950s which led to the inclusion of Purulia in West Bengal (and not southern Bihar, now Jharkhand), it has become the site of this alterity – a distinctive cul-tural region that also serves to shed light on Bengali self-identity. However, as a border zone, it lends itself to a variety of representations, some of which contra-dict each other. Thus it is sometimes seen as a living museum from which Ben-gal's ancient pre-Hindu or rather pre-Vedic and non-Brahmanical past can be re-constituted, at other times, as an extension of Jharkhand and thus of a distinc-tive and authentic *Adivasi* culture (Roychaudhury 1996, Mahato 1978).[8]

The Bangla discourse of folkloristics does not directly address the cultural formations that are emerging in dialogue with the Jharkhand movement. Nor does it address the political terrain that the term *Adivasi* is used to carve out. However, folkloric representations of Purulia do suggest a subtext that needs to be clearly articulated for us to understand the significance of these representa-tions. This chapter analyses three performative genres in folkloric discourse – the *chho* dance, the *jhumur* song and the ritual complex around the goddess Bhadu, specifically her story and her songs – in terms of the representations of community and culture that emerge from them. The selection of genres is deter-mined by the ubiquity of their presence in texts on Purulia. While these genres serve as prisms through which Purulia is viewed as a folklore region, they do not present a homogeneous representation of Purulia. For example, the *chho* dance is supposed to represent the features of an authentic *Adivasi* culture, but Bhadu is not considered to be an *Adivasi* goddess, and the inclusion of her ritual complex in this set requires explanation. The terms 'tribe' and 'folk' are sometimes interchangeable when talking about Purulia – they both refer to some notion of indigeneity – and it is for this reason that I have included Bhadu in my set. For some scholars she is thought to be a folk Hindu version of an older pre-Aryan deity, for others she represents the voice of rural woman folk who were able to preserve older religious forms in their domestic rituals in the face of so-called onslaughts, first from the Aryan and then the Muslim invasions. The inclusion of the Bhadu complex is also important because it allows me to problematize the naturalization of notions of culture and territoriality. The inclusion or exclusion of cultural forms is a political act orientated to the constitution of a cultural region. Folklore discourses are 'ideoscapes', to use Appadurai's felicitous term – mobile carriers of ideologies. They are political acts that aid in the constitution of a cultural geography. This is why I describe Purulia as a folklore region; its culture is produced through acts of folkloric description.

I now give a brief account of Purulia and its relationship with West Bengal. Purulia was part of the Jungle Mahals – the hill areas that ranged from Birbhum, now in West Bengal to Ranchi, in Jharkhand – until this district was dissolved in 1833. It then became part of the district of Manbhum in Bihar. Manbhum, in turn, was dissolved in 1956 and Purulia became a separate district in the state of West Bengal. However, Purulia still has strong cultural links with the state of Jharkhand that was recently carved out of Bihar. This region is of great significance for folklore scholarship. It is home to diverse *Adivasi* groups, such as the Santal, Bhumij, Munda and Mahato.[9] Some of these groups, like the Bhumij, have a long history of interaction with medieval state formations in Central India. This has led to the development of an aristocratic stratum within some of the tribes of this region. Surajit Sinha, one of the first scholars to study this process, called it the 'Rajputization' of the tribes (1995).[10] This process of Rajputization went hand-in-hand with the emergence of a courtly culture that was strongly rooted in the local folk traditions. The courts of the tribal chiefs were important centres of patronage where performers and poets congregated. It is important to remember, however, that the forms that became the object of royal patronage were originally folk forms. When the tribal chiefs disappeared, the musical traditions that they nurtured again became the heritage of the folk. The folk traditions of tribal Central India have a distinctive identity of their own even though this region does not form a unified political entity. (This region is divided between the states of West Bengal, Orissa, Madhya Pradesh, Chhatisgarh and Jharkhand.) Thus, as I have already mentioned, Purulia as a border region has greater cultural affinity with the neighbouring state of Jharkhand than with many of the other districts of West Bengal. This poses an interesting challenge for Bengali folkloristics that has a deep-rooted interest in cultural nationalism; it has always argued that it is the folk culture that gives Bengal its distinctive identity (Dutt 1954; Sen 1920). Purulia is sometimes incorporated within the sphere of Bengali folk culture and at other times is said to be part of a distinctive tribal ethos. The shifts in location are determined by the vantage point from which the particular scholar addresses his/her object. Purulia as an object of folkloric discourse is most often represented by its performative genres and each genre offers a particular perspective from which it may be viewed. This has consequences for the study of culture. Culture becomes a site for border cross-ings and is defined not so much as a collective property of a group but by the discourses that purport to speak for and about it. In this chapter I will show how the culture of Purulia is constituted by the overlapping boundaries between dif-ferent discourses and genres.

In my discussion of the three genres I focus on the writings of Ashutosh Bhat-tacharya, the doyen of Bangla folkloristics and one of the first folklorists to write about Purulia. Other scholars on Purulia usually take Bhattacharya as a reference point in their own writings, whether as support for their own assertions or to engage in polemics. Thus the discourse takes on a dialogic style configuring both Purulia as a social imaginary as well as the public within which the discourse circulates.

Chho dance, primitive culture and authentic tradition

Ashutosh Bhattacharya's writings on Purulia *chho* are framed by a special context. They introduce the dance form to a global audience that has no familiar-ity with this genre. The framing of the *chho* as a tribal war dance, the focus on the masks that the dancers wear, and the music of the drums in his description can all be explained in terms of the interlocutory context in which he wrote (Bhattacharya 1975). The masks and the drum music become dense symbols car-rying the qualities associated with tribalness: the assumption of magical persona represented through the mask coupled with the 'primitive' savagery of the music. In the process, other aspects, such as the singing of a *jhumur* song at the start of a performance in a style that cannot be characterized as warlike, or the use of wind instruments as musical accompaniments, are left out of the description. 'Primitive' is a complex term for Bhattacharya. He sometimes uses it as synony-mous with 'tribal'; at other times it is used to characterize a type of society that is self-contained, isolated and threatened by novelty or change.[11] The shifts in meaning are perhaps inevitable given the fact that he wrote for so many different audiences. However, the representation of the *chho* dance acquires a remarkable fixity even as it circulates among different publics; scholars who take a very dif-ferent stance in relation to tribal societies still tend to represent the dance in the same way. Thus the association between magic and the primitive is valorized by Bankim Mahato (1978). He cites James Frazer's magnum opus, *The Golden Bough*, to claim superiority of the primitive tribal over the believer in false reli-gions. Thus, both authors assume certain core features of the dance behind the obfuscating layers imposed first by Hindu civilization and then by modern tech-nology and mass culture. Purulia *chho* as a living tradition has been influenced by history. The dance themes are taken from epic texts like the Mahabharata and the Puranas, which bears testimony to the long process of interaction between the tribal cultures of Purulia and Bengali Hinduism. Both Bhattacharya and Mahato think that they can strip off accretions imposed by history and modernity to present the authentic, timeless form of the dance.

The theme of authenticity has been taken up by a group of younger scholars. They do not associate it with the notion of tribal culture but rather use the theme to represent Purulia *chho* as a site for a dialogue between folk culture and pan-Indian civilization. Thus Mahua Roychaudhury (1996) and Malati Agniswaran (n.d.) read the *chho* against the Natyashastra (ancient Indian treatise on dance) in an effort to re-create a lost classical dance tradition for Bengal. The cultural activist Pashupati Mahato (2000) criticizes this perspective as a form of internal colonization by the dominant Bengali culture. He says that if there are traces of continuity between Bengali culture and the tribal culture of Purulia it is because tribal culture is primordial. (I will develop this theme in the next section.) However, recent innovations in the dance forms, alluded to in the anecdote with which I begin this chapter, does reveal a concern with 'history'. One of the *chho* troupes have composed a *pala* (dance form) called the 'Santal Bidroho' (Santal Rebellion), which was performed on the occasion of the first folklore conference, held in Purulia in 1978. It did not resonate with the local public and its performance is largely confined to political occasions like party functions and conferences. As a discussion in a folklore journal, *Chhatrak*, reveals (see Basu Ray 1978), the local audience for the *chho* dance was not considered ready for the historicization of the dance form. As we saw, the 'Origin of the Adivasi' *pala* being choreographed in Chorida village was a mythic representation of the *Adivasi* and not a historical one. However, it is not as if history is eschewed completely from the dance.

Masks used to represent Siva as the hunter (*kirata*) in an episode from the Mahabharata depict an idealized Santal mask that was first made by the Chorida *sutradhars* (artisans) as curios to sell at craft bazaars in Purulia and Kolkata (Chatterji 2003).[12] The use of these masks in the dance signalled a new consciousness of historical reality, not so much in the designation of certain characters as Santals, as opposed to the more sanskritic *kirata*, but because a new genre of masks evolved to depict human characters. Masks for the *chho* dance are typically divided into three classes. First, the gods have delicate features and closed mouths: their faces normally express serenity, without any marks of 'human' emotion such as laughter lines or frowns. Second, demon masks have flared nostrils, open mouths with fangs or a solid band of white attached to the mouth to depict teeth. Third, animal masks are used for characters like Hanuman and Jambuvan. While I was in Chorida, I saw a new genre of masks evolving that portrayed human characters like forest dwelling sages, hunters and so on. They were depicted with open mouths in which one could see human teeth: vertical lines were painted on the band of white in the mouth to represent individual teeth. Sages had wrinkles and frown marks painted on their faces. This attempt to introduce a naturalistic 'human' dimension into the dance reflects a consciousness of historical time. It also reflects an awareness of the discourse of folklore that presents Purulia as a 'tribal' region and the *chho* as a tribal dance (Chatterji 1995). Why are Santals used to depict the *kirata* in mythological themes? Why do Santals become the archetypal tribal group in folklore writing on this region? I try and address this question in the next section.

The *jhumur* and the interface between tribe and Hindu civilization

In the previous section I showed how the *chho* dance becomes a symbol of tribal culture by excluding certain features that do not fit the image of the tribal war dance. One of these is the *jhumur* that is sung at the opening of the dance. Representations of the *jhumur* are complex and fragmentary scattered over different discursive sites. References to *jhumur* songs are found in texts about the popular culture of nineteenth century Calcutta (Banerjee 1989). What link do they have with the *jhumur* songs sung in Purulia? On the face of it, authors that mention these songs in the context of popular urban culture do not directly refer to the folk culture in which these popular forms were once rooted.

Ashutosh Bhattacharya (1965) frames his discussion of the *jhumur* genre around the theme of the subaltern. His focus, however, is not so much on the opposition between elite and popular culture. Instead, he uses the *jhumur* form to elaborate on the relationship between tribal and Bengali/sanskritic cultural forms in a way that draws upon the specific features of this border region. Thus he says that the *jhumur* developed within a historical context that fostered Bengali-tribal syncreticism. The tribal groups that inhabit the Chhota Nagpur plateau, where Purulia is located, voluntarily adopted cultural elements from Bengal and created a vibrant, multi-lingual society. The *jhumur* is a product of this cultural hybridity, sung in all the different languages spoken in this region. Bhattacharya is especially interested in the Bangla *jhumur* as a trace of an ancient process of cultural contact. He explores one particular theme prevalent in the *jhumur*, the story of the divine lovers Radha and Krishna. A secular version of this story (with human rather than divine lovers), he says was known in this region before the rise of Bengal Vaishnavism in the sixteenth century, through song forms that readily adapted themselves to the popular musical traditions of Bengal, like the *kirtana*. Bhattacharya uses this as evidence for the hypothesis that the Bengali Hindu influence on this region did not manifest itself as a form of colonization. Rather, it took the form of a voluntary and selective adaptation of themes that were already familiar to the inhabitants of this region. He characterizes this as a form of 'bilingualism' and traces an evolutionary course from the tribal *jhumur* in Santali to the Bangla *jhumur* via the Radha-Krishna theme.

As I have already said, Bhattacharya does not mention the Bangla *jhumurs* that are sung during the performance of the *chho* dance. It is as if the representation of tribal culture when viewed from the vantage point of the dance must necessarily be monolingual, excluding non-tribal elements from its essential form. However, in describing the *jhumur* as a bilingual form there are some factual anomalies. If Santali songs are the first and most primitive form of *jhumur* songs this is not borne out by empirical evidence. The examples of Santali *jhumurs* reproduced in Bhattacharya's account are *dandshalya jhumurs* most commonly sung by Kurmi-Mahatos and Bhumij (Sinha 1997), and Santals do not generally think of the *jhumur* genre as one of their own musical forms (Karan 1995). The Santals function as a symbol in Bhattacharya's text. As debated by Rycroft (2006), they have come to represent the archetypal tribal group in Bangla discourse, perhaps because they are numerically the most dominant tribal group, or because they were the group most often depicted as alter to the Bengalis in the paintings and literary works of the artists who worked in Santiniketan, an institution that has acquired canonical status in Bengal. In contrast, groups that do sing *jhumurs*, like the Bhumij and Kurmi-Mahatos, claim a dual status as both *kshatriyas* (ruling Hindu varna) and tribal, and no longer have mastery over a tribal language. Instead both groups speak a regional dialect of Bangla. Clearly Santals were more suitable for Bhattacharya's model of bilingualism as they speak both Santali and Bangla and have sustained their distinctive identity while still being able to interact with other groups.

Is tribal culture coterminous with folk culture? Bhattacharya makes a distinction between folk and primitive societies on the basis of their relationship to the 'other'. Primitive societies are exclusionary and fragile, threatened by forces of modernity. Folk societies are contemporary and welcome novelty (Bhattarcharya 1962). Are the people of this border region part of folk or primitive society? It is not always clear in Bhattacharya's writings. His accounts of tribal society are filtered through the cultural forms that he describes. When he writes about the *chho* dance it is in the context of an ideal primitive society. But this is not the case with the *jhumur*. It seems to represent the dynamic face of folk society without being part of mainstream Bengali culture. It is also important to note that *jhumur* like the *chho* is not associated with any one group in the region as is the case with the Santali dances. These forms have been appropriated by many different groups including Bengali groups who live in this region, so that it makes sense for a scholar like Pashupati Mahato (1987) to characterize the whole of Jharkhand as 'jhumur desh' (land of jhumur songs) and to speak of a composite folk culture. Cultural forms, even when bound to a particular territory, are thought of as mobile with the capacity for transformation in the face of social change.

Bhadu: the secularization of a goddess tradition

In this section, I discuss the 'Bhadu complex' (see Chatterji 2009). She is a folk goddess worshipped mainly by non-tribal groups. The inclusion of the Bhadu complex in this discussion helps me to illustrate the fluid relationship between the categories of folk and tribe. Bhadu herself, according to Bhattacharya (1965), is supposed to be a product of the change brought about by Hindu colonization on non-Aryan, tribal rituals. However, in keeping with the nationalist interpretation of women's rituals as being the true representations of pre-Aryan Bengali culture, Bhattacharya is able to perceive an ancient agricultural ritual under the veneer of Hindu iconicity (*pautolikta*). A description of the Bhadu complex in monographs on Purulia allows the region to be represented in terms of a confluence between diverse cultural streams (Karan 1995). It also allows me to engage with a set of contemporary folklore writings that are inflected by Marxist ideology. These scholars use the older nationalist ideas about women's rituals reflected in the writings of Dinesh Chandra Sen and Abanindranath Tagore but in contexts that are very different. Thus, the writings of contemporary folklorists in Bengal reflect a concern with the growing popularity of nationalist Hindu political parties in states with a dominant tribal image like Jharkhand, and the participation of tribal groups in communal riots in Gujarat in 2002. The characterization of the folk voice as a secular voice and women's rituals as an embodiment of that voice is related to this concern. I will now describe some of the myths and songs associated with the goddess Bhadu and the folkloric discourse around them.

Bhadu stories have entered the print culture as a result of the interest shown in her by Bengali folklorists and there are several new Bhadu stories that present her as a human being. This does not seem to have affected the ritual or the songs directly, though the emergence of an elaborate iconicity may have some relation to the new interest in her persona. (It seems paradoxical that the growing iconicization associated with the ritual goes hand-in-hand with the humanization of her story.) Bhadu and Tushu *puja* (worship) are the two women's festivals in Chorida, both associated with particular phases of the agricultural cycle, Bhadu with the transplantation of paddy in the rainy season and Tushu with the winter harvest. Scholars like Karan (1995) consider Bhadu *puja* to be a later invention, a secular festival, modelled on Tushu, the 'primordial' agricultural goddess in this region. Bhadu *puja* is performed by women of non-tribal groups.

Bhadu, who is thought to be the beloved daughter of the Maharaja of Kashipur (the capital of Panchakot, an erstwhile state in the Purulia region), died a virgin. Her memory is kept alive through this festival, instituted on her birthday. The enigma of Bhadu's virginity and untimely death has led to many variations in the story that purport to explain it. In these stories Bhadu's divinity and her existence as a flesh and blood woman exist on parallel registers. This coexistence is not thought to be problematic by her devotees. Bhadu partakes of the nature of the archetypal mother goddess whose entanglement in the day-to-day lives of her devotees is celebrated in all goddess festivals in Bengal (Chatterji 1987).

Bhadu *puja*, one of the many festivals of the rainy season, takes place at the time of the transplanting of the paddy seeds in Purulia. In Chorida village, it was performed largely by the *Sutradhar* (carpenter) and the *Bhat* (genealogist) jatis. These two jatis are designated as 'Bengali jatis' in order to distinguish them from the *Adivasi* and lower caste groups in the village. It is performed on Bhadra *sankranti*, that is, the penultimate day of the month of Bhadra, which falls between August and September. The actual *puja* is performed by a group of families who share the costs and the work involved in organizing the puja. The festival continues all night and groups sit with Bhadu, singing songs to her, eating sweets and performing the ritual. The ritual itself is not very elaborate – it involves an *arati* (offering) for Bhadu, performed by one of the women in the group. (Bhadu is worshipped with incense. Incense sticks and a lamp filled with clarified butter are circled around her.) Her feet are anointed with oil, turmeric and *sindoor* (vermilion powder). After the *arati* a cucumber is sacrificed (*bali daan*) before her icon (*murti*). Bhadu is worshipped three times in the course of the night. The first time when her *murti* is installed, then at around 11 p.m. and finally at day break before the *murti* is immersed in the village pond. There is considerable rivalry between the different groups of Bhadu worshippers. Young girls visit each other's Bhadus, singing songs in praise of their own Bhadu while disparaging those of rival groups. It is said that this is the one night in the year when women can roam the streets freely because men are too scared to come out of their houses. This is one occasion when Bengali women can sing songs in public. The songs are mostly joyful, sung in a group. Bhadu is addressed as a young and beautiful woman, sometimes as a young bride come to celebrate the *puja* with her parents and friends.

In most folkloric accounts of the ritual, the songs are supposed to embody the essence of Bhadu *puja*. In fact as noted by Subrata Chakravarti (2001), the songs take the place of *mantras* (ritual chants) in her worship. On the basis of an analysis of these songs he characterizes this event as a secular festival (*utsav*) rather than a *puja*. Bhadu's *murti* is not a sacred icon; instead it is the image of a pretty young girl or a young married woman come to visit her daughter. It has no religious significance but is used only to lend colour to the festival. To demonstrate this, Chakravarti (2001) says that the Bhadu's *murti* has no fixed attributes or symbols that can be used to identify her like other goddesses. He suggests that the festival is a way of setting aside a period of time when women can come together freely, and are freed from the structures of patriarchy that constrain their everyday lives. Bhadu's biography provides the first tentative steps to what, Chakravarti feels, can develop into a path of female emancipation. But this does not address the specificity of her birth, the daughter of the Maharaja of Kashipur. Why should a *kshatriya* woman become the symbol for oppressed womanhood? Chakravarti offers a tentative hypothesis: perhaps because she was popular with her low caste subjects or because she was planning to elope with a low caste man, she was murdered by her kin.[13] In death Bhadu posed an even greater threat to royal authority than she had in life. The only way in which the king could avert a full-blown rebellion was by incorporating Bhadu's death into the ritual calendar. Yet unlike other rituals, Bhadu's festival carries traces of the same quality that characterized her life: it is irreverent and emancipatory.

In Chakravarti's work (2001), the Bhadu myth is an ideological construct, a successful piece of propaganda to discipline and pacify a potentially rebellious population. The establishment of her worship can be interpreted as an attempt to incorporate the source of rebellion into the structure of power. However, Bhadu does retain her exemplary status in Chakravarti's text – if not as a goddess than as a figure that represents all womankind and by extension all subalterns. Not all scholars are able to dismiss Bhadu puja as an act of propaganda. Ashutosh Bhat-tacharya (1965) and those who follow him view it as a tribal agricultural festival that is transformed into a Hindu ritual by the colonizing efforts of the rajas of Kashipur, now in Purulia district. However, it is his writings that have estab-lished the tradition of separating the songs from the ritual. The emphasis on the songs, especially on the lyrics, has helped to crystallize a particular disciplinary perspective which assumes that folklore is necessarily concerned with the search for the authentic voice of the people and that the feminine voice is the privileged site of this authenticity.

Scholars like Partha Chatterjee (1993) and Tanika Sarkar (2001) have said that the nineteenth century nationalist historiography of Bengal posited a domestic space that was thought to be insulated from the modernizing influence of the colonial state. This internal space came to be represented as the ground for national resurgence. The association between domestic space and the women's activities that became the symbolic markers of this space is folklore's contribu-tion to this historiography. Women's rituals and songs become the concrete embodiments of domestic space, the source of a cultural authenticity that is pushed back to pre-Aryan times. Thus Abanindranath Tagore (1943), one of the first scholars to write on women's rituals in Bengal, privileges domestic rituals as examples of pre-Aryan, non-Brahmanical and therefore pure (*khanti*) tradi-tion. To demonstrate this he examines the rhymes that take the place of Sanskrit *mantras* in these rituals and says that they still carry traces of animism. They refer to a time when the world of nature was not separate from the human world and religion and the secular realm were not separate from each other.

The portrayal of folk religion as essentially secular and pragmatic is a stra-tegic device by which nationalist Bengali scholars were able to establish Ben-gal's distinctiveness without repudiating her place within the civilizational mainstream. Folk culture, they claimed, was universal, the folk in all parts of the country and at all times, shared the same concerns which were represented in their beliefs and practices. At the same time the common grammar given to them by Hinduism allows them to use gods and goddesses to represent their concerns and interests. This also allows scholars to use the concept of folk culture or reli-gion as a common thread that binds the diverse aspects of Indian culture.

Secularism is associated with the folk voice in many parts of the world (see Asad 2002). In Bengal today it is used by left-wing oriented intellectuals to counter the cultural nationalism propagated by right-wing political parties. In this context women become suitable representations of the folk. They can be used to represent the category of the subaltern, cutting across such conflicting divisions as class, caste, religion and locality. However the choice of Bhadu as a representative of the 'folk voice' allows for a hybrid representation of folk culture – it becomes a palimpsest that layers an amalgam of influences – tribal, sanskritic and folk. But more importantly, Bhadu is of human origin, which allows for the introduction of 'history' in this discourse. Bhadu allows for the historicization of timeless folk communities. She represents both the eternal and essential folk voice but also the transformation of so-called tribal agricultural rituals like Tushu *puja* with the incursion of non-brahaminical Hinduism into Chota Nagpur.

Cultural fields as zones of debate

The association between secularism and folk consciousness has a long tradition in Bangla folklore. For Dinesh Chandra Sen (1920), one of the foremost folklorists of the nationalist period, the secular, this-worldly orientation of folk literature crystallizes in the Buddhist period, between the third and the tenth centuries, that is, before the 'Hindu Renaissance' brought about in the Gupta period and the advent of Islam in India. According to Sen, this ethos continues to survive in rural Bengal and provides a common bond between Hindu and Muslim peasants. Sen's work was largely confined to East Bengal (now Bangladesh). Post-partition scholars have extended his argument to include Bengal's tribal belt. In Sen's work there was already a recognition of an essentially Bengali consciousness that precedes both Hinduism and Islam – the two great religious traditions of undivided Bengal. He anchors this in Buddhism – a religion that no longer has a living presence here. *Adivasi* scholars, such as P.C. Hembram (1983), working on the Jharkhand region prefer to think of this as emerging out of a natural religion – animism – that informs the orientation of tribal people to their environment. This even allows for an alternate route to the source of Indian civilization. Thus some scholars, for example Hembram (1983) and Mahato (2000), say that tribal people are the true heirs to the Indus Valley civilization because they are the indigenous people of the subcontinent marginalized by later Aryan conquerors.

Left-wing oriented Bengali scholars are caught between these contradictory positions. On the one hand, the work of nationalist folklorists like Dinesh Chandra Sen and Gurusaday Dutt is used to support the contention that folk consciousness is inherently secular. (This precludes, however, any evaluation of their work that would point to the silences within them – such as the fact that tribal people are rarely presented in a positive light.) On the other, there is a need to justify Purulia's inclusion within the wider culture of West Bengal, especially with the formation of the Jharkhand state. Scholars like Shanti Sinha (1997) offer mediating positions. They support Sen and Dutt in their valorization of Bengal's heterodox folk culture, but take this heterodoxy back to the Aryan period. Thus Sinha (1997) notes that it was one of the non-vedic, heterodox streams of Aryans, later called the Vratya – a term that would later inform the concept of *vrata* (women's ritual) – that first entered eastern India and mingled with its tribal population. This led to the emergence of hybrid religious formations like Jainism, Buddhism and Vaishnavism that were inclusive and syncretic in their orientation. Thus, many of the essential features of Hinduism, at least of non-Brahaminical Hinduism, actually originated from tribal culture. I read such statements as attempts to address the genuine concern of activists like Pashupati Mahato (2000) who believe that the 'inclusive' dimension of Hinduism that is universally praised by folklore scholarship has silenced the tribal voice.

However, as Mahato argues (2000), the recent inclusion of tribal people into the category of folk does not adequately address the violence that underlies such processes of assimilation. He calls such processes 'nirbakization' (speechless-ness), a form of cultural forgetting or 'cultural memocide', phrases that fore-ground the inherently violent nature of such acts. In contrast to the scholars mentioned above, he argues for the autonomy of the Jharkhand region of which Purulia District is a part. He is not explicitly arguing for the inclusion of Purulia in the state of Jharkhand, unlike several other scholars (see for example Bosu Mullick 1991) who have a stake in a politically autonomous Jharkhand. Rather, he is arguing for a cultural unity, a unity of aesthetic form across the performa-tive traditions of different tribal groups. I find Mahato's argument extremely interesting. Like the folklorists before him, he too highlights performative genres like *chho* and *jhumur* that are able to circulate between different kinds of cultural and ritual contexts and sees them as sources of cultural exchange between tribal groups in Chotanagpur. Neither does he exclude the interaction between this region and greater Bengal. But in this interaction Purulia becomes the dominant partner: it gives Bengal some of its distinctive folk cultural features without necessarily losing its own place within an alternative cultural field.

In one important aspect, however, Mahato and the other folklorists discussed here have a common perspective. In their writings, the category of cultural 'field' is constituted through a discussion of specific performative genres.[14] In the process of circulation within a discursive field the genres are now part of a new textual tradition and a print culture that has inscribed them in new performative contexts. Conventional folklore scholarship tends to view performative traditions as being embedded in bounded communities. Instead, these genres, once they enter new cultures of circulation tend to create new notions of community and culture. (They address anonymous publics rather than face-to-face communit-ies.) In a sense this new cultural field is a zone of debate in which the performa-tive genres like the *chho*, *jhumur* and Bhadu puja operate as boundary markers. The discursive space around each genre generates a public, to whom its repre-sentations of culture and community are addressed. I have tried to show that the representation of community is variable, determined by the circulation of dis-course around each of the three genres. However, discursive boundaries are not closed. They allow for reflexive interaction between different kinds of textual representations. The choice of these three hybrid genres for discussion in this chapter was determined by this fact, leading to the inclusion of discussions of the goddess Bhadu, who is worshipped by non-tribal groups. Questions of iden-tity are posed within cultural fields constituted by the interplay of textual repre-sentations, oriented to publics that are shaped by the questions being addressed to them, by the reflexive circulation of discourse (see Warner 2002).

Identity-production, one of the sub-themes of this volume on 'Becoming Adivasi', is inextricably tied to the constitution of boundaries (see Cohen 2000). But boundaries are not impermeable. In the process of demarcating autonomous spaces they also produce transitional zones or 'crossings' where different identi-ties meet and sometimes clash. I have not discussed boundaries in the context of identity-formation but rather in terms of the constitution of a cultural field and a discursive space. In this space identity does not emerge in substantial form. Rather it is addressed through motifs embedded in performative genres that embody forms of culture.[15] Thus, an essential 'tribalness' is represented through the music of the drums in the *chho* dance, a tribal/folk Hindu syncretism is uncovered in the erotic play of Radha and Krishna and celebrated in *jhumur* songs, and a folk humanism is evidenced in the Bhadu myth. The themes highlighted in each of the three genres bring to the fore some aspects of the cultural field that is Purulia. In the process they also show us that boundaries are not fixed. Rather the concept of boundary is a shifting frame that gives a temporary coherence to a set of heterogeneous themes and practices.

Notes

1 Baghmundi used to be a small independent kingdom ruled by Bhumij chiefs. The village Chorida, where I lived from 1981 to 1983, was about two kilometres from Baghmundi, formerly the capital of the kingdom and now the block's headquarters.
2 The late Gambhir Singh Mura was awarded the Padma Shri for the dance.
3 As far as I know the *Sharaboli* is known only in Bengal.
4 The term *jati* or rather *jaat* is used to designate both caste as well as tribal groups in Purulia.
5 He was referring to the memorial stones in Bhumij ossuaries. The ossuary of the Baghmundi kings is located in Chorida.
6 Rycroft describes Baghmundi village in the late 1990s. The *Vanavasi Seva Pratisthan* (Forest-dwellers Relief Organization), an outreach branch of the *Hindu Swayam Sevak Sangh*, is now located in the village.
7 Chatterji (1943) is the only author that I know who 'interchanges 'adivasi' with 'bhumiputra'. He also uses 'adivasi' (original inhabitant) in conjunction with 'odhibashi' (resident, inhabitant). Karan (1995) uses terms such as 'janapada' (settlement), 'janagushti' (people) and 'lokayata' (folklore) while talking about border regions like Purulia. 'Tribe' is used by most scholars without any ideological inflection, and is sometimes subsumed within 'folk'. 'Jati', in Bengal, is usually translated as race as in people. In Purulia 'jaat' or 'jati' was used to refer to diverse groups such as Bangalis, Bhumij and Doms.
8 Bangla folklore texts are not very specific about the characteristics of 'Brahmanical religion', and they often use this term to refer to rituals presided over by professional priests who belong to the caste of Brahmans. However scholars like Sinha (1997) also include the performance of 'vedic' sacrifices in this category, and exclude some heterodox Aryans, i.e. Buddhists, from being included in the category of followers of vedic religion. Bengal is said to have been colonized by the Aryans much later than North India and its folk culture is supposed to have preserved traces of her pre-Aryan past (see Sinha 1965, 1997).
9 The Mahato are not officially recognized as a Scheduled Tribe as they designated themselves as 'kurmi kshatriyas' in the 1931 census of India. However, there is a movement in Bengal and Jharkhand to restore their tribal identity (see Mahato 2000).
10 As an anthropologist, Sinha was interested in the caste-tribe continuum, that is, in showing how groups in the middle order of local village hierarchies showed morphological features typically associated with both tribes and castes.
11 For Bhattacharya, 'primitive' is used to characterize a type of orientation to the other. 'Tribe' and 'tribal' especially in the context of the *chho* dance, refer to cultural forms like drum music and the wearing of masks and so on, all of which point to a magical

aura that characterizes the *chho* dance. In some of his writings he claims that low caste groups such as the Doms, who were probably tribals converted to Hinduism, created the dance form.

12 Shankar is described as the original tribal form of the Aryanized Siva in *Patana* (Madavi 2000). The composite name Siva-Shankara points to this form of cultural appropriation.

13 The motif of unsuitable bridegroom is sometimes associated with the Bhadu myth but is seen as someone who is unattainable, or one who is unsuited to fulfil the role of husband. Caste was never an issue in any of the variants of the myth that I heard in Purulia.

14 Bourdieu (1993) describes the 'field' as a structured space of positions.

15 The adaptation of the *chho* dance to the recent video boom in Purulia has led to the inclusion of 'Santali' elements like the *pata naach* in the *Santal Bidroho pala*, thereby reinforcing the stereotype of the 'tribal' dance. Other performance traditions in Bengal have taken the opposite route. The Medinipur Chitrakars, an itinerant community of painters who create narrative scrolls and accompanying songs, have started composing so-called adivasi scrolls with motifs that were once very much part of their own cultural tradition.

References

Agniswaran, M. (n.d.) 'Legends of Kartikeya in Puruliya Chho', http://murugan.org/research/agniswaran1.htm (accessed 16 December 2010).

Asad, T. (2002) *Formations of the Secular: Christianity, Islam, Modernity*, California: Stanford University Press.

Banerjee, S. (1989) *The Parlour and the Streets: Elite and Popular Culture in Nineteenth Century Calcutta*, Calcutta: Seagull Books.

Basu Ray, S. (1978) 'Jhumur', *Chhatrak* (Posh Sankhya), 9–10.

Bhattacharya, A. (1962) *Banglar loksahitya. Volume 1*, Calcutta: Calcutta Book House.

—— (1965) *Bangla Loksahitya. Volume 3*, Calcutta: Calcutta Book House.

—— (1975) *Chhau: Masked dance of West Bengal in America*, Calcutta: Research Institute of Folk Culture.

Bosu Mullick, S. (ed.) (1991) *Cultural Chota Nagpur: Unity in diversity*, New Delhi: Uppal Publishing House.

Bourdieu, P. (1993) *Sociology in Question*, London: Sage Publications.

Chakravarti, S. (2001) *Bhadu*, Calcutta: Loksanskriti and Adivasi Sanskriti Kendra.

Chatterjee, P. (1993) *The Nation and its Fragments*, New Delhi: Oxford University Press.

Chatterji, R. (1987) 'Folklore and the formation of popular consciousness in a village in the Purulia district of West Bengal', Ph.D. dissertation, Delhi University.

—— (1995) 'Authenticity and tradition: Reappraising a folk form', in V. Dalmia and H. von Stietencron (eds) *Representing Hinduism: The construction of religious traditions and national identity*, New Delhi: Sage, 420–41.

—— (2003) 'Category of folk', in V. Das (ed.) *Oxford India companion to sociology and social anthropology*, New Delhi: Oxford University Press, 567–97.

—— (2005) 'Folklore and the construction of national tradition', in D. Noyes (ed.) *Folklore abroad: On the diffusion and revision of sociocultural categories* (special issue), *Indian Folklife*, 19: 3–5.

—— (2009) *Writing identities: Folklore and the performing arts of Purulia*, Delhi: IGNCA and Aryan.

Chatterji, S.K. (1943) (1353 Bangla Shôn, BS) 'Kol jatir sanskriti', *Vishvabharati Patrika*

(1/2), Kartik-Posh, 88–109, reprinted in D. Gosh (ed.) *Bangla samayipatre adi-bashikatha*, Kolkata: Loksanskriti and Adivasi Sanskriti Kendra, 2005.

Cohen, A. (2000) *Signifying Identities: Anthropological perspectives on boundaries and contested values*, London: Routledge.

Dutt, G.S. (1954) *The folk dances of Bengal*, Calcutta: The Estate of late Sri Gurusaday Dutt.

Evans, B. (2005) *Before Cultures: The ethnographic imagination in American literature, 1965–1920*, Chicago: University of Chicago Press.

Hembram, P.C. (1983) *Sari Sarna (Santhal religion)*, Delhi: Mittal Publications.

Karan, S.K. (1995) (1402 BS) *Shimanto banglar lokayaun*, Calcutta: Karuna Prakashon.

Madavi, L.K. (2000) *Patana*, translated into English from Marathi by K. Jamanadas, www.ambedkar.org/patana (accessed on 16 December 2010).

Mahato, B. (1978) 'Chho nach. Ekti shomikha', *Chhatrak (111):* 205–13.

Mahato, P.P. (1987) *The performing arts of Jharkhand*, Calcutta: B.B. Prakashan.

—— (2000) *Sanskritization vs. nirbakization (A study on cultural silence and ethnic memocide in Jharkhand)*, Calcutta: Sujan Publications.

Roychaudhury, M. (1996) 'Banglar loknritto ar Goudiyonritto', *Lokshruti (12):* 89–120.

Rycroft, D.J. (2006) 'Santalism: Reconfiguring 'the Santal' in Indian art and politics', *Indian Historical Review*, 33(1): 150–74.

—— (2009) 'Revisioning Birsa Munda: Visual Constructions of the 'Vanavasi' in Jharkhand', in N.K. Das and V.R. Rao (eds) *Identity, Cultural Pluralism and the State: South Asia in Perspective*, New Delhi: Macmillan Publishers, 261–80.

Sarkar, T. (2001) *Hindu wife, Hindu nation*, Delhi: Permanent Black.

Sen, D.C. (1920) *The folk literature of Bengal*, reprinted in 1985, Delhi: B.R. Publishing Corporation.

Sinha, S. (1965) 'Tribe-caste and tribe-peasant continua in Central India', *Man in India*, 45(1): 8–81.

—— (1995) 'State formation and Rajput myth in tribal central India', in H. Kulke (ed.) *The state in India. 1000–1700*, New Delhi: Oxford University Press, 304–42.

—— (1997) *Lok sangeet sangraha: Jhumur*, Calcutta: Paschim Bangya Rajya Sangeet Akademi.

Tagore, A. (1943) (1350 BS) *Banglar broto*, Shantiniketan: Vishwabharati.

Warner, M. (2002) 'Publics and counter publics', *Public Culture*, 14(1): 49–90.

Part II

Revisiting resistance

Introduction to Part II

Part II invites readers to revisit resistance in order to prompt a rethinking of the linkages between anti-colonial resistance, identity formations in post-colonial societies and historiographic representational practices. As such, the modalities of anti-colonial insurgency, the strategies of colonial counter-insurgency, and the cultural contours of post-insurgency may be addressed from a perspective that is alert to the complex interpenetration of 'history and the present' (see Chatterjee 2002). This would enable a deconstruction of the interplay between histories, temporalities and memories that have been, and continue to be, relevant to an understanding of Adivasi subjectivity (see Guha 1983a; Skaria 1999; Rycroft 2006). It is necessary to consider the presence of insurgency/resistance in historical representations of these pasts since Adivasi initiatives and participation in anti-colonial struggles have helped to generate the conditions for their 'becoming Adivasi' in a de-colonising nation.[1]

How then might an Adivasi-oriented historiography engage with the parameters of resistance as reproduced through Tribal studies and inclusive/corrective approaches to 'minority histories' (see Chrakrabarty 2004). In this context of minority identity-production, what might it mean for these democratising historians – and, in the case of India's Adivasis, also anthropologists – to conflate tribal heritage, history and insurgency? The problem resides in the fact that such conflations might re-legitimate the 'insurgent syndrome', a term invented by Dhanagre (1988) to denote the pre-determined configuring of Adivasi pasts as insurgent, rather than as democratic. Yet in keeping hold of the idea of insurgent temporality and post-insurgent heritage – which are notions sustained by Adivasi reinterpretations and commemorations of their subaltern pasts (see Rycroft 2011, forthcoming) – researchers can engage with Adivasi history whilst also avoiding the allure of political difference (see Sider and Smith 1997). This might mean bringing into play notions such as memory-work or memory-justice that unravel the construction of cultural/legal/political distance between Adivasis and non-Adivasis, and thereby alter the terms through which Adivasi cultural praxis, and related notions such as Adivasi cultural heritage or cultural identity, are articulated (Rycroft forthcoming).

These debates have an important bearing on the construction of collective identities, and on processes of self-identification in contemporary India. While the juxtaposition of insurgency and citizenship in identity-formations may seem dissonant, as argued by Gyan Pandey (2006), such juxtapositions may be more proactive than provocative. This is because they draw attention both to the inter-face between historical responses to subordination and marginality and to legal configurations of the rights of individuals in post-independence nations (Pandey 2006: 4735). Approaching the concept of Indian citizenship from an interest in the legacy, or political effects, of histories of subordination, Pandey's re-conceptualisation of 'the subaltern' in terms of 'subaltern citizenship' is helpful. It allows for a critical distance to be maintained between insurgent pasts (as sub-altern movements) and the post-insurgent present. This does not necessarily obliterate the relevance of temporal and spatial aspects of the insurgencies that may be crucial to some contemporary Adivasi renderings of selfhood. Rather, the terms of subaltern resistance and agency remains pertinent for Pandey, but in ways that do not fetishise insurgent struggle. This kind of approach makes it pos-sible to read Adivasi self-representations of insurgency and collective autonomy in ways that situate these insurgencies, their legacies and memories, as threads that can be woven into more complex patterns of Adivasi belonging that might also encompass other pasts, other subjectivities, and other politico-cultural experiences beyond those of the 'tribe' (Rycroft 2011; see also Rycroft 2005, 2009; Werbner 1998). Setting up a dialogue between Dhanagre and Pandey, one may usefully revisit resistance in the context of an emergent Adivasi studies to allow 'tribal' historiography and subaltern citizenship to connect.

Since the epithet 'Adivasi' has yet to redefine fully those 'tribal' movements in the historical periods that Sarkar and Sen debate in this section, a brief over-view of the related 'tribal' historiography is relevant (see Dasgupta forthcoming). Colonial records and nationalist narratives have structured (and often continue to structure) historical readings of 'tribal resistance'. In official records, this was usually depicted as raids and acts of depredation, as outbreaks of violence and riots, as spontaneous and sporadic outbursts (Guha 1983b; Rycroft 2006). Nation-alist narratives, on the other hand, represented 'tribal protest' within the teleology of the struggle towards *swaraj* (literally, 'self rule') and independence (see Gandhi 1925). Divested of their right to protest independently, Adivasi move-ments remained on the edge of the nation's legitimate history. Those writing within a leftist paradigm relegated tribal movements to the 'pre-history' of the socialist and communist movements in the sub-continent (see Guha 1983a: 14).

By the 1960s however, Indian historians and anthropologists like J.C. Jha (1964, 1967) and K.S. Singh (1966) restored a pro-'tribal' agenda that focused on the Bhumij Revolt, Kol Rebellion, Santal *Hul* (rebellion) and Birsaite *Ulgulan* (rebellion). From an Adivasi studies perspective, both the 'tribal' historiography and the leftist critique of it may be perceived as further marginalising con-temporary Adivasi interpretations and representations of insurgent pasts. Operat-ing within a matrix of nationhood and modernity, K.S. Singh (1966), Stephen Fuchs (1965) and others highlighted the millenarian aspects of 'tribal protest'.

These aspects assumed an 'agrarian' dimension when shared by other communities, and became 'political' only after coming into contact with the national movement. This hierarchy sustained an evolutionary schema, situating colonialism and egalitarian or communitarian form of livings at opposite ends of an ideological spectrum. Thus, K.S. Singh (1983: 211) documents the emergence of Birsa Munda as a 'prophet', against a background of a disintegrating 'communitarian agrarian system' (Singh 1972: xix). Singh's account of Birsaism, traced through a host of engaging folkloristic sources, gave new currency to binaries of insider/outsider, and tribal/non-tribal.

By the 1980s, the Subaltern studies collective set out other directions for the study of tribal movements. Ranajit Guha sought to represent 'a people without a history', those whose histories had been excluded from conventional historical scholarship, but whose historical presence was discernable via a re-reading of colonial discourse (see Chakrabarty 2004). Central to Guha's thesis of 'tribal' subalternity was the oppression by the *sarkar-zamindar-sahukar* nexus (the triumvirate of officials-landlords-moneylenders) (1983a: 8), which prompted the articulation of, in Hardiman's terms, a 'spirit of resistance which incorporated a consciousness of 'the adivasi' against the 'outsider'.' (Hardiman 1987: 15) Whilst this inscription of the outsider in these binary terms is problematic (as it does not necessarily allow for shifts in Adivasi representations of, and negotiations with, non-Adivasis), Hardiman was one of the first historians to follow wider shifts in political representation and replace the 'tribe' with the 'Adivasi' concept, to elaborate the notion of shared histories against exploitation and alienation. While the understanding of Indian nationalism and its relationship with Adivasis had been re-assessed and newer theoretical frames advanced, Skaria (1998) has lamented that the Subaltern collective generally accepted the terms of colonial distinctions although they had inverted their valences.

In the context of the reassessment of Subaltern historiography (see also Ludden 2001), Sangeeta Dasgupta (1999) has emphasised the need to locate the internal tensions within 'tribal' and subaltern communities. Focusing on the Tana Bhagat movement, she has shown how a marginal group identity was mobilised within the Oraons of Chhotanagpur, which also blurred boundaries between the 'tribal' and the 'non-tribal' and has engendered varying responses to shifting political and economic terrains. By bringing into focus the unevenness of the tribe/non-tribe paradigm, the fetishised anti-colonial dimensions of Adivasis can be problematised. It allows for a critique of the concept of Adivasi from within, and points to the importance of studying Adivasi negotiations of tribal and national contours of belonging.

Tanika Sarkar, in this volume, deals with questions of shifting intra-cultural meanings. Revisiting her discussion of Jitu Santal's movement that had appeared as a part of the original Subaltern studies project (Sarkar 1985), she now contests the subaltern approach to Adivasi movements in ways that may inspire new readings of her earlier work. Rather than emphasising either acculturation or continuing 'tribal' traditions, Sarkar now analyses those social, cultural and religious transformations that Jitu sought to impose upon Santals, as well as the radical modernity of his ideas. As she unfolds Jitu's shifting and ambiguous relationships with *zamindars* (landlords), Muslim peasants, Santal sharecroppers, the Indian National Congress, Hindu political organisations, the colonial state and its judicial-legal structure, Sarkar transcends binary oppositions and fixed categories. Here she recasts Jitu as an embodiment of multiple identities and plural affiliations that were contingent, impermanent and changeable, and argues that this initiative of 'self-fashioning' had come from a stratum from within the community that was earlier not in possession of ritual, political or social authority. The rhetoric of historical studies of subaltern groups, as Sarkar poignantly points out, has sometimes been inspired by a romantic exaltation of the potential for freedom. Yet, in the sustained focus on the activity of the leader, the principles of domination and subordination remain in place.

Sen's essay continues some of these points as he analyses the tribal involvement in the rebellions of 1857–8, which have been largely obscured by the tribe-oriented historiography of the 'Jharkhand movement'. By juxtaposing contending narratives – from official correspondence and ethnographic reports to testimonial records drawn from the trials of rebels, and other Adivasi voices recorded during land settlement operations – Sen creatively modifies the official representation of the event as a *zamindar*-led but tribal-supported anti-British movement. An exclusive focus in historiography on tribal leaders, he argues, has erased the intrinsically social character of Adivasi movements as well as their regional-level leadership and organisation. Sen suggests that by rescuing regional-level figures like Gono Pingua and other anonymous 'freedom fighters' from oblivion, the construction of boundaries between 'tribal' and non-'tribal' groups might also be addressed as a core concern of Adivasi historiography.

Note

1 See, for example, the recollection of the *Hul* (Santal rebellion of 1855–7) by descendents of Sido Murmu in *Hul Sengel: The Spirit of the Santal Revolution* (Dir. D.J. Rycroft and J.R. Tudu, documentary film in Santali with English subtitles, 2005) discussed by Rycroft (2011; also see Rycroft forthcoming).

References

Chakrabarty, D. (2004) 'Minority Histories, Subaltern Pasts', in S. Dube (ed.) *Postcolonial Passages: Contemporary History-writing on India*, New Delhi: Oxford University Press, 229–42.

Chatterjee, P. (2002) 'Introduction: History and the Present', in P. Chatterjee and A. Ghosh (eds) *History and the Present*, New Delhi: Permanent Black, 1–23.

Dasgupta, S. (1999) 'Reordering a World: The Tana Bhagat Movement in Chhotanagpur, 1914–19', *Studies in History*, January-June, 1–41.

—— (forthcoming) 'Locating Adivas; Movements in Colonial India: The Oraons and the Tana Bhagats in Chotanagpur', in A. Shah and C. Bates (eds) *Savage Attack: Adivasi Insurgency in India*, New Delhi and Oxford: Social Science Press and Berghahn.

Dhanagre, D.N. (1988) 'Subaltern Consciousness and Populism: Two Approaches in the Study of Social Movements in India', *Social Scientist*, 16(11): 18–35.

Fuchs, S. (1965) *Rebellious Prophets: A Study of Messianic Movements in Indian Religions*, Bombay: Asia Publishing House.

Gandhi, M.K. (1925) 'Bihar Notes', *Young India*, 3 September.

Guha, R. (1983a) *Elementary Aspects of Peasant Insurgency in Colonial India*, New Delhi: Oxford University Press.

—— (1983b) 'The Prose of Counter-insurgency', in R. Guha (ed.) *Subaltern Studies II*, Oxford University Press: New Delhi, 1–42.

Hardiman, D. (1987) *The Coming of the Devi: Adivasi Assertion in Western India*, New Delhi: Oxford University Press.

Jha, J.C. (1964) *Kol Insurrection in Chotanagpur*, Calcutta: Thacker, Spink and Co.

—— (1967) *The Bhumij Revolt, 1832–33*, Delhi: Munshiram Manohar Publications.

Luddon, D F (ed.) (2001) *Reading Subaltern Studies: Critical History, Contested Meaning, and the Globalization of South Asia*, New Delhi: Permanent Black.

Pandey, G. (2006) 'The Subaltern as Subaltern Citizen', *Economic and Political Weekly*, 18 November, 4735–41.

Rycroft, D.J. (2005) 'Memory and History in Jharkhand', *Prabhat Khabar (Santal Rebellion supplement)*, 30 June.

—— (2006) *Representing Rebellion: Visual Aspects of Counter-insurgency in Colonial India*, New Delhi: Oxford University Press.

—— (2009) 'Revisioning Birsa Munda: Visual Constructions of the '*Vanavasi*' in Jharkhand', in N.K. Das and V.R. Rao (eds) *Identity, Cultural Pluralism and the State: South Asia in Perspective*, Delhi: Macmillan Publishers, 261–80.

—— (2011) 'Beyond Resistance: Idioms and Memories of Insurgency in the Adivasi Movement, Jharkhand State, India', in S. Das Gupta and R.S. Basu (eds) *Narratives from the Margins: Aspects of Adivasi History in India*, New Delhi: Pluto Press, 257–76.

—— (forthcoming) 'From History to Heritage: Adivasi Identity and *Hul Sengel*', in M. Carrin and L. Guzy (eds) *Voices from the Periphery: Subalternity and Empowerment*, submitted to Routledge Publishers India.

Sarkar, T. (1985) 'Jitu Santal's Movement in Malda: A Study in Tribal Protest', in R. Guha (ed.) *Subaltern Studies IV: Writings on South Asian History and Society*, New Delhi: Oxford University Press, 136–65.

Sider, G. and Smith, G. (1997) 'Introduction', in G. Sider and G. Smith (eds) *Between History and Histories: The Making of Silences and Commemorations*, Toronto: University of Toronto Press, 3–28.

Singh, K.S. (1966) *The Dust-Storm and the Hanging Mist: The Story of Birsa Munda and his movement in Chhotanagpur*, Firma KLM: Calcutta.

—— (1983) *Birsa Munda and his Movement 1874–1901: A Study of a Millenarian Movement in Chotanagpur*, Oxford University Press: London.

Skaria, A. (1998) 'Being Jangli: The Politics of Wildness', *Studies in History*, 14(2): 193–215.

—— (1999) *Hybrid Histories: Forests, Frontiers and Wildness in Western India*, New Delhi: Oxford University Press.

Werbner, R. (ed.) (1998) *Memory and the Postcolony: African Anthropology and the Critique of Power*, Zed Books: London.

4 Rebellion as modern self fashioning

A Santal movement in colonial Bengal

Tanika Sarkar

Introduction

In 1961, a *Calendar of Events of Local Importance* was prepared for Census operations in Malda, a district situated in the north-western parts of West Bengal. Its function was to map out memorable events in the history of the district, so that respondents to the Census questionnaire – often forgetful about exact dates in their own lives – would recollect the time of personal life events more precisely in the light of happenings of more general importance. Surprisingly, the name of Jitu Santal, leader of several uprisings among Santal sharecroppers between 1924 and 1932, was prominently recollected, and 'the murder of Jitu Santal at Adina' appeared as one of the most memorable events for the year 1932 (cited in Greenough 1982). Clearly, three decades after Jitu's death, his resistance had remained an important milestone for orienting the sense of time for all kinds of local people.

In 1924, Jitu Santal had emerged as the leader of a local anti-landlord movement among Santal sharecroppers. He had also come in contact with local Swarajists (Indian nationalists/Gandhians) and had visited the Faridpur Congress session. By 1926, he had been converted to Hinduism and to Kali-worship by a Swarajist pleader from Dinajpur. He subsequently induced his band of followers to abandon several crucial Santal customs and ritual practices. He also commanded them to accept him henceforward as their fount of law and justice. He told his devotees that a final battle had to be fought to occupy the historic Adina mosque at Pandua before his new and glorious realm could come into its own. In 1928, he conducted a crop looting movement with his followers, telling them that they would be recorded as tenants and would be released from their sharecropper status. In 1932, true to his earlier promise, he led a large band of Santals, occupied the mosque and resisted colonial police for some time until they killed him.

The fact that a Santal rebel remained, for decades, a legendary hero in local memory does question the commonsensical certainty that *Adivasis* inhabited a different and closed world from that of non-*Adivasis*: a divide that sharpened with the emergence of a group of modern, educated elite Indians, whose new identity was seemingly distant from the 'primitiveness' of tribal peoples. We find that, on the contrary, Jitu is embedded within a wide and shared local memory – shared, of course, among unequals – that suggests a more inclusive modern public domain revolving around a spatial unit, rather than an ethno-cultural one. Jitu's legend, moreover, strongly underlines a complex political relationship with the local elite: of sharing, of contesting, as well as of recreat-ing, or trying to recreate, each other's political activism. The politics simultan-eously inhabited very different domains: those of nationalism and Hindu organisations, of land relations, of changing interfaces with the colonial state and its legal-judicial apparatus.

In 1985, I explored the story of Jitu's politics, to show the autonomy of a tribal movement, its ability to compose, on its own terms, a resistance to colonial 'justice' and land policies, as well as to the exploitation of local Hindu landhold-ers (Sarkar 1985). Apart from trying to retrieve the meanings that Jitu and his followers might have ascribed to political and religious terms that were some-times borrowed from elite Hindu and nationalist leaders, I had attempted to understand how and why a movement of tribal sharecroppers had set as its pro-claimed goal the occupation of a historical mosque at Adina. Written in the early phase of Subaltern Studies, my work reiterated some of the typical concerns of that historiography, although it also questioned the tendency to ignore the internal stratifications and power play within subaltern groups, which always position themselves not only in antagonistic opposition to the elites but, equally, to those who are situated below themselves. A revisiting of the narrative is useful, given certain new imperatives.

Here, I would like to probe more deeply those aspects of social, cultural and religious change that Jitu fostered (via his politics) within his community. The pattern of those changes reflects the image of the *Adivasi* rebel, who, to some extent, is in conscious flight from the digits of his ancestral identity. Jitu, like many other tribal peasant rebels before and after him, stitched his cloth of rebel-lion with threads from many sources. He improvised a new Santal identity for his followers that departed significantly and deliberately from the ways of their ancestors. The finely tuned pattern of rejection-cum-retention from plural sources, I would suggest, aspired more towards a new designation of selfhood, rather than the appropriation of external influences through an internal and inher-ited grid of meanings. In the latter frame of understanding, developed during the phase of early Subaltern Studies history writing, an older filter of traditions remained paramount and decisive. I would now emphasize, however, the radical modernity and discontinuity of the fresh composition. The newness constitutes innovation rather than either acculturation or an unbroken continuity of the earlier tradition.

Finally, the modern identity that was hammered out in the course of Jitu's enterprise needs to be named. Or rather, the fragility of all naming needs to be demonstrated. Was Jitu aligned to his tribal community, or to his class identity? Was he a genuinely converted and communal Hindu, or were Hindu symbols mere borrowed trappings that sat rather lightly on a Santal cultural base? Was he a nationalist, close to the politics of the Congress and hence appropriated, or was he using Congress links to fight a different battle that bore little resemblance to Congress intentions? Is there a true, essential core identity that is hidden in the play of multiple affiliations of class, tribe, Hindu, nationalist, peasant and rebel? Or, does the very instability and evanescence of the many possible affiliations suggest a modern predicament where all stable signposts waver, leaving us with the display of plural identities as radically contingent, impermanent, changeable habitations?

Champa and beyond

Santal myths of origin talk about a wandering race, people who were driven from place to place by quirks of fortune. At mythical Champa, a land of plenty and freedom, however, they had rested for a long time, before they were forced out again. Champa recurred as a memory of a lost but retrievable golden age, especially at times of Santal risings that followed in the wake of the great rebellion or 'Hul' of 1855–7: notably, the Kherwar movements, which in the subsequent decades had been inspired by the hope of living once again, as they had in Champa, in independence and without rent payments, except for the small tribute they would bring to their leaders (see Culshaw and Archer 1945: 229).

In Malda district, Santals exemplified the travails of the 'wandering race'. From about 1800, they had started to pour into the district from the region that would become known, following the suppression of the 'Hul', as the Santal Parganas. By the next decade, about 20,000 Santals had settled in eastern Malda and migration continued till 1900. Interestingly, they found a living not in the forest habitat, with which they are inseparably associated, but by clearing forests for settled agriculture. Generally seen as bearers of the slash and burn mode of cultivation, they were actually prized by local landowners of the agricultural area known as the Barind tract for their renowned skill in rice farming. To utilize such skills, in order to prepare Barind for sedentary agriculture, Hindu landowners wooed them with easy terms, nominal rent and often occupancy status in the early years (Carter 1939: 84–5).

The skill and the knowledge that they brought to forest clearing and cultivation, however, were not commensurate with the long-term rewards. After the Barind had become a fertile tract through their labour, the Santals were soon reduced to a sharecropper or *adhiar* status, each taking home only half the crop and providing for his own plough, cattle and accommodation. Land slipped out of their hold through rent demands they could not meet. It was not unusual to find cases of *adhiars* cultivating the same plot for successive generations (Carter 1939: 40–75). A whole range of devices was used to achieve this transformation of Santal relationship to their land. Landlords took recourse to *abwabs* (illegal extraction by landowners, beyond the stipulated rent amount), refused to give proper rent receipts, enforced very high interest rates and employed exploitative and dishonest *gomustahs* (landlords' agents). There was, moreover, distrainment of crops and the use of forced labour as punishment for this. Santals, unused to the dense complexities of legal processes, would submit to the change, thinking that they had defaulted and hence deserved punishment (Carter 1939: 72).

Santals felt that the languages of law, and of property and land relations, were beyond their grasp: like malevolent *bongas* (spirits). The entire new world that came to control their lives so ruthlessly and inexplicably, and that seemed to demand new ritual modalities of propitiation and self-preservation, almost became an other-worldly phenomenon. It would be seen as structurally and operationally similar to older fears, predicaments and anxieties that had been invested in their relationship with Nature, livelihood and community well-being. It would also be very similar in the sheer wilfulness and inexplicability of the forces that operated in these realms. But the *ojhas* (traditional priesthood) and the *manjhis* (village leaders) that used to mediate between *bongako* (spirits) and Santals, and knew how to mitigate the worst of *bonga* malice, now failed to come to terms with the new structure of fear and danger. Their failure left Santals stranded and helpless (Risley 1891: 232).

Historians have suggested that notions of an older 'moral economy', based on a supposedly older order of natural and organic justice, had been composed by English plebeian communities in a particular historical conjuncture. They used this resource to mobilize resistance against the depredations that new agrarian and industrial capitalism inflicted on their material environment from the eighteenth century (see Thompson 1993). My point here is somewhat different. Santal accounts had been pessimistic about all possible worlds. Their lives – as they saw this – had always been serrated by uncertainties. The brief happy sojourn in Champa had been a temporary, atypical reprieve. The history that they constructed about their ancestors does not suggest the linear story of a fall, the loss of a world that had ever been happy or good for an entire time cycle. It indicates a narrative of endless banishments, perpetual wandering and unending homelessness, interspersed with brief spells of shelter and comfort. Their traditional origin myths thus reveal older and continuous uncertainties about the world and the precariousness of Santals within it. Marang Buru, the most powerful spirit in their pantheon, associates with both gods and demons. *Bongako* or spirits ruling the universe are sometimes malevolent beings who eat people up. The conditions of Santal existence indicated to them that higher powers – human and divine – are rarely benign or well intentioned, they require extensive propitiation. What was new in the modern world was that they had lost the key to the propitiatory rites. Jitu did not claim that Champa would be retrieved. He did promise, however, a new world that required new ritual modalities.

As Santals in Malda made the transition from occupancy status to *adhiar*-dom, and as awareness sank in about the ways in which they had helped unwittingly to defraud themselves, a self contempt would accumulate, combining, uneasily, with righteous anger at fraud by the *diku* (the non-*Adivasi*). The Santal's perspective on the process of alienation and dispossession was however ambivalent, made up of anger against the *diku* who robbed his land, and self-contempt for losing out so thoroughly. If the Santal can be so easily led astray, then there is something wrong with his ways. The negative self-image would often drive segments of defeated *Adivasis* to seek out the ways of the very *diko* whom they bitterly blamed for their troubles. From the late nineteenth century, attempts were made to revise tribal custom through waves of conversion to Christianity or Hinduism in recognition of a structural insufficiency that made them vulnerable in changing times (Mukherjea 1943: 381). In the Santal Parganas, the failure of the 1855 uprising led to extensive borrowings from and conversion to Hindu sects and Christianity. Among Bengali Santals, Brahman priests were found to preside over Hindu worship and festivals like the *Charak* (Chattopadhyay 1994: 471).

Mobilization of Santal sharecroppers: the colonial context

Santals in Malda had already composed a rich tradition of struggle against the loss of land. Migration, practised from 1901 onwards as large groups left for Dinajpur, Rajshahi, even the Nepal Terais, was a form of passive resistance. More active forms were initiated from 1910, when *zamindars* (landlords) of *tauzis* (plots) 586 and 587 at Habibpur *thana* (police station) tried to enforce a rent enhancement. Santals at first tried to resolve this peacefully through legal processes. They made a representation to the government about the illegal extractions that the *gomustahs* and the *peadahs* (landlords' musclemen) made from them. Vas, the Collector, was appointed as arbitrator. His enquiries disclosed that landlords had, for a long time, induced Santals to clear Barind jungles at very low rents. Then they demanded an immediate enhancement as the slopes were terraced and the land made ready for cultivation. Vas measured the land and rent was settled at six *annas* per *bigha* (about one-third of an acre) and a provision was made for the payment of arrears. The settlement was a treasured document for what seemed to be an acceptable and just entitlement to Santals who, henceforth, resisted all attempts to revise it (Chattopadhyay 1994: 80).

A colonial legal document was in this case the charter of freedom, which became the basis for future struggle, rather than for a conviction in a legitimate moral economy of the past. When settlement operations began in Malda, there was such tension in the air about imminent changes that District Magistrate Peddie urged that the operation, scheduled for 1932–3, be pushed forward: there were far too many clashes as landlords attempted to destroy *mokarrari* (land held on payment of a fixed rent) possession and increase rent illegally. The administrators on the ground, Vas and Peddie, were more sensitive to the predicament of sharecroppers, documenting in Settlement Reports the various frauds that landlords practised, the oppression of their staff, and the crises in lives of sharecroppers. Colonial courts, however, turned a blind eye to landlord dishonesty and manipulation, which nullified Santal hopes of contractual justice on a modern, legal basis. This disjuncture breaks up any simplified notion of the 'colonial state' and requires a much closer investigation. It was this colonial partisanship (at the judicial level) with landlords that made Jitu proclaim his *bichar* (justice) against that of the state.

The introduction of the Tenancy Amendment Bill in the Legislative Council in 1923 prompted great fears, as well as hopes in different quarters. As the terms of the bill were published, sharecroppers could see some hope of being reclassified as tenants. Landlords dreaded this and as a pre-emptive strike, they tried to break up records of continuous occupation, since that might lead to a change of status. A spate of evictions followed to dislodge sharecroppers from land they had cultivated continuously (Chaudhuri 1979: 198). The phase coincided with a steep rise in agrarian prices. Land, thus, became a precious commodity, and landlords sought pretexts for eviction and re-appropriation of land from sharecroppers, to be made over to more solvent tenants. Rent enhancement suits in Bengal went up from 19,232 to 45,415 between 1928 and 1930.[1] Again, the burden would fall most unbearably on the heads of sharecroppers, faced with hopes of imminent tenancy status as well as a new crisis of rent which led, too often, to a total loss of land. At Dacca, Khulna, Faridpur and Jessore, there were significant struggles, for instance, between Hindu landlords on the one hand, and Muslim and untouchable Namashudra sharecroppers on the other, as the agrarian conflict broadened into religious and caste strife (Sarkar 1987: 38). Jitu's actions with Santal sharecroppers had parallels among several non-tribal peasant and sharecropper movements.

Landlords in the Barind tract, as elsewhere in most parts of Bengal, were overwhelmingly Hindus (Carter 1939: 32). Adjacent communities at Malda – notably Muslim cultivators (Shershabadiyas) who had migrated from Murshidabad to the region at the same time as the Santals, cleared the forests and secured superior tenancy rights, were employed by landlords as henchmen and applauded by the colonial authorities for their economic rationality and work ethic – shared overlapping experiences of exploitation in certain areas. Yet between the Santal and Muslim sharecroppers, there was a radical difference in status and general esteem: all this made for a particularly forceful condition of rivalry that could, and did, outweigh the commonality of landlord-moneylender oppression. Jitu's plans for appropriating the Adina mosque as the goal of his movement could very possibly have derived substantially from this rivalry. There might have been a more immediate, local reason as well. In 1926, a Muslim school teacher in Jitu's part of the district was accused of raping a Santal girl. A clash followed between Muslims and Santals who assaulted the teacher and destroyed school furniture.[2]

Jitu Santal: testimony, tradition and transgression

The 'Jitu Santal' phenomenon is not merely local memory, preserved in the remembrances of the people of Malda. It begins to be anxiously described in the colonial archives from 1924 onwards. His agency appears in the fortnightly accounts of province-wide happenings that the Government of India compiled under the Home Political series. More detailed observations are found in the Home Confidential Political and Political Confidential Records that the Government of Bengal maintained. After the police had accomplished the killing of Jitu and after the movement ended, a Special Officer for Barind was appointed in 1933 by the Government of Bengal to investigate whether the struggle did have some basis in genuine Santal distress. His conclusions, which apparently led to 'somewhat mitigated conditions' there, were recorded in the Survey and Settlement Reports (Carter 1939: 84–5). The colonial state rather excelled at this: first to stamp out protest ruthlessly and then try to soften the blow through investigations and minimal relief, so that trouble would not recur. After Independence, the subsequent West Bengal District Gazetteers traced the narrative of the movement in Malda back to its point of origin in 1924 (Sengupta 1969: 62).

Nationalists records, too, watched Jitu Santal's activities and reported on them: *The Indian Quarterly Register*, the nationalist newspapers, *Amrita Bazar Patrika* and *Bangabani* described his activities in Malda with sympathetic interest. Interestingly, so did the English-owned newspaper, *The Statesman*. If Jitu could not achieve his realm and the appropriation of the Adina Mosque, if he died in enemy fire with his companions, he still somehow captured the imagination of the powers that be. Those who killed him admitted that Barind Santals needed some attention and mitigation of their harsh and unjust circumstances. Yet, the price had not been high enough to lead to effective change. In 1945–6, an enquiry into Santal conditions in the Habibpur-Bamangola-Gajole complex at Barind, which was Jitu's hunting ground, established that most of them had remained sharecroppers with average holdings well below the size of an economic holding: even at the best of times their livelihood could be raised barely above the minimum subsistence levels (Chattopadhyay 1947: 6–8).

Archival reports do not present us with Jitu's own words. They do, however, provide comments, observations and complaints about Jitu from local people in surrounding villages.[3] If some of them, such as tenure-holding Surendra Kumar Talukdar or Puran Ghatwal (a *chowkidar*), were men of local substance and authority, there are also voices and words of local Santals, disenchanted with Jitu or informing the police about Jitu in the hope of rewards: Lalu Santal, Meghrai Sikar Santal, Matla or Salhu. A Christian Santal schoolteacher testified against Jitu and his imposition of a reign of intimidation against 'Christians and Mussalmans and Santals who have not given up hens and pigs'.[4] What is important is that the respondents quoted words spoken by Jitu or by his close associates, and that these words were carefully preserved within quotation marks in the archival documents.[5] Through such transmitted words and their meticulous re-inscription in written archival records, traces of Jitu's utterances were captured and preserved in the secret, confidential domain of official deliberations. The quotation marks would signify when the testimonies were recorded in their pristine form. We may be quite sure that the testimonies would be procured by officials in such a way that their recollection of Jitu's exact speech would be as precise as possible.

It was not very usual for the nationalist media to pursue detailed local investigations, especially at moments when the Congress-led anti-colonial movement fully captured the attention of the press. Jitu, however, did share in that attention because of his seemingly brief connection with Congress and Swarajist agencies.

The *Amrita Bazar Patrika* saw his movement as that of 'reformed Santals', inspired by a Swarajist pleader from Dinajpur.[6] The pro-state *Statesman* laid the blame at the door of Swarajist Hindu agitators: 'The Santals are peaceful, law abiding aborigines, honest to a degree of gullible simplicity and thus easily got at by propagandists.'[7] Applauded for responding to a Hinduisation campaign in one and pitied for the manipulation of an honest aboriginal people in another, in both cases the source of Santal action is attributed to an external non-*Adivasi* agency.

The first two appearances of Jitu Santal in colonial archival documentation forcefully underline the discordant plurality that characterized his activities. In 1924, Jitu Chotka or Jitu Santal of Kochaikandar village in Habibpur *thana* is able to organize an anti-landlord tenant agitation among local Santals. The episode is actually recalled and recorded two years later only after Jitu had also developed some Congress connections. The recollection did not extend to any information about what exactly the earlier tenant agitation had involved. For the state, the more disturbing aspect was that Swarajist agitators supported the movement and sent Jitu to the Faridpur district Congress session and he 'received instruction from them on the art of popular agitation'.[8] It seems that the anti-landlord struggle, by itself, did not cause undue official anxiety. It was the link up between a grass roots local *Adivasi* leader and the Congress organization that was more worrisome.

No doubt the Santal agitation would have been fuelled by rumours about a better deal for sharecroppers which had been suggested by the Kerr Committee. It also seems plausible that the extent of Swarajist opposition to them was not known to Jitu and his followers. So, while the proposal of a colonial agency arouses hopes and stimulates Santal political action against Hindu landlords, their movement, simultaneously, attaches itself to a nationalist organization whose broader support base depended on the very Hindu landlords that Santals were pitted against, and whose official line defended landlord interests in opposition to the suggestions of a colonial administrator. At the same time, however, local Swarajist leaders obviously did not follow the official Party line on land relations entirely, which is why the leader of an anti-landlord tenant movement was courted by them. There was a break in the flow of information and between local and official Party lines that gave Santal politics in Malda this curious turn. Inspired by rumours of imminent change that the colonial administration may introduce and that some colonial administrators championed, they engaged in an anti-landlord movement. But its assumed political form was an alliance with an organization that supported their adversaries and that opposed the colonial state machinery. We find no evidence, however, that local Swarajists actually encouraged Jitu to form a band of anti-landlord tenant agitators. Rather, after Jitu had mobilized a large body of Santal sharecroppers and had attained some local prominence in the Barind area, they sought him out as a possible local ally for the Congress organization.

Kashishwar Chakravarty was a Dinajpur-based pleader and very active among Dinajpur Santals. He had been visiting the neighbouring district of Malda from time to time since 1925 with proselytizing aims. Jitu and Arjun Santal are mentioned as Santal acolytes of this Swarajist pleader who is also referred to as *Sanyasi baba* (ascetic father). Jitu set up a *Sanyasi Dol* (band of ascetics) with Santal sharecroppers of the Habibpur-Bamangola-Gajole range and conducted a Kali Puja, defying police orders, to proclaim his conversion to Hinduism. Though the word *sanyas* (ascetic) was freely used, it seems unlikely that either Chakravarty or Jitu's group were actually ascetics. By 1926, however, all connection between Chakravarty and Jitu disappeared, and Jitu was laying down his own version of the new religion.

The emphasis now shifted away from the tenant agitation towards 'the making of Santals into Hindus' by giving up the use of pigs and fowl, so central to Santal ritual life. Not only would they attain Hinduisation, but they would also attain the clean Shudra status: i.e. the status of agricultural 'low castes' who were pure enough to be *jal chal* (from whose hands, pure born castes would accept water). Santals were to accept Jitu as their sovereign authority, to abide by his form of *bichar* and, instead of paying rent to the landlord, they were to pay Jitu one *kula* (measure) of rice, or about five seers of grain. They were advised to delay the payment of the *adhi* (the share that sharecroppers had to pay to landowners), as Jitu told them that 'those who cultivate in adhi from another will get the lands under the new Settlement as their own jotes or holdings'. Rumours came in, thick and fast, that Jitu's rule would be inaugurated from spring or the month of Phalgun, that Jitu had said that he would go to the fort at Pandua and from there a *larai* (battle) would begin to drive out Muslims and all others who would not join them.[9]

Between 1924 and 1926, Jitu had combined two distinct roles that, in practice, sometimes overlapped. He was the leader of a tenant agitation. He also developed links with a Swarajist and a Hinduisation movement. His tenant struggle was self-created, but he also represented the local face of the Congress, Hinduising nationalist populism that was particularly active in these years especially in the Bihar/Bengal region. The picture had become far more complex by 1926, and we need to separate the different strands of multiple and contradictory politics quite carefully. In 1926, despite the Hinduisation thrust and the suspension of the peasant agitation, in some ways, the concerns of Santal sharecroppers are more pronounced. The Settlement is explicitly mentioned as a resource of hope and justice and a fairly accurate impression is conveyed about the thrust of the Kerr Committee recommendations: sharecroppers might be elevated to tenant status. However, the agency for change is removed from colonial intentions. The Settlement would improve the lot of sharecroppers only if Santals acknowledged Jitu's *raj* (sovereignty).

Jitu told his followers that:

> English Raj is very bad and oppressive and *bichar* cannot be obtained in government courts. [...] Government does not give good justice; it takes too many rupees from the people [...] do not go to the Government with your complaints. [...] The *bichar* of the present government is ... *be aini* [illegal].

You must pay me Rs.3. Then we shall have our own government. I shall be the judge and arbitrator in all disputes.[10]

Jitu was not a traditional *manjhi* (village leader). He was a man without any land.[11] He thus appropriated the role of the headman on the strength of his modern political leadership: of agrarian struggle and of a local Swarajist-cum-Hinduisation movement. He would not only dispense justice, but would also demand the tribute that the *manjhi* is entitled to. At the same time, he also demanded the transference of yet another traditional entitlement. The rent that *adhiars* paid to landlords would now be converted to a tribute to Jitu. Thus his reign would displace a triangulated structure of power: colonial court, Santal *manjhi* and village landlord.

The modes of political action that would lead to this state can also be read as ritual activities that messianic movements prescribe for world transformation. Jitu, in fact, insisted so hard on the ritual avoidance of pigs and fowl, and took such stern measures of social boycott and intimidation against those who still practised it, that Santals reported this in tones of bitter complaint. 'I have not gone to Jitu's meetings,' said Meghrai Sikar Santal, 'as he wants us to give up hens and pigs. Our fathers kept them and if we don't, we won't have enough to eat.'[12] Rumours were circulated, threatening dire consequences. 'Jitu told the people that if they did not give up hens and pigs they would become blind or that they would get cholera.' Or, 'Jitu says kill your hens and pigs, otherwise you will be *Doms* [polluting caste], you will have to undertake the disposal of dead bodies'. On the other hand, if they complied, then 'theirs will be the Raj'.[13]

If Jitu appropriated ritual leadership from traditional community specialists, he also challenged other older hierarchies. He ordered the *mondal* (headman) of Rangamatia to throw away his umbrella in order to demonstrate deference.[14] Jitu's commands seemed to elevate him to the *manjhi* status, not through inherited or consensually procured traditional authority, but through a combination of personal charisma and political leadership. An umbrella is a strong signifier of honour, never to be used by the lower orders, and indisputably associated with the presence of rural bosses. By commanding the headman to divest himself of the symbol of power, Jitu not only declared his own new reign, but also inverted the traditional social order.[15]

A number of headmen, *chowkidars* and Santal chiefs seemed most ready to testify against Jitu to the colonial authorities. A similar rebellion within a rebellion against internal tribal hierarchies and traditional power bases has been noted in a ground-breaking study of early twentieth century Oraon risings in Chhotanagpur by Sangeeta Dasgupta (1999). Oraon protests against British landlords were, she shows, enfolded within struggles against dominant *bhuinhar* chiefs who combined the ritual function of spirit propitiation with British-endorsed privileged tenures and chieftaincy rights. The new Tana Bhagat movement sought to dislodge them from their privileges just as, in a parallel appropriation of nationalist activity, they tried to abolish colonial power through a self-created new ritual regime. The play of power inside the community that modern rebellions induce, and the fracturing of traditional modes of administration and authority that the appearance of new messianic leaders entails, are little noticed in the exclusive focus on opposition between *Adivasis* and non-*Adivasis* in colonial times.

There were, however, other rituals of inversion: a conversion to Kali worship, an annulment of key Santal ritual usages, the occupation of a mosque, intimidation of Muslims and disobedient Santals and their promised expulsion from Jitu's reign, the attainment of a clean *Shudra* caste status, thereby quickly transiting from tribe to caste. Jitu's Raj, brought in through the obedience of the faithful, would not only bestow secure tenancy on his followers, it would also give them clean *Shudra* status, allowing them to offer water to Brahmans. Non-compliance would render them untouchable Hindus. 'If you don't come to our side', he warned, 'you shall be outcasted and will be ... Mussulmans and *Doms* and *Chamars* ('untouchable' castes).'[16] If older *Adivasi* hierarchies had been inverted in favour of personal absolutism, then the hierarchies of caste Hindus strongly inflected Jitu's social thinking and his religious rites. It shows the social influence of the very same caste landlords against whom he led the agitation. It would neither have been directly transmitted by his Swarajist associates nor by his early guru, Kashishwar Chakravarty, who reportedly had Swarajist links. Swarajists, most of the time, were not too obviously associated with caste conservatism.

Jitu's rule: imagining swaraj

Kashishwar Chakravarty would not have been an enduring or decisive influence as he seemed to have disappeared soon from Jitu's life. Yet, he did play a crucial formative role at the initial stages of self-fashioning, providing Jitu with several of the possible blocks of identity-construction that Jitu rearranged differently later on. He was the *Sanyasi baba*, who inspired the idea of a Santal *Sanyasi Dol*, he brought Kali worship to Jitu. Kali, in the understanding of scholars of religion, probably originated as a tribal deity whom Brahmanical religion absorbed into its own mythology. Even after the absorption, Kali retained a strong family resemblance with the more malevolent of the *bongako*. Her re-entry into the tribal sacred universe is, thus, rich in irony (Chakrabarti 2001: 165). Chakravarty came out of a wider movement around this time when Hindu ascetics came close to the Congress movement and functioned as preachers, combining Hinduisation as well as populism among labourers, peasants and tribals. Officials suspected that this was an organized move, planned at a conference of *sadhus* at Nagpur in 1920. Coinciding with the onset of Khilafat (Islamic identity assertion) and Non Cooperation (secular nationalist agitation), a number of them from the Arya Samaj and the Ramakrishna Mission, or from the Dasnami Naga sect, fanned out in the Bihar-Bengal region. At Dacca, a pleader, Anukul Chandra Basu, hosted them.[17] Kashishwar was, similarly, a pleader. We do not know about his sectarian affiliation, though, in his politics, he was suspected of being a Swarajist. It is not clear in the official records why he was called a *Sanyasi Baba*: he could have renounced his old livelihood and taken *sanyas* (ascetic vows).

Jitu's movement was, at first, affiliated to the Satyam Shivam sect that Kashishwar had formed in 1925, 'whose object seems to have been to claim the Santal for the Hindu community rather on the lines of the Arya Samaj'. (Carter 1939: 40) It is not too clear if he inspired the idea of the occupation of the mosque, or whether it was Jitu's own idea. At the time of his active connection with Jitu, there was no mention of such a plan, and that would mesh with his supposed Swarajist inclinations. Jitu announced the plan in 1926, when Chakravarty was no longer a leading figure on the Santal horizon at Malda. It occurred at a time of communal violence in the province and a communal conflict at Barind itself that I referred to earlier. Jitu could, therefore, have added that aspect later on, acting within changed political circumstances, provincial and local. There are strong statements about the expulsion, even killings of Muslims under his Raj. 'We must kill all hens, pigs and Mussulmans', said a Santal.[18] A Christian Santal, on the other hand, believed that the movement was primarily directed at Christians.[19] When a local Christian leased land in Jitu's village, his men prevented him from collecting dues from grass cutting from his plot. A Christian official of the Union Board complained that his servants had been made to leave his service.[20]

What confuses the ascription of communalism to such statements and incidents is that they equally stigmatised the unconverted Santal and promised their expulsion under the new dispensation. A Santal found that his son-in-law threatened to desert his daughter if he did not conform to Jitu's commands. 'In Sikarpur', declared a devotee, 'we shall not keep Santals or Muhammadans any longer'. 'They are trying to make us Hindus by force and we do not want that', complained a Santal plaintively.[21] Does this indicate a total self-severance from an earlier designation that the neo-Hindu finds offensive, just as he finds Muslims, Christians and untouchables gross and polluting? Or is it a flight from those connotations of the past identity which were marked by humiliation and loss? Yet other typical attributes of Santal life were retained: drinking, merry making, dancing and festivities, and the use of bows and arrows and swords

Jitu held meetings at places that were turned into pleasure grounds. Hundreds of men, women and children would come, displaying weapons, playing on flutes and spending a long time just sitting around at leisure under trees (Carter 1939: 40). Social life, too, did not change much. 'The devotees gave up the use of pigs and fowl but persisted with most other Santal customs.' (Carter 1939: 40) If Jitu took a lot from sources outside Santal life, then the resultant bricolage was one whose assemblage was decided only by himself. It resembled no dominant influence or cultural paradigm.

In September 1928, Jitu instructed sharecroppers to loot the *bhadoi* or autumn crop from tracts in the Gajole-Bamangola-Habibpur *thana* area that had been only recently expropriated from defaulting Santal sharecroppers. They were told that they would thereby get themselves enrolled as tenants instead of as *adhiars* in the settlement records. Several cases of crop looting followed and once the entire crop from a six *bigha* plot was carried away. The District Magistrate and a band of armed police rushed there and Jitu was arrested with 60 of his men after several rounds of clashes.[22] The severity of Santal resistance denotes that the looting was motivated not by distress and hopes of gain, but as a necessary ritual action that would inaugurate a change of status. The importance of state deliberations on agrarian laws remains significant as stimulus for rebel action. There is also a nebulous belief that ultimately the state would be persuaded by this mode of protest: the primary enemy, at this point, is, then, the landlord.

In many instances, Jitu's followers seemed to have said, after him, that Jitu's Raj was coming, and so was their Desh. The entry of this Bengali word that denotes homeland indicates the pervasiveness of the nationalist vocabulary that, since Non-Cooperation, had invoked popular movements in the name of freeing the *Desh*: signifying a static object in need of saving. In Santal sentences, *Desh* is an active entity, it is 'coming', to save. Otherwise firmly attached to the notion of immovable substances like earth and soil, it acquires here a dynamic movement. It is both the companion and the condition of Jitu's Raj: they come together to perform the same function for Jitu's *sanyasis*, to liberate them from *zamindars* and rent, colonial courts and the local administrative machinery. The relationship between *Raj* and *Desh* is close but complex. If Raj exclusively signifies Jitu's power and authority, *Desh* would probably encompass all Santal *adhiars* who abide by Jitu's laws.

At this stage, however, the language seems to suggest sweeping transformation by the thick reiteration of negatives: all the things that are to go. When it tries to say what would characterize the new dispensation, we are left with an elevation in tenancy status in colonial records: hardly compatible with the claim that under Jitu's rule the British would also go. The gap between the force of the language and the substantive content is striking. Perhaps there is a hope in a deferred or phased liberation. The Settlement records would inaugurate concrete material changes, but a larger change would follow as the *Raj* is installed. Perhaps, imagination could not conceive of more immediate concrete benefits but still retained the nebulous vision of a larger and total transformation. It is important to remember that, for all the power of the redemptive vision of *Swaraj* or *Ramrajya* (rule of God) that Gandhi enunciated during Non-Cooperation, the substantive shape of it had remained equally elusive. Not even the exact status of the British had been spelt out. The absence left all kinds of imaginaries with space to breathe.

In 1932, earlier hopes associated with tenancy amendment laws had gone. The promise of change through the politics of crop looting had been belied. This time, therefore, Jitu had a new ritual on offer. Or, perhaps, it was not a new ritual after all. From 1926, he had held out the hope that a final, apocalyptic battle would be fought at Pandua and after the Adina mosque was taken over, that Jitu's *Raj* would come. The fourteenth century mosque, a landmark historic and architectural monument located within the old city of Pandua, was a major site of Muslim pilgrimage and was the second largest mosque in Bengal. Dinajpur Muslims had a saying: 'First is Medina, next is Adina.' (Hasan 1970: 5, 37, 68)

Located inside Barind, it would be deeply familiar to Jitu. Jitu and his followers marched up to Pandua on 3 December, occupied the ruins of the mosque and conducted there 'a debased form of Hindu worship' to change it from a mosque to a temple, according to a nationalist source.[23] 'War would begin at Pandua', a follower had said in 1926.[24] We do not know what the form of worship was, but clearly it was unknown and offensive to the Hindu nationalist elite. Even as the mosque was declared a temple, Jitu told his followers to pray, facing the west, a practice unknown to Santals and Hindus, and mandatory among the very Muslims whose place of worship he had occupied.[25]

Along with the Hinduisation of the ruins, he proclaimed himself as Gandhi, and gave *darshana* (sight) to his followers, sitting at the spinning wheel in a Gandhian fashion. His 'Raj', he said, had finally arrived. This was the first time that Jitu had invoked Gandhi's name. But links with Gandhian Santals already existed. Dinajpur-based Santals had been deeply involved with the Congress movement. Civil Disobedience still lingered on, reviving the miracle-making fame of Gandhi, and allowing varied images and messages to be fashioned in his name to fit different contingencies and predicaments. In fact, the greater the distance between the mainstream Gandhian movement and the subaltern one, the more likely it would be that plural and diverse groups would associate, in a protean manner, with his name. Jitu, in search of an appropriate resource for proclaiming the power and magnificence of his imminent Raj, could think of no greater name. Significantly, since the brief flare of interest in the Congress in 1924, we do not find any more evidence of his deployment of Congress associations until 1932.

The last combat had long been promised and Santals knew what would happen. 'The rail will stop', it had been said in 1926, 'and our bows and arrows will carry three *kos* (each approximately two miles in length) and the guns of the English will not fire.'[26] It was no longer Muslims or landlords, then, who would be the combatants, but it would be the English, even though a mosque would need to be occupied as the appointed site for the great war. Was the mosque chosen, then, for its towering grandeur, as a suitable site for Jitu's reign, the grandest place that he could imagine? Was it actually bereft, then, of all anti-Muslim associations? That hardly seems true as Jitu had repeatedly declared that Muslims would be driven out or killed in his Raj. In any case, since the last enemies to be routed would be the English, which is logical enough since Jitu looked forward to absolute power (that would necessarily involve the demolition of the colonial state), the claim to Gandhi's figure, thus, made perfect sense. Who else had, in recent and known past, fought the British harder than Gandhi?

The promise in the message had, of course, been a very familiar refrain in all messianic movements and a familiar motif in older Santal, Munda and Oraon rebellions. It attached a world-transforming consequence to a particular ritual sequence that would immobilize the weapons of the mighty adversary who could not be defeated in a real battle. Earlier, however, this grand finale was a distant horizon, and Jitu told Santals to engage in more concrete, immediate struggles for more limited and vivid results. In 1932, he decided, however, that the time had come for the final effort. It is not certain what made him think so, as the usual portents that usually inspire such apocalyptic expectations were missing in 1932. There was neither any war that Britain faced outside India, nor any hope of its being vanquished by a mighty western power. Civil Disobedience, too, was grinding to a halt. Nonetheless, Jitu decided on the final combat for the Raj. There were no more suggestions of crop looting, or anti-landlord agitation which had characterized his earlier efforts. The *Raj*, the *Desh*, were scoured of all material valences, of all mundane aspirations at this point. There was a sudden inflation of horizon, in the representation of Gandhi as the symbol of Jitu's power, in the construction of the British as the last enemy, in the vision of the future where *Raj* and *Desh* would come.

The ritual did not work. There was a pitched battle between the Santals and the armed police who commanded Jitu to give up the mosque and come out. Jitu refused and the police opened fire, contrary to the prophecy. A Santal arrow killed a constable. Three Santals were shot dead and Jitu was one of them.[27] The movement was over.

Conclusion: Jitu Santal and historical representation

Who were Jitu's men, and who were his enemies? Were his *sanyasis* converted Hindus who had abandoned their Santal designation? It seems so at many points, though Jitu would not entirely identify with Hindus either. If some Hindus had provided inspiration and instruction, they would not be part of the movement, the inner core. His followers were all Santals, and his immediate adversaries were very often Hindus. If a few markers of Santal existence had been demonstratively abjured, many others remained a vital part of the movement. At the same time, his movement absorbed Hindu characteristics, especially the hatred and contempt for lower castes and untouchables. The search seems endlessly circular. The only certainty seems to be that Jitu's men could not be Muslims, low castes and Christians. Initially, the deliberations and the machinery of the colonial state held out some hope. However, at the end, with Jitu claiming absolute power, the existing state needed to give way.

The trajectory of political struggle and cultural change certainly responded to an economic crisis in Santal existence. It also seems to suggest a striking case of a modern self-reform among Santals, in interaction with ideas and images external to the community, but according to terms decided by the *Adivasi* leader, who would select what elements to retain from the non-Santal world, what to discard, what to carry along from the older Santal life and what not to practise. In this pattern of self-fashioning through a new relationship with the older self and the new world, it is not so very different from the reforms that the modern middle class Indians initiated. It was, moreover, an initiative that came out of a stratum from within the community that was earlier not in possession of ritual, political or social authority. The modernity or non-traditionality of the enterprise is evident, as it is in the break with past cultural forms and in the search for resources for self-renewal in other, even adversarial, cultural practices. The sense of insufficiency that this sprang from, the sense of being out of step with the new world that repeated defeats induced, are, again, familiar signs of modern reformism. The framing of the agenda within religious terms and the acquisition of religious authority and aura by the leader had similarly been evident when the elite intelligentsia thrust around, looking for religious anchorage and assurance.

Jitu's allies and adversaries moved around, switching places. The self that was the source and the object of the effort, too, was elusive. At the same time, one aspect of Jitu's affiliation remained constant. His Santal companions were sharecroppers, victims of landlord eviction, betrayed by colonial officialdom. At the same time, class was not the real and necessary core, either, as it was framed within a set of qualifications and restrictions.

Studies of subaltern *Adivasi* groups rarely touch levels below the uppermost layer of the subaltern militants. This exploration of Jitu's movement is no exception to that. In that sense, a predicament of earlier studies of elite nationalism is repeated, in this sustained focus on the activity of the leader. The wishes and needs of the followers are deduced from that. Created by inadequate sources, this superficiality is, however, not sufficiently recognized as a problem. The rhetoric of historical studies of subaltern groups has, sometimes, been inspired by a romantic exaltation of the potential for freedom, for libertarianism. *Adivasi* rebellions are ascribed to the influence of such desires. At the same time, Jitu's movement involved an assertion of absolute personal power, enforced through intimidation, policing and disciplining of recalcitrant subalterns. In the pattern of inversion of existing hierarchies, the principles of domination and subordination remained intact. So were various exclusions and marginalizations.

There is no easy way of characterizing the truth of the movement. It was a movement of sharecroppers whose vulnerability was doubled by their *Adivasi* status. They turned to rebellion when all the powers that be colluded to deprive them of the land that they had cleared and made fruitful. They propelled their defiance by dreams of a transformed world, which would have no *diko*, landlords, rent, courts or police. It would also be a realm without Muslims, *Doms* and *Chamars*.

Notes

1 Census of India, 1931, 5(1): 17.
2 Government of Bengal (GOB), Poll Confidential (Poll Conf), FN 662 (1–2), 1926.
3 For example, evidence from the testimonies of Faisa Mondol, Puran Ghatwal, Surendra Talukdar, in GOB, Poll Conf, FN 622 (1–2), 1926.
4 Evidence of Karo and Hakim Hembrum, GOB, Poll Conf, FN 629 (1–3), 1926.
5 See, for instance, GOB, Poll Conf, FN 629 (1–3), 1926.
6 *Amrita Bazar Patrika*, 24 July 1928.
7 *The Statesman*, 16 December 1932.
8 GOB, Poll Conf, FN 622 (1–2), 1926; Wood to Jarvin, 18 December, 1926.
9 Report of Malda S.P., 26/12/1926; also evidence from Faisa Mondol, Puran Ghatwal, Surendra Talikdar and Salu Santal; GOB, Poll Conf (91–2), 1926, Enclosure 1.
10 Evidence of Kosaldi Sarkar, Bonomali doffadar, Surendra Talukdar, GOB, Poll Conf, FN 629 (1–3), 1926.

11 GOB, Poll Conf, FN 622(1–20), 1926.
12 GOB, Poll Conf, FN 629 (1–3), 1926.
13 Evidence of Karo, Hakim Hembrum, ibid.
14 Evidence of Bonomali and Matla, ibid.
15 On the expansion of meaning of limited gestures of subaltern defiance and about their
    limits, see Guha (1983).
16 Evidence of Saheba, GOB, Poll Conf, FN 629 (1–3), 1926.
17 Report from IB, CID, Bengal, 7/11/1921; Home Department Poll 1922, No 11.
18 GOB, Poll Conf, FN 629 (1–3), 1926.
19 Ibid.
20 Evidence of Kosaldi Sarkar, Bonomali Daffadar and Surendra Talukdar, ibid.
21 Evidence of Karo and Hembrum, ibid.
22 *Amrita Bazar Patrika*, 24 July 1928.
23 *Indian Quarterly Register*, Vol 1, 14 December 1932.
24 GOB, Poll Conf, FN 629 (1–3), 1926.
25 Evidence of Laly Santal, GOB, Poll Conf, FN 622 (1–2), 1926.
26 Evidence of Pomdu, GOB, Poll Conf, FN 629 (1–3), 1926.
27 *The Statesman*, 16 December 1932.

References

Carter, M.O. (1939) *Final Report on the Survey and Settlement Operations in the District of Malda, 1928–35*, Alipur, Indian Office Records.

Chakrabarti, K. (2001) *Religious Process: The Puranas and the Making of a Regional Tradition*, New Delhi: Oxford University Press.

Chattopadhyay, K.P. (1947) *Report on Santals in Northern and Western Bengal, 1945–46*, Calcutta: Calcutta University Press.

—— (1994) *Essays in Social Anthropology*, Calcutta: K.P. Bagchi.

Chaudhuri, B.B. (1979) 'Agrarian Movements in Bengal and Bihar 1919–39', in B.R. Nanda (ed.) *Socialism in India*, Delhi: Vikas, 190–229.

Culshaw, W.J. and Archer, W.G. (1945) 'The Santal Rebellion', *Man in India*, 25: 218–39.

Dasgupta, S. (1999) 'Reordering a World: The Tana Bhagat Movement 1914–1919', *Studies in History*, NS, January–June, 1–41.

Greenough, P. (1982) 'Political Crisis and the Death of Charismatic Leaders in Twentieth Century Bengal', Second Draft for SAFE III, Conference, December.

Guha, R. (1983) *Elementary Aspects of Peasant Insurgency in Colonial India*, New Delhi: Oxford University Press.

Hasan, S.M. (1970) *The Adina Masjid at Hazrat Pandua*, Dacca: Society for Pakistan Studies.

Mukherjea, C.L. (1943) *The Santals*, Calcutta: Indian Research Institute.

Risley, H.H. (1891) *The Tribes and Castes of Bengal*, Vol. 2, Calcutta: Bengal Secretariat Press.

Sarkar, T. (1985) 'Jitu Santal's Movement in Malda: A Study in Tribal Protest', in R. Guha (ed.) *Subaltern Studies IV*, New Delhi: Oxford University Press, 1985, 136–64.

—— (1987) *Bengal 1928–1934: The Politics of Protest*, New Delhi: Oxford University Press.

Sengupta, J.C. (ed.) (1969) *West Bengal District Gazetteers, Malda*, Calcutta: Government of West Bengal.

Thompson, E.P. (1993) *Customs in Common*, Penguin, London, 1993.

5 Reconstructing an event

The Great Rebellion of 1857–8 and Singhbhum Indigenes

Asoka Kumar Sen[1]

Introduction

The early historicization of *Adivasi* anti-colonial movements in Jharkhand is replete with methodological problems.[2] Since the celebration of the centenary of the Great Rebellion of 1857–8, scholars reconstructing narratives of anti-colonial struggles sought to prove that these were truly pan-Indian in character (Majumdar 1962: 196–9).Those belonging to the nationalist and leftist schools tended to subsume these struggles, to use Ranajit Guha's expression, under the 'prehistory' of the national and socialist-communist movements (Guha 1983: 4). Even if nationalism had inspired the making of provincial narratives where tribal or *Adivasi* struggles found space (Datta 1940, 1957: 66–76; Roy Choudhury 1959: 74–9; Das Gupta 2007: 96–119; Sen 2008: 82–107), the historiographic agenda were more or less to enrich the national mainstream.

This subsumption has forced scholars since the 1960s to question why *Adivasis* specifically, rather than 'the masses', were not accorded a place in Indian historiography (Jha 1964: 2–4; Singh 1966: xv–xvii; Baske 1982: 1; Sen 2010: 15–27; Choudhary 2010: 28–42). This resulted in the writing of singular narratives on the Bhumij Revolt, Kol Rebellion, Santal *Hul* (rebellion) and Birsaite *Ulgulan* (rebellion) (Jha 1964, 1967; Singh 1966; Baske 1982). Authors argued that tribal movements in Jharkhand had been assertions of an indigenous political identity, which was threatened by the colonial masters and their native henchmen. Tribal movements were also invoked to serve other specific purposes, such as to identify popular movements in the terms set out by the Subaltern school (Sarkar 1984: 43–8, 1983: 1–2; Guha 1983).

On the whole, these various approaches to writing history no doubt enriched what could be termed 'tribal studies'. But the distracting trend was the hierarchical construction of the Jharkhand movement as constituted by the Kol Rebellion, Santal *Hul* and Birsa's *Ulgulan* (Munda and Bosu Mullick 2003: Introduction). This accorded a lower position to the Great Rebellion of 1857–8 in terms of the historiography of indigenous movements because tribal people were supposedly uninvolved in this uprising and because there was a lack of antagonism versus the local landlords (Thapar and Siddiqui 2003: 50; Bosu Mullick 2003: 257). Such an understanding of tribal participation clearly showed a paucity of historical information. Further, those studying tribal movements highlight cult figures like Ganga Narain (Bhumij revolt), Sido and Kanhu Murmu (Santal *Hul*), Arjun Singh (rebellion of 1857–8 in Singhbhum) and Birsa Munda (*Ulgulan*), and thereby ignore their intrinsically social character and regional-level leadership and organization.

These approaches make two questions very relevant: what was the exact status of the Great Rebellion in the gamut of tribal movements, and is it justified to focus on cult figures alone? I would attribute this misconception to an over-dependence on contemporary official correspondence, administrative reports and subsequent ethnographies. The inadequacy of these sources, I argue, can be substantially removed if two other kinds of records, which I term 'testimonial memory' (Dhadra 1990: 256 63) and '*khuntkatti* memory', are invoked by the historian. These memories are culled from records that were officially commissioned during the trial of a rebel, and during land settlement operations. There are obvious differences in their structure, content and mode of representation. While the first contained the interpretation of the event by officials directly involved with the British military manoeuvres, the other, culled from two different timeframes, have their origin in the memories of the event by *Adivasis* themselves. This chapter therefore becomes a three-fold reconstruction of the 1857–8 rebellion; as I juxtapose these narratives, I attempt to locate the event in different historical perspectives.

The first section of this chapter sketches the contemporary official reading of the event, which represented it as merely a *zamindar*-led but tribal-supported movement. The second collates information on tribal leadership and organization, which official accounts had glossed over. Both of these sources, however, represent the event as a singular anti-colonial movement. To understand its social meaning, the third section focuses on a source, so far unused, and highlights how the rebellion was perceived by local people, not as a linear event but as one marked by simultaneity (in terms of space and demography). I argue that the story of the Great Rebellion, or rather that of any historically significant event, may be creatively modified if it is drawn from strategic local sources.

Official correspondence and administrative reports

Official correspondence and field reports written during and after the uprising,[3] and later ethnographies prepared on their basis (Dalton 1973: 183–4; Buckland 1902: 98–109; Bradley-Birt 1903: 219–28), configured the event as a singularized anti-British uprising of the raja (local ruler) of Porahat, Arjun Singh, who was helped by the tribals of Kolhan.[4] Totalized around him, these texts provide a narrative of a phased movement, which began with the mutiny of the sepoys of the Ramgarh battalion stationed at Chaibasa in 1857. The mutineers looted the government treasury and planned a march towards Ranchi to unite with the rebel sepoys of Doranda. But they were prevented from doing so by the Hos of the neighbourhood of Chaibasa. The messengers of Arjun Singh led the sepoys to Chakradharpur where they were fed and allowed to keep guard over their arms and ammunitions.[5] The combined forces of the British and the chief of Seraikela, which included 3,000 Hos, however recaptured Chaibasa to put an end to this phase of the rebellion (Buckland 1902: 103).

Sources narrated the circumstances leading to the rebellion by Arjun Singh, discussed British military preparations, and enumerated the battles fought and won. We learn how Lt Birch, Senior Assistant Commissioner, Singhbhum, sent *parwanas* (official circulars) to the chiefs of Seraikela and Kharsawan in Singhbhum requesting co-operation to consolidate the British position, and to Arjun Singh to surrender the mutineers. Instead of taking a definite stand, the raja chose to profess loyalty to the British and yet evaded the surrender of troops.[6] During September–November 1857, the raja's employees were busy in fomenting anti-British uprising. Shyam Karan Singh caused a proclamation to be made through the Chaibasa bazaar that 'The people belong to the Almighty, the country belongs to the King and the ruler thereof is Maharajah Urjoon Singh.'[7] Arrows, the emblem of war, were circulated in Kolhan calling upon the tribals to join the raja. Jogu Dewan directed a shopkeeper at Chaibasa to provide rations for 10,000 men. Twelve blacksmiths were employed at Porahat for making iron balls for the raja's artillery.[8] Understanding that the raja was inciting the Hos to rebellion, Lt Birch declared the raja to be a rebel and captured Porahat.[9] Thus, after weeks of uncertainty, Arjun Singh finally assumed leadership of the widespread popular uprising of the Hos of Kolhan and Porahat.[10]

We learn that Ho tribals stood behind Arjun Singh because of 'the immense influence that he and his brother are shown to have possessed'.[11] In response to the symbolic call through the circulation of the war arrows, *Mankis* (head of a *pir* or cluster of villages), *Mundas* (village head) and Ho villagers assembled at Ajudhia, the seat of the raja, and solemnly swore to be loyal to him.[12] It becomes clear that British officials did not reflect on the causes behind the social ferment. These could include an increase in rent, which might have destabilized tribal peasants in the estate of Porahat Khas, operating under the *raiyatwari* settlement (a direct land settlement between the cultivator and the government).[13] In Kolhan the social ferment was more because the indigenes could not reconcile themselves to an alien system of law and justice that Wilkinson's criminal and civil rules had introduced (Sen 1999. 24–37). Similarly, regular payment of rent on the basis of *hals* (ploughs) possessed by families under the new land-revenue administration introduced by Lt Tickell in 1837 and Davis in 1854 was anathema for the people (Sahu 1985: 152–4). It can be presumed that Arjun Singh's personality and his agents' anti-British activities provided necessary opportunity to the Hos to take up arms. Official documents informed that this participation at once converted the raja-led movement into a 'widespread upsurge of the various tribes of Singhbhum' (Buckland 1902: 105–6).

Porahat and Kolhan were key centres of the rebellion. The Porahat rebels were led by Baijnath Singh, the raja's brother, and by Raghu Deo and Shyam Karan, two employees of the Porahat raja. They burnt six villages of the *zamindar* (landlord) of Kera, plundered and burnt unprotected villages, chastised Indian government servants, attacked Anandpur, and drove out the *zamindar*.

They ejected 200 matchlocks of the Seraikela raja from Chakradharpur.[14] The murder of a *jamadar* (labour-contractor*)* and two *barkandazs* (guards) at Jayant-garh in Bar *pir* 'was the signal for an outbreak in Southern Kolhan', reminiscent of the anti-British rising during 1836–7. The British force under the special com-missioner and other officials countered this by arresting two minor rebel leaders. But the Ho insurgents offered an historic fight at Mogra, which compelled the British to change their route of movement. While crossing a dry stream about 4,000 arrow-clad Hos launched a fierce attack on their adversary in which every British official including Capt. Hale and Lt Birch sustained injury. Though 150 Hos had laid down their lives, the insurgents chased the enemy for seven miles defying the volley of gunshots fired by the withdrawing enemy. Despite the advent of *shekhawati* (horse riders) battalion from Raniganj and an additional force of 100 European soldiers, the rebels continued their heroic fight until British troops blocked all the routes of escape to hills and jungles. Arjun Singh and tribal insurgents were forced to surrender in 1859.[15]

This elite account thus focuses on the British, or on Arjun Singh and his men. Moreover, this deludes us to think that the tribal peoples of Singhbhum were lured into anti-British militancy; that they joined the raja out of veneration (Das Gupta 2007: 110–11); and that in the event they simply represented the force of a number, devoid of any agency or leadership. It is perhaps time to question whether the indigenes merely rallied behind the dominant forces to fight for their cause and whether they had indigenous leadership or organization.

The testimonial memory

To know about social organisation and leadership during the Rebellion of 1857–8, I turn to judicial recordings in 1864 which formed part of the letter con-taining the depositions of witnesses, and the arguments posited during the trial of Gono (Gonoo in judicial records) Pingua, the great tribal leader of the rebel-lion in south Kolhan.[16] I have referred to these as testimonial memories. While it may be argued that the courtroom did not allow scope for objectivity as the wit-nesses were either pro-government or forced by circumstance to be so, despite biases within judicial records, these provide the historian with a crucial narrative of a tribal uprising.

In his judgment of March 1864, E.T. Dalton, Commissioner of Chotanagpore, identified Gono as 'the most active adherent of the ex-rajah of Porahat amongst Singhbhum or *Larka Kols* [('fighting Kols')] and the principal agent in spread-ing disaffection amongst them and the leader of the men of that tribe.'[17] The memory of this tribal leader during depositions was vivid and pervasive, spilling beyond Patajaint, his natal village, to other villages in Kolhan and Bamanghatty *pargana* (district) of Mayurbhanj.[18] We learn that Gono was the son of Mata who, along with his other son, had fought the British in 1836–7.[19] After discon-tinuing studies at the Chaibasa school due to poverty, Gono took to 'evil' ways. What motivated him to join insurgency is unclear, but we can imagine that his father's imprisonment and his brother's capital punishment for anti-British acts must have been relevant for him. This had prompted him initially to accompany some *Mundas* and *Mankis* to Porahat, meet Arjun Singh and respond to his call to join the revolt.[20] Presumably due to his family background and turbulent ways, the raja selected him as his 'Sirdar in Singhbhum' by investing him with the *tal-pat* (palm leaf) letter, a turban and a horse.[21]

However Gono's testimony, quoted below, significantly informs us that this link between a non-tribal *zamindar* and an ethnic leader was reciprocal.

> The whole country was in revolt and Passes were held against the British, and there was fighting by order of the Rajah Urjoon Singh. All the Moondahs and Mankis went to the Rajah, I was with them; the Rajah asked us what we were going to do. We replied that the Sahibs have run away and you are now our ruler we will hold to you. Afterwards the Rajah called us and said see I have been hunted from Chuckerdhurpore and from Porahaut and now obliged to live in the jungles. What will you do? Will you fight for me? We said we would fight and swore to do so.
>
> (Gonoo's Testimony, Judicial Department, Proceeding no.31)

This exemplifies Arjun Singh's dependence on tribal support. But why did Gono need the investiture? It may be suggested that although Ho resistance movements were socially organized, these suffered from the lack of a centralized leader. This forced the Hos to fight the enemy at regional levels under their own local leaders. During the 1836–7 movements, we encounter several regional leaders like Poto Sardar, Narra, Burrai, Borah and Pandua, rather than any one representative of the whole community (Singh 1971: 149–53). To earn the status of a more generic leader, Sido and Kanhu Murmu, and Birsa Munda had invoked divine sanction. Gono's ascent to leadership was facilitated when Arjun invested him with the *tal-pat* letter, a turban and a horse. Gono and his followers like Patan Goala and Gooda Manjhi used this letter to garner the support of villagers for him.

This investiture legitimized Gono's position as the acclaimed regional leader of the Ho rebellion in south Kolhan. His name 'was not only in every body's mouth' but his writ ran across the entire region, which the *Mankis*, *Mundas* and villagers could not defy. He went with 100 armed Hos to assist Arjun Singh in Porahat. He then came back to Jayantgarh where, under his orders, the murders of army personnel were committed. He went back to the raja and returned to Kolhan once again to mobilize support for him. Insurgents looted the provisions sent from Chaibasa by the British, which Gono arranged to send to the raja loaded in bullock carts. He was the leader of Ho armed fight both at Seringsia and Mogra. Though Gono considered himself to represent the raja and act on his behalf, he showed ample evidence of independent ways when he sported himself as the 'Chief of Singbhoom', riding the horse given to him by the raja himself.[22] His personal grievances as well as his objections to British rule inspired south Kolhan villagers to unite behind Gono. For waging war against the Queen and for causing the death of a European, Gono Pingua was sentenced to life imprisonment.[23]

Thus, on the one hand, testimonial memory historically reinstated Gono and yet challenged the elite dominance in official documents. Yet, Gono's testimony, coupled with his dependence on the raja for the legitimization of his position, underlined once again the centrality of the raja and the singularized politico-military nature of the upsurge.

The *Khuntkatti* memory

A different image emerges from the third set of colonial records, which has not so far been utilized in rewriting the history of 1857–8. I seek to capture this memory from the *Khuntkatti* papers related to the Tuckey land settlement (1913–18) [24] The central issue then was Kolhan *raiyats'* (cultivator; tenant) right of *khuntkatti* that devolved on the family founding a village from primeval forests. During enquiries people recalled the disturbances of 1830–7 and 1857–8 to apprise whether they were in continuous possession of the villages, or whether they were deprived of the same for participating in these movements.

Information on the rebellion from this officially conducted survey reaches the contemporary researcher through many different intermediaries. Besides the possibility of distortions involved in such recordings, the quantum of data is sparse and spasmodic. Out of the total of 904 villages in Kolhan, only a few remembered the event either independently or along with the disturbances of 1830–7 (Sahu 1985: 40–5, 71–83). Moreover, the narration was generally stereotyped and condensed. Villagers usually mentioned the 'disturbance in raja Arjun Singh's time' and the exodus of the Bhuiyans from their villages (a theme I will return to later).

We may ascribe this diminution to various causes. Due to the absence of a developed mnemonic technique, possibly time took its toll on the corpus.[25] Further, the uprising was remembered as and when it had any relevance to the decision of *khuntkatti*. One may again argue that retention or loss of memory was determined by 'the politics of forgetting.' (Skaria 1999: 109–10) This politics could be constituted by the present-day logic of loyalty to the British, compared with their previous anti-British stance in 1857–8. The result was that Ho memory, rather than illuminating the past, effaced it. This becomes evident from a comparison with testimonial memory. Information, collected six years after the uprising, had shrunk by 1914–16. This means that memory, as a source of history, stands the fear of 'distortion' even by the oral societies, depending on the 'hiatus between event-time and discourse time' (Guha 1986: 33).

The question may be asked as to whether this fragmentary *khuntkatti*-memory deserves the attention accorded in this essay. The rebellion, I argue, had a central importance in Ho life as its continued social use indicates. The tumultuous uprising, like the traumatic experience of 1837, continued to be an 'amplified moment' that the people, devoid of clock or calendar, used as the time-marker (Thompson 1978: 22). This was why it served as a marker for important social and familial occasions, which were seen to have occurred during, before or after the disturbance. One such event related to the founding of the village. Villagers recalled Arjun Singh's fight with the British as the time for the separation of Bara and Chota Lagiya villages.[26] About the foundation of another village it was stated, 'This village was founded before the disturbance in Arjun Singh's time'.[27] Similarly the change of leadership and migration from Kolhan to neighbouring districts of Mayurbhanj and perhaps Keonjhar were related to the rebellion.[28] If the popular understanding of an event should be the quest of historical knowledge, the *khuntkatti*-memory of the rebellion ably serves our purpose by offering an indigenous reading of the event.

Different realities, different narratives

In popular perception, the event was characterized as the mutiny of Arjun Singh, a *golmal* or disturbance, a great fight, the 'Porahat troubles', or as an episode in the greater drama of tribal *ulgulan* (uprisings). While individual officers would inevitably interview people and record their responses, I would suggest that in popular responses the events of 1857–8 were interpreted differently, i.e. not simply as an anti-British uprising staged by Arjun Singh, as official histories have suggested. Differences in terminologies, I argue, represented differences in the popular interpretation of the event itself. Why does this divergence arise? Does it mark a confused and low level of historical consciousness amongst *Adivasis*, or does it characterize a different perception of reality? This problem may be resolved if we apply the distinction between western and non-western narratives as suggested by Skaria. He presents an opposition between pre-modern (or non-western) and western narratives, the latter being characterized by the will to represent a singularized truth by resolving the differences, while the former offered a 'counter-aesthetics of modernity' where a multiplicity of truths emerged as part of a larger sequential narrative (Skaria 1999: 31–2). This multiplicity of truths in tribal and other oral societies represented a cultural pattern that conformed to the ways in which people interpreted and ordered the event from their own social positions. I will explore the issues raised by bringing these sources into creative tension, under seven subheadings.

A golmal (disturbance): Arjun Singh's great fight

Even in its multiplicity we notice the significant commonality of the event being interpreted by Hos as *golmal* (disturbance) that took place during the time of Arjun Singh, who is identified as the raja of Porahat.[29] Thus, the event was a 'disturbance in Arjun Singh's time' or a 'mutiny'[30] or a 'revolt'[31] by the raja.[32] In another village the event was a 'great fight', which 'Arjun Singh had fought with the British'.[33] The two sources earlier referred to also emphasized the centrality of Arjun Singh during this upsurge. But before committing this to a representative status, one should keep in mind the impact of social status in the retention or loss of memory in oral tradition that exaggerates or diminishes the role of individuals, thereby affecting the evaluation of historic events.

Gono Pingua: the rebel as raja's associate

We notice the play of diminution in the case of Gono whose memory survived only in his natal village.[34] But here also it was incidentally mentioned that he had participated in the uprising as an adherent of Arjun Singh; he ran away from the village and was later caught and transported. Gono's son, Putkar Pingua, recalled that:

> during the time of the mutiny the Hos fought with the Raja & the Sahibs came and burned our village & we all ran away. I was young then & the village remained empty for a year. ... My father Gono was caught with the Raja & was transported. Several men were caught & hanged & several were transported.
>
> (TSKP, Patajaint, pp. 3–7, VN 45, KT)

Corroborating the above information, his co-villager Kasi Gour added that Gono was caught with the raja at Jeraikela.[35] Without this particularity, the popular leader of the Kolhan uprising seemed to be ravaged by time, only to be remembered in his village. This implied that Gono and his insurgency were recalled because he was Putkar's father; Putkar belonged to the Pingua *killi*, which was identified as the original clearer of Patajaint, a fact relevant for *khuntkatti* decisions.[36] This conforms to popular historic sensibility being presentist in nature. One may doubt the usefulness of this source, or rather of popular memory, in reconstructing the history of the people. I emphasize however the significance of coalescing different sources for the rewriting of histories. In the present case, one needs to look at testimonial information for a more complete image of Gono.

Popular insurgency and the tale of ruthless reprisal

Due to the above presentist bias, we rarely come across the names of villages where the rebellion had spread. Patajaint and Bara Lagiya[37] were exceptions where people rendered assistance to the rebels. The event is thus not represented as a pervasive popular rebellion as administrative reports suggest.[38] Confusion increases when we find that Seringsia and Mogra, two important seats of uprising during 1857–8, did not retain the memory of the event.[39] We thus have to depend on collateral evidence of British reprisals in the form of arson, loot and plunder as well as the incarceration, transportation and the hanging of the rebels, as proof of the popular character of the uprising.[40] These evidences may also relate acts of counter-insurgency that are missing from the above two levels of rebellion historiography.

Narrative of loyalty

The characterization of the rebellion changes as we take up the *lakhiraj* (right of a revenue-free grant of a village) villages.[41] These recalled the loyalty and assistance rendered to the British by their ancestors when Arjun Singh had mutinied against the British.[42] This loyalty seemingly prompted two villages to term the uprising as simple 'Porahat troubles'[43] and some *Mankis* to render 'faithful services' to the British. In return, they were granted *lakhiraj* rights.[44]

Bhuiyans flee from villages

In most of the Bhuiyan tribal villages, people recalled their exodus from the village rather than the uprising itself. Though some of the villages failed to distinguish between the incidents of 1837 and 1857,[45] in many others, the memory of flight was quite stable.[46] This communal exodus, as the *khuntkatti*-memory suggests, was a ploy to evade the reprisal of Ho insurgents for not responding to the call of joining their ranks.[47] However, to accept this logic would cast the Bhuiyans as either British loyalists or as neutrals, which their historic link with Porahat rajas would not support.[48] About this link Gono said:

> We said we would fight and swore to do so. Then he assembled all the Bhuiyans and Dhorrowas and gave their pay and arms and an army was collected and we went to Ajoodiah with the intention of fighting with Chuckdhar Singh of Seraikelah.
>
> (Gonoo's Testimony, Judicial Department, Proceeding no. 31)

Depositions during *khuntkatti* enquiry further corroborated this link between the Raja and the Bhuiyans.[49] We can therefore presume that that flight was caused by anticipated British retaliation for their tradition of loyalty to the Porahat raj.

Tikan and Captan Saheb visited this site during Mutiny

In the popular representations discussed above, the uprising, in terms of its relationship to other movements, had a predominantly independent identity. But in some other cases, villagers conflated the events of 1837 and 1857 into a single event, from which Tikan (Tickell) and *Captan* (Captain, probably Lt Birch) *Saheb*, representing respectively 1837 and 1857, appeared in tandem. To quote one witness, 'Tikan and Captan Saheb visited this site during Mutiny.'[50] In another village, though villagers related that the original settler had moved from Purnia to Heselkutti after a disturbance, they could not specify whether this was 1837 or 1857.[51] This confusion perhaps underlines the difference in the historical perceptions of the literate and oral traditions. The time-specific literate historiography of 1857–8 had a distinct temporal identity represented by a specific set of occurrences and personalities. But for a Ho what was crucial was the conjuncture of *ulgulan* (rebellion), which subsumed the two distinct events of 1837 and 1857 and personalities. As is suggested by Vansina, a rather complex reality was thus simplified by fusing analogous personalities (Vansina 1985: 19–21). But the crucial question is: why did this not happen in all villages? Is then a 'politics of forgetting' at work in villages where anti-British militancy was very intense, and which villagers strategically softened by undermining the singularity of the rebellion of 1857–8?

Past lingering in the present

It is however not in singular or plural representations alone, but in the interpretation of the timeframe of the event, that *khuntkatti* memory distinguished itself from the other two sources. Official documents narrate that after the last gunshots were fired and trials were completed the uprising came to an end. Villagers then resumed their ordinary pursuits, as if forgetful of the past that had ceased to be meaningful for their present existence. The British continued to pursue the policy of 'judicious management' which 'gradually tamed, softened, and civilized' the 'savages' and brought peace and plenty to the region (Dalton 1973: 184). Thus pre- and post-uprising times joined to create the notion of an uninterrupted continuity, and the upsurge was a forgettable aberration. But in the *khuntkatti* memory, the event extended up to their lived present as it had caused a break in the normal pattern of mundane life. It may be argued that, in this way, ethnic temporal sensibility was shaped both by the present determining the past, and the past being revived to understand the complexities of the present (Rosaldo 1980: 249fn).

The relevance of the rebellion for the villagers was diverse and decisive, affecting for example the composition of and control over several villages. This happened when villages founded and dominated by Bhuiyans, Hos or Gours were settled with others.[52] With this they lost their *khuntkatti* status and village headship,[53] which was generally selected from these families. This undermined the socio-political and economic positions of the concerned *killis* and peoples at the micro village level. I would contend that a change in the regional politics also took place. The power and position of once formidable Bhuiyan community considerably shrank in the Kolhan geo-polity due to their exodus and subsequent developments stated above.

Two other changes may be linked to the event. First, in Singhbhum, migration of socio-economically marginal people to the neighbouring villages and *pirs* was a common event. This peacetime practice seemed to be extended during 1857–8 like the events of 1836–7 when insurgents, as a matter of strategy, and others, out of fear, both temporarily and permanently, fled their villages.[54] The uprising next reinforced the tradition of granting *lakhiraj* rights to the loyal village and *pir* heads initiated after 1836–7.[55] This, on the one hand, strengthened the position of the British because a part of the Ho leadership became permanent supporters. On the other, because of their permanent rights over the lands (as against periodically renewable holdings of others), the socio-political elevation of these families created a cleavage in the ranks of village officials.

Conclusion

The three kinds of sources used in this chapter for reconstructing the story of the Great Rebellion related to differing colonial intentions – reporting the event, recording a trial, and documenting *khuntkatti* proceedings. As such, their form was colonially determined. But the content of the sources greatly differed as contexts and informants changed. In the first, the rebellion was a mere politico-military occurrence that centred on the British and Arjun Singh, where the tribals figured simply as a faceless aggregate. In the second, Gono Pingua lionized the scene, although to underline tribal leadership and organization around the same politico-military pattern. But the third diffused the singularized interpretation and presented a plural reading of the uprising where an extended past tended to invest greater meaning to the upsurge than its limited timeframe. The sources used, when coalesced together, portend to reconstruct a more informed narrative from which certain broad conclusions may be drawn. First, I would conclude that the event was not a mere sepoy or *zamindar*-dominated rebellion. Second, it was tribal-led in the region and can be considered as a rebellion of the indigenes. Third, it was an upsurge where tribals and non-tribals combined against the British Raj.

How then could we situate the rebellion of 1857–8 in the historiography of national, peasant and *Adivasi* struggles? One can invoke here the work of the Santal historian Dhirendranath Baske, who has claimed that tribal movements should be considered within the framework of anti-colonial nationalism (and not set apart). This upsurge merits a higher position, along with the anti-colonial *Adivasi* struggles of 1831–2, *Hul* (1855–7) and *Ulgulan* (1896–1900) because, both at the level of participation and its militancy, it strengthened the wider nationalist movement (Baske 1982: 6). To classify it, however, as an important milestone in Indian peasant movement should be done with some reservations (Jha 1964: 2; Singh 1966: 189; Guha 1983: 22–3). It was true that one of the reasons why Singhbhum tribals rebelled was objection to the colonial land revenue system. But a closer reading of the history of Ho 'peasantization' suggests, first, that during 1857–8, though the community had accepted agriculture as a primary source of livelihood, a large part of the Kolhan and Ho population developed a mixed economy dependent on both cultivation and forest resources. It can also be noted that militancy was more intense among people who pursued foraging and hunting than those inhabiting more agriculturally developed areas.

Studied within the rubric of tribal movements, the chapter contends the dominant trend of valorizing *Adivasi* movements around the cults of Sido and Kanhu Murmu, Arjun Singh and Birsa Munda, in imitation of the dominant narratives of the Indian freedom movement that centralize the personalities of Mahatma Gandhi, Jawaharlal Nehru, Subhas Chandra Bose, etc. Whilst I am aware that to privilege the regional over the national in some ways confirms the limitations of subaltern historic agency, in the Kolhan we have regional-level figures like Gono Pingua who can illuminate the arrested 'minor leaders' of Jaintgarh, and perhaps other such faceless minor leaders, who help us to reconstruct *Adivasi* movements as truly social movements.

Moreover, on account of its display of collaboration between tribal and non-tribal peoples (Arjun Singh and all his men and Patan Goala as Gono's adherent), this movement may impact on those who attempt to construct strict boundaries between tribal and non-tribal groups in their assessment of 'tribal' struggles. I argue that this divide could never be total or essential as it is projected. The construction of oppositional identity is an attempt by the subaltern peoples to redefine themselves. In this process they dislocated themselves from earlier networks of relations, for example when they fought against the local chieftains with whom they once had friendly relations (Tickell 1840: 698). Interestingly, they relocated themselves within the pattern when this relationship was deemed necessary during the rebellion. Similarly the role of Patan Goala emerged out of the network of socio-economic relations that structured Singhbhum rural life. After the villages were originally founded, the Ho invited the Goalas, Tantis, blacksmiths and potters to inhabit their villages to help them run their socio economy. Following Guha's idea of inter-ethnic solidarity, this reading of the rebellion thus situates it closer to non-exclusivist interpretations of 'tribal' movements, which in turn would support a pan-Jharkhandi historic identity (Munda and Bosu Mullick 2003: vii–ix).

Finally what could be the rightful place of the rebellion of 1857–8 in the gamut of *Adivasi* movements? I have detailed how the strength of tribal participation and leadership transformed it from a sepoy mutiny and *zamindar*-led rebellion into a wider rebellion of the *Adivasis* of Singhbhum. This reconstruction rebuts its marginalization in national, subaltern and Jharkhandi historiographies, and argues for its inclusion along with the Kol Rebellion, the Santal *Hul* and Birsa's *Ulgulan* as a historic manifestation of indigenous political identity.

Notes

1 I express my gratitude to Dr Daniel Rycroft and Dr Sangeeta Dasgupta for their comments on an earlier version of this paper. Abbreviations: CS – Craven Settlement; CT – Chakradharpur thana; TSKP – Tuckey Settlement *Khuntkatti* Papers; KT – Kolhan Thana; MT – Manoharpur Thana; TS – Tuckey Settlement; VN – Vasta No.
2 While the terms tribal and *Adivasi* have been used synonymously in this chapter, those who in historical parlance had been identified as tribals or aboriginals prefer to refer to themselves as *Adivasi* and claim that they are descendents of the early settlers of India.
3 Birch to the Secretary; Officiating Commissioner to the Secretary; Dalton to Lushington; Gray to Seton-Karr.
4 Hos dominated Kolhan in Singhbhum district, which was named the Kolhan Government Estate after British gained control of it in 1837.
5 Dalton to Lushington, para. 15; Officiating Commissioner to the Secretary, para. 7.
6 Officiating Commissioner to the Secretary, para. 14.
7 Birch to the Secretary, para. 4.
8 Ibid., para. 9.
9 Dalton to Lushington, para. 31; Officiating Commissioner to the Secretary, paras 9, 14–17.
10 Officiating Commissioner to the Secretary, paras 10–20.
11 Dalton to Lushington, para. 51.
12 Officiating Commissioner to the Secretary, para. 5.
13 Despite the rent hike, the responses of the tribals were varied against their chiefs (Macpherson 1906: 20, 170, 199).
14 Dalton to Lushington, paras 33–4 (Buckland 1902: 105–6).

15 Dalton to Lushington, paras 33–4; Gray to Seton-Karr, para. 18 (Dalton 1973: 184; Buckland 1902: 105–6; Sahu 1985: 84–95).
16 Dalton to Cockerell.
17 Remarks by the Commissioner of Chota Nagpore on the trial of Gonoo, son of Mata, Judicial Department, Proceeding no. 31.
18 We may attribute this vividness to temporal proximity (Vansina 1985: 54).
19 Martun and Rainso's Testimonies, Judicial Department, Proceeding no. 31.
20 Gonoo's Testimony, ibid.
21 Rainso's Testimony, ibid.
22 Martun, Rainso, Chamroo, Konka's Testimonies; Remarks by the Commissioner.
23 U/S 121 and 302 Indian Penal Code.
24 These include *Khuntkatti* Papers, Papers of cases u/s 83 and 85, *Tanaza* Papers and Village Notes.
25 I have in mind the type of mnemo technique referred by Vansina (1985: 44–8).
26 Records of cases u/s 83, Bara Lagiya, VN 2, KT.
27 TSKP, Rugudsai, pp. 3–7, VN 44, KT.
28 Ibid., Kadokora, pp. 3–4, Phutgaon, pp. 3–6, VN 44, KT.
29 Ibid., Bhangaon, pp. 3–7, VN 47, KT.
30 Ibid., Gamharia, pp. 2–8, VN 42, KT.
31 Ibid., Dombloi, pp. 3–5, VN 62, MT.
32 Ibid., Lailohar, Pachpaia, Samtha, VN 2–3, MT.
33 Records of cases u/s 83, Bara Lagiya.
34 TSKP, Patajaint, pp. 3–7, VN 45, KT.
35 Ibid.
36 Ibid.
37 Records of cases u/s 83, Bara Lagiya.
38 Gonoo's Testimony, Judicial Department, Proceeding no. 31.
39 TSKP, Siringsia, pp. 3–6, VN 58, KT, Mongra, pp. 3–5, VN 69, KT.
40 Ibid., Gobergaon. pp. 3–7, VN45, KT, Kotegarh, pp. 3–6, VN 71, KT; Putkar Ho's Testimony, TSKP, Patajaint, pp. 3–7.
41 In nine out of twelve villages this tenure was granted for 'help received in time of trouble', i.e. 1838 and 1858 (Tuckey 1920: 15–16).
42 TSKP, Proceeding Commutation, Kursi, pp. 3–6, VN 16, KT, Dumbisai, pp. 5–7, VN 62, KT.
43 Ibid., *Zirat* Records, Purnia, p. 5,VN 5, KT, Basahatu, pp. 3–4, VN 6, KT.
44 Ibid., Purnia, Basahatu and Murum, Proceeding Commutation, pp. 3–5 VN 12, KT, Kursi, pp. 3–6, VN 16, KT, Dumbisai, pp. 5–7.
45 Ibid., Dobel and Lemra, VN 1, MT, Haribhanga and Saraswatipur, VN 46, KT.
46 Ibid., Lailohar, Pachpai, Dombloi, Kadokora and Manikpur. VN 46, KT.
47 Gonoo's Testimony, Judicial Department, Proceeding no. 31.
48 Dalton 1973: 140; Sahu 1985: 9.
49 TSKP, Chota Nagra, pp. 3–5, VN1, MT, Kotegarh, pp. 3–5.
50 Ibid., Gamharia, p. 2, Heselkuti, p. 6, VN 44, KT.
51 Ibid., Heselkuti.
52 Ibid., Dobel, pp. 3–4, Lailohar, pp. 3–5, Pachpaia, pp. 3–5, Gamharia, pp. 3–8, Patajaint, pp. 3–7, Kadokora, pp. 9–13, Hesabera, p. 3.
53 Ibid., Kadokora, Patajaint.
54 Ibid., Dombloi, pp. 3–5, Patajaint.
55 Ibid., Purnia, Murum.

References

Bihar State Archives, Patna

Spare Copies of Porahat Papers from 1857 to 1862.

Letter of Lt R.C. Birch, the Senior Assistant Commissioner, Singhbhum District to the Secretary to the Government of Bengal, Fort William, 6 October 1857, no. 40.

Letter from Officiating Commissioner of Manbhum and Singhbhum to the Secretary to the Government of Bengal, 29 December 1857, no. 31.

Letter from E.T. Dalton, Commissioner of Chotanagpur to E.H. Lushington, Secretary to the Government of Bengal, 30 September 1859, no. 224.

Letter from W. Gray, Secretary to the Government of India, Home department to W.S. Seton-Karr, Secretary to the Government of Bengal, 18 April 1861, no. 759,

West Bengal State Archives, Calcutta

Judicial Department, Proceeding no. 31, Judicial Department, May 1864.

From Lieutenant-Colonel E.T. Dalton, Commissioner of Chota Nagpore to F.R. Cockerell, Officiating Secretary to the Governor of Bengal, No. 437, 15 March 1864.

District Record Room Chaibasa

Tuckey Settlement Khuntkatti Papers.

Tuckey Settlement Records of Cases u/s 83.

Books

Baske, D.N. (1982) *Saontal Ganasangramer Itihas*, Calcutta: Pearl Publishers.

Bhadra, G. (1990) 'Four Rebels of Eighteen-Fifty-Seven', *Subaltern Studies IV*, New Delhi: Oxford University Press, 229–75.

Bosu Mullick, S. (2003) 'Jharkhand Movement: A Historical Analysis', in R.D. Munda and S. Bosu Mullick (eds) *The Jharkhand Movement: Indigenous Peoples' Struggle for Autonomy in India*, Copenhagen: IWGIA and Birsa, Document No. 108, 244–71.

Bradley-Birt, F.B. (1903) *Chota Nagpore: A Little Known Province of the Empire*, London: Smith Elder.

Buckland, C.E. (1902) *Bengal under the Lieutenant-Governors from 1854–1898*, Calcutta: S.K. Lahiri & Co.

Choudhary, I.K. (2010) 'Situating the Tribes of Palamau in the Revolt of 1857–58 in Jharkhand', in A. Mishra and C.K. Paty (eds) *Tribal Movements in Jharkhand 1857–2007*, New Delhi: Concept Publishing Company, 28–42.

Dalton, E.T. (1973) *Tribal History of Eastern India* (original title *Descriptive Ethnology of Bengal*), Delhi: Cosmo Publications.

Das Gupta, S. (2007) 'Rebellion in a Little Known District of the Empire', in S. Bhattacharya (ed.) *Rethinking 1857*, New Delhi: Orient Longman, 96–119.

Datta, K.K. (1940) *The Santal Insurrection of 1855–57,* Calcutta: University of Calcutta Press.

—— (1957) *Unrest against British Rule in Bihar 1831–1859*, Patna.

Guha, R. (1983) *Elementary Aspects of Peasant Insurgency in Colonial India*, New Delhi: Oxford University Press.

—— (1986) 'The Prose of Counter-Insurgency', *Subaltern Studies II*, New Delhi: Oxford University Press, 1–42.

Jha, J.C. (1964) *Kol Insurrection in Chotanagpur*, Calcutta: Thacker & Spinck.

—— (1967) *The Bhumij Revolt, 1832–33*, Delhi: Munshiram Manoharlal.

Macpherson, T.S. (1908) *Final Report on the operations for the preparation of a record of rights in Pargana Porahat, district of Singhbhum 1905–7*, Calcutta: Bengal Secretariat Press.

Munda, R.D and Bosu Mullick, S. (eds) (2003) *The Jharkhand Movement: Indigenous Peoples' Struggle for Autonomy in India*, Copenhagen: IWGIA and Birsa, Document No. 108.

Rosaldo, R. (1980) *Ilongot Headhunting 1883–1974: A Study in Society and History*, Stanford, CA: Stanford University Press.

Roy Choudhury, P.C. (1959) *1857 in Bihar (Chotanagpur and Santhal Parganas)*, Patna: Gazetteers' Revision Branch, Revenue Department, Bihar.

Sahu, M. (1985) *The Kolhan under the British Rule,* Calcutta.

Sarkar, S. (1984) *Modern India 1885–1947,* Delhi: Macmillan.

Sen, A.K. (2010) 'Resurrecting a Tribal Leader from Oblivion: Gono Pingua and the Revolt of 1857–59', in A. Mishra and C.K. Paty (eds) *Tribal Movements in Jharkhand 1857–2007*, New Delhi: Concept Publishing Company, 15–27.

—— (1999) 'Ideology, Imperative and the Framing of the Rules', in A.K. Sen (ed.) *Wilkinson's Rules: Context, Content and Ramifications*, Chaibasa: Tata College, 24–37.

Sen, S.K. (2008) *Tribal Struggle for Freedom: Singhbhum, 1820–1858*, New Delhi: Concept Publishing Company.

Singh, C.P. (1971) 'The Martyrs of Singhbhum', *Journal of the Bihar Research Society*, 57(1–4): 149–53.

Singh, K.S. (1966) *The Dust-Storm and the Hanging Mist*, Calcutta: Firma K.L. Mukhopadhyay.

Skaria, A. (1999) *Hybrid Histories: Frontiers and Wildness in Western India*, New Delhi: Oxford University Press.

Thapar, R. and Siddiqui, H.M. (2003) 'Chotanagpur: The Pre-Colonial and Colonial Situation', in R.D. Munda and S. Bosu Mullick (eds) *The Jharkhand Movement*, 31–72.

Thompson, P. (1978) *The Voice of the Past: Oral History,* London: Oxford University Press.

Tickell, S.R. (1840) 'Memoir on the Ho Desum (improperly called Kolehan)', *Journal of the Asiatic Society of Bengal*, 11(2): 694–709, 783–808.

Tuckey, A.D. (1920) *Final Report on the Resettlement of the Kolhan Government Estate in the District of Singhbhum 1913–1918,* Patna: Superintendent, Government Printing, Bihar and Orissa.

Vansina, J. (1985) *Oral Tradition As History*, London: James Curry.

Part III

Landscape and Adivasi agency

Introduction to Part III

Part III elaborates environmental aspects of Adivasi subjectivity. Emerging as a distinctive field of enquiry in the 1980s, Environmental studies inflected the trajectory of Tribal and Adivasi-related studies in India. To the already rich literature that had explored the historical relationship between tribes and forests in colonial India (see Sarkar 1980), ecological dimensions were added. Working often in parallel and yet at times converging, both Subaltern and Environmental studies approached marginalised communities and drew their inspiration from political activism. Exponents of the environmental perspective came together with some of the Subaltern historians, and plotted narratives of 'tribal' distinctiveness and dispossession.[1] By 1999 Ramachandra Guha had, however, distanced himself from the 'collective odyssey' of the Subaltern school (2000: xiii; see also R. Guha 1999).

Forest peoples, often equated with 'tribals' or Adivasis – or in the Hindutva (Hindu nationalist) jargon '*vanavasis*' (forest inhabitants) – have dominated the landscape of Indian Environmental history. The initial focus of the discipline, as is well recognized today, had almost entirely been on forest histories and forest policies (see, for example, Arnold and Guha 1995; Grove *et al.* 1998). The lives, livelihoods and cosmologies of the hunter-gatherers, shifting cultivators, nomadic pastoralists and subsistence agriculturalists were explored often beyond the administrative frameworks of Scheduled Tribes and 'Primitive Tribal Groups'. Others, who claimed to be a part of the discipline or, at any rate, were indirectly influenced by it, paid attention to forests in the course of larger socio-economic analyses (Rangarajan 1996; Sundar 1997; Singh 1998; Sivaramakrishnan 1999; Skaria 1999; Pratap 2000). Divested of their rights as custodians of nature, and marginalised due to the importation of a scientific model of forest conservation by the colonial state, the subjects of this history, whose worlds were seen to be entangled with nature, or wilderness or frontier regions, were thought to have been unhinged from their familiar complex mosaic of localised forest uses, and thereby dispossessed of their intimate knowledge of nature. Clearly then, this was a voice of the 'environmentalism of the poor' (Guha and Martinez Alier 1998: 5). It made visible the social costs of environmental degradation borne by those who were located in the margins of society. It also represented the colonial and the post-independence states as premier agents of ecological change – through scientific, modern and in the more recent period, mega-scale technological interventions – and responsible for devastating social and environmental transformations.[2]

As historic watersheds, notably the Indian Forest Act of 1865 (amended in 1878), were identified through the environmental lens, the advent of the colonial state was seen to have marked a period of general decline, and the Indian state was taken to be, at the level of policy and practice, a continuation of the colonial state.[3] Continuities were thus drawn between the colonial and post-independence regimes in institutional frameworks that governed the management and mismanagement of forests, water, wildlife, minerals and other resources (Sivaramakrishnan 1995; Rangarajan 1996, 2002, 2007). The aborted Forest Bill of 1982 has been regarded as a landmark in the emergence of Environmental history as a distinct sub-field. As activists themselves, or as sympathisers of tribe-oriented and eco-Adivasi activism (see Asher and Agarwal 2007), environmental historians generally supported the struggles of the under-privileged groups and searched for the historical antecedents of these struggles in the colonial archives. Such analytical concerns have recently been revisited following the implementation of the Scheduled Tribes Recognition of Forest Rights Act in 2006, generating engaging debates between pro-Adivasi environmentalists, Adivasi activists and non-governmental organisations (Asher and Agarwal 2007: 28–34). Out of these debates and constitutional shifts, important new conceptualisations of the relationship between Adivasis, legal institutions and environmental rights have emerged (Menon 2007).

Early environmental historical research, then, has questioned whether British rule was in fact an ecological watershed by assessing shifts in imperial attitudes to the natural world, and tracing the responses of those dependent upon contested resources to colonial intervention and resource extractions (see Tucker and Richards 1983; Guha 1989, 1994; Gadjil and Guha 1993; Grove 1995; Arnold 1996; Agrawal 1998). A binary model casts the colonisers, the market and the state as agents of ecological degradation, and Adivasis or 'tribal' peoples as nature's Ideal conservators. If the subaltern project had unified 'tribals', peasants and the workers into a dispossessed community, environmentalists sought to posit distinctions between the forests and the fields, between the agrarian sector and the forests and pasturelands (see Bhattacharya 1998: 165).

As they demarcate their field, locate their concerns and move beyond the limitations of the first generation of environmentalism, new issues are however increasingly being taken up. A powerful critique has developed within the frame and outside it. The boundaries between an autonomous nature that supposedly stands outside of human endeavour, and a human agency that is presumed to construct all landscapes, are now blurred. Recognition of the artificiality of categories such as 'arable', 'forest' and 'pasture', and of the forms of livelihoods based on them – 'cultivation', 'hunting-gathering' and 'pastoralism' – facilitates engaging interdisciplinary dialogue (see Agrawal and Sivaramakrishnan 2001;

Dasgupta forthcoming). An acknowledgement of the long histories of changing vegetation, human activities, and state policies drives shared concerns (S. Guha 1999).

The involvement of Adivasis in the Gandhian movement against the Narmada valley dam projects (known as the Narmada Bachao Andolan) has generated a host of inter-disciplinary studies focusing on environmental dispossession (see Gandhi 2003). The multifaceted red-green-Adivasi discourse of social protest that emerged here, and that has also informed departures in joint forest management, can be analysed usefully in the context of other environmental protests involving Adivasis, such as those in Bihar (and later also Jharkhand), Madhya Pradesh (and later also Chhatisgarh), Orissa, Andhra Pradesh, Maharastra and West Bengal (see Gadgil and Guha 1995; Ghosh 2007). The semantics of these have been translated into more recent Adivasi movements, like the Rajmahal Pahar Bachao Andolan (Save the Rajmahal Hills Movement) in Jharkhand, that highlight the complicity of regional states in environmental degradation and social exploitation (Participatory Research in Asia 2004). Sociological studies of such movements, by Amita Baviskar (1995) for example, shatter the popular image of egalitarian village communities as multiple configurations of power are identified within Adivasi societies. Others, like Archana Prasad (2003), have critiqued the reconstruction by environmental historians of 'tribal' history vis-à-vis traditional tribal livelihoods, to reveal problematic continuities between the ideas of late-colonial protectionists, such as Verrier Elwin, and early environmentalist perspectives. As Skaria has pointed out (2001: 265), in its opposition to development, primitivist environmentalism may in fact share some of the same conceptual frameworks as normative development, even as it celebrates the primitive more emphatically.

In its choice of themes too, Environmental history has moved on towards water management, the destruction and preservation of wild life, urban history, health and disease law, and environmental philosophy (see Arnold 2001; Rangarajan 2001; Saberwal and Rangarajan 2003; Satya 2004; D'Souza 2006; Cederlof 2008). Indian environmental history, which had initially drawn its theoretical antecedents from Europe and America, is today in a position to redirect the focus of the West towards larger questions related to colonialism, imperialism, disease, 'race' and ethnicity, as well as ideas of tropical nature (Sutter 2003; see also Sivaramakrishnan 2009; Guha 2000). We contend that the potential of South Asian environmental history to embed its own distinct contribution, keeping in view 'the sheer ecological and cultural diversity of the Indian sub-continent and taking into account the myths and realities of the lived environments' (Arnold and Guha 1995: 7), has almost been fulfilled.

Damodaran and Kjosavik's papers, included within this section, deal with typical themes included within the scope of environmental history and yet add new insights. In the making of colonial forest and agrarian policies in Chotanagpur (Jharkhand), Damodaran points to the tensions underpinning imperial discourse, particularly the official interpretation of the customary rights of Jharkhandi Adivasis. Damodaran examines the differing outcomes of forest policy by looking at the ways in which diverse pressures and interests motivate the protection of forests. She argues that colonial administrators attempted to understand local 'tribal' rights (in the context of forest reservation) and to legislate in favour of these to protect forests. Forest rights in the Chotanagpur context therefore became an important part of the discourse of Ho and Munda exclusiveness as set out by the state and more recently by Adivasis. Thus, customary rights and related folklore, while open to misinterpretation, misrecognition and sustained erosion, did indeed have a basis in the lived environment and were able to reverse colonialism's expansionist agenda. The attempts of the Jharkhand government to award indigenous land claims, not on the basis of oral evidence but specifically on the basis of colonial documentation dating back to the 1920s, demonstrates the vital importance of understanding the colonial interpretation of customary rights.

Kjosavik, on the other hand, interrogates the idea of indigeneity in relation to radical standpoint epistemologies. She aims to relate histories of Adivasi subordination in Kerala to wider politico-intellectual concerns. Despite her different approach to Adivasi agency, Kjosavik, like Damodaran, cites the specific relevance of the Indian Forest Act of 1878 to environmental histories as she probes the ideological and discursive terrains of forest conservation, and identifies how protective environmental measures facilitated the 'legal alienation' of Adivasi lands in the twentieth century. Her research traces how the dominant notion of 'resource frontiers' was elaborated by capitalist (imperialist, colonialist and statist) interests in the Wayanad region of Kerala state in southern India. The scramble for agrarian resources brought about a political situation in which Adivasi interests were totally marginalised, leading to ongoing exclusions in the post-independence era. Kjosavik's paper challenges the ideological foundations of existing accounts of 'tribal' historiography and sociology that refuse to acknowledge the relevance of modern community- or class-consciousness. The article draws on her personal upbringing and extensive ethnographic work in Kerala, and gives visibility to Kurumbar experiences of alienation. These 'tribal' experiences, Kjosavik argues, become 'Adivasi' as they are re-situated within the wider context of leftist mobilisation in Kerala.

Notes

1 A pioneer of Environmental studies in India, Ramchandra Guha contributed to *Subaltern Studies IV* (Guha 1985); David Arnold co-edited, along with Guha, one of the earliest collected essays on Environmental history (Arnold and Guha 1995).

2 John MacKenzie (1997: 215–28) has pointed out that, while US Environmental history has been focused on the impact of capitalism on wild nature, much of non-US historiography shows how colonial and post-colonial states have intervened to use human ecologies.

3 In Kjosavik and Shanmugaratnam's study of indigenous forest rights in Kerala state (2007), such a general approach is modified and takes into account the significance of policy shifts after independence.

References

Agrawal, A. (1998) *Greener Pastures: Politics, Markets and Community Among a Migrant Pastoral People*, Durham: Duke University Press.

—— and Sivaramakrishnan, K. (eds) (2001) *Social Nature: Resources, Representations, and Rule in India*, New Delhi: Oxford University Press.

Arnold, D. (1996) *The Problem of Nature: Environment, Culture and European Expansion*, Oxford: Blackwell.

—— (2001) 'Disease, Resistance, and India's Ecological Frontier, 1770–1947', in J.C. Scott and N. Bhatt (eds) *Agrarian Studies: Synthetic Work at the Cutting Edge,* New Haven: Yale University Press, 186–205.

—— and Guha, R.C. (eds) (1995) *Nature, Culture, Imperialism: Essays on the Environmental History of South Asia*, New Delhi: Oxford University Press.

Asher, M. and Agarwal, N. (2007) *Recognising the Historic Injustice: Campaign for the Forest Rights Act 2006*, Pune: National Centre for Advocacy Studies.

Baviskar, A. (1995) *From the Belly of the River: Tribal Conflicts over Development in the Narmada Valley*, New Delhi: Oxford University Press.

Bhattacharya, N. (1998) 'Introduction', *Studies In History*, 16(2): 165–71

Cederlof, G. (2008) *Landscapes and the Law*, New Delhi: Permanent Black.

Dasgupta, S (forthcoming), 'Locating Adivasi Movements in Colonial India: The Oraons and the Tana Bhagats in Chotanagpur', in A. Shah and C. Bates (eds) *Savage Attack: Adivasi Insurgency in India*, New Delhi and Oxford: Social Science Press and Berghahn.

D'Souza, R. (2006) *Drowned and Dammed: Colonial Capitalism and Flood Control in Eastern India*, New Delhi: Oxford University Press.

Gadgil, M. and Guha, R.C. (1993) *This Fissured Land: An Ecological History of India*, Berkeley: University of California Press.

—— (1995) *Ecology and Equity: The use and abuse of nature in contemporary India*, London: Routledge.

Gandhi, A. (2003) 'Developing Compliance and Resistance: The State, Transnational Social Movements and Tribal Peoples Contesting India's Narmada Project', *Global Networks: A Journal of Transnational Affairs*, 3(4): 481–95.

Ghosh, S. (2007) *Commons Lost or Gained? Forest Tenures in the Jungle Mahals of South West Bengal*, Norwich: University of East Anglia, Overseas Development Group.

Grove, R. (1995) *Green Imperialism: Colonial Expansion, Tropical Island Edens, and the Origins of Environmentalism, 1600–1860*, Cambridge: Cambridge University Press.

Grove, R., Damodaran, V. and Sanguran, S. (eds) (1998) *Nature and the Orient: The Environmental History of South and Southeast Asia*, New Delhi: Oxford University Press.

Guha, R.C. (1985) 'Forestry and Social Protest in British Kumaun, c. 1893–1921', in R.C. Guha (ed) *Subaltern Studies IV*, New Delhi: Oxford University Press, 54–100.

—— (1989) *The Unquiet Woods, Ecological Change and Peasant Resistance in the Himalayas*, New Delhi: Oxford University Press.

—— (ed.) (1994) *Social Ecology*, New Delhi: Oxford University Press.

—— (1999) 'Subaltern and Bhadralok Studies', *Economic and Political Weekly*, 30, 19 August, 2056–8.

—— (2000) *The Unquiet Woods, Ecological Change and Peasant Resistance in the Himalayas*, Expanded Edition, Berkeley and Los Angeles:University of California Press.

Guha, R.C. and Martinez Alier, J. (1998) 'The Environmentalism of the Poor' in R.C.

Guha and J. Martinez Alier (eds) *Varieties of Environmentalism: Essays North and South*, Oxford: Oxford University Press, 3–21.

Guha, S. (1999) *Environment and Ethnicity in India 1200–1991*, Cambridge: Cambridge University Press.

Kjosavik, D.J. and Shanmugaratnam, N. (2007) 'Property Rights Dynamics and Indigenous Property Rights in Highland Kerala, South India: An Institutional Historical Perspective', *South Asian Studies*, 41(6): 1183–260.

MacKenzie, J. (1997) 'Empire and Ecological Apocalypse: The Historiography of the Imperial Environment', in T. Griffiths and E. Robin (eds) *Ecology and Empire: Environmental History of Settler Societies*, Edinburgh: Keele University Press, 215–28.

Menon, A. (2007) 'Situating Law: Adivasi Rights and the Political Economy of Environmental and Development in India', in C. Eberhard (ed.) *Law, Land Use and the Environment: Afro-Indian Dialogues*, Institut Francais: Pondicherry, 363–87.

Participatory Research in Asia (2004) *Tribal Land Rights and Industrial Accountability: Case of Mining in Dumka*, New Delhi: PRA.

Prasad, A. (2003) *Against Ecological Romanticism*, New Delhi: Three Essays Collective.

Pratap, A. (2000) *The Hoe and the Axe: Ethnohistory of Shifting Cultivation in Eastern India*, New Delhi: Oxford University Press.

Rangarajan, M. (1996) 'Environmental Histories of South Asia: A Review Essay', *Environment and History*, 2(2): 129–44.

—— (2001) *India's Wildlife History: An Introduction*, New Delhi: Permanent Black.

—— (2002) 'Polity, Ecology and Landscape: New Writings on South Asia's Past', *Studies in History*, 18(1): 135–47.

—— (ed.) (2007) *Environmental Issues in India: A Reader*, New Delhi: Pearson Longman.

Saberwal, V. and Rangarajan, M. (eds) (2003) *Battles Over Nature: Science and the Politics of Conservation*, New Delhi: Permanent Black.

Sarkar, S. (1980) 'Primitive Rebellion and Modern Nationalism: A Note on Forest Satyagraha in the Non-Cooperation and Civil Disobedience Movements', in K.N. Panikkar (ed.) *National and Left Movements in India*, New Delhi: Vikas, 14–26.

Satya, L.D. (2004) *Ecology, Colonialism and Cattle*, New Delhi: Oxford University Press.

Singh, C. (1998) *Natural Premises: Ecology and Peasant Life in the Western Himalaya 1800–1950*, New Delhi: Oxford University Press.

Sivaramakrishnan, K. (1995) 'Imagining the Past in Present Politics: Colonialism and Forestry in India', *Comparative Studies in Society and History*, 37(1): 3–40.

—— (1999) *Modern Forests: State Making and Environmental Change in Colonial Eastern India*, New Delhi: Oxford University Press.

—— (2009) 'Forests and the Environmental History of Modern India', *Journal of Peasant Studies*, 36(2): 299–324.

Skaria, A. (1999) *Hybrid Histories: Forests, Frontiers and Wildness in Western India*, New Delhi: Oxford University Press.

—— (2001) 'Cathecting the Natural', in A. Agrawal and K. Sivaramakrishnan (eds) *Social Nature: Resources, Representations, and Rule in India*, New Delhi: Oxford University Press, 265–76.

Sundar, N. (1997) *Subalterns and Sovereigns: An Anthropological History of Bastar, 1854–1996,* New Delhi: Oxford University Press.

Sutter, P. (2003) 'Reflections: What Can US Environmental Historians Learn from Non-US Environmental Historiography?', *Environmental History*, 8(1): 25–52.

Tucker, R.P. and Richards, J.F. (eds) (1983) *Global Deforestation and the Nineteenth-century World Economy*, Durham: Duke University Press.

6 Customary rights and resistance in the forests of Singhbhum

Vinita Damodaran

With the aboriginals, jungle rights are ever of supreme importance.

(Macpherson 1908: 5)

In the forest tract of Chalkad
Birsa has gone mad
He has fought the government
In the forest tract.

(A Birsaite song, cited in Singh 2002: 309)

Forest rights and reservations

In a brilliant essay, 'Custom, law and common right', E.P. Thompson recorded how, in English villages during the eighteenth century, communal forms reproduced an oral tradition. This was conceptualised as a customary consciousness through which rights were asserted as 'ours', rather than 'mine' or 'yours'. In this context, 'enclosure as it came to each village was experienced as catastrophic to the customary culture' (Thompson 1993: 179). The highly distinctive customary cultures of the Chotanagpur-based *Adivasis* suffered a comparable catastrophe in the late nineteenth century, not least through the impositions of colonial forest management. The nature of this catastrophe and the response to it, both at the level of the colonial state and of local communities, as I detail it here, helped to define Ho and Munda collective identity. Elsewhere, I have analysed the construction of indigeneity in Chotanagpur in relation to the politics of marginality (Damodaran 2006). Here I assess the contested history of forest management in colonial Singhbhum, to illustrate this phenomenon.

Sivaramakrishnan (1999; 2003) has asserted that the partitioning of landscapes involved in forest reservations was an aspect of modern state formation. In fact, the historical reasons behind forest reservations went beyond this and have been explored extensively by several historians to date (see Grove 1995). Although it was not until 1865 that the formal structure of an Indian Forest Act was set up, the environmental debate in which state forestry originated had already been going on in India and elsewhere in the British Empire for many decades before the promulgation of this act. These debates were dominated not only by a production agenda but also, and as importantly, by conservationists and East India Company surgeons concerned about the relations between deforestation, climatic deterioration, disease, agricultural production and aesthetics. By presenting the act as only a feature of modern state formation the variety of imperial agents and motivations are often obscured. In fact, it is in the context of a modern state agenda within institutions, such as forestry, that many discordant voices came to be heard in the nineteenth century. Not only were these involved in the assertion of different agendas for forestry but also in relation to local rights. Voiced by district officials on the ground, these sometimes displaced the productionist agendas of the state (see Sivaramakrishnan 1997).

Recently, critical revisionist writers have targeted colonial narratives and representations. In particular, they have scrutinised the colonial constructions of ecological 'noble savages', 'pristine forests', isolated 'tribal peoples', and 'customary rights'. While some of these attacks might be legitimate, a closer look at the historical record reveals that we may be too hasty in dismissing colonial narratives in this summary fashion. Colonial discourse did not just conjure up an imaginary landscape, but analysed real landscape differences. In fact, it can be said that the material and the imaginary landscape constituted one another in complex ways. Colonial administrators did participate with the land and the people and were forced to engage with indigenous knowledge systems and contend with multiple ideas of place. The narratives of these travellers, surveyors and officials of the *raj* (British rule) were not merely a representation of place that could be used to root colonial claims to possession, but fostered a far more ambiguous relationship with the place and its native inhabitants (see Kennedy 1996). The ambiguities, contradictions and often acute observations of colonial officials go unrecognised in such post-modern reading. It is against this background that colonial representations of customary rights and constructions of indigeneity need to be seen.

Nancy Lee Peluso (1996; 2001) has criticised colonial constructions of customary rights as having little basis in reality and leading, in the Indonesian context, to the 'racialisation' of the landscape with 'ethnic access' to resource-use (see also Li 1996). This is a problematic position, for the history of debates on customary rights in the Indian context reveals quite clear colonial preoccupations with the detail of local rights and their practice, especially in the context of forest lands. Given the nature of the state and the dominance of the property interest, these rights proved difficult to recover and to legislate in favour of, because they belonged only to practice and to oral tradition. Despite this, colonial officials frequently made genuine attempts to document local rights and land-use customs and to protect some customary practices in the latter half of the nineteenth century. Considered in relation to contemporary *Adivasi* discourses of indigeneity, these attempts are of enormous importance, although they are rarely given adequate attention. The extraordinary attempts of the Jharkhand government to award indigenous land claims, not on the basis of oral evidence but specifically on the basis of colonial documentation dating back to the 1920s, demonstrates the vital importance of understanding the colonial interpretation of customary rights. Interestingly this argument challenges a recent study on property and the environment that proposes that uniform modern property rights in land will inevitably prevail.

In a refreshing new study on forest rights and new forms of forest governance in colonial Kumaon, Agrawal (2005) has emphasised the importance of understanding such colonial interpretations of rights. Using Foucauldian ideas of governmentality he talks of governmentalised local communities, or governmentalised localities, as constituting part of a new regime of control that creates fresh political and economic relationships between centre, localities and subjects. Governmentality thus does not signify the proliferation of oppressive state institutions. Rather, the developments in Kumaon in the 1920s enabled communities to increase their role in environmental control, thereby redefining the relationship between state and locality. This resulted in the production of new environmental subjects and new regulatory communities. In the context of increasing market pressures, Agrawal persuasively tries to argue that these new regulatory arrangements are able to soften and attenuate results, and perhaps even withstand market pressures. In Chotanagpur, during the nineteenth century, the colonial state and officials on the ground made similar attempts to understand and legislate in favour of local rights in the context of forest reservation. While one may not be able to talk of decentralisation of forest governance, as in Kumaon in the 1920s, these attempts need to be understood and analysed by examining particular ecological-historical settings (see Sivaramkrishnan 1997).

While there is an abundance of literature on the history of colonial forestry, much of it is written either from the angle of scientific forestry or of the state developmental agenda, and so the importance of understanding the local ecological-historical settings for these projects is decreased. With the notable exception of Sivaramakrishnan, who is concerned with colonial foresters' acquaintance with the locality, the institution of forestry is rarely conceived of as a matter of governance. Sivaramkrishnan's approach (1997) is focused more on the workings of the colonial state than on the idea of rights. He does, however, record the intense debates in the 1870s and 1880s over forest reservation in the Santhal Parganas. He quotes Oldham, the District Commissioner of the Santhal Parganas, to note that 'the claims of Hillman to uninhabited hills is too substantial a claim and one which has been too distinctly recognised by the government to be set aside.' (1997: 94) It is here, in the context of governance, that we can locate the concern with rights. In his study of Kumaon, Agrawal (2005) emphasises the move of the colonial and post-colonial states away from methods of coercion to other methods of shaping behaviour in the context of environmental resource use. I would contend that this latter approach can be utilised to understand the colonial discourse on rights, as administrators came to think that local rights needed to be settled and preserved in order to facilitate governance. That this realisation was gradual is beyond doubt.

It is clear that when the forest department was constituted in the 1860s the state of the forests in much of India was extremely poor and chaotic, and that the ideas for their administration were extremely vague. In certain areas, the progress of the department was also slow. However, the establishment of the forest department gradually stifled the steady erosion of forest areas in India, a process that was reversed once again only during the Depression of the 1930s and, on a much larger scale, after national independence in 1947. At the forest conference in 1873–4, the defects of the 1865 Act were brought to notice. It provided no procedure for enquiring into and settling rights (which it addressed so vaguely), and did not distinguish between the forests that required close reservation and those that required more general measures.[1] In Chotanagpur, at a conference held in Ranchi in 1882, rules were drafted by the commissioners of Lohardugga, Hazaribagh and Palamau for the management of forests in anticipation that they would have to be explained to the landholders, in relation to deforestation (due to the demand from the new railways).[2]

The drafting of proper forest laws for the different provinces in the period 1869–78 was related therefore to the extent that the long continued right of the user – to the free collection of small produce, fuel, grass, bamboo grazing and shifting cultivation in the wastelands – should be regarded as a prescriptive right. On the other hand, the government (as guardian of all public interests) insisted on the regulation of these rights so as to render possible the good management of the reserved forests in the interests of the country.[3] With forests increasingly being recognised as a revenue resource by the district administration, the clash between foresters and administrators became more apparent. While forest conservancy was adopting a tone that promoted the direct control, systematisation and regulation of the extraction of timber from what was perceived to be a dwindling resource of tropical timber, local administrators often urged caution in overriding local rights to forests. However, the issue of rights continued to be an important one for the district administration. By the 1880s, forests in Chotanagpur were organised under a variety of arrangements, reserved, protected, privatised and leased from the political states. It was generally argued that the interests of the agriculturists were amply safeguarded during the creation of the reserved forest (since in the hilly regions 50 per cent of the forest area was generally excluded from reservation while in the plains the non-reserved area set aside as village commons was three times as large as the reservation). But the history of forest reservation and the evidence of unrest indicate that the interests of small farmers living adjacent to forests were far from secure.

Here, I examine the differing outcomes of forest policy by looking at the ways in which these diverse pressures, the protection of forest for a variety of reasons, the revenue generating possibilities of timber production, and the issue of local rights were played out in a range of contexts in Chotanagpur, notably the Saranda region and the Porahat forest.[4] In the former, the regional administration emphasised the productionist agenda of the forest department through the enforcement of 'reserved forests' while in Porahat, on the other hand, the colonial officials protected the local rights, given the context of conflict between the *raj* and local indigenous communities in the context of 'protected forests'.

The Saranda Forests and the Ho interest

In 1878 the Indian Forest Act was passed extending policies regarding 'reserved forests' and 'protected forests' to all the provinces of British India. Every possible safeguard against infringements (by private rights) surrounded the first class constitution of 'reserved forests', which were secured by a permanent settlement. The second class demarcation of 'protected forests', however, offered less sufficient guarantees for stability and protection. There were also private forests leased from political states. By 1898, 33,738 square miles of forest were closed to all animals, and 28,146 square miles were closed to browsers throughout India. Systematic forestry commenced after the stabilisation of British rule in the latter half of the nineteenth century. As information-gathering in Chotanagpur increased, notably by colonial officials such as Henry Ricketts (1853), S.R. Tickell (1840) and Valentine Ball (1880), new regimes of property were beginning to be put into place. On the completion of the demarcation in 1880–1, the forests of the Singhbhum division comprised Saranda, Kolhan and Porahat. In 1884–5, Chotanagpur division was constituted which embraced the whole of Singhbhum, Palamau and Kodarma. Thus in 1885, 306 square miles of Saranda constituted one 'reserved forest' range, managed by one forest ranger, three forest guards and six *chaukidars* (wardens). The history of 'protected forests' dates back to 1903–5 when 17 blocs were declared protected. There were then various additions and modifications with regard to the area and status of forest. The Kolhan forests were separated in 1906 to form the Chaibasa division. By 1 April 1924, four forest divisions had been constituted with their Head Quarters at Chaibasa for the purposes of control and management of all reserved and protected forests situated within Singhbhum (Phillips 1924: 12).

In Saranda, the reserves were situated entirely in the western third of the district, in the Kolhan government estate, and formed a compact bloc bordered on the north by a belt of cultivated country through which ran the Bengal–Nagpur railway that divided them from the reserves of the Porahat estate, where the two forested tracts met at Goilkera. In the south and south west, the reserves were coterminous with large tracts of forest in Gangpur, Bonai and Keonjhar 'native states'. On the east were the protected forest and cultivated lands of Singhbhum. The reserves were divided into six ranges and twelve blocs, an area of 537 square miles. As Sivaramakrishnan notes, working plans came to symbolise the confidence of the scientific forester, 'but visualising a terrain where science could plan unimpeded the manipulation of the forest compelled a more complete enumeration and disposal of local rights that might obscure the vision' (2003: 258). By 1899, 20,000 square miles of government forests were covered by working plans of which 1,900 were in Bengal.

However, while local governments were urged as part of the working plans to balance the requirements of local communities with the exigencies of forest conservancy and to record all admissible rights of village communities and private persons in local lands, the overriding importance of some forests rendered the idea of rights illusory. The first working plans in Singhbhum were produced in

1903. By 1925 Singhbhum was divided into Saranda, Kolhan, Porahat and Chaibasa with separate plans for each division. It is apparent from settlement reports that rights of village communities were not often recognised. In the context of the Porahat reserved forest, Munda *Adivasis* were evicted from the forested villages. The active *sardars* (leaders) and the Birsaites (followers of Birsa Munda, leader of the *Ulgulan* [rebellion] of 1896–1900) were the most circumscribed.

The first investigation into reserving Saranda forests was sponsored by Dr Anderson in Bengal in 1864. A small addition of 1,370 acres was made with effect from 1 April 1888 (Phillips 1924: 12). Although Saranda was notified as reserved with effect from 1882 and the demarcation was reported as complete, parts of the boundaries remained uncertain for some time. The tract bordered on the former states of Keonjhar, Bonai and Gangpur and a small dispute on the former Bonai state boundary involving 166 acres was settled in favour of Saranda in 1912 (Phillips 1924: 12). As Sivaramakrishnan notes (1999), the natural regeneration of *sal*, the most valued tree in the Bengal forests, became one of the main goals for scientific forestry. However, even in a scheme based on natural regeneration, the forest department attempted to define scientific modes of such regeneration and trained people to protect, enhance and release woody growth. H. Haines's working plan came into force in 1903–4. Six working circles were formed, of which five were worked under the system of selection and improvement, with fellings prescribed for a 15-year period (Phillips 1924: 12). Over large areas the system was simple coppice, the rotation of coppice being 16 years. The production of a sustained outturn of large timber suitable to market requirements, consistent with the maintenance and improvement of the forest, were the general objects of forest management.

H. Haine's working plan was succeeded by P.J. Phillips. The principles of scientific forestry were rigorously applied to these forests, which were regarded as an important revenue resource and rights of local communities were ignored. As the working plan by P.J. Phillips in the 1920s reported:

> the tract was very mountainous, the larger valleys being occupied by village lands while the reserves covered the jumble of higher hills and smaller higher lying valleys, in Saranda villages were fewer and many large valleys were uncultivated and contained fine forests ... in former times this was not the case for topographical maps of sixty years ago show quite a number of villages or old village sites in Saranda, whose names and sites have in most cases long since been forgotten.
>
> (Phillips 1924: 12)

No rights were admitted in the reserves except in Siaba bloc where it was noted that the residents of 138 Kolhan villages were entitled to receive supplies of firewood, thatching grass and fodder grass.

The mention of old village sites here is important for a close examination of the forest revealed that shifting cultivation had been practised extensively here prior to the reservation in 1882. It was estimated that shifting and semi-permanent cultivation had been carried on in the century preceding the report (especially between 1830 and 1882), and that evidence for this was provided by *sasan* or burial stones which were quite numerous. Where *purunga* or true *jhum* cultivation had been carried out (generally on upper and middle slopes) the result was in most cases the production of well-stocked even-aged crops of *sal* trees. On the other hand, where the cultivation was of a semi-permanent nature (*gora*), a savannah type forest occurred in the higher plateau of Ankua and Karampada at about 2,000 ft. The areas here were open and grassy and showed signs of re-colonising with tree species. On the lower slopes the effect of shifting cultivation was seen to degrade the soil and reduce tree cover. One important effect of shifting cultivation was the production of large areas of young woods mostly 40–80 years old.[5]

It is clear from the forest reports of the 1930s that old villages that had existed in these reserves had been cleared prior to the setting up of these reserves in the 1880s. In reserved forest this resulted in the dismantling of previous customary rights relating to shifting cultivation, clearing of villages in lands so demarcated and resettling them elsewhere. Control of the forests required that these shifting cultivators be expelled and in Saranda forest that was what happened (also see Sivaramkrishnan 1997: 84). The creation of reserved forests in Saranda caused the uprooting of many hundred villages. Evidence for this was recorded in Santara, Latua, Loda, Ambia, Ankua, Ghatkori and Karampada, Samta, Tholkabad, Tirilposi and Kodilabad. In Tholkabad for example, Phillips' working plan for the area recorded that the northern half of the compartment was occupied by what were once the *jhum* cultivated lands of Tholkabad situated on a plateau (Phillips 1924: 98). The impact of forest reservation on local people was therefore dramatic. It is clear that the importance of Saranda as a contiguous forest bloc for the colonial government rendered the issue of rights in this context illusory.

It is interesting to note that not all villages were removed to create forest reserves. Some forest villages were retained to provide labour for the forest department. While 27 forest villages were officially recognised, there were other hamlets which existed in order to provide free labour. These villagers were often at the mercy of the forest officials. However, the provisions of the Chotanagpur Tenancy Act did not apply to them and they had no rights to the lands they cultivated (Phillips 1924: 33). In Saranda forests then local rights were ignored in favour of the productionist agendas of the forest department. This was not the case in Porahat where increasing local protest highlighted the impact of forest reservation on local communities. Thus the first decades of forest conservancy in Chotanagpur show a variety of competing interests. While some areas like Saranda were dominated by factors such as timber supply and profits from forests, other areas provided less scope for the removal of timber as they were involved with supplying local needs.

Customary rights in Porahat after Birsa Munda

The story of reservation in Porahat is also interesting though different from the Saranda story with important implications for local rights. Here the reserved forest was sometimes recategorised as protected forests where rights could accrue. Mathew Areeparampil notes that the governing of these 'reserved forests', where no rights could accrue, was often done in very haphazard fashion and many survey errors were made. For example, Heremda in Bandgaon was wrongly declared part of the reserved forest. In Dhalbhum, 138 acres of Mati-gara village was wrongly notified as reserved area. The area was excluded from the reserved forest only in 1938 (Areeparampil 1984: 13–14). Another 160 acres were excluded from the reserved forests of Porahat division after they had been wrongly included in the reserved area. In the case of Chirukubera village in the Porahat *pargana* (administrative district), where the reserved forests were constituted in 1890, revenue from the reserved forest was paid to the local estate holder Raja Narpat Singh. Chirkubera was a *khuntkhatti* village (meaning that it was the tenure of members of the Munda lineage who reclaimed lands) and included the *tolas* (small villages) of Saromsoya, Rontuabera, Sasanbera, Jabu-gadara and Kinduda. All these *tolas* were forcibly removed on the orders of the Raja, and the houses of the villagers and their crops were destroyed (Areepar-ampil 1984: 13–14). Unrest also followed in the case of the creation of protected forests.

J.S. Macpherson reported that the reservation was one great encroachment on *khuntkatti* rights of the Mundas.

> But when the reservation came and with it the evictions, the infringement of their ancient customary rights was obvious and was immediately resented. They made light of the *pattas* [deeds] from the rent receiver and to use the words of the joint forest settlement report, protested that the memorial stones of their ancestors were their pattas.
>
> (Macpherson 1908: 5–6)

Moberly, who was in charge of the operation to demarcate 25 large blocs of protected forest in Porahat, recorded extensive resistance from Mundas and *mankis* (Munda leaders).

> The Mundaris [Mundas] of Karla, Sankai and Todanghatu and Kundruguttu pir [conglomerate of small administrative districts] obstructed the *amins* and when sent for persisted in their obstructive attitude and informed me that they would not permit the lines to be cut, although I warned them that I should be compelled to send for the police unless they promised to assist. An armed force camped in these villages until the lines had been cut and were inspected by me and a certain amount of new cultivation was included in the protected blocs as a punishment.
>
> (Macpherson 1908: 7, appendix 7)

He went on to note that, 'I strongly suspect that the *manki* had organised opposition throughout the *pir*, but I could not get sufficient evidence by which to proceed against him.'

It is clear here that the question of local rights did exercise the colonial government and serious attempts were made to protect them as in the case of the Porahat settlement in 1900. It is within these debates that one can locate changing and contested ideas of property. J.S. Macpherson noted that,

> the reservation had created a general feeling of dissatisfaction and distrust of the government which it will take long to live down. The tenants evicted from a number of villages lost their *khuntkhatti* status for which no grant of *raiyati* [cultivable] lands elsewhere could compensate them. Now when the law recognises their *khuntkhatti* status they clamour that something should be done for them. The opposition to the demarcation of protected forests is due to the fear that eventually the tenants will be excluded from them, and I strongly urge here that no restrictions should be placed on the use of the jungle at least by the residents of the village where it lies, except such as are necessary to prevent its total destruction.
>
> (Macpherson 1908: 6)

That the government had absolutely no right in the Munda *khuntkhatti* villages was apparent to Macpherson who stated that 'the government cannot conceivably have any rights in the waste or forest land in these villages, unless as in some *khuntkhatti* villages in Ranchi, he has forcibly acquired them by seizure, followed by a long period of peaceful possession.' (1908: 6) That the question of jungle rights was important to local people and was a significant factor in the Birsa Munda rebellion of the 1890s was also recognised in Macpherson's comment that:

> with aboriginals jungle rights are ever of supreme importance and in Porahat they are not disposed to accept curtailment of rights or fresh impositions. Birsaism in Singhbhum is due chiefly to interference with jungle rights in Bandgaon and Khas Porahat, and if not vigorous is by no means suppressed.
>
> (1908: 5; see also Damodaran 1995)

The fact emphasised in most reports was that the Mundas evicted from villages or whose village life was circumscribed were later the most active of the *sardars* and Birsaites. These comments reveal the discordant voices within colonial policy and the recognition of the necessity to work with local communities.

For Macpherson then, the customs of Chotanagpur were radically different from other parts of Bengal. As he noted,

> to comprehend rights and customs in Chotanagpur and particularly in Pargana Porahat the most important requisite is to discard completely all ideas of land tenure acquired in other parts of Bengal. The relationship of

landlord to tenant in extensive tracts of Chotanagpur is radically different from the same relation in Bengal and Bihar, the unit of Chotanagpur not being the individual tenant, but a community and the landlord being not the owner of the soil but merely receiver of a charge called rent and having no direct relation with the cultivators.

(Macpherson 1908: 6)

In his report, therefore, Macpherson set out systematically to protect customary rights of local communities against the onslaught of the proprietor. This attempt to settle customary rights, especially with regard to forests, was a result of the impact of the Birsa movement on government opinion. The role of the district administration in recording and emphasising the importance of local rights against the productionist agenda of the foresters is important to note here.

The main focus of Birsa's discontent was the restrictions regarding the protected forests of Piring in the Porahat area. The measures taken to mark off village forests and to prepare a record of forest rights caused much unrest in the region. Petitions were submitted by various *mankis*, Jeta Manki of Gudri, Rasha Manki, Mona Manki of Durkapir 'claiming resumption' of their old rights for free fuel wood, grazing, etc. Birsa himself led a number of *raiyats* from Sigrida village to Chaibasa to petition for remission of forest dues. Men from six other villages had preceded him but nothing came of it (see Singh 1966: 37). The strength of the Birsa movement and the recognition of Mundari *Khuntkhatti* tenure did result in the preservation of some forest rights in the protected forest areas. An effort was therefore made to draw up a record of rights as can be noted in the case of the Porahat settlement.

The Porahat settlement

J.H. Taylor's settlement was conducted under the provisions of the Bengal Act 5 of 1875 and the Bengal Act 1 of 1879. In the course of his operations Taylor drew up a record of rights and duties. It was objected to by the Raja of Porahat with regard to its description of the headman's rights, its prohibition of certain illegal exactions and its definition of forest rights. For each village a separate record of rights was prepared. More than 1,500 objections were received.[6] In Porahat, 195 square miles of forest were marked off between 1880 and 1882 and constituted reserved forest under the Forest Act of 1890. Four years later the rest of the forest and wasteland of the estate was declared 'protected forest' under the Act, not as the forest settlement report noted 'with the object of excluding or diminishing the rights of the tenantry, but with the object of regulating the exercise of these rights and preventing their wanton abuse by individuals to the prejudice of the community.' (Taylor 1904: 33) When Porahat was restored to the raja in 1895, the management of the forest was reserved by government. The report went on to note:

in order that the management of the forest department within the protected area should not unduly limit the extension of cultivation or interfere with

the privileges of *raiyats* [tenants] it was resolved that certain blocs of protected forest should be blocked off for permanent maintenance by the
department and that the remainder of jungle and wasteland be let
uncontrolled.

(Taylor 1904: 33)

Mr Moberly demarcated 25 blocs covering 37 square miles, and subsequently
ten blocs covering five square miles, in accordance with these proposals. The
original proposal regarding the un-demarcated area was that it should be left to
the unrestrained control of the *zamindar* (landlord) and obvious confounding of
the proprietor with the estate and tenantry.

J.H. Taylor and J.S. Macpherson both advanced unanswerable arguments that
the un-demarcated portions of the protected forest should be left to the management of the village headman and *mankis* under the nominal supervision of the
forest department, and that all claims of the proprietor over this area should be
disallowed.[7] Taylor reported that 'unless the village forests were left under the
control of the headman, the management of the forests by the raja, or rather by
his subordinates would be very detrimental to the interests of the tenants'
(quoted in Macpherson 1908: 142). The protected forest was to be managed on
behalf of the village communities, the *zamindar* already having received his
share of the forest in the shape of reserves. Clearly, here one can see a move by
Macpherson and Taylor to establish and protect certain customary rights. In fact,
one can argue that the settlement aimed to limit the rights of the proprietor and
to protect the rights of the *manki*. The *mankis* were military chiefs or original
settlers under whom groups of villages were reclaimed. They survived in only
eight Kolhan *pirs* and in the subdivision of Bandgaon. The *manki* was entitled to
a *nala*, or commission of six *pice* per rupee of the rental, payable through him by
his headman to the proprietor. The proprietor by refusing to pay some *mankis*
their commission had been known to intimidate the others and was known to use
them as instruments of oppression. The rights of the headmen were protected by
hereditary tenure for which they could not normally be ejected.

It was reported after enquiry in Porahat that, though sufficient jungle had been
excluded from the reserves, headmen of villages of that neighbourhood which
contained jungle now objected to it being taken by 'outsiders'. In 1889 the
advent of the railway produced a demand for fuel and timber and unauthorised
sales from the unreserved forests of Porahat and Kolhan began to take place.
Consequently, the Deputy Commissioner arranged that the forest department, in
the interests of the government, and of the villages in which these forests were
situated, should manage the unreserved forests.

Macpherson criticised the decision of the subordinate judge at Chaibasa, who
held that the two headmen in the Sadant *pirs* whom the *zamindar* sued for *khas*
(possession of their villages) had failed to prove a permanent right in the villages. Regarding *raiyati* rights, he settled that the proprietor had no right to interfere in the internal economy of the village, and neither did the village headman
have exclusive rights over this. Vacant holdings were to be settled with villagers.

The headman was not entitled to take *salami* (forced financial exactions) on a resettlement, which in any case were rarely taken in Munda villages. Homesteads, fruit groves, water reservoirs, threshing floors and manure pits, as well as burial grounds, burning grounds and *sarna* or *jahiras* (sacred groves), were not assessed on rent. Macpherson concluded that the villages were founded on the understanding that the cultivated lands alone would be assessed, and an attempt to assess anything else would be an inexcusable breach of custom (1908: 52).

In Porahat then, the jungle and wasteland were protected forest in charge of the forest department. The right of all cultivators to a supply of forest produce for their own requirements was deemed to be beyond discussion. The constitution of the protected forest in the region was subject to rights of the community. The *zamindar* had rights in the reserved jungle but no right of sale in the unreserved forest or right to take any produce from it (Macpherson 1908: 63). As noted, detailed enquiries from village to village proved conclusively that those rights that were admitted had not only been exercised by the tenants from time immemorial but were, in many villages, also connected to the sale of minor forest produce long before 1894. In some *pirs* and in the Ho villages of the Kolhan *pirs*, there was no such custom of sale and the residents of the estate uninterruptedly used the produce of the jungle without restriction.

The recording of customary use placed certain restrictions on the rights of *raiyats* to cut trees for their own use. It was noted that trees of all kinds were customarily cut down in the making of rice land (*don*), but *mahua*, *kusum* and mango trees were always spared in preparing upland cultivation. The following trees were also generally saved: all fruit trees of value, *asan* (when required for Tusser), *palas* and other trees useful for lac cultivation, *arjun*, *sal*, *piasal* and other good timber trees. The latter were of course freely cut for plough and house repairs. The former were spared because they were of more use to the community when standing than when cut. In many villages the *panchayat* (village council) decided which trees might be cut. In villages devoid of jungle no green trees were to be cut. A cultivator wishing to cut a tree of a species reserved by the *panchayat* was required to get the headman's consent. No tree could be cut from the *sarnas* or *jahiras* of the Munda or Ho *Adivasis* and as a rule not even the dry wood of fallen trees could be removed from them (Macpherson 1908: 66–8). It is important to note that, in the greater part of the Pargana, tenants had no right of sale of timber or of uncultivated forest produce. In the Mundari *pirs*, the sale of minor forest produce had taken place uninterruptedly for 30 or 40 years previously, resulting in the denudation of the jungle in neighbouring Ranchi. This was allowed to continue by Macpherson. Where evidence showed that the custom was more recent it was not admitted or entered in the record.

Macpherson also elaborated on the custom of the sacred grove and the strict custom that prevented any cutting in the grove. He recorded the general custom as one where no one may cut down trees here whether green or dry and that not even the dry wood may be taken out of the grove. In Ranchi, the new landlords who were unaware of prevailing custom, cut trees in the *sarna* until they were convicted. The proprietors were disqualified and the commissioner stigmatised it as sacrilegious. Being a new proprietor, the *zamindar* of Porahat also claimed the right to cut trees in the sacred grove and this was also deemed sacrilegious. In Porahat, as Macpherson noted (1908: 70), the *zamindar* was expressly precluded by the terms of his indenture from interfering with the wasteland. This legal enforcement of the status of sacred groves was a very important recognition of local rights and cosmologies.

It was therefore concluded that the government and its successor possessed no right of sale from all unreserved jungle and wasteland, and the produce of it. Further, *zamindars* had no right to take the produce for personal use, nor any right of interference, except to regulate the rights of members of the village communities. Tenants however had unrestricted right to deal with such land and the produce of it in accordance with the customs of the village, and were not liable to render payment, or to take any permission from the *zamindar*. Residents of the estate could take, free for their own use and without permission, all uncultivated forest produce from the waste or jungle of villages except from trees of certain species in some villages where they had been apportioned by the villagers amongst themselves. By custom then all residents of the village had reciprocal rights in the jungles of other villages in the estate (Macpherson 1908: 147). To prevent misconception he hammered home the point that the *zamindar* was not the owner of trees in cultivated land, village sites or *jahiras* nor entitled to any produce or revenue from them and that he had no right to cut them down or sell them under any circumstances.

In order to give practical force to these records of rights, Macpherson required that certified copies of the record be made available to local headmen and, in their absence, to influential tenants. He also made extensive recommendations with regard to the control of ejection of headmen and the appointment of new headmen. Rights in this regard were placed in the hands of the District Commissioner. Such arrangements, he noted (1908: 13), were essential if the record of rights was to have practical value.

> Of all the tenants who have been placed in difficulties by the change of Porahat from a political state to a zamindari in British India, the aboriginals of these *pirs* most require and merit the protection of government by legislation.
>
> (1908: 123)

It is noteworthy that local communities, who feared the imminent seizure of the forests by the state, often misused customary rights. In Ranchi district, it was reported that since the beginning of the forest settlement, local communities, fearing that the settlement would reduce their forest rights, had used their customary rights to sell wood in large quantities denuding the forests in their locality. Interestingly, when the situation proved to have a marked effect on the community and its fuel resources, some local attempts at conservation were recorded. These involved rigid prescriptions against cutting down certain trees.

Unfortunately, the settlement report recorded, these local conservation attempts were few and far between and varied enormously in their effectiveness.

Entangled pasts

The debates on customary rights in the protected forests are far-reaching, for they revealed colonial concerns with local rights, while at the same time designing the most sweeping legislation allocating nearly one-sixth of India's land as forest reserve. While the motives behind this forest legislation have been the subject of much debate, mainly by environmental historians, the discourse of customary rights has received less attention.

While it can be argued that forest rights in the Chotanagpur context became an important part of the discourse of Ho and Munda exclusiveness both by the state and the indigenous peoples themselves, one can take the point too far, as when Peluso and Vandergeest argue that 'the creation of customary rights followed in the presumption of the arriving European's views of the landscapes they found' and that they rarely fitted in with prevailing local ideas about nature and 'were but constructions' with little basis in reality (2001: 801). Interestingly in an argument that works counter to this, Ann Tsing has noted in the context of Indonesia that the Dutch codification of Adat law has been used in more recent times to establish property rights for marginalised forest peoples threatened by forest clearing for transmigration settlement schemes and plantation agriculture (see Richards 2001: 6).

In Chotanagpur customary rights, while open to misinterpretation, misrecognition and sustained erosion, did indeed have a basis in the lived environment which in E.P. Thompson's terms '... comprised of practices, inherited expectations, rules, norms and sanctions both of law and neighbourhood pressures' (1993: 110). Their recognition by the colonial state has to do with the contradictory nature of political power. Thompson (1993: 110) goes on to note that 'unequal as were the terms of power in this conflict, yet power must submit to some constraints because power might bring itself into danger if abuse of customary rights outraged the populace.' The reality of customary rights is not in question here.

One recent book, which examines the links between myths of land relatedness and regimes of property in land, shows the different ways in which 'mythical land relations' are reproduced through the courts. In Australia, for example, contemporary Australian aboriginal groups are obliged to approach the courts to establish land rights. As Abramson and Theodossopoulos point out,

> the dominance of the courts in matters relating to the ratification of land relatedness, means that often with anthropological aid, clansfolk are both able and obliged to translate mythical categories into legal terms. Ancestral tracks and ritual sites become the basis for drawing up boundaries, whilst spiritual guardianship transposes as legal ownership.
>
> (Abramson and Theodossopoulos 2000: 18)[8]

In the case of Chotanagpur, similarly, one can see that brute facts of colonialism were sometimes reversed by recognition of a limited number of customary practices and local land myths.

The entanglement of colonial narratives with indigenous narratives is all too apparent here, generating a complex set of political/cultural formations that have continued to inform both state and popular discourses of identity in the State of Jharkhand today. Nevertheless, the concessions made to indigenous knowledge systems and local identities by the colonial state were insufficient to stem a rising tide of turbulent protest in Chotanagpur. Indeed, the concessions probably encouraged the Ho and Munda *Adivasis* along a pathway towards a mobilisation as minorities that would eventually lead to claims for political autonomy and regional statehood. In the process, a minority culture and minority identities were creatively reworked during struggles to actualise particular rights (see Chakrabarty 2005).

Notes

1 *Indian Forester*, Vol. 10, 1884
2 Ibid.
3 Ibid.
4 Throughout the colonial period, officials debated the links between the forests and local water supply.
5 The final report of J.S. Macpherson on the operations for the preparation of a record of rights in Pargana Porahat of Singhbhum was begun in November 1905 and concluded in April 1907. The report is supplementary to J.H. Taylor's report on the Porahat settlement of 1900–03.
6 J.S. Macpherson has given us a detailed account of the history of the Pargana. Porahat was confiscated in 1858 on account of the rebellion of Raja Arjun Singh. Its revenue administration was made over to the board of revenue and it continued in other respects to be managed as a tributary state. It was incorporated in Bengal by a proclamation of 1892. Raja Arjun Singh died in 1890. By indenture dated 10 October 1895, Porahat was restored to his son Raja Narpat Singh. It was restored with full proprietor rights, subject and without prejudice.
7 DC report, 15 September 1905, DC files, Chaibasa Record Room.
8 It has been argued that this relates to rights as legal process and the proclivities of law to essentialise social categories and identities. In some senses then the process of law might compel collectivities to define themselves in culturally essentialist terms (see also Cowan *et al.* 2001; Clifford 1988).

References

Abramson, A. and Theodossopoulos, D. (2000) *Land, Law and the Environment*, London: Routledge.

Agrawal, A. (2005) *Environmentality: Technologies of Government and the Making of Subjects*, London: Duke University Press.

Areeparampil, M. (1984) *Forest Reservation and Denial of Tribal Rights in Singhbhum*, Chaibasa: Tribal Research and Training Centre.

Ball, V. (1880) *Tribal and Peasant Life in Nineteenth Century India*, first published in 1880 as *Jungle Life in India, or The Journeys and Journals of an Indian Geologist*, reprinted in 1985, New Delhi: Usha Publications.

Chakrabarty, D. (2005) 'Politics unlimited: the global adivasi and debates about the political', in B. Karlsson and T. Subba (eds) *Indigeneity in India*, London: Kegan Paul, 231–42.

Clifford, J. (1988) *The Predicament of Culture*, Cambridge MA: Harvard University Press.

Cowan, J.K., Dembour, M.-B. and Wilson, R.A. (eds) (2001) 'Introduction', in J.K. Cowan Dembour, M.-B. and Wilson, R.A. (eds) *Culture and Rights: Anthropological Perspectives,* Cambridge: Cambridge University Press.

Damodaran, V. (1995) 'Famine in a forest tract', *Environment and History*, 1(2): 129–58.

—— (2006) 'The politics of marginality and the construction of indigeneity in Chotanagpur', *Postcolonial Studies*, 9(2): 179–96.

Grove, R.H. (1995) *Green Imperialism, Colonial Expansion, Tropical Island Edens and the Origins of Environmentalism,* Cambridge: Cambridge University Press.

Indian Forester (1884) Volume 10.

Kennedy, D. (1996) 'Imperial history and post colonial history', *Journal of Imperial and Commonwealth History*, 24: 345–63.

Li, T.M. (1996) 'Environment indigeneity and transnationalism', in R. Peet and M. Watts (eds) *Liberation Ecologies, Environment, Development and Social Movements,* London: Routledge, 339–70.

Macpherson, J.S. (1908) *Final Report on the Operations for the Preparations of a Record of Rights in Pargana Porahat, District Singhbhum, 1905–1907,* Calcutta: Government Printing.

Peluso, N.L. (1996) 'Fruit trees and family trees in an anthropogenic forest: ethics of access, property zones and environmental change in Indonesia', *Comparative Studies in Society and History*, 38: 510–48.

Peluso, N.L. and Vandergeest, P. (2001) 'Genealogies of the political forest and customary rights in Indonesia, Malaysia and Thailand', *Journal of Asian Studies,* 60(3): 761–812.

Phillips, P.J. (1924) *Revised Working Plan for the Reserved Forests of Saranda and Kolhan Divisions in Singhbhum*, Patna: Superintendent of Government Printing.

Ricketts, H. (1853) *Report on the District of Singhbhum,* Calcutta: Bengal Military Orphan Press.

Richards, J.F. (2001) 'Introduction' in J.F. Richards (ed.) *Land, Property and the Environment*, Oaklands: ICS Press.

Singh, K.S. (1966) *The Dust Storm and Hanging Mist*, Calcutta: KLM.

Sivaramakrishnan, K. (1997) 'A limited forest conservancy in southwest Bengal, 1864–1912', *Journal of Asian Studies*, 56(1): 75–112.

—— (1999) *Modern Forests: State Making and Environmental Change in Colonial Eastern India,* Stanford: Stanford University Press.

—— (2003) 'Scientific forestry and genealogies of development in Bengal', in P. Greenhough and A. Tsing (eds) *Nature in the Global South: Environmental Projects in South and South East Asia*, Durham: Duke University Press, 253–88.

Taylor, J.H. (1904) *Final Report on the Survey and Settlement Operations in the Porahat Estate*, Calcutta: Government Printing.

Thompson, E.P. (1993) *Customs in Common,* London: Penguin.

Tickell, S.R. (1840) 'Memoir on the Hodesum', in *Journal of the Asiatic Society of Bengal*, 9(2): 694–710.

7 Standpoints and intersections

Towards an indigenist epistemology

Darley Jose Kjosavik

Introduction

Drawing on the notion of intersectionality developed by black feminists and the insights from field research on indigenous peoples' (*adivasi*) development in Kerala, India, this chapter develops a situated standpoint of the indigenous peoples, which I shall call indigenist standpoint epistemology. At the outset I introduce the premise of standpoint epistemologies. This will be followed by a discussion of proletarian standpoint and feminist standpoint epistemologies and move on to the situated standpoint. Based on these premises then, I attempt to delineate an indigenist standpoint epistemology and argue that this epistemological position arises at the intersection of class and indigeneity. Further, I argue, this epistemological position could contribute to gaining a more complete historical understanding of the *adivasi* development question and generate knowledge that could contribute to the emancipatory development of indigenous peoples and other under-classes. The historical processes that shaped this intersection in a specific geographical region in Kerala are analysed. I also argue that the indigenist standpoint has the potential to provide a more emancipatory conceptualisation of indigeneity than those offered in post-colonial and statist accounts.

Standpoint epistemology: a political project

Positivist/empiricist research presupposes a 'neutral', 'objective' and 'universalist' epistemology, where rules of logic and observational criteria are used for delineating 'true' knowledge from mere belief and speculations (Kuhn 1970). This orthodox epistemology had been criticised by Marx and Engels (1975a, 1975b, 1975c, 1976) and Lukács (1971) for privileging the experiences of the capitalist class and by western feminists for privileging capitalist and male experiences (Hartsock 1983, 1997, 2003; Harding 1991, 1998; Smith 1987). Black feminists have sought to unravel the dominance of capitalist, male and white experiences and worldviews (Crenshaw 1992; Collins 1998). Alternative epistemologies advanced from these critiques came to be known as standpoint epistemologies – proletarian standpoint, feminist standpoint and situated standpoint respectively. The basic premise of these epistemologies is the position that the experiences of the oppressed and marginalised groups possess epistemological advantage in the search for knowledge since they are least likely to have a vested interest in maintaining the illusions about the world. Thus the cognitive superiority of the subordinate standpoints arises from their differential 'experiential space', since society is characterised by structured heterogeneities (Mills 1988).

Mills (1988) argues that it may not be possible for this detached knower to move freely between these structured spaces, as one tends to be constrained by the kind of experiences one has and the concepts one is likely to develop, being located in a certain position in the social structure. Areas of experience, which are outside this realm, may not be accessible through the world of the Cartesian knower and the ways of knowing designed by the dominant group. Therefore, the argument of standpoint epistemology is that since the subordinated groups have access to these areas, it potentially gives them a more real picture of the dynamics of the social world. Following the realist metaphysics of Marxism, the alternative sets of experiences have epistemic significance; they are not indifferent as regards the kind of knowledge that is produced about the world. The dominant groups are thus characterised by experiences that result in fostering illusions about the social world. On the contrary, the experience of the subordinate groups has the potential to produce more adequate conceptualisations of the social world; the epistemic privilege comes from the structured nature of oppression. A standpoint, however, is not self-evident or obvious to someone by virtue of being merely a member of the subordinate social group; one has to struggle for it. A standpoint is also not limited to members of subordinated classes/groups. It can be struggled for and achieved by others as well, through critical thinking and self-reflection, and engaging with the liberation struggles of subordinated groups at various levels (Harding 1986, 1998; Collins 1998).

Standpoint epistemology is a political project, an emancipatory epistemology to challenge hegemonic ideologies and beliefs. Given the realist ontological premises, standpoint epistemology inextricably interlinks social experiences to the material dimensions of the world thereby acknowledging what Bhaskar (1975, 1989) calls the transitive and intransitive objects of knowledge. Thus, it retains the normative element of knowledge, and does not sabotage the project of science in discovering 'truth' or objective knowledge. However, standpoint aspires for 'strong objectivity' as opposed to the 'weak objectivity' of traditional science (Harding 1986, 1987, 1990, 1998). As argued by Roy Bhaskar (1989) and Andrew Sayer (2000), critical realism is evidently compatible with standpoint epistemology (Kjosavik 2005a). Both are emancipatory political projects committed to science in the quest for objective truth – truth being 'adequacy of explanation' for critical realism and 'strong objectivity' for standpoint theorists. Both reject judgemental relativism, thereby retaining the normative element of science. It is this normative element that legitimises the emancipatory project of critical realist ontology and standpoint epistemology. I shall now attempt to delineate elements of indigenist standpoint epistemology.

Towards an indigenist standpoint

I draw on the notion of intersectionality to develop a situated standpoint of the indigenous peoples, which I shall call indigenist standpoint epistemology. I have also drawn on the empirical insights from my study on indigenous peoples' development issues in Kerala (southern India) to delineate some of the key elements of this standpoint. Much research on *adivasis* tends to be either descriptive ethnographic studies limited to specific communities or localities without making external connections, or extensive surveys largely of a positivist/empiricist kind (see Elwin 1964; Sinha 1982; Chattopadhyay 1972; Roy Burman 1975; Singh 1982; Kunhaman 1982; Sivanandan 1989; Shah 1992). In such studies, the underdevelopment of the *adivasis* seems to emerge as a 'natural' condition of existence divorced from history and the larger political economy (Kjosavik 2005a). Saha (1986: 291), however, posits the *adivasi* development issue in terms of the 'unequal integration of these tribes into the broader society'.

I argue that the indigenous peoples are situated in a social location at the intersection of class and indigeneity, and this social location largely precipitates the current development dilemmas faced by these peoples. In the case of indigenous peoples, following the intersectionality concept of Collins (1998), class and indigeneity can be seen as phenomena that mutually construct one another. Intersectionality thus provides an interpretive framework for thinking through how intersections of class and indigeneity shape the experiences of indigenous peoples across social and geographical contexts. It is to be emphasised that the communities that exist at this intersection are not theoretical categories, but historically constructed through material-social processes. The object of study, from an indigenist standpoint, will be the intersection of the class-indigeneity oppression rather than a separate assessment of either class exploitation or ethnic subordination.

Indigenous peoples' material existence at the class-indigeneity intersection is characterised by a double alienation; alienation from their own past means of production (land, forests and other natural resources) and constant alienation from the product of their labour consequent to their present engagement in the market relations of production and consumption. This is coupled with systematic discrimination and constant disadvantage in the labour market following adverse incorporation into the political economy of the nation state. Thus, indigenous peoples' material-social experiences at the class-indigeneity intersection, and their becoming conscious of the mutual construction of class and indigeneity in their everyday engagement in production, provides potential for a more complete understanding of the structured nature of social relations that exist in the world. As phrased by Haraway (1991: 191): 'The standpoints of the subjugated are not 'innocent' positions. On the contrary, they are preferred because in principle they are least likely to allow denial of the critical and interpretative core of all knowledge'. Indigenist standpoint is an explicitly political standpoint in that it aims to engage in knowledge production and struggles to eliminate all forms of domination.

It is possible to understand class-indigeneity intersectionality by analysing class relations based on the historical and concrete lived experience of those whom social scientists call indigenous peoples, to question how their class experiences have been shaped by their indigeneity and how indigeneity in turn has been shaped by their class experiences. Following Marx (1963: 124) and Collins (1998), one can also assess whether indigenous peoples 'live under economic conditions of existence that separate their mode of life, their interests and their culture from those of other classes', and whether indigenous peoples continue to bear the intergenerational costs of adverse incorporation into the dominant political economies and the associated ideology and practice of ethnocentrism.[1] Thus, I would posit that the group positionality of indigenous peoples is determined less by the theoretical categories that are constructed within distinct discourses of class and indigeneity, and more by the actual lived experience of the indigenous people at the intersection of class and indigeneity. For instance, the representations of *adivasis* by colonial administrators and anthropologists invoke them as 'primitive' communities without contact with the outside world, living in isolation (see Hamilton 1820; Dalton 1872; Bradley-Birt 1905; Lacey 1931). Postcolonial representations of *adivasis* followed along the same primitivist lines, though often with a change in the terminology to 'Scheduled Tribe' and with a more integrationist ideology (see Bailey 1960; Chattopadhyay 1972; Dube 1972; Mathur 1972; Prasad 1980; Roy Burman 1982; Vidyarthi 1982). On the other hand, Béteille (1974) laboured hard to understand if *adivasis* belong to the peasant class, while Ambasta (1998) argued for their proletarian class position. Kjosavik and Shanmugaratnam (2004) point out that *adivasis* were conceptualised as frozen (proletarian) class in the Kerala model of development.

Economic outcomes are indeed fundamental to conceptualising economic class relations of indigenous people. A more realistic analysis of class formation would, however, involve an intersectional analysis that is also sensitive to institutionalised ethnocentrism, slavery and bonded labour as mode of production, alienation of indigenous people from their past means of production, and other factors shaping the social location of indigenous peoples as a group.

In Marxist tradition, class analysis is heavily influenced by its origins in the racially and ethnically homogeneous European societies, as well as the construction of class categories based on an individual's relation to capital and labour. Race, ethnicity, caste and other such factors were largely outside the ambit of such a conceptualisation of class. In the Indian context, ethnicity and caste have been historically intertwined in complex ways to produce and reproduce economic inequalities. The institutional mechanisms of organising and reproducing unjust power relations of class, ethnicity and caste have been similar: separation and exclusion of both geographical and socio-economic space. If the focus of class analysis is groups with identifiable histories, then it could be seen that indigenous peoples participate in class relations in particular ways, meaning that class analysis can be 'more finely crafted into intersectional categories' (Collins 1998: 215) such as class-indigeneity intersectionality or class-caste intersectionality. Thus actual group histories become pertinent to class analysis.

In Marxist social theory, class describes or represents a relation among social groups with unequal power; classes are set in oppositional relationships such that one group's privilege is dependent on another group's disadvantage, one class or group exploits the other, or benefits from the other's disadvantage, or excludes the other from equitable social and economic rewards. These groups are largely defined by their location within historically specific power relations, not from choices made by individual group members as regards identity or belonging (Collins 1998). Historically, in the Indian context, the notion of 'Indigeneity' (being *adivasi*) or 'Tribal-ness' and 'Low caste' were formed in an allegedly inferior way of constructing groups in relation to 'dominant' ethnic groups and 'upper' castes (Kjosavik 2005a).[2] The group relationships within class-indigeneity intersectionality persist at an intergenerational level, though patterns of this intersectionality may be distinctive in any given era or historical time frame. However, the basic relations of opposition among groups that are constructed within these intersections and linked by them remain constant through history (Collins 1998).

Therefore, following Collins (1998), it can be argued, as long as the basic relations of intergenerational disadvantage and privilege in which indigenous peoples and the ethnically dominant groups 'find themselves' persists, it is a class relation. It would be fruitful to explore how indigenous people participate in class-indigeneity intersectionality at any given time in the Indian context, especially in oppositional relations with other groups. Such an approach would have a dual emphasis on fixity and change (Collins 1998). The fixed nature of class-indigeneity intersectionality is highlighted by the intergenerational nature of family inequality when the children of indigenous people and dominant groups largely replicate the economic status of their parents including their relation to the means of production. On the other hand, class-indigeneity formations also change, particularly in the context of the politics of inclusion and integration through affirmative action and other means (Kjosavik and Shanmugaratnam 2004). Opportunities for struggles are thus continuously being remade. The Kerala model of development initiated by the Left political movement and institutionalized by the Left government, the radical left movement of the 1960s (Naxal movement), the Land Alienation Act 1975, and the decentralised planning initiated in Kerala in the mid-1990s provide instances of such remaking of opportunities for struggle (see Kjosavik 2005a, 2006, 2010a, 2010b; Kjosavik and Shanmugaratnam 2004, 2006, 2007). In this way, historicising class-indigeneity relations as specific power relations helps understand how class-indigeneity relations change over time. It also highlights the role of human agency in bringing about such changes.

To understand group formation based on class-indigeneity intersectionality, it is important to recognise '... the centrality of group culture and consciousness in developing self-defined group standpoints' (Collins 1998: 217). Shared disadvantage and shared interests by themselves are not sufficient conditions for such group formation, but as Marx (1963: 124) pointed out a long time ago, 'economic conditions of existence that *separate* their mode of life, their interests and their culture from those of the other classes' remain important (emphasis added). It requires development and proclamation of group consciousness, and the groups must recognise the oppositional relations with other groups in the system of power relations. The economic conditions of existence of indigenous peoples in India definitely *separate* their mode of life from the dominant groups, and they have historically recognised themselves as a group with shared group interests constructed in opposition to the dominant ethnic groups in India. The consistent struggles of indigenous peoples through the colonial period and continuing struggles in the post-colonial period bear testimony to this oppositional consciousness. The standpoint that arises at the intersection of class and indigeneity through this consciousness and struggles is the epistemologically privileged indigenist standpoint.

Class-indigeneity intersection: experiences of the *adivasis* of Kerala

An understanding of the double alienation experienced by *adivasis* could be obtained by an analysis of the historical processes that shaped class-indigeneity intersection in a specific geographical region in Kerala. The location of the *adivasis* of Kerala in the class-indigeneity intersection cannot, however, be problematised without taking account of the pre-colonial relations of exploitation, and the colonial mode of production under British rule, which linked the colony to the metropolis through capitalist relations controlled by the metropolis. The generation of surplus and its transfer from India to Britain was achieved through the reinforcement and strengthening of the pre-colonial relations of exploitation within Indian feudalism under the colonial regime (Kosambi 1956; Banaji 1972; Habib 1974; Alavi 1980; Saha 1986). Saha (1986) uses the term sub-colonial mode of production to conceptualise the mode of production in 'tribal' areas; the reinforced relations of exploitation in the colonial mode of production in the pan-Indian social formation was passed on to the *adivasi* areas. Therefore, in the sub-colonial mode of production, the *adivasis* were subject to double colonialism; they were forced to produce surplus for the feudal landlords and for the British capitalists.

An analysis of the historical processes that shaped the intersectional experiences of *adivasis* in the Wayanad region of Kerala is presented in the following section. The Wayanad region was subject to pre-colonial relations of exploitation and sub-colonial mode of production. There are six different *adivasi* communities in Wayanad: *Kurumar*, *Kurichiyar*, *Paniyar*, *Adiyar*, *Kattunaicker* and *Urali*. These communities had historically different relations with land and forests. *Kurumar* and *Kurichiyar* were traditionally agriculturists, *Paniyar* and *Adiyar* were agrestic slaves and bonded labourers of feudal landlords, *Kattunaicker* were hunters and gatherers and *Uralis* were artisans. *Paniyar* constitute the largest *adivasi* community in Wayanad (comprising 45 per cent of the *adivasi* population), followed by *Kurumar* (20 per cent), *Kurichiyar* (17 per cent) and *Kattunaicker* (11 per cent).[3] *Adiyar* and *Uralis* constitute the remaining 7 per cent. Currently, the majority of *adivasis* are engaged in casual agricultural wage work, mostly on private farms and government and private plantations, while a small number work as permanent workers in plantations owned by the government. A small percentage of *adivasis* are cultivators on tiny holdings. Some *adivasis* migrate seasonally for agricultural wage work to the border regions of the neighbouring State of Karnataka.

The makings of the Wayanad resource frontier and the dispossession of the adivasis

'A frontier is an edge of space and time', and in a resource frontier landscape elements are wrested 'from previous livelihoods and ecologies to turn them into wild resources, available for the industries of the world' (Tsing 2003: 5100). In Wayanad, the colonial period (1805–1947) was marked by the disenfranchisement of the *adivasis*. The protracted imperial discourse on land rights in the nineteenth century resulted in the final allocation of ownership rights to land, forests and the resources thereof to three power groups – the colonial state, the *janmis* (landlords) and the *devaswoms* (temples).[4] The livelihoods, the ecologies and the geographies of the *adivasis* were usurped as a starting point for making this resource frontier. The material processes of frontier making had already begun, and had run parallel to the property rights discourse, setting precedents through practices, 'inventing' traditions and thereby predetermining the outcome. The frontier-making process was marked by the co-option of the ecologies, geographies and labour processes into the dynamics of the world market. This was achieved by a series of simultaneous processes starting with logging and export of timber to feed the British shipping industry, for military purposes, and for laying down and running the imperial railway network.

In 1824 the forestlands of Madras Province were opened up for coffee cultivation (Ravi Raman 1997). In Wayanad, massive deforestation occurred following the establishment of the first coffee plantation in 1840. Large areas were later opened up for tea and cinchona plantations. The potential of the Wayanad forests as a source of valuable timber had been reported by several European travellers such as Hove and Lord Valentia, in the late eighteenth and early nineteenth centuries (Kunhikrishnan 1987). However, by the late 1850s the best timber had been cut away from the lower slopes of Wayanad and felling was in progress on the higher slopes (Cleghorn 1861). It is thus evident that considerable deforestation had already occurred within half a century of the British occupation of Wayanad.

The 'salvage frontier'[5] project began with the establishment of a Forest Conservancy for the scientific management of forests. Dr Cleghorn, who was appointed the Conservator of Forests of the Madras Presidency on 19 December 1856, suggested the introduction of an efficient protection scheme and general forest management prescriptions for sustained supply of valuable timber to meet the imperial requirements (Stebbing 1922). The villains were identified – shifting cultivators and timber merchants. 'With reference to that urgent need, the protection of the forests from the improvident acts of the people and the destructive ones of the timber merchant', Cleghorn 'made strong and wise suggestions to counter and put a stop to these evils' of shifting (*kumri*) cultivation and indiscriminate and uncontrolled cutting of trees by the merchants as well as the colonial officials (Stebbing 1922: 302). But in fact it was the British attitude towards forests and the policies the British had followed since the conquest of Wayanad that had resulted in the large-scale deforestation.

The next step in salvaging the frontier came with the Indian Forest Act 1878, the purpose of which was to extend state control over the remaining forests, thereby protecting the forests from the forest-dependent population and 'saving' it exclusively for the extraction of revenue by the colonial government. The Forest Act marked the culmination of a colonial discourse on rights to forests. Baden-Powell, based on a highly selective and legalistic reading of Indian history, proposed total state control over all forests (Guha 1996). He argued that as the 'Oriental Sovereigns' had the right to dispose of forests and wastelands as they pleased, the same rights could be claimed by the British successor (Baden-Powell 1875, cited in Guha 1996). This position was widely acceptable to the forest officers of the time, as they perceived this as the only option to save forests from 'individual self-interest and short-sightedness' (Guha 1996: 93). On the other hand, the Madras government rejected state intervention, arguing that tribals and peasants should be allowed to control the forestland. One member of the Madras Board of Revenue went so far as to say that the state had no right over uncultivated lands that were invariably 'village property, not village privilege' (Guha 1996: 94). Both these extreme views were, however, rejected by Brandis (1875, cited in Guha 1996), who advocated a restricted takeover of forests by the state. He based his arguments on the grounds of justice, of respecting customary rights of villagers, and of efficiency. He urged the administration to demarcate as state forests only large and compact areas of valuable forests free of rights of other persons, and to leave the smaller areas located near the villages under the control of village communities (Brandis 1869, cited in Guha 1996). His intention was to create three broad classes of forest property in line with the European experience – state forests, village and other community forests and private forests.

At the end of the discourse, however, it was the colonial hegemonic interest of controlling people, and revenue extraction that prevailed over the rights of indigenous people and village communities; the Indian Forest Act 1878 was largely based on the ideas put forward by Baden-Powell. The result was the statisation of large tracts of forestlands. The colonial discourses on land rights in Wayanad resulted in the designation of large tracts of forestlands as the *janmam* or private property of the landlords, thus delegitimising the *adivasi* rights to forests and even wastelands. Baden-Powell (1972) raised serious criticism of the Madras government for not asserting state claims on forests and wastelands consequent to what he saw as the wrong upholding of the *janmam* claims. Following the Indian Forest Act of 1878, however, large tracts of forests in Wayanad were brought under state control either by purchase or lease (for a period of 99 years) of *janmam* forests, in addition to the escheat forests that were already under state control.[6] The twin processes of privatisation and statisation effectively dispossessed the indigenous peoples of Wayanad and precluded them from asserting any claims to their ancestral forestlands. State forests were classified as reserve forests and protected forests. While reserve forests were used exclusively for the extraction of timber, the protected forests were leased out or sold to British planters to establish plantations after deforesting the area. At the same time, the indigenous peoples' access to state forests was severely curtailed, whether it was for grazing or collection of fuelwood, fodder, food materials or minor forest produce. The outcome was a total alienation of *adivasis* from their forest based means of production.

The late frontier processes and the production of an adivasi proletariat

The enactment of the late frontier began in the 1930s, with the rush of rich planters from southern Kerala who were looking for opportunities to invest in commercial plantations (see Tharakan 1976). The wild, unruly rainforests continued to be transformed into well-disciplined, well-pruned and well-trained expanses of tea and coffee that directly linked the frontier to the metropolis. The 'civilising the savage' project, largely unsuccessful in the early frontier processes, gathered momentum. The 'wild' forest people got trained and disciplined together with the rows and columns of coffee and tea. Even the 'wildest' of them, the *Kattunaicker*, who were nomadic hunters and gatherers, eventually changed their rhythms to the ringing bells of the plantations.[7] Thus, the making of the resource frontier was simultaneously a proletarianising process for surplus exploitation. By the time the late settlers, largely peasants and landless labourers from the midlands and coastal areas of Kerala, began to arrive after independence in 1947 with the active encouragement of the state, the taming of the *adivasi* labour had progressed. Expanses of wilderness, however, remained in the form of reserve forests, revenue forests and revenue lands, and private forests, yet to be conquered and tamed, which the new settlers set out to do. The frontier went wilder than ever with the land rush; it teamed with speculators, the timber mafia, middlemen of all shades, traders, moneylenders and entrepreneurs. The resource became 'fugitive': you captured the resource and claimed rights on it; might was right. It was captured in a variety of ways, and the result was the alienation of the remaining lands controlled by the *adivasis*.[8]

Stories of the heroic deeds of the 'enterprising, hardworking peasants taming the rugged nature, fighting wild animals and struggling with the hostile earth to reap golden harvests' spread far and wide in Kerala, carried through the newspapers, radio, magazines and other publications, as well as via migrants who went back to visit their home villages, and the occasional visitor who went to see the settler *in situ*. As a young girl growing up in a midland Kerala village from which several families had migrated to Wayanad, I had listened to the stories about the out-migrant families and the *nallakaalam* (good times) they were having in Malabar they told my parents and grandparents, during their occasional visits to the home village. The *adivasis* were largely absent from these accounts. The narratives presented the frontier as empty spaces devoid of pre-existing lives and livelihoods, with abundant resources waiting to be captured.[9] They invoked images of a *terra nullius* extending to the horizons. The stories inspired a spirit of adventure and nurtured the land-dreams of the midland Kerala peasant, which prompted continued exodus. The later winds that came down the hills also carried stories of ruthlessness and violence in the scramble for resources; the civilised were going savage.

As the frontier making processes intensified in Wayanad, the wresting of previous livelihoods became complete. The *adivasis* were 'liberated' from resources and released into the labour market to compete with the newly arrived labour from the midlands. An almost total alienation of the *adivasis* from land, their major means of production occurred. In the newly constituted labour market they were marginalised and intensely exploited as they did not possess the skills demanded by the frontier resource-making processes. Thus, their status as proletarians is different from the classical Marxian proletariat that is able to compete in an open labour market, and hence doubly exploited in the sub-colonial relations of exploitation that persisted even after independence. The double alienation of the *adivasis* – alienation from the means of production and alienation from the product of their labour – became complete. By virtue of not being the classical proletariat, *adivasis* were subject to 'double exploitation' or 'twin exploitation' of their surplus labour – the first exploitation arising from the very participation in the labour market and the second by being the marginalised labour. The class-indigeneity intersection is thus characterised by twin exploitation and double alienation.

Lands and landscapes kept changing as farming systems were transformed. Cropping patterns and practices that maximised profits in the short run were adopted by planters and rich peasants, while poor peasants selected crops and practices that enabled 'survival today'; soil mining, run-off and pollution by agro-chemicals followed, even before the frontier making was completed. While the state actively encouraged the frontier-making process, it simultaneously engaged in a salvage frontier project as well. The post-independence state passed The Madras Preservation of Private Forest Act in 1949, in an attempt to regulate the frontier-making process. According to this Act, the owners were not allowed to convert contiguous forestlands of more than 100 acres to any other land use (Vasudevan and Sujatha 2001). This Act also included wastelands and communal lands. Thus, in the salvage frontier project, whatever was left of the *adivasi* livelihoods was once again wrested from them. The reserve forests continued to be exploited by the state and encroached upon by the settlers, while it was protected from the indigenous communities. The revenue forests were either leased out to settlers or encroached upon for cultivation. Large extents of revenue forestlands were leased out to private firms and public sector companies to raise industrial woodlots. In 1971, the state took over the private forests to protect the forest ecosystem and to redistribute the degraded lands to landless people. Intensive conservation activities were undertaken as well, with the establishment of the Wayanad Wildlife Sanctuary. Thus in the Wayanad frontier, the resource-making, resource-destruction and resource-conservation processes were going on simultaneously.

The illegal–legal continuum and the legal alienation of adivasi lands

A frontier, by definition is wild and lawless, or at best characterised by fuzzy boundaries between what is legal and illegal. The illegal–legal distinction was largely redundant as regards the Wayanad frontier: here these were not dichotomous categories but a continuum. However, from the perspective of the immediate frontier makers (the in migrants or the settlers and other active agents), it would seem that 'illegal' was a non-existent category. For them the encroachments on *adivasi* lands (lands controlled and cultivated by *adivasis*), state property (revenue forests, revenue lands, reserve forests), private property (agricultural lands and forests owned by landlords), or *dewaswom* lands (owned by temples) were merely pre-legal phenomena. It would seem that they operated with the conscious assumption that what was pre-legal 'today' would become legal 'tomorrow'. When I asked an elderly settler in Wayanad whether he was worried about getting evicted by legal procedures from the private forestland he had encroached on in the 1950s, he answered:

> We were not worried about eviction. There were a large number of families encroaching on various kinds of lands in Wayanad. We knew that it was impossible for the government to evict us, as it would lead to political turmoil. We were sure that it was simply a matter of time before we obtained legal rights to our soils, on which we had shed much sweat.
>
> (Elderly settler)

This passionate statement is reminiscent of Locke's labour-mixing thesis on property rights. Locke (1924) argued that it was labour that put value on land, and therefore the one who mixed his or her labour with a piece of land had the right to claim private property rights over it. Locke posits his theory in the context of a State of Nature and as applicable to first appropriations from Nature. In the case of the Wayanad frontier, however, unlike the Lockean premises, much of the lands on which labour-mixing arguments were invoked by settlers to claim property rights, were already mixed with previous labour, that of the *adivasi* communities, in the form of shifting cultivation, settled agriculture, animal herding, hunting and gathering, collection of fuelwood, fodder, medicinal herbs and other minor forest produce. Marx (1970) makes a distinction between the labour involved in hunting and gathering, and that involved in agriculture. The labour process involves humans and nature, resulting in an interchange between the two. This relationship, however, varies with the nature of the production process. In the agricultural production process, land is not taken as given, but is itself produced by labour. It would seem that property rights claims that invoke the Lockean labour-mixing argument privilege the latter form of labour to the peril of the hunting and gathering communities, as experienced round the globe.

In Wayanad, the discourses on property rights claims in the post-independence period, were played out among the planters, the settlers, the landlords and the state, and did not engage with the previously 'mixed' labour or 'first appropriation' claims of the indigenous people. It was the organised power derived from the political and economic clout of the planters and settlers that was largely responsible for elevating the status of their land from pre-legal (illegal) to legal. Though these encroachments were illegal, the government of Kerala chose to use the term 'regularisation' in the state procedures for granting titles, thus pre-empting or neutralising any illegal connotations either to the act of encroachment or the process of legalisation.

Towards an emancipatory conceptualization of indigeneity

The indigenist standpoint at the intersection of class and indigeneity would allow us to develop a more emancipatory conceptualization of indigeneity. I have argued elsewhere (Kjosavik 2005b) that the concept wars over 'indigeneity' revolve around three properties attributed to indigeneity by scholars, activists and policy makers: (1) essentialist property – an essentialist notion that constructs indigeneity as consisting of certain essential unchanging cultural contents transmitted from generation to generation; (2) descriptive property – a concept that posits indigeneity as being embodied, through descent from original inhabitants or of those that inhabited the territory at the time of conquest or in-migration; and (3) normative property – suggesting that the subjugation and marginalisation of these communities ought not to have occurred, and its effects ought not to have precipitated their intergenerational subjugation and marginalisation by the now dominant social groups.

In my view it is the third property that holds the key to substantive politicisation and, when combined with the second property, it is capable of politically articulating indigeneity from a materialist perspective, if we bring in the concept of exploitation from the Marxian class theory. I shall now state four elements that are to be considered in a materialist theorisation of indigeneity, which captures the double alienation at the class-indigeneity intersection, experienced by the indigenous people.

1   The people we refer to as indigenous are constituted by the descendants of either the original inhabitants or of those who occupied the land at the time of conquest and new settlement, and at times descendants of other conquered people that moved into the area. They are thus historical communities and are not constructed or imagined communities.

2   These people have been dispossessed of their means of production – land, forests and other resources, and subordinated to the dominant groups and this situation is intergenerationally reproduced and continuing.

3   The resources alienated from them are now largely subserving global and local capitalist interests.

4   These people are now largely integrated into the capitalist relations of production as suppliers of labour power. The surplus value they produce are appropriated by the global capital and its local intermediaries. That is, their labour is exploited within the existing production relations, characterised by relations of exploitation that permeate the continuing sub-colonial mode of production at the local level.

Such a conceptualisation of indigeneity has the potential for the development of a revolutionary consciousness, which would facilitate the forging of class alliances with other working class movements. Class politics has now largely given way to identity politics in the form of New Social Movements, which may be termed cross-class movements. We are currently in a rapidly globalising neoliberal world where workers are increasingly being exploited and thrown out of the labour market, and indigenous peoples the world over are increasingly alienated from their remaining resources. The double-exploitation of their labour is more intense and simultaneously they are being thrown out of the labour market even before they enter. The struggle then would be for a fair share of the global means of production, a fair participation in the realm of production, and a fair share of the surplus produced. The key question then emerges: is political mobilisation based on identity politics capable of addressing this situation? I would argue that alliances based on class politics are all the more relevant at this juncture. A materialist conception of indigeneity would facilitate an alliance of working class movements and indigenous people's movements in their struggles. An indigenist standpoint epistemology could be the starting point for knowledge production in this direction.

Notes

1   The term adverse incorporation is used to mean incorporation from a position of disadvantage.
2   See Saha (1986) for a historical account of the formation of lower castes and *adivasis*.
3   Records of the District Planning Office, Sulthan Bathery.
4   *Devaswoms* were controlled by the Chieftains (local rulers) or their upper caste representatives, who acted as de facto *janmis*.
5   This term is borrowed from Tsing (2003).
6   Escheat land was the land formerly owned by Pazhassi Rajah, who fought a protracted war against the British over control of Wayanad. After the Rajah's defeat the property owned by him was taken over by the British Government.
7   See Cooper (1992) for an account of the processes by which the British 'colonised' time.
8   This paragraph is based on discussions with the elders of the *Kurumar* community.
9   Academic accounts on internal migration in Kerala tend to represent the host regions as previously empty spaces, and largely ignore the fact that there were *adivasi* lives and livelihoods embedded in the frontier spaces.

References

Ambasta, A. (1998) *Capitalist Restructuring and Formation of Adivasi Proletarians: Agrarian Transition in Thane District (Western India) c. 1817–1990*, PhD Thesis, The Hague: Institute of Social Studies.

Baden-Powell, B.H. (1875) 'On the Defects of the Existing Forest Law (Act XIII of 1865) and Proposals for a New Forest Act', in B.H. Baden-Powell and J.S. Gamble (eds) *Report of the Proceedings of the Forest Conference, 1873–74*, Calcutta: Government Press.

—— (1972) *The Indian Village Community*, Delhi: Cosmo Publications.

Bailey, F.G. (1960) *Tribe, Caste and Nation: A Study of Political Activity and Political Change in Highland Orissa*, Manchester: University Press.

Béteille, A. (1974) *Six Essays in Comparative Sociology*, New Delhi: Oxford University Press.

Bhaskar, R. (1975) *A Realist Theory of Science*, Leeds: Leeds Books.

—— (1989) *Reclaiming Reality: A Critical Introduction to Contemporary Philosophy*, London: Verso.

Bradley-Birt, F.B. (1905) *The Story of an Indian Upland*, London: Smith, Elder and Co.

Brandis, D. (1869) 'Explanatory Memorandum on the Draft Forest Bill', dated 3 August 1869, in Forests, B Prog. Nos 37–47.

—— (1875) *Memorandum on the Forest Legislation Proposed for British India (Other Than the Presidencies of Madras and Bombay)*, Simla: Government Press.

Chattopadhyay, G. (1972) 'The Problem of Tribal Integration to Urban Industrial Society: A Theoretical Approach', in K.S. Singh (ed.) *Tribal Situation in India: Proceedings of a Seminar*, Simla: Indian Institute of Advanced Study, 486–93.

Cleghorn, H. (1861) *The Forests and Gardens of South India.* London: W.H. Allen & Co.

Collins, P.H. (1998) *Fighting Words: Black Women and the Search for Justice*, London: University of Minnesota Press.

Cooper, F. (1992) 'Colonizing Time: Work Rhythms and Labour Conflict in Colonial Mombasa', in N.B. Dirks (ed.) *Colonialism and Culture*, Ann Arbor: The University of Michigan Press, 209–45.

Dalton, E.T. (1872) *Descriptive Ethnology of Bengal*, Calcutta: Government Press.

Dube, S.C. (1972) 'Inaugural Address', in K.S. Singh (ed.) *Tribal Situation in India: Proceedings of a Seminar*, Simla: Indian Institute of Advanced Study, 28–33.

Elwin, V. (1964) *Tribal World of Verrier Elwin*, Oxford: Oxford University Press.

Guha, R. (1996) 'Dietrich Brandis and Indian Forestry: A Vision Revisited and Reaffirmed', in M. Poffenberger and B. McGean (eds) *Village Voices and Forest Choices: Joint Forest Management in India*, New Delhi: Oxford University Press, 86–100.

Habib, I. (1974) 'The Social Distribution of Landed Property in Pre-British India', in R.S. Sharma (ed.) *Indian Society: Historical Problems*, New Delhi: People's Publishing House.

Hamilton, W. (1820) *A Geographical, Statistical and Historical Description of Hindostan, Vol. I*, London: John Murray.

Haraway, D.J. (1991) *Simians, Cyborgs, and Women: The Reinvention of Nature*, London: Free Associations Books.

Harding, S. (1986) *The Science Question in Feminism*, New York: Cornell University Press.

—— (1987) 'Conclusion: Epistemological Questions', in S. Harding (ed.) *Feminism and Methodology: Social Science Issues*, Indianapolis: Indiana University Press, 181–190.

—— (1990) 'Starting Thought From Women's Lives: Eight Resources for Maximizing Objectivity', *Journal of Social Philosophy*, 21(2–3): 140–9.

—— (1991) *Whose Science? Whose Knowledge? Thinking from Women's Lives*, New York: Cornell University Press.

—— (1998) *Is Science Multicultural? Postcolonialisms, Feminisms, and Epistemologies*, Indianapolis: Indiana University Press.

Hartsock, N.C.M. (1983) *Money, Sex, and Power: Toward a Feminist Historical Materialism*, London: Longman.

—— (1997) 'Standpoint Theories for the Next Century', in S.J. Kenney and H. Kinsella (eds) *Politics and Feminist Theories*, London: The Haworth Press, 93–101.

—— (2003) 'The Feminist Standpoint: Developing the Ground for a Specifically Feminist Historical Materialism', in S. Harding and M.B. Hintikka (eds) *Discovering Reality: Feminist Perspectives on Epistemology, Metaphysics, Methodology, and Philosophy of Science*, London: Kluwer Academic Publishers, 283–310.

Kjosavik, D.J. (2005a) *In the Intersection of Class and Indigeneity: The Political Economy of Indigenous People's Development in Kerala, South India*, PhD Thesis, Norwegian University of Life Sciences, Aas, Norway.

—— (2005b) 'Theoretical Constructions and Politicisation of Class and Indigeneity', Disputas Lecture, 3 December, Norwegian University of Life Sciences: Aas, Norway.

—— (2006) 'Articulating Identities in the Struggle for Land: The Case of the Indigenous People (*Adivasis*) of Highland Kerala, South India', Paper presented at the International Symposium 'At the frontier of land issues: Social embeddedness of rights and public policy', 17–19 May, Montpellier, France.

—— (2010a) 'L'articulation des identités dans les conflits fonciers: le cas des Adivasis des hautes terres du Kerala, Inde du Sud', in P-Y. Lemeur and J. Jean-Pierre (eds) *Politique de la terre et de l'appartenance. Droits fonciers et citoyenneté locale dans les sociétés du Sud*, Paris: Karthala.

—— (2010b) 'Politicising Development: Re-Imagining Indigenous People's Land Rights and Identities in Highland Kerala, South India', *Forum for Development Studies*, 32(2): 243–68.

Kjosavik, D.J. and Shanmugaratnam, N. (2004) 'Integration or Exclusion? Locating Indigenous Peoples in the Development Process of Kerala, South India', *Forum for Development Studies*, 31(2): 232–73.

—— (2006) 'Between Decentralized Planning and Neoliberalism: Challenges for the Survival of Indigenous Peoples of Kerala, South India', *Social Policy and Administration*, 40(6): 632–51.

—— (2007) 'Property Rights Dynamics and Indigenous Communities in Highland Kerala, South India: An Institutional-Historical Perspective', *Modern Asian Studies*, 41(6): 1183–260.

Kosambi, D.D. (1956) *An Introduction to the Study of Indian History*, Bombay: Popular Prakashan.

Kuhn, T. (1970) *The Structure of Scientific Revolutions*, Chicago: University of Chicago Press.

Kunhaman, M. (1982) *The Tribal Economy of Kerala: An Intra-Regional Analysis*, M. Phil. Dissertation, Centre for Development Studies, Trivandrum.

Kunhikrishnan, K.V. (1987) *The British Indian Forestry: Malabar Experience*, M.Phil. Dissertation, University of Calicut, Calicut.

Lacey, W.G. (1931) *Census of India, 1931*, Vol. VIII, *Bihar and Orissa Part I, Report*, Patna: Superintendent of Government Printing.

Locke, J. (1924) *Two Treatises of Government*. London: J.M. Dent and Sons Ltd.

Lukács, G. (1971) *History and Class Consciousness: Studies in Marxist Dialectics*, London: Merlin Press.

Marx, K. (1963) *The Eighteenth Brumaire of Louis Bonaparte*, New York: International.

—— (1970) *Capital Vol. 1*, Moscow: Progress Publishers.

—— (1976) *Capital: A Critique of Political Economy*, Vol. 1, London: Penguin.

Marx, K. and Engels, F. (1975a) *Collected Works*, Vol. 1, London: Lawrence and Wishart.

Marx, K. and Engels, F. (1975b) *Collected Works*, Vol. 3, London: Lawrence and Wishart.

Marx, K. and Engels, F. (1975c) *Collected Works*, Vol. 4, London: Lawrence and Wishart.

Mathur, K.S. (1972) 'Tribe in India: A Problem of Identification and Integration', in K.S. Singh (ed.) *Tribal Situation in India: Proceedings of a Seminar*, Simla: Indian Institute of Advanced Study, 457–61.

Mills, C.W. (1988) 'Alternative Epistemologies', *Social Theory and Practice*, 14(3): 237–63.

Prasad, M. (1980) 'Impact of Urbanisation on a Tribal Village: A Case Study of Tusmu in Chotanagpur', in B. Singh and J.S. Bhandari (eds) *The Tribal World and its Transformation*, New Delhi: Concept, 83–97.

Ravi Raman, K. (1997) 'Intervention in the Western Ghats: An Inquiry into the Historical Processes of Loss of Biodiversity and Community Sources of Livelihood', in P. Pushpangadan, K. Ravi and V. Santhosh (eds) *Conservation and Economic Valuation of Biodiversity*, New Delhi: Oxford University Press.

Roy Burman, B.K. (1975) *Historical Ecology of Land Survey and Settlement in Tribal Areas and Challenge of Development*, New Delhi: Council for Social Development.

—— (1982) 'Transfer and Alienation of Tribal Land', in B. Chaudhuri (ed.) *Tribal Development in India: Problems and Prospects*, Delhi: Inter-India Publications.

Saha, S.K. (1986) 'Historical Premises of India's Tribal Problem', *Journal of Contemporary Asia*, 16(3): 274–319.

Sayer, A. (2000) *Realism and Social Science*, London: Sage.

Shah, G. (1992) 'Tribal Issues: Problems and Perspectives', in B. Chaudhuri (ed.) *Tribal Transformation in India, Volume II: Socio-Economic and Ecological Development*, New Delhi: Inter-India Publications.

Singh, K.S. (1982) *Economies of the Tribes and Their Transformation*, New Delhi: Concept Publishing.

Sinha, S. (1982) 'Re-thinking about Tribes and Indian Civilization', in B. Chaudhury (ed.) *Tribal Development in India: Problems and Prospects*, Delhi: Inter-India Publications, 3–13.

Sivanandan, P. (1989) *Caste and Economic Opportunity – A Study of the Effect of Educational Development and Land Reforms on the Employment and Income Earning Opportunities of the Scheduled Castes and Scheduled Tribes in Kerala*, PhD Thesis, Centre for Development Studies, Trivandrum.

Smith, D.E. (1987) *The Everyday World as Problematic: A Feminist Sociology*, Boston: Northeastern University Press.

Stebbing, E.P. (1922) *The Forests of India Vol. I. The Progress of Conservancy and the Development of Research in Forestry*, London: John Lane – The Bodley Head Limited.

Tharakan, P.K.M. (1976) 'Migration of Farmers from Travancore to Malabar From 1930 to 1960: An Analysis of its Economic Causes', M. Phil. Dissertation, Centre for Development Studies, Trivandrum.

Tsing, A.L. (2003) 'Natural Resources and Capitalist Frontiers', *Economic and Political Weekly*, Vol. XXXVIII (48): 5100–6.

Vasudevan, C.V. and Sujatha, V. (2001) *Forest Laws of Kerala*, Cochin: Ganesh Publications.

Vidyarthi, L.P. (1982) 'Problems and Prospects of Tribal Development in India', in B. Chaudhury (ed.) *Tribal Development in India: Problems and Prospects*, Delhi: Inter-India Publications, 375–85.

Part IV

Politics, participation and recognition

Introduction to Part IV

Part IV explores how Adivasis contend with discourses of development as well as those tribe-oriented ideas of governance that can be simultaneously upheld and disavowed by the nation state. To those concerned with upholding the human rights and politico-cultural rights of 'subaltern citizens', the notion of community is of central importance. Discursive and social processes become important analytical fields, and could be explored in terms of 'identisation', identity-politics and recognition. These are terminologies that are familiar in development studies and political theories concerning minorities (Pieterse 2004; Fraser 2000; Appadurai 1996; Calhoun 1994). The ways in which Adivasis represent themselves as 'Indigenous', 'tribal', 'autochthonous', 'Adivasi', 'subnational' or 'regional' point to the inflections between transnational, national and more localised political contexts.

In a provocative article, Nancy Fraser states: 'Everything depends on how recognition is approached.' (2003: 23) In order to understand the ways in which identity-politics may disrupt existing discourses, analysts need to tackle the multiple uses and effects of the 'idioms of recognition' (Fraser 2003: 21–2). Shared, on the one hand, by activists pressing for identity-oriented resolutions to social conflicts and political injustices and, on the other, representatives of neo-liberal, national and regional interests, these idioms are viscerally mobile. They can extend into the divergent discourses of resistance, community empowerment, participation and development by virtue of a 'common grammar' (Fraser 2003: 23) that gains efficacy as it moves into disparate political contexts.

Carol Mueller's analysis (2003) of 'recognition struggles' becomes very relevant here. Taking forward Alberto Melucci's concept of 'identisation', a process through which the boundaries of identity/difference are set into political motion, the concept of identity comes to gain legibility through '... the contingent definitions of means, ends, and fields of action that exist in a state of tension arising from a system of social relationships as well as systems of meaning.' (Mueller 2003: 276) Social antagonisms and oppositions (see Laclau 2006) are thus able to mobilise diverse communities in ways that transgress a priori configurations of class and ethnicity. In many ways, this point is crucial to any analysis of

Adivasi mobilisations in post-independence India. These include those movements that are definably Adivasi or Indigenous, such as the early Jharkhand movement or sub-national assertions in North-eastern states, and those that reveal extensive Adivasi participation but aim towards ends that are not specifically geared towards Adivasis, such as Naxalism (Maoist revolution in India). Movements against Naxalite insurgencies, such as Salwa Judum in Chhatisgarh state, have also involved Adivasis (see Guha 2007).

The shifting ideological terrains of elitist institutions should not, however, become the basis for studies of recognition struggles, as Barbara Hobson (2003) has pointed out. This is because such institutional knowledge might not comprehend the nuanced political languages of the 'minority' representatives (Hobson 2003: 6). Rather, the ambivalent language of struggle requires analysis in complex counter-ideological spaces (Rycroft forthcoming). An example of this may be the deployment of the notion of Adivasi self-rule, or Indigenous self-determination, by Adivasi activists in the state of Jharkhand. On account of the chequered history of the Adivasi movement in Jharkhand since the 1950s (Panchbhai 1982), and the interpenetration of nationalist and regionalist ideologies (Corbridge 2003), this notion of self-determination becomes relevant both for subaltern actors aiming to sustain counter-hegemonic strategies of collective re-empowerment and for regional elites (Mitra 1992), who can harness its potential for their own identity-politics. The idea of an Adivasi political representation therefore requires careful unpacking, as the contributors in this section show.

Bengt G. Karlsson discusses the recent articulation, by Indigenous leaders in northeastern India, of the concept of 'traditional institutions'. As an anthropologist who carefully reads the political nuances of such Indigenous markers, Karlsson situates recent debates on ethno-nationalism and insurgency within the wider frameworks of Indigenous governance and democracy, such as the Review of the Workings of the Indian Constitution for the North-eastern Region. After the formation of the state of Meghalaya in 1972, and in view of the United Nations' Decade for Indigenous Peoples (from 1994), the traditional political institutions of the Khasi, Jaintia and Garo communities, Karlsson claims, have become a critical site of contest between traditional leaders and those advocating state power. This has resulted in competing systems of authority at local and regional levels. The issue extends to the Autonomous District Councils that were set up through the 6th Schedule of the Indian constitution, as a way to usher in a decentralised administration. The political apparatus of the post-independence state is called into question by the traditional leaders, who some critics consider to be anti-democratic. Karlsson thereby offers an understanding of multiple and fractured North-eastern indigenous subjectivities.

In David Mosse's research on the anthropology of development in western India, the notion of traditional power is less evident. Instead, Mosse discusses the economic and social relationships built up between Bhil Adivasis and development project partners. Using Bruno Latour's analytic of translation (1986), he traces how the hegemonic power of development technologies, economies and discourses is mediated and at times strategically legitimated by a diverse range of Bhil Adivasi villagers. The assessment comes in the wake of Mosse's close engagement with a British government-funded initiative to implement local power in India's 'tribal' regions. Mosse cites histories of Bhil responses to colonial exclusions and national integrations in order to address the question of Bhil agency. The article makes visible analytical possibilities that criss-cross the development and the historical terrains.

Amit Prakash focuses on the Jharkhand region, and more specifically the relevance of Jharkhandi regionalism to shifts in the 'politics of development'. Jharkhandi regionalism refers to demands for increased levels of Adivasi autonomy (and self-rule) in the southern districts of erstwhile Bihar and in some adjoining districts. It asserts an inclusive Adivasi heritage that is less concerned with particular 'tribal' difference and more with a pan-Indigenous mobilisation against internal colonialism (see Corbridge 2003). Located at the interface between Adivasi assertion and state power, 'the politics of development' is specific to Jharkhand and yet may also be read in other social contexts. It has emerged since independence through the tensions between, on the one hand, calls for centralised rule and pan-national development, as advocated by Jawaharlal Nehru and the Congress party, and, on the other, patterns of de-centralisation as envisaged by Adivasi participants in the parliamentary process. For Prakash, the 'politics of development' is an analytical approach that may facilitate a nuanced engagement with Adivasi responses to the perceived pitfalls of national ideologies.

References

Appadurai, A. (1996) *Modernity at Large: Cultural Dimensions of Globalization*, Minneapolis: University of Minnesota Press.

Calhoun, C. (1994) 'Social Theory and the Politics of Identity', in C. Calhoun (ed.) *Social Theory and the Politics of Identity*, Oxford: Blackwell Publishing, 9–36.

Corbridge, S. (2003) 'The Ideology of Tribal Economy and Society: Politics in the Jharkhand, 1950–1980', in R. . Munda and S. Bosu Mullick (eds) *The Jharkhand Movement: Indigenous Peoples' Struggle for Autonomy in India*, Copenhagen: International Work Group for Indigenous Affairs, 131–70.

Fraser, N. (2000) 'Rethinking Recognition', *New Left Review*, 3: 107–20.

—— (2003) 'Rethinking Recognition: Overcoming Displacement and Reification in Cultural Politics', in B. Hobson (ed.) *Recognition Struggles and Social Movements: Contested Identities, Agency and Power*, Cambridge: Cambridge University Press, 21–32.

Guha, R.C. (2007) 'Adivasis, Naxalites, and Indian Democracy', *Economic and Political Weekly*, 11 August, 3305–12.

Hobson, B. (2003) 'Introduction', in B. Hobson (ed.) *Recognition Struggles and Social Movements: Contested Identities, Agency and Power*, Cambridge: Cambridge University Press, 1–17.

Laclau, E. (2006) 'Ideology and Post-Marxism', *Journal of Political Ideologies*, 11(2): 103–14.

Latour, B. (1986) 'The Powers of Association', in J. Law (ed.) *Power, Action and Belief*, London: Routledge, 264–80.

Mitra, S.K. (1992) *Power, Protest and Participation: Local Elites and the Politics of Development in India*, London: Routledge.

Mueller, C. (2003) ' "Recognition Struggles" and Process Theories of Social Movements', in B. Hobson (ed.) *Recognition Struggles and Social Movements: Contested Identities, Agency and Power*, Cambridge: Cambridge University Press, 274–91.

Panchbhai, S.C. (1982) 'The Jharkhand Movement among the Santals', in K.S. Singh (ed.) *Tribal Movements in India: Volume 2*, New Delhi: Manohar, 31–52.

Pieterse, J.N. (2004) 'Ethnicities and Multiculturalisms: Politics of Boundaries', in S. May, T. Mahood and J. Squires (eds) *Ethnicity, Nationalism and Minority Rights*, Cambridge: Cambridge University Press, 27–49.

Rycroft, D.J. (forthcoming) 'Memories: Around Performance Ethnography in India', in S. Chaudhuri (ed.) *Memories and Moments in Fieldwork*, submitted to Sage Publications.

8 Sovereignty through indigenous governance

Reviving 'traditional political institutions' in Northeast India

Bengt G. Karlsson

Northeast India is a region of violent separatism and has, since Independence, been the scene of various armed struggles, the most well-known being the still ongoing Naga movement for sovereignty.[1] According to estimates, among *c*.200 ethnic groups in the region, there are as many as 60 active insurgency outfits fighting for autonomy. In the comparative Minorities at Risk project, Ted Robert Gurr and his colleagues refer to a larger 'Central Asian uplands' region – consisting of the Northeastern borderlands and the hill tracts of Bangladesh and Burma, and also Tibet and the Xinjiang province in China – which is said to have the '[T]he largest number of ongoing and prospective ethnic wars anywhere in the world.' (Gurr 2000: 286) Autonomy or self-determination, in one form or another, is indeed on the agenda of more or less all mobilised communities in Northeast India. Some organisations pursue a rather low-key type of cultural mobilisation, whereas others have taken to arms, to pursue their struggle for sovereignty. The overall logic is that of territorial nationalism, i.e. for each ethnic group or nation to have a land of its own. As the reality on the ground does not provide any ready-made ethnically homogenous territory, this logic spurs what appear to be unsolvable conflicts, not least those relating to boundaries, between communities. It can of course be argued that the present impasse of escalating inter-ethnic violence would require new collective imaginings or serious attempts to think beyond the idea of the territorial nation. There are voices that advocate the strengthening of a multi-ethnic, civic polity in Northeast India, but the entire political logic of the region nevertheless seems to push things towards further ethnicisation of communities (cf. Karlsson 2001, Baruah 2003).

I would like to take note of a recent trend in how autonomy demands are being voiced in the region. First, self-determination demands are increasingly being articulated in the global language of indigenous rights.[2] Second, the ethnic organisations struggling for sovereignty insist increasingly on the re-activating of so-called traditional political institutions, claimed to be a superior and more democratic alternative to the modern (Western) institutions that have been put in place after Independence. This turn towards what I would like to call 'indigenous governance' is an interesting development that draws attention to possible content of self-determination and thus not only focuses on the outer form (i.e. merely insisting on getting their respective ethnic homelands). In this chapter, I will discuss a recent attempt in Meghalaya to strengthen the role of traditional chiefs and their councils as governing bodies. This movement is a well-organised urban, elite initiative that increasingly is becoming a visible political force in the state. As the argument of the spokespersons goes, the 'traditional institutions' have always been there and they have proven over time to be effective (their very survival is cited as a proof of their efficiency). They have, however, been undermined by the new administrative set-up under the state government and the autonomous district councils. Because of the poor performance of the modern institutions of governance, it is high time to recognise and empower the traditional or customary ones. This, the leaders of the movement claim, would ensure genuine grassroots democracy and facilitate real development as well as bring an end to the political turmoil and the insurgency in the state.

Meghalaya is a small hill state situated between the Brahmaputra valley in the north and Bangladesh in the south. The population is roughly two million people and as about 85 per cent belong to so-called tribal or indigenous peoples – the main ones being Khasi, Jaintia and Garos – Meghalaya is commonly described as a 'tribal state'. During the past decade, there has been much debate in the state about the revival of traditional political institutions. Obviously, not all share the optimism of the leaders of the traditional institutions movement. The most commonly made critique relates to the absence of women as well as 'non-tribals' in the traditional decision-making bodies. Other commentators take the present hype about reviving traditional institutions as just another political gimmick, an ephemeral agenda soon to pass. Perhaps, but, as I will argue, several contemporary actualities might make this revival a more lasting and significant event. The well-crafted discourse of the movement seems to resonate with popular sensibilities in the state.

In this paper, I give a brief account of how the leaders of the movement make their case. I followed the leaders during an active phase of campaigning in late 2003, participating in meetings and workshops, and then conducting follow-up interviews and collecting written materials. The campaign ended with a grand assembly in Smit, a place of great symbolic significance for the Khasis, on 14 January 2004. About 40,000 people took part in the assembly, referred to as the Durbar Ri or 'People's Parliament', which thus turned out to be the show of strength the organisers had hoped for. The explicit purpose of the assembly was to get people's approval for a massive development scheme that the leaders had planned with the help of a consultancy group in Bombay, based on project proposals which had been submitted by village heads from all parts of the state.[3] This event was followed up by a second Durbar Ri in 2007. This time it was held in an equally significant place, the famous sacred forest of Mawphlang and the organisers created huge interest worldwide by bestowing a green award upon former US Vice-President Al Gore for his campaign against global climate change. Several national and international media picked up the story, with imaginative headlines like the one by the Associated Press, 'Tribal kings in remote Indian state give environmental award to Al Gore.'[4] The BBC journalist Subir Bhaumik reported that 'The award will be handed over at the second Dorbar Ri

(People's Parliament) on 6 October near a sacred forest at the village of Mawp-lang, which has been preserved untouched for more than 700 years.'[5] As one of the leaders and member of Indian parliament Robert Kharshiing explained, '[w]e are hoping that the association with Gore would bring global attention to the pre-dicament facing the people of this remote corner of earth.'[6] More than 200,000 people were reported to have participated.

Awakening of the grassroots

When I talk about the leaders of the traditional institutions (TI) movement, I refer in fact only to a handful of persons, of which the two most active were Laborious Manik S. Syiem, President of the Federation of Khasi States and also the Syiem (traditional chief or ruler) of Hima Mylliem (though presently under suspension, as will be discussed later), by profession a college lecturer, and John F. Kharshiing, spokesperson of the Federation and previous youth leader and social worker from a well-known Shillong family.[7] The latter is also the younger brother of Robert Kharshiing. Further, I refer to Purno A. Sangma, the most well-known political figure from Northeast India, earlier speaker of the Indian parliament and previously one of the top leaders of the Congress party. Sangma, who left the Congress party in 1999 as a protest against Sonia Gandhi's leader-ship, has become a vocal advocate for empowering the traditional institutions.[8] Sangma is also a member of the Indian parliament (he was re-elected in the 2004 Lok Sabha elections as one of the two MPs from Meghalaya). In his capacity as member-in-charge of the Commission to Review the Workings of the Indian Constitution for the Northeastern region, Sangma has a special importance here. The report of the commission has become an important document for the move-ment, as we will see.[9] The political analysts familiar with the names mentioned above would most likely note the personal motives for them to fish in these waters. One can always assume personal agenda in the pursuit of politics, but we are still left with the question of why leaders try to capitalise on certain issues – and not on others – at a particular moment in time. To understand this, one needs to consider the larger social and historical context in which these assertions are being made or through which certain modes of action are made possible and desirable. As a general sociological premise, one should be wary of reducing the significance and meaning of human actions to the intentions or interests of the actor. Actions, as the philosopher Hannah Arendt reminds us, always exceed the actor's intention (1998: 233). The role of traditional chiefs and their council has been a contentious issue since the independence of India, but it has gained an unforeseen actuality during the last decade. The significance of this is what inter-ests us here.

Laborious Manik S. Syiem gives the following account of how the TI move-ment has developed.[10] Things started to build up in 1993 with the United Nations' year for the world's Indigenous Peoples. This, as he puts it, became the 'eye-opener'. 'We realized the need to maintain the traditions in order to move ahead, hence our slogan, 'revival for survival'.' Dressed in turban and traditional clothes, along with a group of young boys, he went on a tour around the Khasi Hills with the message to revive the traditions. But the time was not ripe to push things then. It took until the year 2000 for the movement to take a more definite shape. After a series of consultations they arranged a meeting or durbar in his Hima (state) to discuss whether people still wanted to follow the customs and traditions.[11] 'Should the traditional institutions be kept, or simply be done away with? This was the question we asked.' And the answer of the Durbar Hima (the meeting of the people in the state) was one of full support of the traditions.[12] 'From there', he continues, 'we thought first about going directly to Delhi, but then realized that to gain strength we need to have the whole state behind us and thus also get the support of people in the Jaintia and Garo Hills.' 'In the year 2000, the Commission on the Constitution also came up, and we decided to try to influence them rather than approaching the parliament.'

These developments relate to what Laborious Manik S. Syiem describes as the first phase of the movement. After this, the District Council intervened and in 2001 managed to get him suspended from his office and replaced by an 'Acting Syiem'. Some of the other traditional chiefs got scared and feared that that they would meet the same fate of being suspended. But as the Federation of Khasis States supported them, they soon got going again. To quote Laborious Syiem once more,

> This is our second movement. We call it now 'Peoples Movement for Grass-roots' Democracy'. The political parties can show that they have the ballot box. Our movement is peoples' movement, not that of the ballot box. So, how can we show Delhi that we have peoples' support? The Durbar is our base. This is us. This is what we will show Delhi.
>
> (Syiem interview, 2004)

As he describes it, it is not only a question of grassroots' democracy, but of Khasi democracy, a unique system that they are proud of, and which they want to preserve and develop. Central in this system is that power is firmly grounded with the people through the Durbar, which is described as an arena free from party-politics that strives for consensus and transparency in all its dealings.[13]

The first objective of the movement is to get constitutional recognition of the traditional governing bodies, which then will pave the way for the second objective of getting direct government funding to these bodies. As a way of establishing the necessity of such recognition, John F. Kharshiing has at several meetings during the campaign narrated the following anecdote:

> I have just returned from USA, where I had been invited to discuss grass-roots' democracy: All over the world people are talking about grassroots' democracy. A Red Indian Chief asked me what we were following. I said, 'the Indian Constitution'. 'Are You mentioned there, are Your chiefs and councils named there', he continued to ask me? 'No', I said. 'If You don't exist in writing, You don't exist at all', he then told me.

According to Kharshiing, the present invisibility of the traditional institutions derives from a 'constitutional anomaly', and this is the 'root cause' of the matter.[14] This takes us back to the complexities relating to the native Khasi states inclusion into the Indian Union. As Kharshiing explains, the end of British rule over India, on 15 August 1947, did not bring the desired freedom for the Khasi people. The 25 Khasi states had, prior to Independence, started to 'prepare themselves for their own form of governance', above all by organising themselves into the Federation of Khasi States. However, what took place, in Kharshiing's words, was nothing but a 'betrayal': they had been 'made to believe' that the Khasi states would be able to maintain sovereignty and political autonomy at the lapse of the British paramountcy, but in the end, they had lost all of this and became a part of the province of Assam. The key events in the story, and this goes for Khasi historiography in general, are the shady dealings surrounding the signing of the so-called 'Instrument of Accession' and in addition the pressures on the Khasi States to sign the 'Instrument of Merger' (see Giri 1998; Syiemlieh 1989). The states did finally agree to sign the first but not the latter and, as the story goes, they have thus in legal terms never fully joined India. The Khasi states objected further to the Sixth Schedule and by introducing this without their consent, the Indian government violated the terms laid down in the Instrument of Accession. It is here that we have the 'constitutional anomaly',[15] which is said to have haunted the Khasi people ever since, and out of which the present violence and insurgency in the state emanates.[16]

Independence and the new administrative order

The new administrative order that was established after Independence in most parts of the Northeastern hills got its constitutional form through the Sixth Schedule. What are then the central features of the Sixth Schedule? In short, it can be described as an institutional mechanism developed for the (then) hill districts of Assam, allowing a certain amount of political and financial self-governance, while at the same time bringing the different hill peoples of these geo-politically sensitive frontier tracts firmly under the larger Indian administration. The 'autonomous district council' (ADC), with most of its members democratically elected and only a handful directly nominated by the governor to safeguard minority interests, is the key institution of the Sixth Schedule. The ADC has powers over large numbers of subjects relating to public administration, usage of land and natural resources, and is entitled to collect taxes, run its own courts and make laws. The district council is further empowered to appoint or replace chiefs or headmen, something which, as we will see, remains highly controversial. Even so, the ADC commonly appears as a rather toothless tiger, whose modus operandi is heavily dependent on the state government. Lack of financial autonomy is often cited as the major limitation of the district councils. The governor of the state has also the superseding powers and can, for example, temporarily adjourn an ADC. Laws passed by the district council have to be approved by the governor as well as by the state government.

More or less from its inception, the Sixth Schedule has been the subject of critique and debate amongst indigenous peoples, officials and anthropologists. For some commentators, it is the most progressive attempt to grant self-determination for tribal and indigenous peoples, whereas others see it as a more circumscribed form of autonomy, largely because of the powers vested with the governor as well as with the state government. There is, however, a consensus regarding the very poor performance of the ADCs; it is argued that the councils have not been able to function in a satisfactory way. There are, for example, common charges of corruption or misuse of funds, of 'bad leadership' in general, and that the elected members of the councils bother more about their political career than about the welfare of the people.[17] The political development in the region proves that the ADCs did not satisfy the hill peoples' aspirations for self-determination, as movements for statehood soon sprang up in various parts of the Northeastern hills.[18] The development during the 1960s, with increased violence, apparently made it necessary for the central government to re-organise Assam and subsequently to make the hills district into a number of separate states.[19] As part of this process, Meghalaya came into being as a separate state in 1972, then comprising three ADCs: the Khasi Hills, the Jaintia Hills and the Garo Hills district councils. When the Khasis, Jaintias and Garos thus got their own 'tribal' state, the question arose as to whether the district councils had become obsolete and should be dismantled (Dutta 1984, Vol. 1: 100). The ADCs, however, remained in place, which, as we will see, has led to a rather confusing situation with multiple and overlapping layers of governance.

The previously mentioned National Commission to Review the Workings of the Constitution points in their report to such an 'overlap of authority' and 'conflict of interest' between the state assembly and the district councils in Meghalaya. For example, local issues such as road repair, electricity supply or waste disposal are said to be shuffled back and forth between the state and the district council administrations. On top of this, the report further acknowledges the existence of a third tier of governance, i.e. the traditional ruling systems in Meghalaya, represented by the Syiems in Khasi Hills, the Dolois in Jaintia Hills and the Nokmas in Garo Hills. As the Commission report argues, if one includes the traditional tribal governing institutions, 'there are not *two* but *three* competing systems of authority – each of which is seeking to 'serve' or represent the same constituency' (National Commission 2001: para. 2.2.30, emphasis added). Interestingly, the Commission recommends a strengthening of the traditional political institutions as a measure to ensure self-governance and to thwart militancy. 'For this to happen', the report suggests, 'the traditional systems of governance will have to be included and given specific roles and opportunities, instead of being marginalised as they have been for decades' (ibid.: para. 2.2.37). This statement is of great political significance, in that it supports and confirms what the TI leaders have been saying. To remind you, P.A. Sangma, who chaired the Commission for Northeast India prior to this engagement, had taken a public stand in favour of the empowerment of the traditional chiefs and their governing bodies.

To favour the traditional institutions is commonly taken in Meghalaya as a critique against the district councils, as these two bodies have been in conflict since the latter came into being. With the district councils, the powers of the chiefs were radically reduced as discussed above. As the political scientist L.S. Gassah puts it, the ADC today treats the traditional chiefs as 'its subordinate officials' (1998: 7). That the ADC is empowered to appoint and remove chiefs and headmen is, and has been, one of the most contentious aspects between the two bodies. From the perspective of the traditional bodies, these are matters exclusively for the respective durbar to decide upon. The ADC should have nothing to do with this. But as things stand today, the 'Appointment and Succession of Chiefs and Headmen Act, 1959', passed by the Khasi-Jaintia Hills Autonomous District Council, authorises the district council to intervene in this process. Laborious Manik S. Syiem calls this Act 'a draconian piece of legisla tion', of which he is the latest victim. His suspension has over the past few years been taking ever-new turns and is now awaiting a settlement by the High Court. Without going into the many intricacies of this case, it is rather obvious that Laborious Syiem's political engagement plays an important role in his suspension. The Executive Committee of the Khasi Hills Autonomous District Council has recently also issued a warning against traditional chiefs' involvement in politics, and particularly in any 'anti-district council activities'. The Executive Committee states that such involvement is illegal (referring to the above mentioned Act) and could lead to the removal of the chief. In this context, the district council authorities even threaten the Syiems for their membership in the Federation of Khasi States, claiming that after the Sixth Schedule was introduced, the Khasi States ceased to exist, and that the continued activities of the Federation go against the Indian Constitution.[20]

Traditional institutions

There are certainly many who would not go along with the recommendations of the Commission and, thus, in different ways refute the governing potential of the traditional political institutions. It is important to note that 'traditional institutions' is a term that is used in the debate by the actors themselves, and thus is not a theoretical or analytical concept that I have introduced. Most commonly, the term is applied in a generic sense without any details about these institutions. In this way, a great variety of customary arrangements, functioning in different ways in different parts of the state, are being brought together under the notion traditional institutions. There are important differences between the three main ethnic communities, but also within them. These institutions have further undergone changes over time and might function in quite a different way from how they are supposed to function. This is obviously not the place to provide any such details, but let me just very briefly touch upon what is commonly talked about as the traditional political institutions among the Khasis.

In general, this is a three-tier system spanning the village council (Durbar Shnong), an intermediate level (Durbar Raid) and the state level (Durbar Hima).[21] At each level, there is a presiding officer: the headman or Rangbah

Shnong at the village level, the Sordar at the Raid level and the Syiem at the Hima level. As with the Garos, the village council consists of the adult male members in the village, preferably one from each household. Women do not participate in the village durbar or at the higher-level durbars. Even though much has been written on these institutions, it is difficult to find any detailed ethnography or accounts on how the durbars actually function today. What we commonly get instead are elaborate outlines of how they ought to function, or supposedly functioned in the past. A commonly highlighted feature is the centrality of the durbar, that decisions are taken by the durbar and not by the presiding officer, be it the headman or Syiem. As the historian David R. Syiemlieh puts it,

> The highest decision making bodies in the political and administrative set-up among the Khasis were the *Durbars*. There is no written law about the functions, composition and working of the *Durbars*, for they work according to *Ka Riti*, a constitution which has grown out of past usages and practices. Every stage of administration from the village to the state has its own *Durbar*. The Khasi *Durbar* even today is a solemn affair. There is no walking out of a *Durbar*. Decisions are unanimous. Should there be a disagreement the issue is dropped.
>
> (Syiemlieh 1989: 5–6)

At each level there are a number of different functionaries that, like the presiding officers, are appointed by the durbar. The procedure varies in different parts of the Khasi Hills, but in general it appears that most positions are reserved or prioritised for persons belonging to certain clans or lineages, commonly the original or founding clans in that particular area (Nongkynrih 2002: 75–6).

The exclusion of women and the reservation of executive functions within the Durbars to persons from certain clans are often quoted as examples of the democratic deficit of the traditional institutions. Particularly the first is used as an argument against the claims of the TI movement; i.e. how can the traditional institutions provide an avenue to grassroots' democracy when half of the population, the women, are excluded from these bodies?[22] The common response by the TI leaders is that the traditional institutions are flexible, they allow change and are indeed changing, and further that women today have started to participate in the durbars and even holding executive functions within them.[23] This, however, is still an exception. But again, it is important to note that lack of female participation is not a problem solely for the traditional institutions, but is a more general social feature that applies to the ADCs as well as the state assembly. As the sociologist Tiplut Nongbri argues, even if women in the matrilineal Khasi, Jaintia and Garo societies in several aspects have a better position than Indian women in general, there is nevertheless a strong ideological prejudice against their involvement in politics (Nongbri 2003: 204–5). Another point of critique against the present functioning of the traditional governing bodies is the lack of transparency and accountability. For example, in financial matters, it is said that the taxes, royalties and fees that these bodies collect are never accounted for. How in this 'age of scams and corruption', the well-known journalist Patricia Mukhim asks, can the durbar be 'exempted from public auditing?'[24] Another problem that people have raised is that many of the local headmen lack education and appropriate skills to function in a modern bureaucratic setting. Those headmen who have education often choose to leave their village and settle in urban areas. Most of the local persons that have expressed such a critique to me would still hold that the traditional institutions do have a place and a role to play particularly as a local level governing body. It is then more a question of transforming these institutions, to make them more inclusive and thus allow women as well as persons from other communities to play an active part in the durbars, and further to make the durbars accountable and open for public scrutiny.

An interesting exemption from this, as well as a fundamental rejection of the governing potential of the traditional institutions, is expressed by Apurba K. Baruah, Professor in Political Science at the North-Eastern Hill University in Shillong, in his recent work. Baruah is carrying out a research project with colleagues on the functioning of these institutions on the local level. The project is implemented in collaboration with London School of Economics' 'Crisis States Programme'. Baruah's overall argument relates to the non-democratic nature of the traditional bodies, that they, besides excluding women and 'non-tribals' in general, are based on communitarian principles that are incompatible with 'modern liberal democratic values' (2003, 2004). John Harriss, the LSE partner, states similarly that 'the traditional political institutions are not democratic', and further that these institutions above all have to do with 'tribal identity' and as such become drivers of 'separatism' and 'conflict' (2002: 5).

Indigenous governance – towards a conclusion

In the words of the Commission report, the political future of Northeast India hinges on people choosing 'self-governance' rather than 'separation' (National Commission 2001: para. 1.6). In the case of Meghalaya, the report recommends that the traditional system of governance be strengthened to achieve the former and thus to pre-empt militant separatism. This, then, is basically what the TI movement claims, but very much the opposite of what Baruah and Harriss argue. The discussion on traditional institutions is commonly framed in black and white terms, i.e. whether the traditional institutions are good or bad, democratic or autocratic, fuelling or containing separatism, and finally whether these are worth preserving or better discarded altogether. As a researcher, one needs to move beyond such simplifications and, at least temporarily, abstain from value judgements. In this chapter, my concern is more about why the traditional political institutions have become such a contentious issue today and less about whether these are good or bad.

As I indicated at the outset, there are several larger processes behind the turn towards 'indigenous governance', that is, to seek sovereignty through traditional governing institutions. In short, I believe that the most important ones are the overall crises of the developmental state (its failure to deliver) and the overall questioning of the state as a benevolent regulator of social life and, in concordance with this, the emergence of the global indigenous peoples' movement and the increased international recognition of indigenous rights.[25] The main aspiration of indigenous peoples worldwide today is self-determination, in most cases through peaceful means and within the parameters of existing nation-states. As Ronald Niezen argues in his 2003 book on international indigenism, self-determination is largely to be achieved through 'constitutional reform and the implementation of treaties and agreements between indigenous and state governments.' (2003: 194) This is also true for the TI movement in Meghalaya, which sets it apart from the insurgency organisations in the state, which seek self-determination through armed struggle. The TI leaders in Khasi Hills stress the need to rectify the injustice following from the violation of past agreements between the Indian government and the native chiefs through constitutional reform, that is, recognition of the traditional political institutions in the Indian constitution. According to Niezen, the main issue for indigenous leaders is not whether their people will be led 'wisely or foolishly', but rather whether their people will be able to determine their own future or 'will continue to be ruled by outside powers.' (2003: 195) To govern oneself is thus the prioritised goal, regardless of whether this would turn out to be the most effective or liberal form of governance. The state government, as well as the district councils, are in the hands of the tribal or indigenous peoples of Meghalaya. In such a situation, one would assume that further stress on self-determination is superfluous. But, arguably, this is not the case. The TI leaders advocate increased sovereignty through the traditional political institutions. According to them, the durbar represents a superior form of governance, free from the deceitfulness of modern party politics. The headman and his council are said to be closer to the grassroots and thus better placed to cater for the needs and aspirations of the people. As such, these bodies are claimed to be more effective and democratic than the governing structures put in place after Independence.

One can certainly question these claims and, as mentioned, read the turn towards indigenous governance as a worrying sign that spells further social cleavages and ethnic conflicts in these troubled Northeastern borderlands. But there are also other contingencies to be explored. It could be argued that an unforeseen outcome of the TI movement could be a shift of focus from ethnic territoriality and the politics of boundaries to what the historian Arif Dirlik calls 'place-based imaginations' and, possibly, explorations of new forms of locally grounded sovereignty (1999). The traditional councils need, as the critics stress, to be reformed and made more inclusive in order to get democratic legitimacy and, if such a change does eventually occur, the empowerment of these institutions can indeed bring about a widening of civic space in Meghalaya. The point here is not to argue for any of these scenarios, but merely to suggest that the revival of traditional institutions is a more complex and socially significant event than most commentators and scholars seem to believe.

Notes

1 The Naga people's independence movement is the longest armed struggle in India, beginning soon after India gained Independence in 1947.

2 The English term 'indigenous peoples' has come into usage in India during the past two decades, often used along with and synonymous to the more well-known terms 'tribal' and *adivasi*. The importance of the term, however, is the new global context it speaks to (and draws on) with increased recognition of indigenous peoples as collective rights bearing subjects under international law (cf. Karlsson 2003; Karlsson and Subba 2006).

3 See 'Meghalaya tribal lobby in fund hunt', *Telegraph,* 16 January 2004.

4 Wasbir Hussain, Associated Press, *Yahoo News India*, 31 October 2007.

5 'Al Gore wins Indian tribal award', *BBC News*, 30 August 2007.

6 Quoted by Biswajyoti Das, *Reuters,* 'India tribe to honour Al Gore on global warming', 29 August 2007.

7 *Hima* is the name of the traditional Khasi states, i.e. Hima Mylliem is the state of Mylliem. I follow the common practice of translating Hima in English as 'state', though this might be questioned from a political science point of view.

8 Sonia Gandhi's foreign origin is the main problem for Sangma.

9 The report or Consultation Paper by the National Commission to Review the Working of the Constitution relating the Northeast is entitled 'Empowering and Strengthening of Panchayati Raj Institutions/Autonomous District Councils/Traditional Tribal Governing Institutions in North East India', dated 21 December 2001.

10 Interview in Shillong, 8 December 2004.

11 Durbar (alt. dorbar) refers to meetings of the traditional councils that are organised on different political levels as will be discussed later. These types of durbars have little in common with the elaborate court rituals associated with the Mughal durbars, which the British later transformed and made use of to assert symbolic authority over the Indian subjects. For the latter, see Cohn (1983).

12 According to estimates as many as 5,000 people representing 700 villages were present at the Durbar (see, for example, a later report in *Grassroots Option*, Monsoon/Autumn 2002).

13 This latter was a central theme of a talk that Laborious Manik S. Syiem gave at a seminar on 'Urban Governance and Traditional Institutions' at the North-Eastern Hill University in Shillong, 2 December 2003. See also his paper 'Khasi Democracy: an unwritten constitution' (unpublished, dated 15 June 2001).

14 The citation is taken from a paper entitled 'The Struggle for Recognition', which John F. Kharshiing presented at a workshop in Shillong, 31 May 2001; he later presented a copy of the paper to me. Most of these themes have also been brought up during the campaign, though in a less elaborate form.

15 'Constitutional anomaly' was first used by Mohammad Saadualla, who pointed out in a meeting of the Constitutional Assembly, September 1949, that placing the Khasi states under the Sixth Schedule without any settlement with the Khasi Chiefs that had signed the Instrument of Accession, amounts to a 'constitutional anomaly' (Chaube 1973: 87).

16 See, for example, 'Memorandum', by the Federation of Khasi States to the National Commission for Review of the Working of the Constitution, signed by President Laborious Manik S. Syiem (Syiem of Mylliem) and Secretary Dr B.S. Syiem (Syiem of Khyriem), 22 July 2000, p. 4.

17 For a wider discussion, see Chaube (1973: 96–8) and Dasgupta (1997: 364–5). For Meghalaya, see particularly Dutta (1984).

18 The Naga leaders rejected the Sixth Schedule outright, sticking to their demand for full sovereignty.

19 The Indo-Chinese war in 1962 probably also pressurised the Centre to find solutions that could prevent further outbursts of violent separatism (Baruah, 2003: 51).

20 See *Shillong Times*, 9 March 2004.
21 In many places, there is also a fourth tier consisting of sub-village or locality within a village.
22 This has been the main point of discussion in most of the seminars and workshops on traditional institutions I have participated in, and also something that people have communicated in private discussions.
23 Laborius Manik S. Syiem has for example made this point on several public occasions, as well as in personal discussions/interviews with me.
24 In an editorial, 'Traditional Institutions – a critique', *Shillong Times*, 3 October 2003.
25 For a larger discussion on present challenges of the state, see Blom Hansen and Stepputat (2001) and J. Friedman (2003).

References

Arendt, H. (1998) *The Human Condition,* Chicago and London: The University of Chicago Press, 2nd edition. First published in 1958.
Baruah, A.K. (2003) 'Tribal Traditions and Crises of Governance in North East India, with special reference to Meghalaya', *Crisis States Programme*, Working Paper No. 22, London School of Economics, http://www.crisisstates.com/download/wp/WP22AB.pdf (accessed 20 December 2010).
—— (2004) 'Ethnic Conflicts and Traditional Self-Governing Institutions: A Study of Laitumkhrah Dorbar', *Crisis States Programme*, Working Paper No. 39, London School of Economics, http://www.crisisstates.com/download/wp/wp39.pdf (accessed 20 December 2010).
Baruah, S. (2003) 'Citizens and Denizens: Ethnicity, Homelands, and the Crisis of Displacement in Northeast India', *Journal of Refugee Studies*, 16(1): 44–66.
Blom Hansen, T. and Stepputat F. (eds) (2001) *States of Imagination: Ethnographic Explorations of the Postcolonial State*, Durham and London: Duke University Press.
Chaube, S. (1973) *Hill Politics in North-East India*, Bombay: Orient Longman.
Cohn, B.S. (1983) 'Representing Authority in Victorian India', in E. Hobsbawm and Ranger, T. (eds) *The Invention of Tradition*, Cambridge: Cambridge University Press, 165–210.
Dasgupta, J. (1997) 'Community, Authenticity, and Autonomy: Insurgency and Institutional Development in India's Northeast, *The Journal of Asian Studies*, 56(2): 345–70.
Dutta S.K. (1984) *Report of the Commission of Inquiry on Autonomous District Administration in the State of Meghalaya, Vols I & II*, Shillong: Meghalaya Government.
Dirlik, A. (1999) 'Place-based Imaginations: Globalisation and the Politics of Place', *Review: Fernand Braudel Center*, 22(2): 151–87.
Friedman, J. (ed.) (2003) *Globalization, The State, and Violence*, Walnut Creek: AltaMira Press.
Gassah, D.S. (1998) *Traditional Institutions of Meghalaya: A Study of Doloi and his Administration*, New Delhi: Regency Publications.
Giri, H. (1998) *The Khasis under British Rule (1824–1947)*, New Delhi: Regency Publications.
Gurr T.R. (2000) *Peoples versus States: Minorities at Risk in the New Century*, Washington DC: US Institute of Peace Press.
Harriss, J. (2002) 'The State, Tradition and Conflicts in the North Eastern States of India', *Crisis States Programme*, Working Paper No. 13, London School of Economics, http://www.crisisstates.com/download/wp/WP13JH.pdf (accessed 20 December 2010).

Karlsson, B.G. (2001) 'Indigenous Politics: Community Formation and Indigenous Peoples' Struggle for Self-Determination in Northeast India', *Identities*, 8(1): 7–45.

—— (2003) 'Anthropology and the "Indigenous Slot": Claims to and Debates about Indigenous Peoples' Status in India', *Critique of Anthropology*, 23(4): 403–23.

Karlsson, B.G. and Subba, T.B. (eds) (2006) *Indigeneity in India*, London: Kegan Paul.

Niezen, R. (2003) *The Origins of Indigenism: Human Rights and the Politics of Identity*, Berkeley/Los Angeles/London: University of California Press.

Nongbri, T. (2003) *Development, Ethnicity and Gender: Select Essays on Tribes in India*, Jaipur and New Delhi: Rawat Publications.

Nongkynrih, A.K. (2002) *Khasi Society of Meghalaya: A Sociological Understanding*, New Delhi: Indus Publishing Company.

Syiem, L.M.S. (2003) 'Urban Governance and Traditional Institutions', Talk at the North-Eastern Hill University in Shillong, 2 December.

Syiemlieh, D.R. (1989) *British Administration in Meghalaya: Policy and Pattern*, New Delhi: Heritage Publishers.

9 Aid, Adivasis and aspirations for development in western India

David Mosse

Introduction

In *Cultivating Development*, I took the case of participatory development in Adivasi-dominated regions of India to re-assess the decade-long history of a British aid project.[1] This took place between 1990 and 2003 in the Bhil western region, and I was involved as a social development consultant. My aim was to ask not whether development works, but *how* it works. How, in this case, are the very different interests of Bhil villagers, an Indian public sector agro-input production and marketing giant, and a British aid agency brought together through a project discourse that hid diverging ambitions and buried ideological divisions? The focus of the book was aid policy and the debates in the anthropology of development. In this chapter, I take up one strand of the argument which concerns the place this development intervention had within the historical trajectory of Bhil society of eastern Gujarat, south Rajasthan and western Madhya Pradesh. National or international development policy only works if it is translated into the different ambitions and intentions of those bureaucrats or beneficiaries who it enrols. Indeed, participatory policy models do not and *cannot* shape actual practice in the way that they claim. Rather, I assert that they are ignored, resisted, 'consumed' or 'tactically used' (Mosse 2005: 16).

This chapter therefore asks how an external drive to participatory development was translated into the social conditions and ambitions of Bhil Adivasi communities. It questions how these communities, and their project collaborators, consume 'participatory development'. It also assesses how Bhils translate between their material/cultural concerns and the policy goals of international development. Here I use 'translation' in Bruno Latour's sense (1996), suggesting the agency of development collaborators in shaping patterns of power that are not premised on centre/periphery or other such binaries. The conjoining of the notion of 'development' with the social category 'Adivasi' invokes powerful and opposed visions. On the one hand, international aid agencies or non-governmental organisations (NGOs) are unwitting partners with nationalist modernisers in efforts to extend facilities, technologies or educational resources to Adivasis in the name of reaching out to the marginalised, by giving opportunities to underprivileged sections of society, or by integrating tribal communities into the mainstream. But these ambitions might also be cause for deep concern among those at the margins who see in development the work of instruments of social regulation, the extension of state power, bureaucratic and commercial exploitation, or the cynical promotion of religious nationalist agenda among indigenous and tribal peoples. Here resistance might be the only appropriate response, illustrated in activist involvement in various social movements: 'Remoteness tends to be the best insurance against poverty' (Padel 2000: 289; see also Ferguson 1994).

Such opposed views direct attention away from careful ethnographic examination of the ways in which development programmes and Adivasi society actually intersect in particular contexts. Going beyond these divisions it is possible to show not only how development agencies impose their own definition of the problem, and strive to produce beneficiaries in their own image (while protecting favoured policy goals and producing 'success' in their own terms), but also to assess how Adivasis enrol outsiders onto *their* agenda and, through their 'consumer practices', consent to development interventions making something quite different of them (de Certeau 1984). It is this social dynamic of development that is the focus of this chapter.[2]

Designer development

The trick of development is to arrange things so that events appear to be the outcome of planned intention, and therefore to make policies, or rather the policy-makers or politicians, the authors of a history of a kind whose causal chains lead back to managed budgets. Indeed, development success derives from the creative capacity of policy to connect economic and historical processes of change to its own normative schemes. It requires that community members, fieldworkers, government advisers and experts of various kinds are enrolled and collude in making certain knowledge, models and technology (often those of expert outsiders) the privileged agents of change. To be effective at this, a high degree of ambiguity and interpretive flexibility has to be build into the language of policy itself. But the process has to begin, as any development intervention does, by defining places, peoples and problems in ways that are compatible with currently popular and politically viable solutions. Here I am writing about a rural development project which produced a narrative of tribal underdevelopment and change, around the twin solutions of improved agricultural technology and participation.

In 1990, a team of British project design consultants, of which I was one, conceived of the Bhil Adivasi region as the environmentally degraded home to a catalogue of deficiencies correctible by improved agricultural technologies. However, as a *participatory* project it could not, as other colonial or state development efforts had, trace these to farmer ignorance, traditional agriculture or tribal backwardness. As a new 'Farmer First' programme, drawing on the work of Paul Richards and Robert Chambers *et al.*, it understood indigenous farming practices as sophisticated and adapted to resource systems which were complex, diverse and risk-prone. In these practices, farmers flexibly combined multi-crop regimes, livestock and trees in order to reduce risk, and were themselves experts, active experimenters and critical judges of modern technology. The real problem, we judged, was that tribal cultivators were victims of a defective state system of agricultural research and extension promoting technologies, which were ill-adapted to the needs of poor upland tribal farmers. State-implemented soil and water conservation (SWC) interventions, and an exclusionary forest policy also victimised them.

So it would be farmer *participation* – in setting the research agenda, experimentation and evaluating technology – that would renew tribal farmers' interest in their land. This approach aimed to develop and deliver a basket of relevant technologies for Bhil Adivasis to choose from, promising a positive spiral of improved productivity and reduced out-migration, to return Bhils to their vocation as settled agriculturalists. Although colonial stereotypes of lawless criminal Bhils had been banished from contemporary development discourse, the legitimising story of tribal underdevelopment that we project workers (donor adviser, consultants, fieldworkers) told ourselves was by no means free from standard historiographic and administrative representations of Bhils. Through these we received notions of innocence, isolation and wildness (opposed to the ordered plains society). The story of Adivasis being driven to the cultural periphery of the forest tracts, from where they became *dacoits* (raiders), prepared the role for outsiders to become their 'civilisers', their rescuers from exploitation. But in our project design, Bhils were not only historically exploited Adivasis, whose vulnerable subsistence livelihoods were in need of protection; they were also entrepreneurial farmers in search of improved technology and new markets.

Successful programme designs manage to encompass such divergent disciplinary and ideological perspectives. In our case, this was accomplished by the supremely ambiguous policy idea of 'participation' which, for example, allowed a certain kind of consultation and client-oriented experimentation in agricultural research to be linked with the idea of radical social change. It therefore could address historical relations of exploitation by money lenders, traders, labour contractors and local agents of the state that had for long conspired to exclude Bhils from the benefits of the state's anti-poverty schemes. Further, this interpretive flexibility of design was the key to enrolling different agents and supporters with divergent interests onto a project, which is necessary for 'success'.

As will become clear, this also makes outcomes uncertain. 'Participation' could have the paradoxical effect of creating patronage and increasing external control. But in the project's official view, participation was about offering Bhils more local control, local access and empowerment, enhanced group capacities and social capital, awareness, skills and self reliance. In this view such changes could be generated through the work of Community Organisers and village volunteers, and through the new technology, the effects of which could be sustained by farmers' organisations. As the British Overseas Development Administration (ODA) project document of 1992 (now the Department for International Development, DfID) summed up the design: 'the basic premise is that sustainable development can only be achieved by enhancing local self-reliance through institutional and community development'. Of course this participation theory buried a multitude of counterviews, not only those of foreign consultants and donor advisers of different persuasions, but also those of the Indian partner agency through which the programme was to be executed. This agency was a national agro-input manufacturing and marketing giant whose development vision, of increased inputs for commercial agriculture and spin-offs into agro-based industries linking it to farmer clients, was fundamentally at odds with the ODA planners' new participatory poverty-focused agenda and low/no-cost low-input technology. Such differences were concealed by careful conceptual work in design and skilful brokerage as the project unfolded.

As a piece of policy work, the project design was highly successful. This meant in particular that its focus on natural resources development, poverty reduction, participation and non-state private-sector actors expressed the then favoured trends in British aid policy, such that the project was effectively 'made in Britain'. It would be a mistake, however, to imagine that the conceptual work of policy anticipates and directs programme action, or even that failure in the execution of policy creates a 'gap' between theory and action that can be narrowed by 'best practice'.

Bhil society

Any international aid project has above all to satisfy the political needs of its development agency. As a matter of priority, therefore, its actions and events come to be interpreted in terms of authorised policy models. However, this project also stood as part of a long trajectory of outsider interventions in the Bhil region. It was perceived by its Bhil beneficiaries as 'opportunity' and as 'threat' and, interestingly, as a set of possible relationships: from patronage, protection, employment and market access, to exploitation and theft. To better understand this it is necessary to draw on the work of subaltern historians who have helped overwrite colonial narratives of tribal isolation, marginality and rescue, by examining the way in which Bhil identity was and is the product of relationships with outsiders, be they colonialists (enforcing systems of taxation and forest demarcation), usurious moneylenders, Gandhian reformers, Christian missionaries or Hindu nationalists.

As noted by Hardiman (1987: 181) and Skaria (1999: 270), the erosion of livelihoods that followed forest demarcation had, by the twentieth century, generated its own long history of Bhil uprisings, involving attacks on government offices, and protests against the Forest Department by setting fire to the forest. Along with state monopoly over timber, colonial forest policy involved an administrative turn against Bhil shifting cultivation and gathering. 'Under the steady influence of a British officer, it was envisioned that tribes would abandon their wild and wandering ways, take to settled agriculture, and become steady, yeoman cultivators.' (Skaria 1999: 198) With settled agriculture Bhil communities developed another significant long historical relationship, namely with traders/moneylenders, or *sahukars*. In fact, in pre-British times *sahukars* already had a critical role in the expansion of settled agriculture in the forested Bhil domains. As Hardiman points out (1987: 96–7), *sahukars* maintained hegemony through economic compulsion and paternalism rather than coercion. While clearly exploited, Bhils were not bitter towards *sahukars* as a class; the relationship with their *sahukar* was a valuable asset, it was necessary and 'natural'.

The transformation of 'wildness' from a discourse of rule to one of exclusion, the historical replacement of forest livelihoods by *sahukar*-financed cultivation, and the move from independence to debt and dependence, together had the effect of turning 'Bhil' and *jangli* into negative ascriptions. People themselves began to reject such identities in what Skaria describes as a 'deep malaise among forest communities' (1999: 255). Several 'Bhil' communities came to prefer identities like Mina or Bhilala, which emphasised connections (historical or mythical) with the regionally dominant Rajputs (Baviskar 1995; Deliège 1995). A few converted to Christianity. The 'Bhil malaise', together with intensified exploitative economic relations, also contributed to a series of social reform and religious movements or rebellions from the mid-nineteenth century. Most of these focused on the goddess (*mata, devi*), and their exponents demanded self-improvement, the living of pure and clean lives, the elimination of meat-eating, alcohol and animal sacrifices to animist deities and ancestral spirits, which were all considered as aspects of 'inferior' Bhil culture (Jain 1991). To Skaria, these movements suggest a distancing from 'wildness', now associated with marginality, and a hostility to (yet cultural emulation of) upper castes who subordinated the Bhils in new ways (Skaria 1999: 256). The goddess cults flowed into the stream of Gandhian nationalist reforms, which left their mark in the form of Adivasi schools, *bhajan mandlis* (devotional groups), and changed dress or dietary codes.

In some villages today, followers of reformed practices identify themselves as *bhagats* claiming status over 'ordinary Bhils', emphasising education, thrift and prosperity. In some areas *bhagat* Bhils now constitute a separate *jati* restricting marriage with non-*bhagats* (Rao 1998). Even if they did not 'awaken' Bhils themselves, these pre-independence movements awakened political organisations to the need to mobilise Adivasis in order to capture power (Sharma 1990 cited in Weisgrau 1997: 41). In the 1990s, Hindu nationalist organisations (the Sangh Parivar) found fertile ground in the 'Bhil malaise' for the political rhetoric of pan-Hindu unity (Weisgrau 1997: 70). This took a violently communal form in April 2002, when the strategic Hindutva-isation of Adivasis meant they were mobilised to attack and loot Muslim (Bohra) moneylenders and traders in eastern Gujarat (Lobo 2002). Such dilemmas and religious movements continue today as Bhils struggle to reproduce valued agricultural livelihoods, but are only able to do so through large scale seasonal labour migration primarily to urban construction sites that is organised through contractor brokers on extraordinarily exploitative terms, where they experience prejudice, stigma and criminalisation with new intensity (Mosse *et al.* 2005).

The point is that Bhils struggled to maintain livelihoods and forged their identity in the context of a history of relationships with dominant groups in society;

and continue to do so today. Adivasis have had to contend constantly with the categorisations of dominant others, whether British officers, Gandian national-ists, missionaries, bureaucrats, communalist politicians and, as I argue in this chapter, agents of rural development. Bhil identity and 'locality is constituted in and through relations to wider systems, not simply impinged upon by them' (Li 1996: 165). The state, market and political parties are not external to Bhil iden-tity and community but constitute them internally and historically. And so do development projects, which I will suggest are as much about forging relation-ships as the introduction of schemes.

While development professionals embarked on a project premised on goals of self-reliance, empowerment, the development of community capacities (and in which the agency of outsiders was under-emphasised in favour of local partici pation), Bhil villagers were predisposed to regard the initiative primarily in terms of relationships with outsiders as patrons or exploiters, their agenda and the resources they could bring. This contradiction between the project model and the historical reality had important implications for the social processes and effects of the project. I want to look at three aspects of this: first, the processes of 'participatory planning' by which project workers aimed to establish programme priorities; second, the experience of one programme, that of savings and credit; and third, the economic and cultural effects of these development interventions. In each case, the official discourse reveals and conceals a very different logic of practice. Projects and their effects are translated into the different meanings and historical trajectories of Adivasis in the Bhil region.

Participatory rural appraisal and the goddess

The participatory approach of this project was premised on the notion, popular-ised by Robert Chambers, that by using the right techniques (primarily those of Participatory Rural Appraisal or PRA) outsiders could release local people's knowledge so as to transform top-down planning and reverse the hierarchies of power in development (Chambers 1997). It is not surprising, however, that our first ventures into Bhil villages with the exoteric paraphernalia of PRA were met with suspicion. Our initial efforts revealed the many development ghosts that haunted the Bhil landscape: fear of the loss of land rights from dam construction and flooded valleys, land acquisition for industry, or the eviction of forest-land 'encroachers'. Villagers were no strangers to the manipulating interests of out-siders. Indeed, their first tactic was not to share their knowledge but to discern the motivation of outsiders that, in this case, appeared deviously clothed in the rhetoric of participation, facilitation or handing over control to local people. There were accusations that project workers were proselytising Christian mis-sionaries, which had become a pervasive idiom of mistrust in the region.

But such mistrust did not linger long, since it was quickly apparent to village leaders and other people of high status, such as local headmen, office holders and members of dominant lineages, that the project's 'participatory planning process' (its PPP) could be turned to their individual advantage by manipulating the definition of 'community needs'. Indeed their interests — for example, the development of valley bottom land or tree nurseries under their control — featured prominently in the village plans drawn up by project staff, who urgently needed collaborators and beneficiaries to secure their own reputation as efficient fieldworkers in the eyes of their bosses. These Bhil men were rich in what Arjun Appadurai (2004) calls 'the capacity to aspire', that is the ability to navigate the links between their own immediate needs and the wider goals of another's project, so as to draw down individual benefits. Correspondingly, poorer households, socially marginal lineages and women were not only relatively excluded by the public exercises of the project's PPP, but lacked this capacity to aspire. Women fieldworkers, whose own reputations were at stake, confided that Bhil women did not seem to know how to shape their expectations. On the one hand, they imagined big infrastructure developments, irrigation schemes, hospitals and the like but, on the other, their expectations were individual and personal. The mutual enrolment of project and participants was more complex in the case of women who could not easily translate their desires into readable form.

Although in this participatory project the official emphasis was on learning from people and having them set the development agenda, ultimately the PPP can be regarded as a means to bend local needs to a pre-existing (external) analysis of problems and available solutions sometimes at variance with local needs. For example, farmers in these upland villages were most concerned with maintaining soil fertility, emphasising the importance of cattle and fodder, and gave priority to capturing water in valleys for irrigation. But village planning exercises invariably focused on soil erosion as a cause of declining productivity and the need for physical soil and water conservation (SWC) works, along with improved crop varieties. Villagers willingly complied with external priorities and technologies, endorsing outsider impositions with 'local knowledge' because this was, at least for some, an effective means to access new resources. So Bhil farmers would concede to a soil erosion discourse and to community conservation (of soil and trees) in the hope of the delivery of key investments to enhance individual household endowments of land and water (e.g. wells, lift irrigation) and to meet the urgent and immediate need for off-season labour provided through physical soil and water conservation works.

One could argue, then, that the instruments of participatory planning were a means less to reveal than to *modify* farmers' knowledge so that it led to desired conclusions/solutions (SWC or improved varieties) that were present before the analysis began. In the end, villagers spoke through PRAs as we wanted them to speak. Participatory planning involved a kind of disciplinary technique producing right thinking. Indeed, amidst the templates, charts, statistics, rational planning frameworks, diagnoses and prescriptions, and printed work-plans, all geared to producing information and rationalising decisions for an external agency, it would not be surprising to discover that Bhil villagers were unaware that these exercises were all about privileging *their* knowledge (see also Fiedrich 2002: 93–5). In fact, Bhil farmers became 'indigenous' experts through complying with project systems. In this there was perhaps also, as Novellino suggests, a *confessional* element, in which Bhil farmers admitted inadequate, environmentally destructive practices and the need for improvement and imported models of agriculture, forestry or soil conservation (Novellino 2003: 286–7). Bhil farmer practice is simultaneously honoured and discredited in relation to superior models of knowing introduced by educated well-dressed outsiders guided by foreign experts.

As symbolic enactments, PRAs and related activities signalled how Bhils could become proper beneficiaries. But these were also dramas for consumption by a wider audience of outsiders that the project needed in its network. A 'demonstration PRA' was an essential part of any public event, donor visit, celebration of national holidays, etc., organised by the project. Colourfully laid out in selected village sites, it symbolised the transformation of marginal Adivasis into modern development beneficiaries for a VIP audience, yet concealed the politics of development. Such events therefore dramatise underdeveloped backwardness and project success. They draw attention to aspects of project work that simulate the authenticity of local places and local people.

I do not, however, wish to imply that Adivasis were unchanged by these 'participatory' encounters, nor that they were easily manipulated into passive acquiescence with outsiders' designs. First, for Adivasi villagers the experience of 'modern' rational planning, of representing problems and possibilities apart from structural constraints (e.g. crop varieties from debt relations) could be liberating in a certain way (see Fiedrich 2002: 99). For sure, Bhil farmers were not going to acquire new practical expertise through PRA encounters, but in communicating to outsiders, in putting practices into words (or diagrams), they might reflect on their practices in new ways so as to allow innovation (see Bloch 1991: 193). And the process of translating an individual, often fragmentary, experience of a difficulty into the collective awareness of a problem with a view to change involved new understanding. Second, Bhil villagers (initially elites) were skilled manipulators and adept translators of idiosyncratic local and personal interests (in wage labour, wells, pumps, loans) into legitimate demands, ensuring the necessary compromises to sanction schemes and satisfy project criteria of success and worker performance. Indeed, increasingly the project relied upon a cadre of semi-professionalised village brokers, record-keepers, group leaders and mediators with project staff to achieve this dovetailing of bottom-up and top-down.

While, as noted above, some people were slower to respond to the signals and templates that project workers were using to convey how to be a proper development beneficiary (and through lack of this 'capacity to aspire' they lost out), many read the project very well. They anticipated outsider points of view in their self-representation. For example, in the local histories drawn up in PRA 'timelines', new project villages proclaimed themselves fitting subjects of development. On the one hand, such histories emphasised needs arising from deforestation and soil erosion and, on the other, they signalled openness to modern technology. In these 'timelines', the past was marked by ecological decline, while present and future time was measured in terms of the arrival of technology in the villages (the first diesel pump; the first use of urea; the first bicycle, radio, flour mill, TV and so forth). There were stories of 'social progress' too, the end of buffalo sacrifices to the goddess *mataji*, the first use of shirts or tiled roofs, the first '10th pass' student or the first government job. These were histories of progress to which the project was invited to contribute its benefits and technologies.

In such development encounters, Bhil villagers contended with outsider judgements, and found new cultural forms for aspirations and identities. Once again, by adopting the conventions and technologies of outsiders, these villagers were aligning themselves with cultural practices through which alliances could be forged with benevolent members of the dominant class. And the significance of this is that it repeats the pattern of Bhil relations with outside agents that is manifest in various Bhil reform movements, and the *devi* cults in particular (see Hardiman 1987: 164). Indeed, Baviskar, writing about a revival of the devi or *mataji* phenomenon in 1992 (1995: 97–103), comments that it was not so much about adopting caste Hindu practices or (as Hardiman suggests) a democratisation of upper-caste values, but a carefully considered contingent capitulation to dominant ideology. The project itself began in 1992. In one village I witnessed a threatening stand-off between developers and villagers as the goddess arrived in the place project staff had prepared for their opening PRA. Demanding devotion, 'cleaner' dress, purer dietary codes, the goddess appeared to express community resistance to development interlopers. But a few years later it seemed that the cult of the PRA and the cult of the *devi* had more in common than we realised: the goddess cults provide a mould for the interactions of development in which external agenda come to speak through local voices (Baviskar 1995: 79). In both, Bhils contended with outsider evaluations of them, drawing on these to represent themselves and their social aspirations. Through both PRA and the *devi* cult, Bhils would tactically adopt the values of upper caste and educated outsiders as a means to escape the marginality imposed by the exploitation and objectification sometimes of these same outsiders. Both the goddess cult and the project's PPP introduced Bhils to new language, knowledge and ways of communication with outsiders, aspirations and self-evaluations.

Self-help groups and patronage

As this or any development programme puts in place its *own* procedures, systems of accountability, professional divisions and hierarchies of authority it becomes difficult — often impossible — to turn ideas of participation, self-help or local control into practice. 'System goals' such as the preservation of rules and procedures, or maintaining systems of rank and administrative order take precedence over 'policy goals' of community driven development (Quarles van Ufford 1988), and the reproduction of class relationships between staff and villagers (as management and labour, patrons and clients) over those of facilitated self-reliance. In fact, project systems worked to minimise administrative risk associated with Bhil farmers developing their own way of doing things, making their own decisions, taking their own risks and making their own mistakes. In practice, what the project needed were reliable clients, not autonomous partners.

Bhil villagers themselves also acted to turn 'self-help' initiatives into a means to perpetuate patronage and social protection from external benefactors. Perhaps it is not surprising that villagers preferred project patronage and the delivery of concrete benefits over facilitated self-help. They readily discarded the disciplines of participation to make themselves project employees and clients, and refused to extend their systems of reciprocal labour exchange (*halma*), used for land clearing or house building, to project work such as SWC. Self-help, low subsidies, local contributions, project withdrawal or cost-recovery were hardly self-evident ideals to villagers accustomed to maximising gains from high-subsidy state programmes. The very mention of recovery could evoke the fearful memory of revenue officials imposing repayment demands for 'bunding work' executed by the state decades earlier. Although they were now familiar with the official rhetoric of 'people's participation' (*jansahbhagita*), in common parlance 'participation', *bhagidari*, implied simply that a contribution (of money or labour) had to be made; and the extent and nature of villager's *bhagidari* (contribution) was a matter for negotiation and agreement with outsider patrons. Risk-averse villagers had no more incentive than staff to diversify and innovate and they complied with the standard packages, subsidies and wage labour on offer, carefully matching their 'needs' to the administrative exigencies of the project agency. This reproduced an invisible disjuncture between village realities and project systems concealed in the rhetoric of participation. This is especially clear in the case of the project's microfinance programme.

Nothing symbolised the transformation from tribal 'hand-to-mouth' under-development to self-reliance better than the 'moral discipline' of saving. By the project's fifth year thousands of 'self-help' groups had been formed, based on lineage-hamlet social units. These involved some savings activity (especially linked to wages from project works) but had also become the primary vehicle for project investments, credit for agro-inputs, group controlled assets and enterprises (pumps, threshers, flour mills, shops, etc.). In official policy, the self-help groups (SHGs) were increasingly conceptualised around a donor-favoured model of enterprise promotion among risk-taking individuals accountable to their group. However, it was soon clear that by this standard these SHGs were mostly failing miserably. While savings levels were low, SHGs had accumulated large funds from project investments. But these external funds were hardly circulated among members and failed, as was intended, to meet a widening range of credit needs of their members. This situation was all the more surprising given that these Bhil villages had a vibrant indigenous financial institution (*chandla*) which was able to mobilise substantial capital for individual needs, businesses or bride-price. Why did so much income (at least from the better-off households) find its way into *chandla* payments, and so little into SHG savings accounts? Why, when group funds had accumulated considerable capital, was so little rotated as credit? The answer may be to do with the different relationship between money and social obligation in the two systems.

In *chandla* money *is* social obligation (payments simultaneously meet and generate obligation) through personal networks. There are no funds or deposits. Money works by constantly circulating, generating more obligation and more money within particular social networks. It is the social network and its accumulated obligation that offers a fail-safe insurance arrangement for those in the circle. Voluntary savings into a project-supported group fund involved no such obligations, and borrowing only weak ones (hence poor repayments).The only means to generate security through SHGs was through financial *accumulation* (deposits) and perpetuating a relationship with the project. Groups did indeed maximise the accumulation of funds (and assets) from the project as a form of social security, and insurance against uncertainty or enterprise failure (or project withdrawal). For large parts of the year these funds simply sat as unutilised capital in bank accounts. The majority of SHGs were adopting conservative strategies perpetuating themselves as clients of the project (rather than operating with autonomy), maximising the acquisition of further grants, assets and project initiated enterprises. The latter may have been economically marginal, but that was not the point; they sustained a relationship between project patrons and Adivasi client groups. Indeed, the range of activities of an SHG (and the size of its fund) was a measure of the intensity of engagement and the strength of the group–project relationship. 'Passive groups' were those without activities. Arguably, for villagers, project money in their group accounts represented a project interest in them, and was a guarantee of continuity in the relationship. As such it was not available to generate other obligations within the community through lending. If lent, project funds would/could not be recovered, and their dissipation might threaten the relationship with project patrons: patrons could lose their interest, villagers their reputation as trustworthy clients and custodians; or, worse, dangerous obligations could be created, meaning that patronage could turn into claims on land or labour.

This strategic use of external financial resources is consistent with Geof Wood's (2003) argument that poor people facing chronic insecurity prioritise the maintenance of relationships with people (patrons or projects) having better access to resources and offering social protection in the short term, even though this limits their capacity for longer-term economic mobility. It is unsurprising that Bhil villagers with a long history of economic insecurity and exploitation, living in a region of underdeveloped markets and currently experiencing the loss of protective patronage (as *sahukars* turn to increasingly exploitative economic relations), sought to secure and protect relations with new patrons rather than to strive for autonomy through independent enterprise, or that they adopted the risk-reducing strategy of maximising material benefits in the short term (for example, from wages or wells). And who is to say that wanting patronage and resources from the project is less a sign of empowerment than wanting to manage your own resources (Fiedrich 2002: 65)? At the same time, from the project side, organisational conservatism encouraged such relations of patronage with Bhil groups.

So when measured against the standards of the new microfinance model, the project's groups were very poor performers. They had low saving, poor recovery and fund rotation, and a propensity to multiply questionable group activities rather than lending for individual enterprise. However, judged from a point of view in which securing social protection and stable patron–client relations are central, the very features that defined group failure – dependence, accumulating funds, multiple collective enterprises – were the markers of effectiveness, just as a really good SWC programme was one that spent budgets, gave employment, pump-primed groups and sustained relationships.

As with the matter of handling financial resources, it was clear that villagers did not view new technology as separate from their relationship with project patrons (cf. Burghart 1993); its adoption or, for example, the maintenance or demonstration plots could signify their status as appropriate clients. While this contradicts the principles of participation and self-help, it is perhaps not a our prising livelihood strategy among Bhil communities where survival has long depended upon forming alliances with those with better access to resources – *sahukars*, *rajputs* and today NGOs and their projects (Weisgrau 1997: 93). Moreover, this project functioned in a wider political context of development as patronage. The competitive environment of Adivasi districts in which NGOs or departments try to secure clients for their programmes is infused with notions of territoriality, loyalty and obligation.

The economic and cultural effects of an aid project

There is no question, however, that a majority of Bhil households interviewed in a series of detailed village studies we undertook in 1996–8 considered that they were benefiting significantly from this project. Of course there were downsides: the loss of land to SWC, complaints about the rising cost of cultivation from expensive new seeds and inputs, and increased workloads (especially for poorer, younger women) brought by irrigation, new winter season crops, vegetable growing, or restricted grazing from joint forest management (JFM) enclosures. But for many, the increase in food security from better crop yields meant a reduction of outflows for food grain (in the lean season). JFM brought fodder and fuel to shareholders, and project works gave urgently needed wage labour. To be sure, the principal economic gains from many project activities accrued to households in proportion to the quality (that is, lower valley rather than upper slope) as well as quantity of land they possessed. Moreover, the poorest (including the land poor) received less of the project's subsidies, while contributing more to common assets through their own subsidised labour on project works. Indeed, richer families gained most, and mostly from increased agricultural incomes especially from irrigation and winter season crops. Poorer families gained least, primarily from wage labour, while the gap between the very poorest, including long-term migrants and others, appeared to be widening. But at the same time, what the project offered, especially wages and low-cost credit, was also of greatest importance to the livelihoods of the poorest and most heavily indebted households.

While Bhil villagers appreciated such benefits, the evidence of these field studies showed that they did not endorse the project's theory about what it was doing, i.e. its legitimising policy model. First, the project expected to enhance agricultural livelihoods and reduce seasonal labour migration to urban construction sites, but the actual effect of the project was probably to deepen the interdependence of agriculture and labour migration by pushing a trend towards greater reliance on cash incomes (Mosse *et al.* 2002). In some villages, overall migration increased. New cultivation and new lifestyles demanded more spending. Bride-price too was inflating, and with it the demands of *chandla*. Second, while its philosophy urged self-sufficiency and an alternative low-cost, low-subsidy approach that promoted rain-fed technology and low external inputs, the project further opened the door to input agriculture, productive credit and cash cropping. The most tangible economic benefits derived from the *external* provision of subsidised inputs/credit, irrigation (lift schemes, wells, pumps and check dams) and employment. Third, there was a contradiction between the project model's emphasis on independently managed SHGs and the project's effect, which was to create dependent groups through investment and patronage which were drawn into conservative villager strategies geared to security and social protection. Fourth, our project design emphasised the gains from agricultural *research* and new crop technology that would increase yields without the need to change cultivation practices or additional inputs. The model was breeding-based rather than agronomy-based, and generated a context-free knowledge of crop performance from paired comparisons and controlled crop-cutting experiments. But once the new technology was re-embedded in the complex micro-environments, conditions of seed supply, networks of obligations, deficits or debts, family relations or market connections that constituted Bhil cultivation practices, the scientifically proven yield advantages could fail to appear as livelihood benefits. The benefits of technology development refused the general application. Nonetheless, the project's participatory crops programme, using farmer evaluations in breeding, testing and popularising new varieties, was in fact a huge success and a major advance on prevailing regulatory frameworks with wide applications for policy and bureaucratic practice.

The paradox of this success is that it came from challenging the scientific status of Indian agricultural research by recognising its context in institutional (research station) politics, while giving scientific status to farmer knowledge by ignoring *its* context. Participatory crop selection and breeding did not simply re-label the 'local' as 'scientific'. Rather it involved 'dis-embedding' farmer knowledge and judgement so that it could acquire a global (scientific) significance, and then 're-localising' it (see van der Ploeg 1992 cited in Desai 2004). Farmers' judgements about the performance of new varieties were 'scientific', not just because they were based on relevant experience and wider criteria (duration, disease resistance, price, etc.) but because they were separate from the context of institutional politics that distorted conventional agricultural research and regulatory frameworks. But at the same time, the participatory science construction of the rational scientific farmer necessarily ignored the kind of ethnographic evidence that indicates the contextual way in which South Asian farmers actually make crop choices and judgements about technology.

Certainly Bhil farmer views on new seeds were equivocal, at least five years after when the studies were done. There was considerable interest, but those who habitually home-saved seed were not keen on expensive seeds that had to be purchased, even on credit. Improved seeds only did well in particular soil and moisture conditions, while yields varied greatly across farmers' fields. Uncertainty, especially in the face of variable monsoon rains, meant that the dramatic economic gains modelled for plant breeding in the long term could disappear in the short term and locally, as could the seeds' generalised advantages, which include drought resistance and yield. Here, they were treated as a small situation-specific addition to available options for cropping.

Working in one of the project's exemplar villages in 2002–3, Kirit Patel (2007) found that varieties claimed to be highly successful by their project promoters just three to four years earlier had almost entirely disappeared from farmers' fields. Patel's work deepens understanding of the problem of our expert Participatory Plant Breeding (PPB) models. These presumed a world of choice in which farmers would meet the demands of a harsh and variable ecology (steep slopes, water scarcity) by changing their portfolio of varieties. They just needed more choices. But in relation to their staple crop, maize, Bhil farmers could not imagine themselves in a supermarket of maize varieties. They had a nutritionally-reasoned commitment to a particular type of grain – *katholi* maize.[3] Much could be learned from this for future crop improvement programmes, but the point here is that expert preoccupation with successful design and its outcomes precluded engagement with Adivasi experimental models that contradicted project ones, and that meant that despite considerable investment, soon after the project withdrew, not a single improved maize variety was found competing with local ones.

In any case, Bhil villagers did not in fact emphasise seed technology, or even soil and water conservation structures, in accounting for the initially recorded greater yields in their maize or rice fields. Far more important in their view was the new access to project credit through the self-help groups at low cost without collateral silver or the need for brokers and the *timely* purchase of seeds and fertiliser that this allowed. (There is little doubt that the uptake of improved seeds was significantly influenced by their ready availability on credit in villages.) What was really important for the poorest (often excluded from credit entirely) was that groups provided the means to acquire purchased inputs, such as fertiliser, *for the first time*. Almost all villagers (80 per cent) were members of groups because they could provide flexible and unmediated access to cultivation loans/inputs when needed without lengthy negotiation.[4] They offered freedom from the social burden of dependence upon moneylenders precisely in situations where they were most vulnerable, such as when in urgent need of critical cultivation inputs, or when the power of usurers over them was most keenly felt. Villagers sought freedom from harassment for repayment, freedom to decide when to sell their crops and, above all, freedom from the anxiety of protracted loan negotiations that critically delayed inputs and reduced yields.

For all of the above reasons, even though they received a smaller proportion of available group credit, the perception of benefit was skewed towards the poorest Bhil households who were most at risk from loss, who had fewer options and who depended upon self-help group loans to the greatest degree. Better-off households built security by investing in networks of social obligation, but for the poor, who lacked such networks, membership of a project-backed group afforded a substitute security (and reduced vulnerability) by way of credit to meet urgent cultivation, food or emergency (e.g. medical) needs, not to mention entitlement to work on project schemes. At best, group membership would reduce a little the everyday dependence on usurious *sahukars,* which was probably a precondition for income gains from agriculture or enterprise of any kind. For poorer households, if group membership were important this was because it could reduce exploitative dependence, by providing substitute social networks, and by bringing people into a relationship with project benefactors. For the better-off it was the latter that was the principal benefit. Regardless of their viability as farmer managed microfinance institutions, self-help groups were a means to perpetuate the relationship with the project patron.

When villagers insisted to researchers that the self-help groups were the most significant benefit provided by the project, it was the groups' ability to stand for access to a range of other project benefits and not just the economic gains of credit for agro-inputs that was important. But these new institutions and their routines had wider significance which lay not in the project interventions themselves (still less in its designs), but in wider processes of change and cultural negotiation which they symbolised and into which they fed. I want finally to turn to these.

Self-help or self-betterment

Bhil villagers repeatedly emphasised the cohesive and supportive aspect of project self-help groups, and the unity that they brought to villages in contrast to earlier times of disputes and family quarrels, by saying things like, 'if someone's roof needs repairing urgently before the monsoon, group members will offer help without asking for liquor'. Villagers pointed as well to the sociality of meetings, discussions and planning, when members of scattered households (especially women) came together. Now it is by no means obvious what these proclamations mean, if we set aside the possibility that this 'unity' was either the effect of power concentrated by project, or a projection for outsiders (see Mosse *et al.* 2002: 215–16). The self-help groups were not after all new associations. They were no more than the meeting of existing close-knit hamlet and lineage groups. At one level it appears that these expressions of unity indicate licence of an alternative mode of collective action in Bhil villages.

In this regard it is significant that, along with the celebration of group unity, there was a parallel commentary on the decline of other forms of reciprocal exchange and social obligation: the *halmo* system of labour exchange with liquor or food was being replaced by hiring wage labour; livestock were being sold for cash rather than consumed, gifted or sacrificed in fulfilment of social or religious obligations; and SHGs themselves offered freedom not only from *sahukars,* but also from the terrible pressures of *chandla*, whose obligations extracted forced payments or threatened social isolation. It begins to look as if SHGs were institutions allowing a form of cooperation and mutual support that was independent of burdensome social obligations, and in which voluntary savings and project subsidies substituted for social obligation. This was especially attractive to the poor with weak social networks.

There is a further point here. SHGs not only forged new types of collective action, they also offered a *cultural critique* of old ones. The discipline of meetings and savings was opposed to lavish spending on festivals, animal sacrifices or bride-price. The order of schedules, ledgers, minuted resolutions, rules and fines especially repudiated disorderly collective action mediated by *daru* (distilled liquor). Interestingly, abandoning alcohol was often ranked as the most significant change brought about by the project. Alcohol was connected to ill-health, debt, social conflict and, most seriously for women, with domestic violence. In fact, women directly linked the social discipline of group processes with reduced domestic violence and the reduced need to return to their natal homes to escape abuse. The promotion of SHGs appeared to displace and morally de-legitimise existing social capital mediated by alcohol. Was this a problem? It depends on who you asked. For women, and those with weak networks (e.g. of *chandla*), SHGs were a new form of association offering freedom from the burden of mutual obligation and alcohol-related domestic violence, as well as links to project patrons.

The decline in alcohol and abuse was important because it was central to women's physical and emotional well-being; but its centrality to Bhil villagers' 'change narratives' may also be related to the wider issues of identity and self-improvement with which it resonated. After all, alcohol has long been a core symbol of Bhil underdevelopment, and renouncing *daru* a Brahmanic virtue and idiom of progress and modernity, for example in the numerous *devi* cults, and in Gandhian and other social and religious reform movements (see Hardiman 1987). The project as a whole, but its SHG groups in particular, were contexts in which Bhils learned 'to see themselves as they understand others to be seeing [and judging] them' where they had to contend with 'cosmopolitan criticism (on radio, in offices, when they travel as "hicks" to the city)', and where they complied with outsiders' constructions of progress and civility (Pigg 1996: 180). Hardly surprising, then, that their narratives of change deal in the currency of stereotypes and negative Adivasi self-images, and key symbols and processes of improvement:

> Five years ago I was sick often and used to drink a lot. Since the project started I have stopped drinking and am healthy, this is because of exposure visits. [We] are not wearing torn clothes any more, there is a great change in life, especially because of the meetings. Now men sit together and discuss and help to solve each other's problems, regardless of clan. ... Some men in the village have started to wear trousers or shorts instead of *lungis* [cloth garments]; they have started to sit together for group meetings and have learned new things.[5]

Through meetings (commonly in the presence of field staff) villagers not only made decisions, passed resolutions and petitioned the project, they also bettered themselves in a specific way. As noted in relation to PRA timelines, project staff and Bhil villagers together constructed the project, and especially its SHGs, as a modernising force, and in doing so looked back on a tribal life of isolation, fear, ignorance, conflict, alcoholism and domestic violence. The project provided the context in which outsiders bringing new structures and routines (groups, meetings, formats), new leadership and new rules, brokered aspirations of modernity among marginal Adivasis. In the project, technologies too, whether seeds, SWC or diesel pumps, were a medium through which Adivasis, supposedly culturally different and of 'another time', became modern and contemporaneous with project agents (see Skaria 2003). Elsewhere, missionaries and Christian conversion have played this role, or Hindu nationalists or Gandhian social reformers, each in dangerous competition and conflict with the other (Karlsson 1999, 2000). Each offers a new economy in social life, release from ritual and social obligations (and expenses), a new order and orientation and a 'better' way of being. Adivasi development and religious change, or conversion, are often idioms of each other. In both, the renunciation of alcohol is a prime marker in the Adivasi story of modernisation.

Bhil endorsements of distinctions between a modern puritan middle-class lifestyle of thrift, account keeping and cleanliness, and customary tribal backwardness served tactically to maintain a relationship with the project patron. Ironically, the development practices through which project workers most clearly established and advertised to others their dealing with the apparently authentic (but actually simulated) 'local' and 'indigenous' – PRA, PVS, SHGs – were precisely those which for Bhils were avenues to the 'modern'. The point is that, despite our ideals of participation, in development poor people become 'empowered' not in themselves, but through relationships with outsiders having better access to resources; and not through the validation of their own existing knowledge and actions, but by seeking out and acknowledging the superiority of modern technology and lifestyles, and by aligning themselves with dominant cultural forms (cf. Fiedrich 2002). As Hardiman writes of the pre-Independence *devi* cults among Bhils, 'assimilation to dominant values ... provided a meeting point between the adivasis and certain progressive members of the dominant classes ...' eventually linking them to the wider nationalist movement (1987: 164).

In project villages, people also commented on the fact they had begun to consume differently. 'Everyone in my family has developed city tastes, like potato', says one man; 'earlier they used to eat wild food, now they don't like to eat this stuff.' The renunciation of *daru*, bathing regularly, wearing *dhotis*, eating rice or potatoes, planting improved varieties or adopting other signs of a modern lifestyle modelled for them by project workers – these were behavioural norms and patterns of consumption that were important because they facilitated and signalled alliances and new routes to power. Here objects (and practices) are given meaning and value because, as Douglas and Isherwood argue, they allow households that possess them greater 'discretion in interaction with outsiders and hence greater ability to maintain desired social relationships' (1978). Correspondingly, 'to be poor is to be poorly connected through things to other people, to fail to mount the necessary rituals of consumption' (Fardon 1999: 139, citing Douglas and Isherwood 1978). Orientation to 'modern' patterns of consumption (or practices, or beliefs) also implies new social differentiation according to lifestyle; new distinctions and new exclusions, that 'introduce a kind of marbling of cosmopolitan status into village life' (Pigg 1996: 173, cf. Bourdieu 1984). This was noted in relation to the status claims of reformed Bhagat Bhils, expressed in diet, dress styles and education. And here the project has its own social (as well as economic) effects by modelling and differentiating access to high-status consumption patterns. It is significant that, in the context of the increased impor tance of consumables – soap, tea, fertiliser, cloth – better-off households spoke of project benefits in terms of greater interaction with the market (selling surplus and spending on consumables). Poorer households, however, spoke of benefits in terms of going to the market less and a reduced need to borrow or to purchase food-grain for survival.

Conclusions

I have taken up one thread from a complex development project story, which concerns the contradiction between participatory development's professed goals of self-reliance and local control, and a set of actual project and cultural practices that are all about forging relationships with powerful outsiders for patronage and social protection. These are, in turn, consistent with historical strategies of poor Adivasis in the western region. Such a contradiction is easily concealed as project actors are constrained to promote the view that their activities result from the realisation of policy goals, of new technology and participation. But in itself such policy does not generate practice. Rather it offers a representation, a significant interpretation of events, one that actually erases the personal, contingent, hybrid agencies, struggles, connections and interactions of actual practice by portraying events as the outcome of rational intention guided by expertise (see Mitchell 2002: 77).

In the project, the new relationship of patronage and input supply was interpreted as an improved seed technology. 'Participation' concealed the political effects and the power of the project outsiders, who were portrayed as the beneficiaries' agents. In order to work, policy models and programme designs have therefore to be *transformed* in practice. They have to be translated into the different logic of the intentions, goals and ambitions of the many people and institutions they bring together. Locally, for example, participation is translated into patronage, new seeds into sources of credit. Correspondingly, policy models are poor guides to understanding events, practices and effects associated with development interventions. This project was not a hidden hand consolidating self-reliance; it was a powerful external source of patronage interacting with regional and historical processes of change. For its Bhil beneficiary communities, it was a means to access external resources, to articulate broader social ambitions and cultural re-evaluation as well as individual economic and political mobility.

Notes

1 This chapter extracts and develops one line of argument from Mosse (2005). I would like to thank Pluto Press for their willingness to allow me to draw materials from various chapters of my book.
2 Of course, such a binary distinction between 'developers' and 'beneficiaries' sets aside the many other contradictory perspectives among donors, scientists, bureaucrats and field-staff in any field of development and which are explored in Mosse (2005).
3 First, Bhil farmers worked hard to adapt environments to allow cultivation of this particular grain – levelling increasingly fragmented field plots, etc.; second, they exploited the variability present within the existing *katholi* variety to adapt to different environments (small seeds for sloping land; large ones for the flat); and third they preserved the quality of seeds (at risk through cross-pollination) through rigorous seed selection practices that were incorporated into daily social life (hence the typical display of cobs outside Bhil houses and the group interactions over seed sorting). While the project's Participatory Plant *Breeding* model for maize expected adaptation and yield increase through preserving genetic purity by the careful differentiation of the identity and source of new varieties, Bhil farmers applied a sophisticated taxonomic knowledge (based on *morphological* classification and an understanding of the interaction between biological and agro-ecological factors) to the selection of seeds from existing varieties after each harvest. This eroded the very basis of project technical success.
4 Taking into account the interest payments, the gifts of liquor, cash or chicken to loan brokers, lost wages and the compulsion to sell crops early at low prices to repay the loan (and so borrow again for food at the end of the season), it would cost well over Rs350 to secure a seasonal loan of Rs500 from a moneylender, but only Rs25 from the group.
5 Comments made during interviews in project villages during 'impact assessment village studies' in 1996–7.

References

Appadurai, A. (2004) 'The capacity to aspire: culture and the terms of Recognition', in V. Rao and M. Walton (eds) *Culture and public action*, Stanford, CA: Stanford University Press, 59–84.

Baviskar, A. (1995) *In the belly of the river: tribal conflicts over development in the Narmada valley*, New Delhi: Oxford University Press.

Bloch, M. (1991) 'Language, anthropology and cognitive science', *Man* 26(2): 183–98.

Bourdieu, P. (1984) *Distinction: a social critique of the judgement of taste*, Cambridge: Cambridge University Press.

Burghart, R. (1993) 'His lordship at the cobblers' well', in M. Hobart (ed.) *The growth of ignorance: an anthropological critique of development*, London: Routledge, 79–99.

de Certeau, M. (1984) *The practice of everyday life*, Berkeley: University of California Press.

Chambers, R. (1997) *Whose reality counts? Putting the first last*, London: Intermediate Technology.

Chambers, R., Pacey, A. and Thrupp, L.A. (1989) *Farmer first: farmer innovation and agricultural research*, London: Intermediate Technology Publications.

Deliège, R. (1985) *The Bhils of western India: some empirical and theoretical issues in anthropology in India*, New Delhi: National Publishing House.

Desai, B. (2004) *Local brokers: knowledge, trust and organisation in the practice of agricultural extension for small and marginal farmers in Rajasthan, India*, PhD thesis, SOAS, University of London.

Douglas, M. and Isherwood, B. (1978) *The world of goods: towards an anthropology of consumption*, London: Routledge.

Fardon, R. (1999) *Mary Douglas: an intellectual biography*, London and New York: Routledge.

Ferguson, J. (1994) *The anti-politics machine: development, de-politicisation and bureaucratic power in Lesotho*, Minneapolis: University of Minnesota Press.

Fiedrich, M. (2002) *Domesticating modernity: understanding women's aspirations in participatory literacy programmes in Uganda*, DPhil thesis, University of Sussex, UK.

Hardiman, D. (1987) *The Coming of the Devi*, New Delhi: Oxford University Press.

Jain, P.C. (1991) *Social movements among tribals: a sociological analysis of Bhils of Rajasthan*, Jaipur: Rawat Publications.

Karlsson, B.G. (1999) 'Entering into the Christian dharma: contemporary "tribal" conversions in India', Paper presented at the Conference on 'Cultural Interactions', Oxford, September.

—— (2000) *Contested Belonging: an indigenous people's struggle for forest and identity in sub-Himalayan Bengal*, London: Curzon Press.

Latour, B. (1996) *Aramis, or the love of technology*, trans. Catherine Porter, Cambridge, MA and London: Harvard University Press.

Li, T. Murray (1996) 'Images of community: discourse and strategy in property relations', *Development and Change*, 27: 501–27.

Lobo, L. (2002) 'Adivasis, Hindutva and post-Godhra riots in Gujarat', *Economic and Political Weekly* 37(48): 30 November–6 December, 4844–9.

Mitchell, T. (2002) *Rule of experts: Egypt, techno-politics, modernity*, Berkeley: University of California Press.

Mosse, D. (2005) *Cultivating Development: an ethnography of aid policy and practice*, London & Ann Arbor, MI: Pluto Press.

Mosse, D., Gupta, S., Mehta, M., Shah, V. and Rees, J. (2002) 'Brokered livelihoods: debt, labour migration and development in tribal western India', *Journal of Development Studies*, 38(5): 59–88.

Mosse, D., Gupta, S. and Shah, V. (2005) 'On the Margins in the City Adivasi Seasonal Labour Migration in Western India', *Economic and Political Weekly*, 40(28): 3025–38

Novellino, D. (2003) 'From seduction to miscommunication: the confession and presentation of local knowledge in "participatory development"', in J. Pottier, A. Bicker and P. Sillitoe (eds) *Negotiating local knowledge: power and identity in development*, London: Pluto Press, 273–97.

Padel, F. (2000) *The sacrifice of human being: British rule and the Konds of Orissa*, New Delhi: Oxford University Press.

Patel, K. (2007) *Cultivating diversity on farm: examining de facto conservation of agrobiodiversity in a tribal region of western India*, PhD Dissertation, University of Guelph, Canada.

Pigg, S.L. (1996) 'The credible and the credulous: the question of 'villagers' beliefs' in Nepal', *Cultural Anthropology*, 99(2): 160–201.

—— (1997) 'Found in most traditional societies – traditional medical practitioners between culture and development', in F. Cooper and R. Packard (eds) *International development and the social sciences: essays in the history and politics of knowledge*, Berkeley: University of California Press, 259–90.

Quarles van Ufford, P. (1988) 'The hidden crisis in development: development bureaucracies in between intentions and outcomes', in P. Quarles van Ufford, D. Kruijt and T. Downing (eds) The hidden crisis in development: development *bureaucracies*, Tokyo and Amsterdam: United Nations and Free University Press, 9–38.

Rao, A. (1988) *Tribal social stratification*, Udaipur: Himanshu Publications.

Richards, P. (1985) *Indigenous agricultural revolution*. London: Allen and Unwin.

Sharma, B.K. (1990) *Peasant movements in Rajasthan (1920–1949)*, Jaipur: Pointer Publishers.

Skaria, A. (1999) *Hybrid histories: forests, frontiers and wildness in Western India*, New Delhi: Oxford University Press.

—— (2003) 'Development, nationalism and the time of the primitive: the Dangs darbar', in K. Sivaramakrishnan and A. Agrawal (eds) *Regional Modernities: the cultural politics of development in India*, New Delhi: Oxford University Press, 215–37.

Van der Ploeg, J.D. (1992) 'The reconstitution of locality: technology and labour in modern agriculture', in T.K. Marsden, P. Lowe and S. Whatmore (eds) *Labour and locality: uneven development and the rural labour process. Critical Perspectives on Rural Change Series IV*, London: David Fulton, 19–43.

Weisgrau, M.K. (1997) *Interpreting development: local histories, local strategies.* Lanham, MD, New York and Oxford: University Press of America.

Wood, G.D. (2003) 'Staying secure, staying poor: "the Faustian bargain"', *World Development*, 31(3): 455–71.

10 Politics, development and identity

Jharkhand, 1991–2009

Amit Prakash

Introduction

In democratic developing countries such as India, policies and programmes for the development of a region and/or social group should address two related issues. First, they must endeavour to raise the living standard of the population of the target region and/or social group; second, try to generate a popular feeling of betterment of living standards. Achievements in the implementation of development policy will not serve the purposes of containing socio-political conflicts or generating increased legitimacy for the state unless society views these as such. Challenges to the legitimacy of political regimes born out of socio-political conflicts increase what Kohli calls the 'crisis of governability' (Kohli 1990). In light of this crisis, this chapter analyses the linkage between (a) the changing development profile of the 18 districts that once formed the Jharkhand region of Bihar (since 2000, the State of Jharkhand), and (b) the articulation of a new Jharkhandi identity, as expressed through the electoral support for Jharkhandi political parties since the 1990s. I will argue that while there may not be a direct correlation between the performance of development policy and identity-articulation in Jharkhand (or, for that matter, any given region, state or nation), the patterns of the political process underline the existence of a complex entanglement between these two factors, in terms of the relationship between state and society.

The politics of development and identity

It would be difficult to defend a contention that there has been no improvement over the last half-century in the overall living standards of the population of Jharkhand as a direct result of the development policy of the Indian state. Respondents interviewed in the Jharkhand region during my fieldwork in 1996 and again in 2006, agreed that, over the past few decades, there has been a marked improvement in the living standards of most people in the Jharkhand region.[1] They also recognised the central role played by the government's development policy but expressed their stark disappointment with the slow pace and inefficiency of the state's development efforts. Evidently, the feeling of betterment amongst them was marginal. The successes of the development policy could have generated, and to some extent did generate, a certain degree of legitimacy for the nation state. However, this process has gradually been undermined over the past two decades. Thus, an effort to understand the reasons behind the government's failure to harness the legitimising effect of the improvement in general living conditions of the population is required. This leads us to another malaise in the model of development adopted in India.

> All plans of development have greater chances of success if the relevant cultural and social factors are integrated into planning ... social and cultural factors must be so presented that they are plainly appropriate to the problem at hand and are clearly useful to the makers of development decisions ...
>
> (Narayan 1988: 81)

Despite Jawaharlal Nehru's interest in 'tribal' cultural distinctiveness, the model of development adopted in India after Independence did not have a place for socio-cultural factors. The development model premised on centralised rational bureaucratic planning and implementation of industry-led development was hardly suited to the development requirements of the 'tribal' areas (listed under Schedule V) and other backward regions. The absence of meaningful contributions by the local communities in the policy process in terms of addressing the local needs and utilising locally available resources led to plans being drawn that were unsuitable for a sustained development effort. The high 'transaction costs' of the development effort are also pertinent in such a model of development. Since locally available resources were hardly utilised in the planning and implementation of development programmes, it was too expensive to sustain a long, coherent and vigorous development effort of the state, not to mention the possibilities of corruption that it engendered.

The overall consequence of this model of development was that the local communities became passive beneficiaries of the state's development policy instead of being active partners. Consequently, there was no feeling of betterment and whenever matters worsened, the population simply looked up to the state for more handouts instead of making joint efforts with the development policy machinery to ensure better availability and management of resources. Consequently, there emerged a 'politics of development'. The political resources at the command of the local communities were channelled to secure an increasing amount of development funds as relief or short-term programmes and not as an investment into sustainable developmental activities. An exchange of resources which could have occurred at an early stage between the local communities or identities and the state to generate a long-term development plan, as well as legitimacy for the regime, was delayed. Consequently, the local communities gradually began to resort to agitational politics in order to generate some meaningful exchange of resources with the state.

The Jharkhand movement, which was rooted in a distinctive Adivasi heritage and culture, has therefore emerged as one of the avenues for this exchange of resources between the electorate of the region and the state.[2] Since the Jharkhandi groups do not, for many reasons, command enough political influence in the executive and legislative structures of the state, they demanded political and administrative autonomy in order to deliver better development policy implementation in the region. Owing to the inability of the rationalist state to respond successfully to this movement based on a distinctive heritage, the demand for autonomy found greater support, culminating in the creation of a separate State of Jharkhand in the year 2000. The Jharkhandi leaders, however, were not ready to divorce themselves from the issue of Adivasi identity. They successfully managed to merge the issues of Jharkhandi identity with the poor performance of the development bureaucracy. The issue of Jharkhandi identity is invoked to generate political support which is more inclusive than exclusive in nature (Prakash 2001). Despite being premised on tribal heritage and culture, the leadership is quick to include the non-tribal population in the category of Jharkhandi because of the overall numerical minority of people of tribal origins:

> The opponents of the Jharkhand propagate that after the creation of the Jharkhand State, the outsiders will be expelled. This propaganda is aimed at breaking the unity of the people of Jharkhand and at disrupting the Jharkhand movement. ... People of hundreds of *jatis* are original residents of the Jharkhand region but Jharkhand does not belong to them only. All those people who are living here for years ... have the same claim to the region as the original residents.
>
> (Soren 1992: 20–1)[3]

Thus, the leaders of the Jharkhand movement have used a peculiar mixture of identity-politics, populism and the poor developmental profile of the region to seek electoral support. Whether the people of the region see any relation between the poor developmental profile of the region and the demand for regional autonomy is also important to understand the salience of the Jharkhandi identity in the politics of the region. People in the Jharkhand region assert that the government of the State of Bihar at Patna did not invest enough resources in the Jharkhand region and hence wanted a separate State for faster economic development.[4] Clearly, the identity of being a Jharkhandi is bolstered by this attitude since it defines another dimension in the 'us' and 'them' dichotomy.

Overview of the politics of development and identity: 1950s–1990s

By the time India gained Independence in 1947, the Jharkhandi leaders had succeeded in creating a political community in south Bihar in the hope of engaging with the independent Indian state, in a manner that parallels Indian nationalists' engagement with the colonial state (Prakash 1999). However, the socialist credentials of the Indian state gave the nation a degree of political legitimacy and support that the Jharkhand Party (JHP) was unable to undermine. The overwhelming control of the state over the economic and information resources assisted this legitimacy. The Jharkhandi community was clearly the recipient of largesse allocated by the state, which the Jharkhandi leaders were unable to affect owing to their weak political position in the legislatures. Hence, the Jharkhandi population had to depend on the plans that the state drew up for them instead of having a meaningful role in the development planning for the region. The politics of development and identity in Jharkhand in the period 1947–91 is thus complex and marked by multifarious political articulations and contests, and overall poor growth of development indicators (Prakash 2001: chs. 4–6). A brief delineation of the main characteristics of the politics of development during 1947–91 is crucial in order to locate the later discussion for the period 1991–2004 in its historical and politico-economic context.

The development profile of the Jharkhand region in 1951 was quite poor, as it was in most parts of India. However, indicators of socio-economic development – such as death, birth and infant mortality rates, agricultural and industrial production, employment patterns, and literacy and education rates – were better in the Jharkhand region than in Bihar as a whole in 1951. However, even in 1951, the Jharkhand region was contributing a disproportionate share of revenue to the coffers of the State of Bihar while receiving only a miniscule proportion of developmental investment. This pattern continued over the next five decades, lending credence to the Jharkhandi argument that the region was an internal colony of Bihar.

Indicators of socio-economic development during 1951–91 tell a similar story. Admittedly, while most indicators show a substantial improvement over the four decades 1951–91, the rate of improvement in Bihar as a whole far outstripped the improvements in the Jharkhand region. This differential is true in most indicators with two important exceptions. The first is the growth in literacy and education, which were better in the Jharkhand region than in Bihar as a whole. This factor has an important role to play in the intensification of the Jharkhand movement and the central role that the All Jharkhand Students' Union (AJSU) played in the movement in the 1980s. Second, there was a disproportionate growth in the proportion of tax revenues collected from the Jharkhand region, which also contributed to the sharpening of the Jharkhand movement on account of the intensified alienation of the Jharkhandi population from the state government of Bihar.

While the developmental patterns of Bihar were marked by a lack of substantial change, the politics of the region was anything but staid (Prakash 2001: 85–131). In the 1950s, the JHP's agenda of autonomy and statehood for the Jharkhand region had found enthusiastic support amongst the region's electorate. The JHP not only performed exceedingly well in both the 1952 election, by winning three of the eight seats (or seven of 12 if the multi-member constituencies are included) and the 1957 election, by winning eight of the 12 seats.[5] During this decade the JHP virtually laid down the law for the region but gradually lost popular support. Despite its enthusiastic popular support, the JHP failed to convince the States Reorganisation Commission to recommend the creation of a separate State of Jharkhand and increasingly started to depend on tribal premises for mobilisation. Keeping in mind the region's poor developmental growth, this shift needs to be assessed in a demographic context marked by a declining proportion of Scheduled Tribes in the population of Jharkhand. All three factors ensured that the JHP was increasingly marginalised in the decades to come.

Between 1961 and 1991, the Jharkhandi electorate experimented with a wide spectrum of political formations, from the Congress Party (Indian National Congress, INC) to the extreme Left, yet the issues of local development, Adivasi autonomy and regional statehood did not hold sway in terms of the nation's political imperatives. The political process during this period was fractured across various political formations active in the region. The failure of the JHP to secure a separate state led the electorate to adopt the developmental vision of the INC. While the issues of autonomy and statehood never quite lost their appeal amongst the region's electorates, by the early 1960s these voters realised that there were wider political impediments to their implementation, which made them move away from regional parties. Further, the numerous Jharkhandi parties that emerged – all claiming to be the true inheritors of the ideology of the JHP – ensured that the movement fell into almost complete disarray. Thus the phase of national party building was truly underway in Jharkhandi politics. The INC performed well in the 1962 election and even better in the 1967 (partly due to the fact that JHP had merged with the INC in 1963) and 1971 elections. The 1977 election found the national pattern being repeated in Jharkhand with Bharatiya Lok Dal (BLD; Indian peoples' party) leading the way and Jharkhandi parties being more or less absent from any serious contest.

Despite two decades of support to the INC's development vision, the rate of growth of the development profile of Jharkhand did not show any significant improvement. The electorate therefore also discarded the INC and the 1980 election again saw support for a wide variety of political formations, from INC to Janata Party (Peoples' Party) to the rejuvenated JHP. The INC, however, was back in favour in the 1984 election winning all the Lok Sabha seats from the Jharkhand region.[6] This election marked a break in the political process in Jharkhand. The 1989 election saw the entry of a new actor – the Bharatiya Janata Party (BJP; Indian peoples' party) – on the political horizon of Jharkhand, and this brought back the issue of autonomy and statehood onto the political agenda of the region with proposal for smaller States, even if the BJP's construction of the Jharkhand region as Vanachal (and of Adivasis as 'vanavasis' or forest dwellers) went directly against the grain of the ideology of Adivasi self-rule.[7]

Another feature of the political process of Jharkhand in the 1980s was the three-pronged strategy articulated by the electorate. On the one hand, electoral support was extended to national parties, particularly the INC and BJP, which would form the government at the Union level and could legislate for a separate state. On the other hand, electoral support at the State level was extended to the regional parties likely to form the government at the state level in the hope of influencing a better developmental response. Simultaneously, sizeable political support was extended to agitational politics of AJSU and Jharkhand Co-ordination Committee (JCC). The blockading of mineral transportation from the region was a part of this strategy which served the purpose of bringing the issue onto the national agenda, leading to the creation of the Committee of Jharkhand Matters (COJM) in 1990 by the Union Ministry of Home Affairs in an attempt to find a solution to the issue of development. It comprised all the major political figures of the historic Jharkhand movement irrespective of their official party affiliation. Besides, there were many other experts ranging from anthropologists to social activists who served on the COJM. The important political figures of the Jharkhand movement who were members of the COJM were Dr R.D. Munda, Dr A.K. Singh, N.E. Horo, Shibu Soren, B.B. Mahto, B.P. Kesri, S.S. Besra, Prabhakar Tirkey, Santosh Rana, Suraj Mandal, Shailendra Mahato and Dr Stephen Marandi. The joint secretaries to the ministries of Rural Development, Tribal Development and Home Affairs represented the central government while the government of Bihar was represented by the secretaries in the ministries of Home Affairs and Tribal Welfare and the Regional Development Commissioner of the Jharkhand region (see Prakash 2001: ch. 7).

The politics of development and identity in the 1990s and beyond

The pattern of growth in the development profile of the Jharkhand region did not change significantly in the decade 1981–91. Over this decade, the demographic balance altered to make politics on tribal lines even more difficult, since by 1991 only 27.66 per cent of the population of the Jharkhand region were of tribal origin. Literacy continued to represent the successful component of public policy in the region. By 1991, more than 33 per cent of the population of the region were literate. This growth in literacy was matched by a growth in further educa-tion. The Jharkhand region continued to outperform Bihar as a whole as far as literacy was concerned. There was a decline in employment in the Jharkhand region with just about 32 per cent of the population being employed in 1991 (over 36 per cent in 1981). An increasing percentage of the population depended on agriculture; thus, a declining percentage of the population was employed in the non-agricultural sector. Despite a rise in the number of persons employed in agricultural activities, there had been a decline in the irrigation potential of the Jharkhand region during the decade 1981–91. This decline can also be noticed in land irrigated by government canals. The overall development profile of the Jharkhand region had declined over the previous two decades.

In such a developmental scenario, the elections to the Lok Sabha (Lower House of the Parliament) were held in 1991. While continuing some of the facets of the 1989 election, with the BJP owing to its promise of a separate state winning five of the 14 seats (with more than 30 per cent of average votes), the 1991 election also marked the virtual exclusion of the INC from any serious electoral contest in the region. In the 1991 election, the INC did not win any parliamentary seats (despite receiving 18 per cent of the average votes) while the

Jharkhand Mukti Morcha (JMM; Jharkhand Freedom Front), a regional party that advocated Adivasi self-rule, won six. Faced with a sluggish and inert developmental scenario, electoral support for Adivasi autonomy and regionalism was therefore stronger in this election.

As far as the pro-autonomy JMM was concerned, electoral support was poor in 1991 compared with the 1989 election in terms of vote share, but the party did win six of the 14 seats in the region. The JMM's average vote percentage in the seats they won declined to 36.79 per cent (from almost 49 per cent in 1989), while they polled an average 29.28 per cent in constituencies where they had presence amongst the first five candidates. The Janata Dal (JD), by virtue of being the party in a position to influence development policy implementation at the local level, continued to receive some degree of electoral support in the region. However, by 1991, the political process of the region crystallised into a clear support for the BJP, which was promising a separate state, and the JMM, ensuring that this promise was not forgotten by the BJP in the national parliament.[8]

The BJP's clear articulation of the demand for a separate state yielded rich dividends for the party in every election since 1991. The Lok Sabha election in 1996 saw a stronger electoral support for the BJP with JMM once again being relegated to the political backwaters, not to recover for the next three elections. In fact, the BJP, with its national standing and its clear potential to form the government at the Union level took the wind out of the sails of the JMM, the only active Jharkhandi party in the region. In the 1996 elections, BJP candidates were elected from 12 of the 14 Lok Sabha constituencies in the region with an average of 33 per cent of the votes.[9] The JMM and the INC won one consistency each. The INC thus failed to convert its 16 per cent of the average votes polled in all constituencies in Jharkhand into seats during this election. Clearly, the inadequate performance of the development machinery over five decades had encouraged and re-articulated the popular support for the idea of Adivasi autonomy. But having issued a clear promise of, and having the potential to deliver, statehood in Jharkhand – challenges that no other party with any chance of forming the government at the Union level had yet embraced – in 1996 the Jharkhandi electorate gave unprecedented support to a relative newcomer, the BJP.

As far as the JMM was concerned, it seemed to become increasingly marginalised. While the demand and mobilisation for a separate state was led by Jharkhandi groups, including the JMM and the AJSU, owing to the virtual highjacking of their agenda for statehood by the BJP, such political groups have been unable to claim that they alone were the legitimate proponents of the Jharkhandi political opinion. Consequently, since the 1991 elections they have been increasingly marginalised in the electoral politics of Jharkhand. Likewise, their vote share in the 1996 elections declined further and the JMM polled about 32 per cent of the votes in the sole seat won. Average votes polled by the JMM in Jharkhand declined to 14.4 per cent, while the average votes polled in the constituencies with a presence amongst the first five candidates declined to only

15.5 per cent. This was a far cry from the large electoral support that the JMM and other such parties had enjoyed in the 1980s.

The 1998 general elections continued the same electoral pattern with very few significant differences.[10] While the INC slightly improved its presence in the region by winning two seats with 17 per cent of the average vote, the BJP was the undisputed winner in the electoral contest of 1998. The BJP's candidates were elected in 12 of the 14 constituencies in the region, with more than 45 per cent of the votes. It must be noted that, by this time, all major political actors in the Jharkhand region had come around to supporting the idea of a separate state in Jharkhand. However, the BJP, with its astute mix of a small states agenda, patronising of tribal institutions and fielding of Scheduled Tribe candidates, finally created a situation in which the JMM increasingly became politically marginalised. Further, since it was increasingly becoming clear that the electorate had by now decided to support fully the statehood agenda, only national parties with significant numbers in the Lok Sabha would be relevant. This is exactly what the results of the 1998 elections underline.

Consequently, the JMM was unable to win a single seat in the region in the 1998 elections. The average votes polled by the JMM across all the constituencies declined to 14.4 per cent. However, the vote share of the JMM in those constituencies where it had a presence amongst the first five candidates rose significantly to 22.5 per cent. Such a rise in the vote share did not translate into a higher number of seats won by the JMM on account of the extreme polarisation of the political process of the region during the 1998 election.

The large mandate given by the Jharkhandi electorate to the BJP did not translate into significant gains for the population of the region. The Union government did not last a full term and elections were called for once again in 1999, and there was little change in the pattern of electoral outcome in the region. The BJP won 11 of the 14 seats in the region with 45 per cent average votes while the INC won two seats with average vote share of 23 per cent. RJD won only one seat with an average vote share of 8 per cent. BJP candidates were elected by a larger proportion of the votes in almost all the seats won by them. The JMM continued to be increasingly marginalised in the electoral contest during the 1999 elections, not winning any seats.[11] Further, the JMM also faced an all-round decline in the average votes polled. In the constituencies in which the JMM had an electoral presence amongst the first five candidates, the average votes polled fell to 12.88 per cent from 22.5 per cent in 1998. Besides, the overall average votes polled by the JMM in all the constituencies of Jharkhand region declined to 11.9 per cent from 14.4 per cent in 1998.

Clearly, the four elections held in the 1990s were dominated by the BJP in Jharkhand. Since the major difference between the electoral positions of BJP and other political parties active in Jharkhand region was the promise of a separate state, it is perhaps not wrong to deduce that the electoral support for BJP's clear articulation of a separate state in Jharkhand carried the day for the party. In fact, the attraction of the separate state promised by the BJP held so much of a sway in these elections that the political formations that had led the demand for such a separate state since before Independence were marginalised. Whether such shifts in electoral support from the JMM and INC to the BJP demonstrate short-term instrumentalist voting by the electorate, not a more far-reaching shift in electoral patterns of the recently created State of Jharkhand, will emerge in the analysis of the results for the 2004 and 2005 Assembly elections.

Turning attention to the development profile of the erstwhile Jharkhand region of Bihar and the new State of Jharkhand in 2001, some central indicators are available to evaluate the changes in the development profile of Jharkhand between 1991 and 2001.[12] The population of Jharkhand grew at a decadal rate of 23.19 per cent between 1991 and 2001 (24 per cent during 1981–91) compared with 28.43 per cent decadal growth of Bihar. The sex ratio of Jharkhand in 2001 was 941 compared with 922 in 1991. Literacy rates continued to perform well in Jharkhand. While the literacy rate in Jharkhand in 1991 was 33.65 per cent, it had risen to 54.13 per cent in 2001 (literacy figures for Bihar for 1991 and 2001 were 21.1 per cent and 47.53 per cent respectively). Similarly, female literacy in Jharkhand rose from 20.8 per cent in 1991 to 39.38 per cent in 2001, while the respective figures for Bihar were 18.63 per cent and 33.57 per cent. Clearly, as far as literacy was concerned, Jharkhand far outperformed Bihar during 1991–2001. Perhaps employment rates in agricultural and non-agricultural sectors are the most crucial indicators as far as economic development is concerned. Jharkhand continued the patterns of earlier decades with much higher non-agricultural employment levels compared with Bihar. While 22.22 per cent of Jharkhand's population were employed in agricultural activities in 1991, the same figure in 2001 was 25.16 per cent.

Similar growth was also noticeable in agricultural employment in Bihar, with 23.95 per cent of the population of Bihar being employed in agriculture-related activities in 1991, rising to 26.21 per cent in 2001. However, the most significant difference can be noted in non-agricultural employment. In Jharkhand, 9.12 per cent of the population was employed in non-agricultural activities in 1991 (Bihar: 5.75 per cent); by 2001, 25.16 per cent of the population of Jharkhand was employed in this sector (Bihar: 7.67 per cent). Thus, the overall employment scenario in Jharkhand had grown at a much higher rate than Bihar. This overall positive trend in the socio-economic development of Jharkhand during 1991–2001 formed the backdrop of the parliamentary elections of 2004. This election was important for being the first election in the new State of Jharkhand and also for the significant political re-configurations that seem to emerge from the result of this election.

By the time the general elections were held in 2004, the new State of Jharkhand had been in existence for over three years and the BJP, the largest beneficiary of the pattern of electoral support in the 1999 election, was in power at the State level (as well as at the Union level as a part of the National Democratic Alliance).[13] However, the trends and patterns of electoral support for the BJP in the 1999 elections did not continue in the 2004 elections.[14] BJP candidates were elected only from one constituency in Jharkhand, that of Koderma from which Babulal Marandi, the former Chief Minister, was elected with 44 per cent of the votes polled. The BJP polled less than half of the 1999 average vote share at 22 per cent.[15]

Further, JMM and other Jharkhandi political groups (such as the AJSU and the revived JHP led by N.E. Horo) re-emerged on the electoral horizon of Jharkhand after more than a decade of political irrelevance. Although a number of Jharkhandi political formations were in the fray, only the JMM was able to win seats in the region. The JMM's candidates were elected from four of the fourteen Lok Sabha seats in the region. Further, the JMM polled an average of almost 47 per cent of the votes polled in the seats won by its candidates, which was quite respectable. However, this performance by the JMM in 2004 election does not reflect a rise in popular support for the Jharkhandi political opinion in the State. In fact, the average electoral support for all the Jharkhandi parties in constituencies in which they had a presence amongst the first five candidates declined to 8.24 per cent in the 2004 election from 12.88 per cent in 1999. Since Independence, this is the lowest level of electoral support for Jharkhandi political parties in constituencies in which they had a presence amongst the first five candidates. Further, the overall electoral support for Jharkhandi political parties in all the constituencies of Jharkhand declined to 4.12 per cent in the 2004 election (11.96 per cent in 1999 elections). This poor level of electoral support for Jharkhandi political groups was the second-lowest in all the general elections since 1952. Clearly, all is not well with Jharkhandi political groups in Jharkhand. The largest beneficiary in the shifting patterns of electoral support in the new State of Jharkhand in the 2004 general election was the INC, which was elected in six of the fourteen constituencies in Jharkhand with an average vote of about 26 per cent.[16] In fact, the Jharkhand political dynamics seem to have reverted to those of the 1970s and 1980s, when INC dominated the elections in Jharkhand.

However, the transformation is more complex. Some of the patterns of the 2004 elections reinstate the conditions of acute political disarray noticed in the 1960s. The first important thing to note is that the BJP seems to have reversed its fortunes by securing eight of the 14 seats in the State while polling only 27 per cent of the total votes polled. The INC, on the other hand, was able to win only one seat while polling 15 per cent of the votes cast. At first glance, it seems to be a complete sweep for the BJP, as in the 1990s. On the other hand, the lack of a high percentage of votes polled by the BJP indicates that its good performance in the 2009 polls in terms of seats won was due to the complete political disarray amongst other parties active in the region. The INC's troubled relationship with RJD and JMM was one important factor. The alliance with JMM also reflects the absence of a political strength and agenda within the INC.

As far as Jharkhandi political opinion was concerned, a complex picture emerges. In terms of winning seats, JMM was the only Jharkhandi party which won two of the 14 available Lok Sabha seats. Further, in these two seats, the Jharkhandi political parties substantially lost electoral support by polling only 28 per cent of the votes (compared with 46 per cent in 2004). Average votes polled by all Jharkhandi parties across all constituencies in Jharkhand rose significantly to 24.6 per cent in 2009 compared with a mere 4 per cent in 2004. Further, in constituencies in which Jharkhandi parties marked a presence amongst the first five candidates, the votes polled for Jharkhandi parties rose from 8 per cent in 2004 to 28.7 per cent in 2009.[17]

Thus, despite significantly increasing their vote share in almost all constituencies in the State, Jharkhandi parties were unable to translate their electoral support into seats. The prime reason for this was the complete splintering of the Jharkhandi political space. The JMM faced stiff contest from a number of parties, all of which claimed to be representing the Jharkhandi ideal. Chief amongst such new parties were Jharkhand Vikas Morcha (Prajatantrik) (JVM), AJSU Party (AJSUP), Jharkhand Janadikhar Manch (JHJAM) and Jharkhand Jan Morcha (JHJM). These parties therefore fragmented the Jharkhandi vote share in a way that affected the outcome of the polls. Here it must be noted that such fragmentation of the Jharkhandi political opinion was earlier noted in the 1960s and 1970s, a period during which the Jharkhand movement all but disappeared from the political landscape of the State. Matters were not helped by the complete absence of an agenda of transformation amongst the Jharkhandi parties – a legacy of the Jharkhand movement phase that they have yet to overcome.

Implications of the developmental and political patterns

The changes in development profile have been the central factor in the dynamics of the political process of the Jharkhand region. However, this relationship is not one of a direct correlation but of a contingent and complex variable. The planners of development policy in the early 1950s had hoped that a vigorous development policy would weaken demands for autonomy on cultural lines. However, the poor implementation of the policy and the inadequate improvements in the development profile had encouraged the electorate to demand Adivasi autonomy and regional statehood. Under these circumstances, the issues of Jharkhandi identity were raised to augment the political resources controlled by the electorate. The fortunes of the Jharkhandi groups who have stood for Adivasi self-rule and a separate State of Jharkhand reflect these dynamics.

The INC had been partially successful in focusing attention on the development needs of the region (as opposed to the identity issue) and had gained significant electoral support for such a policy in the late 1960s, 1970s and early 1980s. However, the party lost the legitimacy and support generated by its pro-poor rhetoric (and some concrete efforts) due to the developmental inertia in the region. Hence, in the late 1980s and 1990s, the electorate of Jharkhand were willing to experiment once again with the various political parties that were present in the region, including the Jharkhandi political groups. The BJP entered the electoral horizon of the Jharkhand region precisely at this time and the reasons which led to the decline of INC also partially explain the success of the BJP. The BJP projected itself with the slogan 'You (the electorate) have tried all parties time and again, try us once' to appeal to those who had been let down by all political groups in the region too many times, as far as their developmental requirements were concerned. Further, the BJP also stole the thunder of the

Jharkhandi political opinion by offering its own concept of a separate State in Jharkhand under the name of 'Vananchal' (forested region) to appeal to the *Hindutva* (Hindu nationalist) ideologues and non-tribal electorate in the region; the plans for a State came to fruition in 2000.

The failure of the political parties in the Jharkhand region to offer avenues for the exchange of resources between the electorate and the state, and the consequent decline in the development profile added another dimension to the relationship of dependence in the region. In the 1990s, the electorate split the political resources that they controlled into three components. In the 1991 and 1996 elections, State-level electoral support was extended to Janata Dal or Rashtriya Janata Dal (National Peoples' Party, RJD) which was in office at the State level and could have influenced public policy implementation.[18] In the Lok Sabha elections, this political support was extended to the BJP as it was the only national party that was promising the creation of a separate State of Jharkhand. The third component of the strategic use of political resources by the electorate consisted of forcing the two parties to remember their promises during the term of office. This was manifested in the support for the agitational politics of the JMM, the JCC and the AJSU, consisting of economic blockades and general strikes. This kind of agitational politics forced the state to listen to the Jharkhandi electorate, since these agitations often required coercion by the state in order to keep the mineral lifeline of the country running. Such coercion undermined the legitimacy of the state and the regime. Consequently, the regime in office was forced to take urgent policy measures to contain future strife.

This three-pronged approach in the late 1980s and the 1990s has yielded better profits for the people of the Jharkhand region than all others. Such strategic use of political resources has led the state to engage in a more meaningful exchange of resources with the population of the Jharkhand region. As a result, the Committee on Jharkhand Matters (COJM) was established and, by 1995, the Bihar Vidhan Sabha (Bihar Legislative Assembly) legislated to create the Jharkhand Area Autonomous Council (JAAC); finally. the separate State of Jharkhand was created in 2000 (see Prakash 2001: ch. 7). The splitting of political resources at the command of the electorate has thus forced the state to respond with better policy measures.

The Lok Sabha election of 2004 underlines the continuation of the pattern of strategic use of the political resources at their command by the electorate. Once the State had been created in 2000, the electorate saw little use for the BJP, not least due to the policy shortcomings of the BJP government at the State level. Further, issues such as the domicile policy for government employment did not help the BJP in securing larger electoral support. The improvements in socio-economic profile in 1991–2001 notwithstanding, the BJP was unable to offer a road map for the development of the State. The Jharkhandi political parties on the other hand were not a very attractive political choice for the electorate on account of the fact that the rationale for their existence (the creation of a separate State of Jharkhand) had disappeared and they had never offered an alternative vision for the development of the State. Further, the RJD, which was in power at the State level when Jharkhand was a part of Bihar, did not offer a viable alternative on account of its inability to contribute to the development of Jharkhand, despite being in power for almost a decade. The INC therefore emerged as a dominant player in the new State.

Thus, overall, any predictions that may have been made about electoral support to the BJP's 'Vanachal' and *vanavasi* constructions in Jharkhand have been belied. The BJP's appeal to the electorate in Jharkhand was limited to the party's promise for a separate State of Jharkhand. Once that was realised, the electorate shifted support to the developmental vision of the INC, something which was tried intensively in the 1960s and 1970s with little success. Conversely, the idea that the ethnic aspects of the Jharkhandi identity – which had formed the basic premise for the quest for regional autonomy – have become irrelevant also appears false. Continued support to the JMM is only one aspect of this argument. The role of the Adivasi movement in Jharkhand in legally safeguarding the Scheduled Areas and implementing the Panchayati Raj (Extension to Scheduled Areas) Act (known as PESA) is another. Such Adivasi political and cultural concerns are also evident in the large-scale popular support for Birsa Day (the remembering of the Adivasi freedom fighter Birsa Munda), and for *Hul* celebrations, such as the large commemoration of the 150th anniversary of the Santal Rebellion (of 1855–7) in June 2005. The complex entanglements of identity and development are thus yet to play themselves out fully in the politics of the new Jharkhand state. The contours of this politics of development are fluid and complex, as demonstrated in the results of the 2009 elections wherein complete political disarray of the Jharkhandi political opinion is the only pattern that emerges, with multiple political actors flogging the politics of identity without a glimmer of an agenda of social transformation and social change. Jharkhandi parties like the JMM are finding it increasingly difficult to reinvent their relevance in contemporary Jharkhandi politics. These weaknesses of the opposition ensure that the BJP and the INC fight their national electoral battles in Jharkhand and, in the process, trample upon any remaining idea of Jharkhand.

Notes

1 For instance, the MP from Ranchi, a Congress Party worker in Chaibasa and a female forest-produce collector in the rural interior of Dumka district, all agreed that 'There has definitely been some development ...' (interviews in the Jharkhand region in January and May 1996).
2 While a number of terms are used to refer to the tribal population, such as tribes, Adivasi, aborigines, or autochthones, social science has 'not examined the term 'tribe' in the Indian context rigorously' (Shah 2004: 92). Hence, the discussion about tribal population in India has largely followed the government categorisation of Scheduled Tribes (STs) and more recently, the politically-articulated term 'adivasi' seems to have been accepted by all, including the tribals themselves.
3 The term *jati* does not have a corresponding English equivalent. It is also used quite loosely in the Indian languages. It can mean caste, community, group of people or tribe, depending on the context. In this extract, it implies tribe.
4 This contention has been an important issue and is evident in most speeches and writings of the leaders in the Jharkhand region. For instance, in a speech at a public meeting, the JMM Lok Sabha candidate for the 1996 election for Ranchi constituency

said 'Bihar government makes little effort for our development, that is why we are demanding the creation of a Jharkhand State', Public Meeting in Sonahatu Block in May 1996.

5 In 1952, when the Lok Sabha had 489 seats, India was divided into 314 single-member constituencies, 86 double-member constituencies and one three-member constituencies. In 1957, with 494 seats in the Lok Sabha, there were 312 single-member constituencies and 91 double-member constituencies. The reservation of seats for Scheduled Castes and Scheduled Tribes was the main reason for the creation of double-member constituencies (see Singh and Bose 1984: 13).

6 The results of the 1984 elections need to be treated with caution as this election was truncated by the assassination of Indira Gandhi. Hence, most parts of the country saw an unprecedented 'sympathy vote' in favour of the INC leading to the largest majority in the Lok Sabha ever. Thus, this result may not be a part of a long-term electoral trend in the Jharkhand region.

7 The BJP clearly articulated its view of smaller states only in its election manifesto for the 1991 Lok Sabha election and in the *Resolution Regarding Creation of New states of Uttaranchal and Vananchal* tabled on 5 March 1993 in the Lok Sabha. However, politically, the issue was very much alive in the 1989 election.

8 In the election manifesto for the 1991 Lok Sabha election, BJP promised: 'The BJP recognises that regional imbalances have developed in some states because of their size. The party would appoint a commission to report on formation of smaller states which are economically and democratically viable. Initially, BJP will have Uttaranchal, Vanachal and Union Territory of Delhi as three new states of the Indian Union …' (Bharatiya Janata Party 1991: 3).

9 *Statistical Report on General Elections, 1996 to the Eleventh Lok Sabha*, Vol. I (National and State Abstracts & Detailed Results), New Delhi: Election Commission of India, n.d.

10 *Statistical Report on General Elections, 1998 to the Twelfth Lok Sabha*, Vol. I (National and State Abstracts & Detailed Results), New Delhi: Election Commission of India, n.d.

11 The JMM did not win any seats in the 1999 elections. However, Shibu Soren of the JMM won the Dumka parliamentary seat in a by-election after it was vacated by Babulal Marandi on 8 March 2001 following his swearing in as the first Chief Minister of the newly created State of Jharkhand.

12 All data used in this chapter for the year 2001 have been taken from Census 2001, available from the Census Commissioner of India at www.censusindia.net.

13 The Bihar Reorganisation Act, 2000, provided that the newly constituted Legislative Assembly of Jharkhand would have a term coterminous with that of the Bihar Legislative Assembly as those MLAs in the Bihar Assembly elected from the Jharkhand region formed the bulk of the MLAs in the Assembly of Jharkhand.

14 *Statistical Report on General Elections, 2004 to the 14th Lok Sabha*, Vol. II, New Delhi: Election Commission of India, n.d.

15 Ibid.

16 Ibid.

17 All data cited for the 2009 election have been collated from various sections of the Election Commission website, www.eci.nic.in, owing to unavailability of official reports as yet.

18 The Janata Dal split in 1997 after charges of corruption were levelled against the then Chief Minister, Laloo Prasad Yadav. Consequently, he formed a new party, the Rashtriya Janta Dal (RJD), which was in office in Bihar with Rabri Devi as the Chief Minister until the Vidhan Sabha Elections 2005.

References

Bharatiya Janata Party (1991) *Manifesto of the Bharatiya Janata Party for Lok Sabha Election 1991*, New Delhi: BJP Central Office.

Kohli, A. (1990) *Democracy and Discontent: India's Growing Crisis of Governability*, Cambridge: Cambridge University Press.

Narayan, S. (1988) *Movements Development: Police and Judiciary in Tribal World*, New Delhi: Inter India Publications.

Prakash, A. (1999) 'Contested Discourses: Politics of Ethnic Identity and Autonomy in the Jharkhand Region of India', *Alternatives: Social Transformation and Humane Governance*, 24(4): 461–96.

—— (2001) *Jharkhand: Politics of Development and Identity*, New Delhi: Orient Longman.

Shah, G. (2004) *Social Movements in India: A Review of Literature*, New Delhi: Sage Publications.

Singh, V.B. and Bose, S. (1984) *Elections in India: Data Handbook on Lok Sabha Elections*, London: Sage.

Soren, S. (1992) 'Jharkhand Rajya ka Sawal?' (The Question of Jharkhand State), in S. Narayan (ed.) *Jharkhand Movement: Origin and Evolution*, New Delhi: Inter-India Publications, 19–27.

Part V

Mainstreams and margins

Introduction to Part V

Part V examines how Adivasi identities have been appropriated by dominant groups, whether these are located within or outside the conventional boundaries that demarcate spaces of Indigenous and tribal belonging. As noted by Homi Bhabha (1990), the notions of margins and minorities can and do interpenetrate. The space of the margin is often appropriated by dominant cultural formations or narratives, which may include '... those justifications of modernity – progress, homogeneity, cultural organicism, the deep nation, the long past – that rationalize the authoritarian 'normativizing' tendencies within a culture in the name of the national interest ...' (Bhabha 1990: 4). Using Bhabha's approach, one can set out an analytical context concerning how Adivasi subjectivities are reified, and how their interests are appropriated by dominant groups (Xaxa 1999).

The concept of a national 'mainstream' suggests that there is – and that there has historically been – an ideological gulf between Adivasis and non-Adivasis, or between Adivasi interests and non-Adivasi interests. This sense of Adivasi difference and distinctiveness vis-à-vis a national mainstream emerged during the 1920s and 1930s, when non-dominant group identities were represented in administrative terms as 'minorities' (Roy 1946; Grigson 1944), and situated outside the imaginary borders of the dominant Hindu community (see also Guru and Chakravarty 2005: 139–40). Further, from the 1930s to 1950s, the Indian National Congress broached the topic of sub-national group identification via hegemonic processes that aimed to erase or disavow insurgent pasts. Specific Adivasi movements have, however, reclaimed and re-imagined insurgent pasts (see Rycroft 2011). Such imaginaries might be seen to contradict the values of India's mainstream, characterised by the veneration of a 'centre' that enables India to achieve pan-regional and intercultural unity.

Nationalists, such as Jawaharlal Nehru, the first Prime Minister of independent India, reasoned that sub-national group interests could be reconciled with national interest through the policy of affirmative action. In rational secularist terms, Nehru drew up five principles for 'tribal' integration and development that have enabled 'tribal' rights and heritage to gain visibility. This *Panchsheel* approach provided the initial ethical framework for the early 'five year plans' that sought to bring Adivasis within the ambit of the liberal socialist state. The initial *Panchsheel* framework was protectionist, elaborating notions of tribal genius and tribal rights, and set out the terms for a mutual recognition of tribal participation according to the practices of traditional tribal institutions. It was also socialist and humanist, allowing for the human condition to hold sway over purely economic developmental interests (Singh 1989). These development measures reconfigured the 'tribal' within a new rule-of-difference, which privileged cultural relativism and oversaw a generation of 'welfarist anthropology' (Debnath 1999: 3112). Paradoxically, however, this was a narrative as much of social containment as of welfare. For Adivasis, this meant being re-administered from the 1950s onwards as Scheduled Tribes, a constitutionally sanctioned entity earmarked for special political, economic, and cultural measures that might secure, through the involvement of the nation state and its anthropologists, a semblance of egalitarian development.

For some critical anthropologists, such as Biswanath Debnath, these factors have defined the inscription of 'tribal' subordination within post-colonial development and anthropological narratives:

> The poverty of ideas in anthropology has been created by an overzealous nationalistic cause. The two societies of India – one of the Hindu elite and the other tribal – remained separate but gradually became intertwined in a complex web of unequal economic linkages. It is this interlocking process which the Indian elite, including anthropologists, refer to as 'integration', and constantly flag as a desirable objective to pursue and achieve.
>
> (Debnath 1999: 3112)

Keeping this developmental rationale in view, Suranjit Saha (1986: 287–91) has set out the historical context of the relationship between 'tribal society and the national mainstream' as 'the problematic of integration'. In a manner that anticipated Debnath's critique, Saha argued that the idea of integration is 'operationally counterproductive' on account of its non-reflexive approach to development (1986: 287). Thus, the relations between the state (or the dominant society more generally) and Adivasis might foster antagonisms as well as alliances, and in turn lead to Adivasi critiques of state intervention as internal colonialist, or paternalist and acculturative (Saha 1986: 287–8). The negation of indigeneity at the expense of 'tribal' recognition implied that Adivasi selfhood and subjectivity could not be fully presented either in the Scheduled Tribe concept, or through related provisions and acts.

Other analysts, namely G.C. Rath, have taken the discussion on national integration forward, situating the problem as a response to divergent terms of cultural and political representation:

> Whilst isolation aims at conscious separation of tribe from the potential political and economic mainstream and assimilation tends to the tribe's partial and involuntary subservience, integration in contrast is a respectful

merger with the mainstream, staking a claim to an equal share of power and resources as other citizens.

(Rath 2006: 76)[1]

In the past two decades, right-wing religious nationalists in India have discredited Adivasi claims to indigenous subjectivity, as this usurps the presumed antiquity of the Hindu majority. They have also disavowed the legal status of the Scheduled Tribes and Scheduled Areas that are posited as continuations of colonial attempts to administer 'aboriginal' regions in India as 'backward tracts'. It is presumed by Hindu nationalists that such protectionist measures give legitimacy to the view that the 'tribals' own a cultural heritage that is distinct from (and a threat to) that of the nation's. This has led to a Hindutva (Hindu ness, or Hindu nationalist) mis-appropriation and reconstruction of Scheduled Tribes (or 'tribals') as *vanavasis* (forest dwellers), and much secularist analysis (see Bilgrami 1998; Baviskar 2005; Sarkar 2005; Teltumbe and Gatade 2005; Ramachandran and John 2005; Rycroft 2009). Critical of colonial administrative anthropological enquiries, and consequent attempts to situate Adivasis outside the imaginary borders of the dominant Hindu community, Hindu nationalist leaders and some sociologists/anthropologists (see Ghurye 1943) and modernists (see Rycroft 2006) have implemented more assimilationist ideologies and programmes.

At the other end of the political spectrum, left-wing critics have demonstrated the anti-secular slant of assimilation, and also aimed to dismantle the culturalist principles of the liberal *Panchsheel* paradigm (Rath 2006: 68). From their perspective, unless it was subjected to a rigorous economist critique, national integration would incorrectly privilege a linkage between 'minority' identities and economic deprivation. Again, 'Ultras' or guerrilla left-wing organisations such as the Naxalites (Maoists), sympathetic to Adivasi struggles against exclusion from the national mainstream, aim to revolutionise the 'tribals', but do so in such a way that discredits Adivasi customary institutions as vestiges of colonial rule (Guha 2007). In all of these discourses – liberal, the right wing and the left wing – the language of centre and periphery has gained efficacy historically, at the expense of Adivasi-specific imaginings.

As debated by Akeel Bilgrami, the concept of 'mainstream' has implications for political and cultural theorists who apprehend nationalism as:

a modern state of mind in which the very ideal of 'nation' has built into it as a form of necessity the ideal of nation-state, with its commitment to such things as development, national security, *rigidly codified forms of an increasingly centralized policy, and above all the habit of exclusion of some other people* ...

(1998: 383, emphasis added)

The culture of national de-colonisation was often premised upon cultural nationalism, or 'culturalism'. This ideology has underpinned the perception and celebration of 'tribal heritage' in national discourses and institutions (see for example Mann 1993). In pre-independent India, cultural nationalism would often take the form of populism, since a populist approach to community construction would enable a wide range of people to think of themselves as belonging to the same de-colonising nation, albeit from a culturally-specific position (see Skaria 2003: 232–3). As such, it often privileged dominant cultural forms that gave new relevance to predominantly Hindu values and traditions, over marginal heritages, such as those relating to Adivasis. Yet with the anthropological bias of Tribal studies after independence, an alternative tribe-specific populism emerged, emphasising village-level self-rule (Rath 2006: 79). This concept of local auto-nomous councils had earlier attracted numerous political thinkers, from Brajen-dra N. Seal, to Mohandas K. Gandhi, and W.V. Grigson (Rycroft forthcoming). Since the early 1990s, the idea of *gram swaraj* (village self-rule) has become an important site for current Adivasi engagements with secular nationalism. The wide-ranging debates accompanying the Panchayati Raj (Extension to Scheduled Areas) Act of 1996 (known as PESA) have provided the grounds for Adivasi negotiations of state de-colonisation through de-centralisation. PESA both avows local Adivasi leadership and customary laws, and yet also disavows wider regional claims for Adivasi self-rule (Dreze and Sen 2002; Sundar 2005).

With the return to minority identity politics in the 1990s – a pan-Indian polit-ical shift that accompanied the crisis in secularism epitomised by the controver-sial Mandal Commission of 1989 (and a resurgent Hindu nationalist movement that opposed it) – democratic regional movements as well as the counter-hegemonic Naxalite causes became the divergent foci for Adivasi assertion (see Kothari 2001). The rise of plural '… caste, ethnic, tribal and gender identities …' in political debates from the 1970s onwards shows how social movements and '… distinctive histories, constituencies and ideologies …' all interpenetrate in the negotiation of statist master narratives, giving rise to the need to compre-hend multiple interpretations of belonging (Ray and Katzenstein 2005: 9, 11; see also Guru and Chakravarty 2005: 141). Through minority representation, such groups are transformed into communities within the nation. These processes also present opportunities to re-interpret the margins of the nation. Within this frame-work of mainstreams and margins, the practices of representation are thus crucial to an understanding of how political and cultural articulation works, and why its social effects are of analytical importance. Our contributors to this concluding section show how the rhetoric produced through a discourse of mainstreams and margins has become part of the cultural policy – those conditions of governance as pertaining to national de-colonisation and tribal welfare – in modern India.

Abhijit Guha provides a nuanced descriptive ethnography of how political parties in West Bengal celebrated the 200th year of the Chuar '*bidroha*' or rebel-lion in 1998–9. The rebellion was represented in colonial records as a tribal-peasant revolt and has since defined the subaltern aspects of the history of Midnapur district. Basing his study on reports drawn from the Bengali daily, *Sambad Pratidin*, and on pamphlets and articles published by political activists and academics, Guha analyses the divergent narratives of the Chuar rebellion in order to provide an insight into how people, across time, space and socio-political affiliation, viewed, acted upon and used a past event for partisan purposes. Guha views the celebration of the *bidroha* as a kind of contemporary social drama in which the political parties and their leaders pursued their self-interests by raising allegations against opponents and by showing their respective capabilities for mass mobilisation, keeping future electoral battles in mind. He raises questions concerning socio-political representations of insurgent pasts in order to discuss the interface between anti-colonial resistance and political identities in contemporary India.

Shah's entry point is different, as she shows how poorer sections of the Adivasis were marginalised by dominant sections of their community. Based on ethnographic fieldwork, Shah studies the immediate aftermath of the separation of Jharkhand from the state of Bihar, and what the formation of Jharkhand meant to some of its Munda Adivasi people. Recognising different layers (identified along economic, educational and caste lines) within the Adivasi and wider Jharkhandi society, Shah discusses the divergent sets of imaginations that coexist and interrelate with one another. Questioning the relationship between the region and the state, she draws attention to the multiple imaginings of and articulations of regionalism. Jharkhandi responses were structured according to different contexts, which were distinct and yet overlapped. Adivasis of Jharkhand existed as inhabitants of a specific village; as tenants in relation to *zamindars*; as members of kin groups and clans; as part of an Adivasi group; and as constituents of a regional community. Jharkhandi regionalism advanced a programme of opposition that was premised on the notion that Jharkhand was an internal colony of Bihar State. The demand for Jharkhand thus evolved into a regional movement enjoying the support of a range of people, but with the common consent that the area's identity derived from the exploitation of its population and its distinct cultural heritage. While Jharkandi activists who had spearheaded the struggle for autonomy reimagined the regional community through the re-invention of indigenous rituals, symbols and traditions and thereby helped the people of a specific village to identify with a regional community, some of the images of the Jharkhandi community that were reproduced by these activists were starkly at odds with the social experiences of the villagers, and further alienated them.

Note

1 However, anthropologists and anthropological thinking in the colonial period, or shortly after it, cannot necessarily be fitted into these moulds (see Dasgupta 2007).

References

Baviskar, A. (2005) 'Adivasi Encounters with Hindu Nationalism in MP [Madhya Pradesh]', *Economic and Political Weekly*, 26 November, 5105–13.

Bilgrami, A. (1998) 'Secularism, Nationalism and Modernity', in R. Bhargava (ed.) *Secularism and its Critics*, New Delhi: Oxford University Press, 380–417.

Bhabha, H.K. (1990) 'Introduction: Narrating the Nation', in H.K. Bhabha (ed.) *Nation and Narration*, London: Routledge, 1–7.

Dasgupta, S. (2007) 'Recasting the "Oraons" and the "Tribe": A Study of Sarat Chandra Roy's Anthropology', in P. Uberoi, S. Deshpande and N. Sundar (eds) *Anthropology in the East: Founders of Indian Sociology and Anthropology*, New Delhi: Permanent Black, 131–68.

Debnath, B. (1999) 'Crisis of Indian Anthropology', *Economic and Political Weekly*, 30 October, 3111–14.

Dreze, J. and Sen, A. (2002) *India: Development and Participation*, New Delhi: Oxford University Press, 359–60.

Ghurye, G.S. (1943) *The Aborigines, So-called and their Future*, Bombay: Popular Book Depot.

Grigson, W.V. (1944) 'The Aboriginal in Future India', *The Journal of the Royal Anthropological Institute of Great Britain and Ireland*, 74(1–2): 33–41.

Guha, R.C. (2007) 'Adivasis, Naxalites, and Indian Democracy', *Economic and Political Weekly*, 11 August, 3305–12.

Guru, G. and Chakravarty, A. (2005) 'Who are the Country's Poor? Social Movement Politics and Dalit Poverty', in R. Ray and M.F. Katzenstein (eds) *Social Movements in India: Poverty, Power and Politics*, Lanham: Rowman and Littlefield Publishers, 135–60.

Kothari, S. (2001) 'Sovereignty and Swaraj: Adivasi Encounters with Modernity and Majority', in J. Grim (ed.) *Indigenous Traditions and Ecology: The Interbeing of Cosmology and Community*, Harvard: Harvard University Press, 453–64.

Mann, R.S. (1993) *Culture and Integration of Indian Tribes*, New Delhi: M.D. Publications.

Ramachandran, T.K. and John, P.T. (2005) 'The Sangh Parivar's Initiatives in the Tribal belt of Wyanad in Kerala', in A. Teltumbe (ed.) *Hindutva and Dalits: Perspectives for Understanding Communal Praxis*, Kolkata: Samya, 300–3.

Rath, G.C. (2006) 'Nehru and Elwin on Tribal Development', in G.C. Rath (ed.) *Tribal Development in India*, New Delhi: Sage Publications, 65–91.

Ray, R. and Katzenstein, M.F. (2005) 'Introduction: In the Beginning, There was the Nehruvian State', in R. Ray and M.F. Katzenstein (eds) *Social Movements in India: Poverty, Power and Politics*, Lanham: Rowman and Littlefield Publishers, 1–31.

Roy, S.C. (1946) 'The Aborigines of Chota Nagpur: Their Proper Status in the Reformed Constitution', *Man in India*, 26(2): 120–36 (first published in 1936).

Rycroft, D.J. (2006) 'Santalism: Reconfiguring 'the Santal' in Indian Art and Politics', *Indian Historical Review*, 33(1): 150–74.

—— (2009) 'Revisioning Birsa Munda: visual constructions of the '*vanavasi*' in Jharkhand', in N.K. Das and V.R. Rao (eds) *Identity, Cultural Pluralism and the State: South Asia in Perspective*, Delhi: Macmillan Publishers, 261–80.

—— (2011) 'Beyond Resistance: Idioms and Memories of Insurgency in the Adivasi Movement, Jharkhand State, India', in S. Das Gupta and R.S. Basu (eds) *Narratives from the Margins: Aspects of Adivasi History in India*, New Delhi: Pluto Press, 257–76.

—— (forthcoming) 'Indian Anthropology and the Construction of 'Tribal Ethnicity' Before Independence', in S. Gupta (ed.) *Nationhood and Identity Movements in Asia: Colonial and Postcolonial Times*, New Delhi: Manohar Publishers.

Saha, S.K. (1986) 'Historical Premises of India's Tribal Problem', *Journal of Contemporary Asia*, 16(3): 274–319.

Sarkar, T. (2005) 'Problems of Social Power and the Discourses of the Hindu Right', in R. Ray and M.F. Katzenstein (eds) *Social Movements in India: Poverty, Power, and Politics*, Lanham: Rowman and Littlefield Publishers, 62–78.

Singh, K.S. (1989) 'Jawaharlal Nehru, Tribals and Their Transformation', in K.S. Singh (ed.) *Jawaharlal Nehru, Tribes and Tribal Policy*, Calcutta: Anthropological Survey of India, 1–11.

Skaria, A. (2003) 'Development, Nationalism and the Time of the Primitive: The Dangs Darbar', in K. Sivaramakrishnan and A. Agrawal (eds) *Regional Modernities: The Cultural Politics of Development in India*, Stanford: Stanford University Press, 215–36.

Sundar, N. (2005) ' "Custom" and "Democracy" in Jharkhand', *Economic and Political Weekly*, 8 October, 4430–4.

Teltumbe, A. and Gatade, S. (2005) 'Gujarat: In Search of Answers', in A. Teltumbe (ed.) *Hindutva and Dalits: perspectives for Understanding Communal Praxis*, Kolkata: Samya, 275–99.

11 Using the past to win the present

Peasant revolt, political parties and the print media in leftist West Bengal

Abhijit Guha

… many indeed most, of the symbols that are politically significant are overtly nonpolitical. Often, the less obviously political in form symbols are, the more efficacious politically they prove to be.

(Cohen 1979: 87)

Opening the curtain

During 1998–9, an upsurge of interest and activism was observed among leaders of political parties in West Bengal as they celebrated the 200th anniversary of a peasant revolt, popularly known as the 'Chuar Rebellion'. The Medinipur town and the adjoining areas of the erstwhile Medinipur district, located in the south-western part of West Bengal, became the main centre for the celebration of this revolt.[1] This peasant revolt of 1776 is regarded as one of the earliest of rebellions against the exploitative revenue policy of the British East India Company. Local kings and tribal chiefs, who paid a tribute to the Mughal rulers rather than a regular form of revenue, ruled the area when the rebellion took place. In the pre-British period, these kings and chiefs had their own armies and police force. The soldiers of these armies received tax-free lands from the chiefs for cultivation and, in turn, provided protection to the rulers in times of warfare. These tax-free lands were known as the 'Paikan' lands; *Paik,* in Bengali, refers to a 'guard' or to the 'police'. The land revenue policy introduced by the Company, which tried to force the local chiefs and kings to collect taxes on these Paikan lands, created a strong resentment among the rulers and their traditional soldiers. They ultimately broke out in violent rebellion, and this was termed as the 'Chuar', or the 'Paik' rebellion (Roy 1966: 46–7; Das 1972: 103–50).

The 200th anniversary of the 'Chuar' or 'Paik' rebellion that spread over the vast forest tracts of south-western Bengal and parts of present-day Jharkhand State (then termed 'Jungle Mahals') in the second half of the eighteenth century, was celebrated primarily by the Communist Party of India (Marxist) (CPI (M)) and the Congress Party. Leaders from these parties addressed large public meetings and seminars, and made sincere efforts to associate themselves symbolically with this pioneering agrarian revolt. The leaders tried to link these events with the ongoing struggles of the downtrodden and toiling masses in the countryside

(Bhunia *et al.* 1998; Sarkar *et al.* 1998); these people, they argued had been exploited, oppressed and brutally exterminated by the colonial rulers (see Roy 1966: 46–7, 115–28). Interestingly, the area around an old temple in Karnagarh, 8 km from Medinipur town, which is situated 129 km from Kolkata, was selected as the centre stage for this drama. The main deity of this temple is the goddess Mahamaya, who is worshipped by many who come from surrounding areas to this temple on auspicious days of the Bengali calendar. According to one of the early accounts of this rebellion written by a British administrative official, J.C. Price (1953: 1–12), this Karnagarh area was under the *zamindari* (estate) of Rani Shiromoni. The temple, with its adjoining areas, was one of the major centres of the Chuar rebellion. The word *chuar*, it needs to be pointed out, literally means 'uncivilized', 'barbaric' or 'wicked' in Bengali. The celebration of the 200th anniversary of the Chuar rebellion in 1998–9 in Medinipur, and the visit of the state level political leaders of the Congress and the CPI (M) to the town and in and around the old Karnagarh temple marked the beginning of a political ritual veiled under non-political masks.

The Chuar *bidroha* was an armed peasant revolt that gave much trouble to the British colonial administration during the second half of the eighteenth century. It broke out in the erstwhile Medinipur district and across the entire stretch of the Jungle Mahals covering the districts of Bankura, Purulia and parts of eastern Bihar (O'Malley 1908: 37, 41–2, 44–5). The first wave of the Chuar *bidroha*, which took place outside Medinipur, started around 1765, and not in 1799, as has been depicted by the contemporary political parties of West Bengal during the celebrations of 1998–9. Rani Shiromoni was only one among other important leaders who had participated in the *bidroha*. However, none of the leaders of the political parties highlighted these aspects of the rebellion in their pamphlets and speeches before the media. There is no historical justification behind fixing 1799 as the year of the Chuar *bidroha*. The focus on the year 1799 reflects a colonial bias for two reasons: (i) Rani Shiromoni, who was suspected of supporting the *bidrohis* (rebels), was brought to Midnapore under arrest on 6 April 1799; and (ii) by the middle of June 1799, the colonial administration began to get the upper hand in suppressing the rebellion, though sporadic attempts at revolt continued up to the first decade of the nineteenth century.

Political parties at the national and local levels

Before entering into a detailed description of the political rituals performed by the political parties towards the celebration of the Chuar *bidroha* (rebellion) at Medinipur, it is necessary to make certain observations on the parties in the contemporary Indian political scenario. Political parties operate in India at two levels: the national and the regional levels. The Congress is the largest national political party. Regarded as a centrist party, it is now in power at the centre with support from leftist parties like the Communist Party of India (CPI) and the CPI (M). The Bharatiya Janata Party (BJP; Indian peoples' party), another national level party, is considered to be a right-wing party, with a strong allegiance towards the Rashtriya Swayamsevak Sangh (RSS; National Association of Volunteers), a militant Hindu chauvinist party responsible for the demolition of the Babri Masjid at Ajodhya, a small town in Uttar Pradesh.[2] The BJP is regarded by leftists and the Congress in India as a party that appropriates non-political symbols from rituals and mythological narratives to achieve political success at a popular level. It is now in opposition at the centre after its electoral defeat in 2004. However, at the time of the celebration of the Chuar *bidroha* at Medinipur in 1998–9, this party was in power at the centre, while the Congress and the two communist parties were in opposition. The two communist parties of India, the CPI and the CPI (M), though not as large as the Congress and the BJP in terms of their numerical strength, could be regarded as national political parties since these have their organizations in almost all the states of India

In West Bengal, the CPI (M)-led Left Front Government (LFG) has been in office for the last 33 years. By winning elections with a huge majority, they have achieved a fair amount of bargaining power in the Congress-led central government. In the State Legislative Assembly of West Bengal, the Congress and the BJP are both on the opposition bench, and there is no election alliance between the Left and the Congress against the BJP. The Trinamul Congress (founded on 1 January 1998), a true regional party that has no influence outside the state, although formed out of the Congress party in West Bengal in order to sharpen the opposition to the LFG, is in election alliance with the BJP. At the time of the celebration of the Chuar *bidroha*, the BJP was in power. The Trinamul leader, Mamata Banerjee, was then Railway Minister, and the Trinamul Congress was in power in the Medinipur Municipality during 1998–9. The Jharkhand Party could also be regarded as a regional party because of its restricted influence in parts of West Bengal, Jharkhand and Orissa. Out of the many factions in the Jharkhand Party, the faction that is the most powerful in West Bengal is the Jharkhand Party (Naren), named after the Santal leader, the late Naren Hansda. Here, the Jharkhand Party (Naren) is strongly opposed to the ruling Left parties and is in election alliance with the BJP and the Trinamul Congress.

These various national and regional political parties were involved in the celebration of the 'Chuar Bidroha' in their own ways. Despite their differences in ideology (communists professing the dictatorship of the proletariat; the Congress favouring a secular state; and the BJP advocating a Hindu India) and their relationship with other parties at the national and state levels, these political parties have each tried to appropriate the past to serve their own electoral agenda. In this case, however, the BJP was not an important player for two reasons: (1) it does not have any significant organizational or political power in West Bengal; and (2) there is hardly any element of Hinduism that it could derive from these insurgent historical narratives. The major players in the celebration of the Bidroha were the Congress and the CPI (M) because of their important positions in the political scenario of the state. In terms of political strength, the CPI (M) is the largest political party in the state, and also in Medinipur; the Congress is in second position. The CPI, because of its limited organizational strength in the state as well as in Paschim Medinipur District, was also a marginal player in the celebration. The state and district level leaders of the CPI (M) and the Congress were involved in the celebration because the issue of the Chuar *bidroha* was picked up for the first time by the Congress in order to criticize the LFG on the floor of the state assembly, and also before the press. The Congress alleged that the left parties, particularly the CPI (M), which claimed to support the struggles of the tribal peoples and the peasants of our country, had given no importance to the Chuar *bidroha*: they had not paid homage to one of its leaders, Rani Shirom-oni, nor incorporated the events of the rebellion in the school history text books. The allegations made by the major opposition party in the assembly were polit-ical, and specific to the Paschim Medinipur district, where the violent opposition of the Jharkhand Party (Naren) had already troubled the CPI (M). The CPI (M) thus had to answer this political challenge by one of its major opponents, and its leadership faced this challenge in an interesting way.

As I will analyse, the leaders of the party, both at the state and district levels, manipulated the public sphere via the media (and not their own party organs). They attempted to show through various activities that included the formation of celebration committees, the publication and distribution of pamphlets, the organ-ization of seminars and visits to locations associated with the rebellion, that they were connected to the Chuar *bidroha* at both ideological and academic levels. The Congress responded to such performances of the CPI (M) leaders in a similar manner. The showing of strength, and the verbal duels between the CPI (M) and the Congress, formed the main theme of this political drama. The entry of the Jharkhand Party and the Trinamul Congress in this drama was of marginal importance. The Jharkhand Party (Naren), which had a number of followers from the tribal populations, contested the use of the term 'Chuar' by the leaders of the CPI (M) and Congress. Their interest, however, lay not in celebrating this rebellion in West Bengal, but in commemorating the 'Santal Hul' (Santal rebel-lion of 1855–7).

Methodological arguments

This study is based on the methods of social anthropology. I have chosen the episode of the celebration of the 200th anniversary of this peasant rebellion by the major political parties in West Bengal in order to construct a descriptive eth-nography (see Geertz 1973: 3–30), in which the day-to-day happenings around the anniversary are analysed to shed light both on the political culture of the state and on the interface between anti-colonial pasts and political identities in con-temporary India. The main intellectual inspiration behind the selection of the episode comes from the ethnographic studies on political symbolism conducted by Abner Cohen (1979) and Marc Abeles (1988). Cohen constructed the ethno-graphy of the daily activities of visitors who went to see V.I. Lenin's mummified body in erstwhile USSR, and showed how the power of the socialist state was reinforced through the use of non-political symbols (Cohen 1979). Marc Abeles, in a later work, conducted an ethnographic study of two specific tours of the former French President, Francois Mitterrand, in which he depicted the dress, style of walking, interviews with media persons and the television coverage of the president's tours before the elections. His analysis emphasized how the president had used non-political imagery and symbols to recreate his own past in order to win the present political battles against the opposition (Abeles 1988).

In this study, and using Victor Turner's analytical language, my aim is to view the celebration of the Chuar *bidroha* as a kind of contemporary 'social drama' (1974). As such, I will assess how the political parties and their leaders present themselves before the public and the print media in order to pursue their self-interests. I am particularly interested in exploring how they raise allegations against opponents, display their respective capabilities for mass mobilization, and keep future electoral battles in mind. The materials for this study have been primarily drawn from reports of the national and regional newspapers, particularly *Sambad Pratidin* (a Bengali daily), which gave the most vivid and picturesque running commentary on the various activities of the leaders of the political parties. *Sambad Pratidin* became one of the most important players in this celebration. Other sources include pamphlets and other material published by activists of political parties. The author's personal encounters with activists from political parties, and his own presence in Medinipur town as an observer of incidents centring on the celebration, also provided material for this study.

The chapter is arranged around two broad themes. First, I narrate the succession of events as these progressed through time, to highlight the activities of the political leaders as revealed through media reporting. Second, I deal with some of the narratives of the Chuar *bidroha* as found in the various texts ranging from scholarly accounts to pamphlets and leaflets of the political parties. These two themes are closely interconnected. Together, they provide a holistic description of how people, across time, space and socio-political affiliation, have viewed, acted upon and used a past event that had an important bearing on their lives. In the concluding part of the chapter, I raise some questions concerning socio-political representations of insurgent pasts and make an attempt to answer these within the context of the local political scenario of the state.

How the drama began

In late 1998, the Congress party raised concerns regarding the history syllabus at schools in West Bengal. The state and district level leaders of the party placed concrete demands before the state government and the administration of the erstwhile Medinipur district. A committee, under the name of 'Chuar Bidroha O Rani Shiromonir Atayatyager Disatabarsha Udjapan Committee' (Committee for the Bicentenary Celebration of Chuar Revolt and the Self-Sacrifice of Rani Shiromoni), consisting of known leaders of the Congress party, put forward the demands. This strategy was adopted to give a non-political appearance to the demands, and also to show that researchers were involved in raising the issue before the administration. The committee placed its demands before then Minister for Information and Culture Buddhadev Bhattacharya (presently chief minister of West Bengal) on 23 November 1998 and the District Collector of Medinipur on 26 November 1998. The demands were:

1   An account of Rani Shiromoni, the legendary leader of 'Chuar revolt', should be included in the history textbooks of the secondary level school syllabus in West Bengal.
2   The whole of the Karnagarh and its adjoining area in the erstwhile Medinipur district should be given immediate recognition by the government as a heritage site, and the government should also take steps to protect this site.
3   A museum should be developed to commemorate the bicentenary of the 'Chuar Revolt', which was represented as an uncompromising struggle of the people of India against the colonial regime.
4   The whole of the Karnagarh area should be developed into a National Tourist Centre.
5   A statue of Rani Shiromoni should be placed in Delhi, the capital of India.

The information minister took up the demands of the Congress in good spirit, as press reports indicate. The director of the State Archaeology Department came to visit Karnagarh and submitted a report to the relevant government department. The real drama, however, was to begin after this routine administrative action. The structure of the drama contained the following elements: (a) the showing of strength by political parties during election campaigns; (b) the delivery of public lectures by state and national level leaders of the parties; (c) the blaming of opponents in public by familiar and much used rhetoric; and (d) the attempts to show a moral commitment to the historic 'Chuar revolt' against colonial exploitation. On the surface, however, there was always a non-political and non-party appearance in the speeches, tour programmes and press statements of the rival political parties, mainly of the Congress and the CPI (M). I will elaborate on each of these dramatic elements in my ethnography of political symbolism. Let me first detail the succession of events as revealed through the reports published in a state-level Bengali newspaper, the *Sambad Pratidin*, during February–December 1999.

The chronicle

Two actors, the media and the political parties, performed the political ritual around the bicentenary celebration of the Chuar *bidroha* in Medinipur. The ritual can be subdivided into three phases: (i) initiation, (ii) high point, and (iii) closing. In the initiation phase, one of the opposition parties, the Congress, raised the issue by placing the demands before the Left Front Government (LFG). This acted as a stimulus and the dominant partner, the CPI (M) of the LFG, began to organize mass campaigns at the Medinipur town by holding public meetings, forming a committee, publishing leaflets and announcing future programmes. During the second phase of the ritual, the political parties, particularly the Congress and the CPI (M), organized tours and visits of their heavyweight leaders to Karnagarh, one of the centres of the rebellion. In this phase, a ritual fight with political opponents, which was in a rudimentary stage, took place. The Jharkhand Party also came into the scene at this stage and criticized the CPI (M) for its middle-class attitude towards what they considered to be an '*Adivasi* movement', i.e. a mobilization of indigenous and tribal (rather than strictly peasant) claims to autonomy. The CPI (M) leaders took the opportunity to criticize the Congress on this occasion. In the third and the closing phase, political parties left the stage and the West Bengal government constructed a tourist lodge in the name of one of the legendary leaders, Rani Shiromoni, who was arrested by the colonial administration in 1799 for supporting the rebels. The elected councillors of Medinipur town, belonging to the Trinamul Congress, made the demand to the central railway minister for a local train to be named Rani Shiromoni. Soon afterwards, a train began to travel between Medinipur and Kolkata. The succession of the various events of the ritual, as reported by the *Sambad Pratidin, Ajkal* and *The Statesman* may now be enumerated.

22 February 1999

A 95-member committee, including 13 District Committee members of the CPI (M), was formed to celebrate the 200th anniversary of the Chuar *bidroha*. The district secretary of the CPI (M) announced that anyone could be a member of this 'historical committee' by paying a subscription of only Rs10/-, and the target was to enrol 50,000 members.

1 March 1999

A 121-member committee, which included some freedom fighters, was formed under the initiative of the state and district level Congress leaders in Medinipur town. The Congress leaders announced some future programmes for popularizing the first historic anti-colonial struggle of the peasants. The leaders of the party also blamed the CPI (M) for politicizing the bicentenary celebration of the Chuar *bidroha*.

2 March 1999

The minister for information and culture declared that the state government would take up the 200th anniversary celebration of the Chuar *bidroha* during his discussion with the Congress leader Dr Manas Bhuniya. In the same news item, it was reported that the Celebration Committee, formed under the leadership of the Congress, made a deputation to the district magistrate of Medinipur, which contained, among other items, the suggestion to form an all-party committee for organizing the celebration of the Chuar *bidroha*. This news item also reported the reply given by the CPI (M) district secretary against the criticisms made by the state Congress leaders about the party's role towards the formation of the 'Chuar Bidroha Celebration Committee'.

5 March 1999

The minister of information and culture announced a four-point programme to pay homage to the Chuar *bidroha*, which included the all-round development of Karnagarh and the publication of an authentic document on this peasant struggle. The news item reported that the state secretary of CPI (M) would visit Medinipur shortly.

9 March 1999

The CPI (M)-led 'Chuar Bidroha Celebration Committee' organized a seminar at Medinipur Zilla Parishad Hall where CPI (M) State Secretary Anil Biswas gave a lecture in which he emphasized the class analysis of the *bidroha*. This news item, published in the *Sambad Pratidin*, was one of the most remarkable of reports. It carried a photograph of the CPI (M) state and district secretaries in the midst of the archaeological remains of Karnagarh, along with a literary report of their visit to the actual site of the rebellion.

10 March 1999

Sambad Pratidin carried yet another literary report in which the journalist described the meeting of the CPI (M) state secretary and the priest of the Karnagarh temple. The title of the news item was also significant. It can be translated as follows: 'The pious priest becomes a devout follower of the communist leader.' The journalist quoted the priest as having said: 'Karnagarh is no more a religious place, it now carries history.'

11 March 1999

Then Chief Minister of West Bengal and legendary leader of the CPI (M) Jyoti Basu announced that he would visit Medinipur since the activities that were being organized to celebrate the completion of 200th year of the Chuar *bidroha* were 'Good Work'. The journalist reported that Jyoti Basu would visit Medinipur in the last week of March or in the first week of April and would address a big meeting in the town.

12 March 1999

Sambad Pratidin reported the statement made by a CPI (M) member of parliament (MP), Lakshman Seth, regarding the importance of the Chuar *bidroha*. The MP demanded the inclusion of 'Chuar Bidroha' in the school history textbooks, and stated in parliament that the central and the state governments should jointly celebrate the *bidroha*. The journalist also reported that Seth had drawn the prime minister's attention to this issue.

14 March 1999

Then Prime Minister Atal Behari Vajpayee had a long discussion with the CPI (M) MP, Lakshman Seth, and assured him that the Central Government, led by the BJP, would make all arrangements to accord the due honour to the Chuar *bidroha* and its notable leader Rani Shiromoni. The concluding paragraph of this newspaper report was significant and can be translated as follows:

> The historical events around Karnagarh had been drawing the attention of the different sections of the society since the publication of news reports in the *Sambad Pratidin*. There might be hostile competition among the Congress, CPI (M) and the BJP on the observance of their programmes but this was not that important. ... The matter had achieved a new dimension after the Prime Minister's positive assurance.

29 March 1999

Half a dozen CPI (M) heavyweight leaders, including then Chief Minister of West Bengal Jyoti Basu addressed a huge public meeting at Medinipur on the Chuar *bidroha*. Basu announced a bundle of future programmes to give proper honour to the *bidroha*, which included reporting the incident in the school textbooks and the establishment of a women's college at the site of the *bidroha*. The chief minister, in his characteristic style of populist speech, said:

> Nobody knows this history. I, too, didn't know. Just the other day, I enquired about the matter with one government employee in my office. He also admitted his ignorance about the matter. It is necessary to bring this history to public knowledge.

The chief minister used this occasion to criticise the BJP who, according to Basu, 'is distorting the history of India and never participated in the freedom struggle of the country'. But quite significantly, the chief minister pointed out that the term 'Chuar' was a derogatory one. The journalist reported that a CPI (M) secretariat member, Biman Bose, had paid his visit to Karnagarh on this occasion.

7 April 1999

Four heavyweight Congress State Assembly members (MLA) visited Karnagarh and demanded the construction of a tourist centre in the historical site in Medinipur. This report of *Sambad Pratidin* also carried a photograph that showed the Congress leaders in one of the architectural remains at Karnagarh. The team consisted of Tirthankar Bhakat, who had been repeatedly designated as a research scholar in history sponsored by a fellowship of the Indian Council of Historical Research (ICHR). Bhakat was actually a prominent leader of the youth wing of the Medinipur District Congress and obtained his Masters' degree in Political Science from Vidyasagar University; he did not complete his ICHR funded PhD programme. These facts were, however, never disclosed in any newspaper and more interestingly, nor by rival political parties like the CPI (M), the Jharkhand

Party (N) and the BJP. We came to know from this news item that the Director of the daily *Sambad Pratidin* was present with the Congress leaders, and admired political leaders of the CPI (M) and Congress for giving importance to the issue of the Chuar *bidroha* and Rani Shiromoni. In the afternoon, the celebration committee, already formed by the Congress party, organized a seminar and circulated a colourful folder, which contained papers that briefly narrated the historical background and the major events of the Chuar *bidroha* along with the demands of the committee. At the end, the journalist mentioned that the District wings of the Trinamul and the BJP had become very active by bringing their heavyweight leaders to Karnagarh. On the same day, another popular Bengali daily, the *Ajkal*, carried a report that highlighted the speech of Naren Hansda (a Santal MLA from the Jhargram subdivision of Medinipur who belonged to the Jharkhand Party) who was invited to talk at the meeting organized by the Congress-led celebration committee. The report said that Hansda, while praising the heroic rebellion, lashed out at both CPI (M) and Congress for using the term 'Chuar' to designate the anti-colonial struggle of the *Adivasis*, since the term was used by the then ruling class to denigrate the indigenous and tribal peoples of India. The Congress leaders, who were present at the meeting, admitted Hansda's 'legitimate grievance'. Interestingly, this issue was not mentioned in the *Sambad Pratidin*.

8 April 1999

One of the most prestigious English dailies, *The Statesman* published a lengthy report with the title: 'Hansda threatens stir over 'derogatory' term.' It is better to quote from the report:

> Mr. Hansda said that the poor Pykes, Digars, Sardars and the Tribals residing in the jungle mahal of Midnapore took part in the Bidroha ... to defame them all, the British gave this 'derogatory' term *chuar* (uncivilized). ... But there is no difference in the outlook of the Congress and the CPI (M) over the matter as they retained this insulting term injuring their sentiment 52 years after Independence.

6 December 1999

This news item could be regarded as the last one in this series in the *Sambad Pratidin* because interest in the issue had already subsided, and no political party showed much interest in the 'Chuar Bidroha' after April–May 1999. It was reported in this news item that a number of elected women councillors from various political parties of Medinipur town (many belonged to the Trinamul Congress) put forward a demand to Central Railway Minister Mamata Banerjee that the Purulia Express train between Kolkata and Purulia should be renamed as the Rani Shiromoni Express, since this train travelled through the heartland of the Chuar *bidroha*.

The above chronicle has been constructed as a narrative of the initiation (22 February 1999–5 March 1999), high-point (9 March 1999–8 April 1999) and the closing (6 December 1999) of a political ritual, which centred on the celebration of an *Adivasi* movement in a district of West Bengal. Against this backdrop, in the next sub-section, I will describe the tour of the CPI (M) state secretary in Karnagarh, as reported in the print media.

The grand tours and the great meeting

The speeches and tours of the CPI (M) and the Congress leaders in Medinipur during March–April 1999 in connection with the celebration of the Chuar *bidroha*, and the description of the events in the *Sambad Pratidin*, demonstrate how a historic event could be picked up and used in the campaign against political opponents under the garb of non-political issues. The CPI (M) leaders, in particular, tried to show their active participation in the heroic past of the people of Medinipur. On 9 March 1999, the anchor story on the front page of the daily carried a lengthy report with a photograph. The photograph shows the *punjabi*-clad ('punjabi' is a traditional Indian garment worn by men to cover the upper portion of the body) State Secretary of the party, accompanied by Dipak Sarkar, the then district secretary, in the midst of a barren place covered with thorny bushes and shrubs. In the background, some broken structures of an ancient building are visible. The caption in the photograph reads: 'The CPI (M) state secretary, Anil Biswas, at the devastated fortress of Rani Shiromoni at Karnagarh. The district secretary Dipak Sarkar accompanied him. From the region which is soaked with the memories of Chuar rebellion'. The news report vividly depicted the tremendous hardship of the leader who got down from his comfortable car under the scorching sun, and collected information about the architecture of the historical fortress of Rani Shiromoni. After painstaking field observation, Biswas told the reporters: 'One should not write the history of the freedom struggle in India by sitting within the archives, if one wants to write it afresh. One should visit the places where the fire of the rebellion broke out and the archaeological remains still exist.' Undoubtedly Biswas, who is not a professional historian but a seasoned politician, tried to convey a number of political symbols under the cover of a non-political appearance.

This was done in two ways. First, by this dramatic act, the CPI (M) secretary made a sincere attempt to impress upon the intelligentsia that he was also a down-to-earth researcher of the struggle of the poor peasants of a region located far away from the metropolis. Second, by walking on his feet to reach this historical spot in a rural area of Medinipur, Biswas tried to show that he had contact with the people and ordinary party workers, and that he did not have any conservative attitude towards religious personalities, like the temple priest. By and large, Anil Biswas at Karnagarh became a serious field worker doing socio-historical research on a neglected and yet one of the oldest chapters of peasant struggle in Bengal. It is significant to note that the CPI (M) party's Bengali daily,

Ganasakti, did not undertake the business of this projection in order to maintain the non-political image of the secretary of the party.

Almost within a month, the state level Congress leaders from Kolkata reached Karnagarh, and visited the same places toured earlier by the CPI (M) heavy-weights. But the Congress leaders highlighted the history of the struggle from a different angle. While the CPI (M) luminaries had reinterpreted the past in the light of class analysis, the Congress leaders sought to make the history of the rebellion resonate in the contemporary social milieu by demanding the inclusion of the Chuar *bidroha* in school textbooks, and by urging for the development of the historic site into a tourist centre. The CPI (M), on the other hand, tried to reassert its position by organizing a colourful procession of *Adivasis* on the streets of Medinipur town on the day of the public meeting addressed by Jyoti Basu. There were, however, similarities between the strategies of the Congress and the CPI (M): (i) the formation of big celebration committees comprising researchers in history and people from different sections of the society; (ii) tours of heavyweight leaders to Karnagarh; (iii) making public statements in the print media in quick succession; and (iv) politically attacking the opponents.

The celebration of the Chuar *bidroha* reached its climax when the CPI (M) Bengali daily organ, *Ganasakti*, delivered a gimmick to its readers in the last week of March 1999. On 27 March 1999, on page 5, the *Ganasakti* carried a headline, which can be translated as follows: '200 YEARS OF CHUAR REBEL-LION: ON SUNDAY FIVE LAKH PEASANTS' GATHERING IN MED-INIPUR TOWN.' It was reported that Jyoti Basu would come to this meeting and there *'will be five lakh peasants'* (500,000; my emphasis) in the Judges Court Ground of the town. Incidentally, on 29 March 1999, the *Ganasakti* did not provide the actual number of people who had gathered in the meeting addressed by Jyoti Basu.

The aftermath

The aftermath of this political ritual is interesting. The media, however, did not give much importance to these events. On 22 July 1999, just a few months after the celebration, the Tourism Development Corporation of the Government of West Bengal established a tourist lodge in Medinipur town under the name of 'Rani Shiromoni Paryatak Abas' (Queen Shiromoni Tourist Lodge). On the wall of the lobby in the lodge, there is a big light-yellow rectangular board on which we find a stylized sketch in green ink of the side face of a woman wearing a large ring in her nose. She seems to be Rani Shiromoni. A text appears below the face, which depicts the 'Chuar Rebellion' and also provides a short biogra-phy of the Rani and her humble background, along with her courageous leader-ship during the rebellion. It is important to note here that the State Assembly Election was held on 21 May 2001.

In November 2002, a 'bar' for serving beer and liquor at the 'Rani Shiromoni Tourist Lodge' was opened. When the Tourism Development Corporation decided to open the bar, the Chairman of the Congress-led Midnapore Municipality, Nazim

Ahmed, raised the objection that the Government should not serve and sell liquor in a tourist lodge named after Rani Shiromoni, one of the leaders of the 'Chuar Rebellion'. The Ganatantric Mahila Samity (the Women's wing of the CPI (M)) of Medinipur and a local club also objected to the decision to open a bar within the premises of the tourist lodge. The Tourism Department, however, opened the bar within the tourist lodge under the name of 'Kangsabati', and it is now quite popular. 'Kangsabati' or 'Kasai' is the name of an important river in the district, which flows on the southwestern side of the Medinipur town. There was no further deputation from the Congress party or the Ganatantric Mahila Samity. I collected this anecdote from the inhabitants of the town, and also from the employees of the Rani Shiromoni Tourist Lodge. The local train named Rani Shiromoni runs between Bankura and Howrah railway stations on every day of the week.

The third and the latest event in the series is the unveiling of a sculpture at the entrance of the Midnapore Railway Station by Probodh Panda, the CPI Member of Parliament from Midnapore, on 26 January 2006 (The Republic Day of India). The sculpture was planned and executed by members of the Art College of Midnapore. The sculpture, on a dark brown quadrangular piece of cement, shows armed policemen on horseback attacking bare bodied men on the ground, shooting arrows from their bows. There are some faces jutting out in between these two groups of fighting men, and a branched tree without any leaf in it is carved out. A thick rope for hanging the rebels to death is also visible. The text of the commemorative inscription under this piece of sculpture reads:

> In Memory of the Martyrs of the First Historical Battle of Deliverance against the British Rule in India
> Chuar Bidroha in its First Phase – 1768 AD
> Chuar Bidroha in its Second Phase – 1798–1799
> Nayek Bidroha 1806–1816
> Leadership Under – Durjan Singha, Gobardhan Dikpati, Rani Shiromoni, Mohanlal and Achal Singh.

The sculpture and the text clearly reveal that the power of the icons, 'Rani Shiromoni of Karnagarh in Medinipur' and the 'Chuar Rebellion of 1799' have largely lost their efficacy to the users of these symbols. References to other leaders, to places outside Medinipur and to other phases of the rebellion, including the Nayek Bidroha, have now come into existence.

The narratives of bidroha

I have described the current events around the celebration of the Chuar *bidroha* in 1999 in Medinipur in the style of a 'thick description' of the various events. We have seen how the different political parties manipulated various non-political images and symbols and competed with one another to get an edge over their rivals. We have also observed how the activities of the political parties led to the climax of the drama, and ultimately ended up in large gatherings, a part of present day political rituals. Let us now take up another dimension of this drama. In this endeavour, we will look at academic texts written by Bengali scholars, and re-read some of the texts produced by the intellectuals of the political parties in the form of leaflets and brochures. Let us start with the academic narratives.

Our first text is a Bengali encyclopaedia, which is regarded as an authentic compendium on socio-economic and historical topics: *Bharatkosh*, published in as early as 1967, was edited by a galaxy of scholars including the anthropologist Nirmal Kumar Bose, the historian Nihar Ranjan Roy, and the linguist Suniti Kumar Chatterjee. In the third volume of the encyclopaedia is a one-page entry entitled 'Chuar Hangama' [*Hangama* in Bengali means 'disturbance']. A translation of the text in English would reveal the attitude of a section of the Bengali academicians in the post-colonial period towards the Chuar *bidroha*. I provide a translated version of the text.

> The wild races, which inhabited the Jangal Mahal of the Medinipur district and its adjoining western and northern forest clad regions, were collectively called the Chuars. They did not practise cultivation; they used to hunt animals and birds and sold forest produce and used to maintain livelihood by robbery whenever they got the opportunity. They were brute and cruel to such an extent that the word chuar became synonymous with savagery and cruelty.
>
> (*Bharatkosh* 1967: 385–6)

Interestingly, the book *Bharater Krishak Bidroha O Ganatantric Sangram* (1966), written by the leftist scholar Suprakash Roy and published a year before the *Bharatkosh,* is a contrast to the above article. Writing about the second 'Choar' revolt (1798–9), the author notes:

> The very word "choar" which we have always regarded as a bad name, and designated it in all our best dictionaries as "crooked and low caste", which neglected an unknown group of "barbaric" human beings who virtually wiped out the immensely powerful British rulers from a large region of Bankura and Medinipur districts. Suffice it to say that the story of this revolt could not make a place in our traditional history.
>
> (Roy 1966: 115)

It is interesting to note that a radical scholar like Roy could not avoid using the term 'chuar' or 'choar'. For him, it was an enigma as to how this word became derogatory in the Bengali language. He therefore made a conjecture. In the words of Roy: 'Probably being furious by the exploitation they became ghastly in appearance and merciless to their exploiters which led the then *zamindars* and their obedient historians of Bankura and Medinipur to designate these people by this derogatory appellation.' (1966: 115) There are many linguistic and literary evidences to contest Roy's conjecture. The semantics around the word 'chuar' can be traced to the Jain tradition, and are to be found in the writings of medieval Bengali poets.

Suniti Kumar Chatterjee, in his monumental work *The Origin and Development of the Bengali Language*, writes:

> The Pali Jataka and Tri-pitaka literature which gives a faithful account of Aryandom in India in the centuries immediately before the Maurya period, mentions sixteen great nations, among which Pundra, Vanga, Radha or Suhma have no place. Jain tradition as preserved in the *Ayaranga Sutra* describes Ladha and Subbha as countries inhabited by a wild and churlish people. In fact, the tradition, that the Radha people of West Bengal were wild and barbarous, is present down to middle Bengali times e.g. Mukunda-rama writes (*c.*1580) in his *Candi-Kavya*, 'Ati nichakule janama jatite choar/ keho na paras kore loke bale Radha.' (Birth in a very low caste, a Chohad/ No one touches (me), people call (me) a Radha.)
>
> (Chatterjee 1926: 67–8)

Given this long tradition of referring to the *Adivasis* of the large forest-tracts of the Jangal Mahals as 'Chuars', it was not an easy task for Bengali academics and political leaders to wipe out this derogatory nomenclature from texts and speeches. In none of the pamphlets published by the CPI (M) and the Congress during the celebration of the 'Chuar bidroha' in Medinipur (hundreds of copies of which were distributed in Medinipur) was there any analytical discussion on the use of the derogatory term by Bengali academics.

A reading of the pamphlets reveals the immediate political intention behind the celebration. One finds hardly any difference in those texts on the historiographical contents regarding the socio-economic causes of the revolt. CPI (M) and Congress pamphlets (Sarkar *et al.* and Bhunia *et al.*) mention the existence of tax-free lands for the lower castes and tribes of the Jangal Mahal, and the convergence of the interests of the local *zamindars* with the subalterns in their violent struggle against the colonial land revenue policy of the British rulers. However, there were two important differences in the pamphlets. In the Congress pamphlet, there was a vivid description of the devastations caused by the rebels, and the helplessness of the British administration. But the CPI (M) pamphlet emphasized the wider national, even international, background of the revolt. Both CPI (M) and the Congress pamphlets, however, did criticize the land revenue policies of the East India Company. Second, and quite interestingly, the Congress text mentioned the traditional antagonistic agrarian relationship between the *zamindars* and the peasants, but mentioned that both these classes became united under the attacks of the bigger and more virulent enemy, the British. The writer of the CPI (M) pamphlet did not undertake any agrarian class analysis of the rebellion in terms of the alliances between the lower castes and tribes with the landlords. The similarities between these texts are not very difficult to locate. Both pamphlets mention that the Chuar *bidroha* remains an unknown and neglected chapter in history, and lament this situation. The CPI (M) text directly blamed the Congress, while the Congress pamphlet mentioned that they had already placed their demands before the state government for the proper recognition of this heroic peasant struggle.

The pamphlet composed by the Jharkhand Student Federation (published by Naren Hansda on 2 May 1999) is different in many respects from that of the CPI (M) and the Congress. This text thoroughly criticized the use of the term 'Chuar' by the ruling class and their allies, and demanded that this term be banished and the revolt be renamed as the 'Freedom Struggle of the Jangal Mahal'. In this text, we also find a description of the cruelties of the British army:

> At last in 1799 the then Viceroy-General Wellesley sent two big divisions of army equipped with modern arms encircled the rebels and devastated them by two pronged attack. The British army burnt the villages of the rebels and hanged them in the trees.
>
> (Hansda 1999)

The Jharkhand Student Federation's pamphlet expressed its strong resentment against the plans that proposed to develop tourist centres in the place where the revolt took place. Again, this was the only political group in West Bengal which did not make any attempt to celebrate the bicentenary of the Chuar *bidroha*. The Jharkhand Students Federation demanded the writing of a 'neutral history' at an early date (Hansda 1999).

Lastly, I would like to mention another important text, which described the 'Chuar Rebellion' in an encyclopaedic manner. This description is found in a 216-page book published by Paschimbanga Bangla Academy in 1986, and later reprinted in 1996 (authors unknown). The title of the book is *Muktir Sangrame Bharat* (India in the Freedom Struggle) and it contains short descriptions of many movements of the people of India from 1757–1947. Jyoti Basu, the then chief minister of the West Bengal government, wrote the foreword for the book. On page 15, under the title of 'Chuar Rebellion of Medinipur and Bankura (1798–9) and the Layek Rebellion of Medinipur (1816)', we find an entry on the 'Chuar Rebellion'. There is a black and white photograph above this entry which shows a broken high structure in an open field and the caption reads: 'The Ground for Hanging the Chuar and the Layek Rebels'. In this entry the author(s) noted:

> The British and a section of the zamindars of Medinipur termed the primitive and lower caste inhabitants of the Jungle Mahals of Medinipur, Bankura and Manbhum as 'Chuars' out of sheer disregard. These people depended on the wealth of the forest and cultivated in a primitive manner.
>
> (Muktir Sangrame Bharat 1996: 15)

Interestingly, this entry mentioned the name of Durjan Singha as one of the leaders of the 'Chuar rebellion' but it did not mention Rani Shiromoni, nor did it give any special importance to Karnagarh or Medinipur as one of the centres of the rebellion. Again, this entry does not mention the first wave of the rebellion that took place in 1765.

Epilogue

So far, we have moved from the past to the present, and back again to the past, in order to narrate a contemporary political ritual in West Bengal. Let us now raise three questions to reflect upon the contemporary mindset of the political leaders of West Bengal. The questions can be arranged in the following order:

1   Why should 1799 be chosen as the year for celebrating this peasant struggle of the 'Jungle Mahals', particularly when the year was a symbol of victory for the colonial state?
2   Why were Medinipur and Karnagarh given prime importance when there were many other places within and outside the district where the rebellion had broken out?
3   Why should the derogatory word 'Chuar' continue to be used in textbooks, encyclopaedias, politicians' speeches and newspaper reports?

The answers to these questions could be searched within the context of the contemporary political scenario in the State of West Bengal, and particularly in the Paschim Medinipur district. First, although the CPI (M)-led LFG has an overwhelming organizational power in almost every corner of the state, the western part of Paschim Medinipur remains a troublesome pocket for the Left since the Jharkhand Party (Naren) has a following in this area. Second, in the Medinipur town, the Congress continues to be a powerful political opposition to the left parties. The majority of the elected members of the Midnapore Municipality (the local government) still belong to the Congress and to the Trinamul Congress. Thus, when the Congress attacked the LFG for not paying any homage at the state level to the Chuar *bidroha* and its legendary leader, Rani Shiromoni, the CPI (M) took this as a golden opportunity to fight the lion in its own den. Midnapore town became the ideal political arena to fight the Congress and the Jharkhand Party on an issue that would appeal to the tribals of the district who formed the support base of the Jharkhand Party (Naren). The use of the derogatory term 'Chuar' in the various texts revealed the typical middle class and upper caste Hindu mentality of the Bengali political leaders and academics. The leaders of the Jharkhand Party (Naren) transformed this weakness of the middle-class Hindu Bengali mind into attractive political capital. They could not, however, fully exploit this because the CPI (M) leaders addressed the linguistic/ideological issue in their public speeches, thereby appropriating the Jharkhand Party's own agenda.

In the midst of the clamour and grandeur of the bicentenary celebration of the Chuar *bidroha* by the major political parties of West Bengal, no academic was found to raise these pertinent questions, which could have opened up a more critical reinterpretation and appreciation of one of the earliest peasant movements in eastern India.

Notes

1 For administrative convenience, the district of Medinipur was divided in 2002 into East and West Medinipur, or Purba and Paschim Medinipur. Medinipur town is the district headquarters of the present Paschim (West) Medinipur district.
2 The demolition of the Babri Masjid, an historic Muslim monument, for the establishment of a Hindu temple in the same location by the right wing BJP can be viewed as a form of Hindu Fascism, and as a violent performance of a political ritual under the mask of the dominant religion of India. The enactment of this ritual drew its nutrients from the mythical past of India depicted in the famous epic, the *Ramayana*.

References

Abeles, M. (1988) 'Modern Political Ritual: Ethnography of an Inauguration and a Pilgrimage by President Mitterand', in *Current Anthropology*, 29(3): 391–404.

Anon. (1996) *Mukter Sangrame Bharat*, Kolkata: Paschimbanga Bangla Academy.

Bharatkosh (1967) Vol. 3, Kolkata: Bangya Sahitya Parishad.

Bhunia, M. *et al.* (1998) 'Choar Bidroha O Rainy Shiromoni Smaranay' (pamphlet).

Chatterjee, S.K. (1985) *The Origin and Development of the Bengali Language*, Calcutta: Rupa & Co. First published by Calcutta University in 1926.

Cohen, A. (1979) 'Political Symbolism', *Annual Review of Anthropology*, 8: 87–113.

Das, N.N. (1972) *History of Midnapore, Volume I*, Midnapore, Medinipur Itihas Rachna Samity, 103–50.

Geertz, C. (1973) *The Interpretation of Cultures*, New York: Basic Books.

Hansda, N. (1999) 'Itihase Upekshita Pratham British Birodhi Ganasangramer Dwisatabarsha Utjapan' (pamphlet).

O'Malley, L.S.S (1908) *Bengal District Gazetteers: Bankura*, Calcutta: Government of West Bengal.

Price, J.C. (1953) *The Chuar Rebellion of 1799*, reprinted in A. Mitra (ed.) *District Handbooks: Midnapur*, Appendix IV. Originally published in 1874.

Roy, S. (1966) *Bharater Krishak Bidroha O Ganatantric Sangram*, Kolkata: Book World.

Sarkar, D. *et al.* (1998) 'Medinipur Jelaye Chuar Bidroher Duso Bachar' (pamphlet).

Turner, V. (1974) *Dramas, Fields, and Metaphors: Symbolic Action in Human Society*. New York, Cornell University Press.

12 Who cares for a new state?

The imaginary institution of Jharkhand[1]

Alpa Shah

Introduction

On the stroke of midnight, 15 November 2000, India's 28th state, Jharkhand, was created. At 12.05 a.m. Governor Prabhat Kumar took his oath and later paid tribute to all the martyrs of the Jharkhand movement who had contributed towards independence from Bihar. The Jharkhand movement is often described as one of India's oldest autonomy movements with the first demands being made in 1928.[2] The long struggle for independence was initially professed around the idea that the culturally autonomous tribal, or *adivasi*, people of the area should have the right to a separate state.[3]

Later, given that the demographic reality of the region meant that a significant Jharkhandi population did not count as Scheduled Tribe, at least according to the census, the promoters for independence became more inclusive. As Sudipta Kaviraj (1993: 15) argues more generally of nationalism, to become practical Jharkhandi regionalism needed a programme of opposition in which an abstract and general sense of injustice was central. Jharkhandi regionalists advanced a new rhetoric of internal colonialism against the State of Bihar: while the development machinery of Bihar performed disproportionately poorly in Jharkhand, Bihar was reaping the benefits of Jharkhand's mineral, land and forest resources. The demand for Jharkhand thus evolved into a multi-ethnic regional movement enjoying the support of a range of people, but with the common consent that the area's identity derived from the exploitation of its population and its distinct cultural heritage (Bosu Mullick 2003: viii). This view formed one basis of the struggle for Jharkhand's independence from Bihar within the Indian federal union – that the region should be restored to those that rightfully owned it and could best manage it – its true 'sons of the soil' (Jha 1990; Weiner 1988).

I arrived in India on 15 November 2000 to pursue fieldwork in rural Jharkhand. As I read the front page of the newspapers, 'The Pioneer' and 'The Economic Times', at a friend's house in Delhi, I realised the mixture of celebration and anxiety that would welcome me in Ranchi, Jharkhand's capital, a few days later. The first government was a National Democratic Alliance (NDA) led by Bharatiya Janata Party (Hindu Nationalist, BJP) Chief Minister Babulal Marandi, and not by Shibhu Soren, leader of the Jharkhand Mukti Morcha

(Jharkhand Liberation Front or JMM) party that had led the long fight for independence. Nevertheless, the fact that Jharkhand had finally separated from Bihar was a cause for great celebration by many in Ranchi with euphoria and merry-making from activists of different parties for days thereafter. What I did not realise in those early days in Delhi was the fact that many of the *adivasis* I would later meet in rural Jharkhand did not care, and moreover often did not know, about these major political changes.

A few weeks after Jharkhand's separation from Bihar, I moved to live in the village I call Tapu, less than 50 kilometres from Ranchi city. On one of my first market days I walked from Tapu, through the degraded forest, to the market in the town of Bero. I was with Mangra Munda who had made an effort to dress in his market best.[4] His skin was glowing against his clean white shirt and *longyi* (wrap around cloth), and his hair was slick – oiled, parted and neatly combed. As we walked, I noticed that he was barefoot. I asked Mangra why he had come without his slippers (sandals or flip-flops). He said he had lost so many in the market by leaving them somewhere and then forgetting them. He wasn't used to wearing slippers, and now had decided to give up wearing them to Bero. I laughed and said that the Jharkhand State was now formed, and Tapu would therefore develop. Shops would open in the village and Mangra would be inundated by people trying to sell him slippers. He however replied on a serious note:

> I've been hearing that there may be some change in *sarkar* (the state) – has the Jharkhand *sarkar* been formed? In any case, what does it matter? What development will it bring? As far as I'm concerned, it is probably only going to bring our *soshan* (exploitation) closer.

Mangra's comments left me silent. They led me to reflect on the processes of the construction of Jharkhandi regionalism, and its appropriation by the BJP. Jharkhand's movement for autonomy has shaped its construction as a separate region. While Jharkhand was not claiming autonomy as a national state in its own right but wanted separation within the Indian union, Jharkhand's independence was fought on a similar basis to that of many nationalist movements – the idea that the region has a distinct population that shares a history and culture, and that its body of citizens should exercise sovereign control over themselves. As Sudipta Kaviraj (1993: 3) argues of nationalism, the idea of regionalism also stitches together social groups or communities of people who would not have thought of themselves as a single people having one political identity. After the emergence of regionalism, they are somehow supposed to imagine themselves in this way. The case of Jharkhand sheds light on the complex and contradictory processes that take shape in the formation of a region.

In this chapter, I look at the immediate aftermath of Jharkhand's separation from Bihar, and what the formation of Jharkhand meant to different people in Jharkhand. Why did some of the *adivasis*, the Mundas of Tapu in this case, not care about the separation of Jharkhand State? How did the views of these people about the formation of Jharkhand coexist and inter-relate with at least two other sets of imaginations of Jharkhand – one held by a higher caste village elite and the other by educated *adivasi* activists living in the more urban centres of Jharkhand? To look at these questions, I use ethnographic fieldwork conducted between November 2000 and June 2002 when I was based in Tapu, along with insights from earlier periods of fieldwork in 1999 and later visits in 2004 and 2007. Much of the detailed ethnography from which the arguments of this paper emerge are developed elsewhere in my work and in particular in my monograph, *In the Shadows of the State: Indigenous Politics, Environmentalism and Insurgency in Jharkhand, India* (Shah 2010). In this chapter, I wish to draw attention to the multiple imaginings of a region, the complex relationships between these imaginings, and the way in which these are produced and reproduced. In doing so, I would like to conclude by making some tentative suggestions about how we could analyse the relationship between the region and the state.

Who cares about Jharkhand? The Mundas of Tapu

Regionalism can mean a variety of things to different people. To Mangra and most Mundas in Tapu, the idea of Jharkhand represented, above else, a change in the state, *sarkar*. To investigate their understandings of Jharkhandi regionalism it is vital to analyse their imaginings of the state.

Sarkar was both an abstraction and a practice that the Mundas in Tapu considered beyond the moral pale, did not wish to engage with, and generally wanted to keep away from. While I have explored this distancing from the state in more detail elsewhere (Shah 2007), in this chapter, I discuss some of the Munda attitudes to the state. Jharkhand has had a long history of being dominated by outsiders from the region – mainly Brahmins, Rajputs and Vaishyas from Bihar. These upper castes colonised state positions, developed mining industries and organised petty trading businesses in rural Jharkhand. In many cases they took over *adivasi* land. While the state bureaucracy expanded and increasing development resources were pumped into rural areas, it was mainly these migrant communities who benefited, and rarely the lower sections of the *adivasis* (Weiner 1988).

The outsiders who dominated the state were culturally very different from the locals, and had little respect for their ways of life. They often looked down on *adivasi* communities, constructing them as inferior *jangli jatis* (literally meaning wild, savage, forest castes) who participated in dirty, impure and inferior practices, key examples of which were considered their potential militancy, sexual promiscuity and drinking habits.[5] These outsiders often treated *adivasis* as dispensable: Jharkhand is noted for its history of repressive police shootings on tribals protesting against state development projects, land seizure, and the heavy influx of outsiders (Das 1992).

Though different from their colonial predecessors, who often romanticised *adivasi* cultures through the classically patronising imagery of the noble savage (Skaria 1997), these migrant communities dominated the state in Jharkhand in many ways and continued the oppressive colonial displacement of *adivasis* from the area. While the colonial displacement was in the interests of trade or development (*adivasis* from Jharkhand were notably taken to work in the tea and indigo plantations of Bengal, Assam, Bhutan and Burma, and on railway and road building projects), today Jharkhand is infamous for controversial *adivasi* displacement from forests and from areas demarcated for development projects, mining and for the construction of dams.

This political economy of state–*adivasi* relations has parallels elsewhere in the country, and observers in different regions have noted the *adivasi* fear of, and desire to keep away, from the state (Hardiman 1987: 6; Mosse 2005: 51). However, it was not always clear to the Mundas who was included in the category of *sarkar*. Some explained that the British colonial government, the Angrez (English), were part of *sarkar* and might even have brought *sarkar* to the area. Others considered the various NGO workers who worked in the area as *sarkari*. While there was an ambiguity about how *sarkar* came to the region, whom it included and what its functions were, *sarkar* was clearly feared by some Mundas.

Soshan, exploitation, the term Mangra had used, was the most frequent one with which Mundas described the state. Mundas often debate as to whether *sarkar* has become more sophisticated than it was in colonial times in exploiting them. Many Mundas argued that in the past, *sarkari* officials took people to far away lands as labour or locked them up in cells. *Soshan* (exploitation) now takes new forms. *Sarkar* has developed laws for registering land, taken over rights to the forests, arrested and fined people who breached forest rules. While the *sarkar* claimed that *adivasi* rights were protected in court, courts were, in practice, manned by foreigners, and legal processes simply unaffordable. Mundas attributed *sarkar* and its associations to an 'outside' and 'alien' world. Given a choice, most Mundas preferred to have nothing to do with *sarkar* and its officials, expected nothing from them, and did not accept the idea that *sarkar* could serve the public effectively.

Jatru Munda, standing proudly by a pile of roof tiles he was baking for a new wing of his mud house, once told me, 'I like to think that I can do everything for my family. Why would I be interested in the brick houses provided by *sarkar*?' Most Mundas thought they did not need the state. They had their own leaders who could settle disputes and run the village. They ate food from the forests and their land. Forest resources and mediation by local spiritual healers provided cures to illnesses. And the Mundas earned money for the purchase of things that they could not produce themselves by working as agricultural labour or on construction schemes run by the higher caste village elites, and sometimes seasonally migrating to work as casual labour.

In recent years, a few members of the younger generations have been educated and have left Tapu to go to school and college in Bero and its vicinity. Through this process of education, they bring back to Tapu different values and aspirations from those of their parents. Aspirations that are more akin to that of the children of the village elite (the *zamindar* descendants who are usually of higher caste, discussed in the next section) and that leave them with the desire to get state sector jobs or become businessmen. These younger generations, aspiring to join village elites, have more contradictory understandings of the *sarkar* and often look down on the ideas of their relatives and parents, putting them down to 'illiteracy'. Their kin, however, retaliate that the youth are disenchanted with village life and this is further evidence of the *sarkar*'s increasing power to mislead the new generations. In fact, many explained that by grabbing those who aspired to engage with it, the *sarkar* had brought an amoral, self-interested kind of politics into village life, further dividing it.

To Mundas, Jharkhand State was something of interest to the village elites who engaged with the state and the dirty politics associated with it. But it was not something of concern to them. Jatru and many of his friends and family, like Mangra, tried to stay away from all things they associated with the state whether it was development, the police or the courts. In fact, like Mangra, many were suspicious that, as history had shown them, these latest changes might only bring *sarkar* closer and make it a more powerful force over their lives.

The idea of Jharkhand to the Mundas was hence intimately related to changes in the state. The desire to distance themselves from the state shaped their lack of interest in the state being Jharkhandi rather than Bihari. This lack of interest was not simply the result of Mundas thinking that the state could not change for the better. Rather, it was the result of Mundas feeling that the state itself had not, was not and should not be a part of their lives. In short, the Mundas' lack of regionalist sentiment for the idea of Jharkhand was the result of their alienation from the idea of the state itself.

Hooray for Jharkhand! The village elites

'Go ask the Yadavs', was the most frequent remark from the Mundas of Tapu when I wanted to know more about the impact of the creation of Jharkhand. While Mundas made up about 60 per cent of the Tapu population and were tenant descendants of servants brought by the *zamindars* or landlords of the village, Yadavs, who formed about 20 per cent of the village population, were descendants of the *zamindars*. Though the Yadavs were not the highest caste, they were regarded in the area as significantly higher on the caste hierarchy than Mundas and certainly treated locally with the same status as the high caste *zamindar* descendants of the surrounding area. I call these ex-*zamindars* elites here because of the status they derived from their ancestry and because most were significantly more wealthy in terms of land and capital than the tenant descendants. Moreover, unlike the Mundas, they aspired to rise up the class hierarchy. In this part of Jharkhand these elites were generally from the higher castes or from educated *adivasi* families who had been revenue collectors in the past.[6] Unlike their poorer counterparts, these village elites were not only acutely aware of Jharkhand's independence from Bihar, but were also thrilled about the possibilities they thought these changes could bring.

One great hope, reiterated by many who aspired to rise up the class hierarchy, was that Jharkhand's separation would result in new economic opportunities.

The abolition of *zamindari* (landlordism) in the early 1950s had meant that these elites faced a gradual impoverishment and increasingly attempted to sustain their lifestyles through resources related to the activities of the state – whether directly (as in through government jobs) or indirectly (for instance through government contractorships). As the state decentralised, and money started to come into the area in the name of the rural poor, contracts of the Ministry of Rural Development, for example, had become particularly important as involvement in their implementation offered potential to accrue significant financial gain through the illicit siphoning off of funds (Shah 2009). Many of the rural elites became local leaders and brokers to state development schemes. These elites hoped that with the formation of Jharkhand, the decentralisation of the state would lead not only to the possibility of more jobs in government but also increased development funds being pumped into the rural landscape, resulting in greater opportunities to increase their bank balances. They celebrated the creation of Jharkhand State as it was hoped that these changes would increase their ability to colonise the local state.

There is a conscious awareness amongst the village elite that Mundas hold a different view of the state to themselves. However, it has often appeared to me that, in front of Mundas, they sought to perpetuate, perhaps even exaggerate the narrative of state alienness, corruption and exploitation (Shah 2007). State, and in particular, rural development resources for 'the poor' are most often captured by exclusive networks of state officers and village elites. This exclusivity, and the misinterpretations it encourages about the roles and practices of the state, is perhaps central to local control of state resources by members of the elite. Indeed, although difficult to evidence, it is possible that village elite utilise and play on Munda imaginings in order to reinforce and further their control of the local state.

The struggle to reimagine Jharkhand: *adivasi* activists

Encouraged by these higher caste village elites, then, Mundas feel divorced from the idea of Jharkhand as they see it as being connected with the idea of the state. There are, however, possibilities for changes in this view that may result from a different category of *adivasis*. These are middle class *adivasi* who have a different kind of elite status because they are educated and have usually moved to settle in the cities, have jobs in government and may even own small businesses. Historically, many of the *adivasis* of this background come from families who converted to Christianity or have had ancestors who were dominant landowners in the villages they came from and/or were village authorities. Since many people from this background have also been the influential vanguard of the Jharkhand movement, I call them activists here and now turn to possible transformations led by this elite.

The first moves for a separate state in Jharkhand were the result of social and educational work of Christian missionaries from the late eighteenth century in the area. They created a different class of *adivasis* promoting tribal cultural heritage, demanding better educational facilities and job opportunities for tribal students,[7] and making claims for a separate state in the Indian federal union. Since the first demands were made in 1928, the movement went through stages of varying strengths and factions (Prakash 2001). However, when Jharkhand finally gained independence it did so not led by this elite but at the behest of a Hindu nationalist government, the Bharatya Janata Party (BJP), considered by many as the party of the outsiders.[8] Many city-based, educated and usually *adivasi* Jharkhandi activists, on the one hand, celebrated the cleavage of Jharkhand from Bihar. On the other hand, however, they were also furious that separation was achieved by an 'outside' government that they saw as having little regard for the region's *adivasi* communities and their history of mobilisation for autonomy. The way in which separation was achieved, they argued, undermined the idea of Jharkhand as a state in which *adivasis* would be protected. Provoked by lessons from elsewhere in India[9] and hence threatened by the incorporation of *adivasis* into the Hindu nation, these Jharkhandi activists have been concerned more than ever in promoting a separate imagined Jharkhandi community with a shared language, history and culture.

Like most visionaries of nationalism, they are involved in the work of purification to imagine the idea of Jharkhand. The result has been their reinvigorated campaign to establish a Jharkhandi regional identity, an indigenous identity. They also argue for the notion that all Jharkhandis have a history of living in the same place, being sons of the soil (Munda 2000a), and sharing a regional language, Nagpuri. They also argue for the protection of a shared livelihood and *adivasi* cultural heritage centred on their '*jal, jangal, jamin*' (water, forest and land). This heritage is enshrined in the establishment of an *adivasi* religion, Sarna, whose essence is claimed to be worshipping nature (Munda 2000b). They also assert that Jharkhand's *adivasis* areas share ancient systems of self-governance, such as the Santal *manjhi-pargana* (village leader, district leader) system, that they are busy revitalising at a range of political levels.

Sudipta Kaviraj (1993: 14) argues that nationalist identity is fundamentally a product of colonialism, and that colonial writers constructed an India to present to Indians looking for an identity. In Jharkhand, the ethno-regionalism produced by the activists is also significantly a historical product of colonialism. Colonial-era writing on tribal populations, such as those of the anthropologist/lawyer Sarat Chandra Roy or the anthropologist/administrator Verrier Elwin, have been highly influential in the indigenous identity constructions that lie at the heart of present day Jharkhandi ethno-regionalism. Of course, to gather a fuller understanding of *adivasi* identity in Jharkhand, one needs to question how anthropological representations are internalised by *adivasi* activists, and how they relate to histories of *adivasi* resistance to colonial and post-colonial policies and practices.

While these movements for imagining Jharkhand usually begin in the cities, they can spread through kinship to more remote rural areas through the engagement of these activists in villages where they have families and friends, and through their involvement in non-governmental organisations and through the participation of rural *adivasi* elites. It is thus possible that these imaginations of

Jharkhand will filter to villages like Tapu where the poorest *adivasis* may gain new visions of what it might mean to have the State of Jharkhand, therefore transforming their understandings of the state itself.

Some of the imaginations of the Jharkhandi national community being proposed by the *adivasi* activists might square with the visions of poorer *adivasi* villagers. In Tapu, for example, a revitalisation of the self-governance system of the *parha* by members of the *adivasi* activists in recent years has had some support from ordinary villagers (Shah 2010). While this can be seen as one sign of success for the *adivasi* activists to celebrate, I would like to sound some warnings here. The first is that their re-appropriation in the politics of local leaders, for example MLAs (members of the state's legislative assembly) in Bero, who are trying to mediate the boundary between the state and the rural *adivasis*, might result in the local MLAs being discredited by poor *adivasis*, such as the Mundas of Tapu, and hence also lead to their discrediting the revitalisation of the *parha*. The second is that, in the case of the *parha,* the local systems of self-governance are significant for these sections because they represent a different kind of politics from the amoral politics that they associate with the state. The Mundas valorise an alternative form of politics, a politics that is indivisible from the sacred realm, and where the authority of the *parha* is underpinned by its connection to the spiritual world (Shah 2010). And lastly, in attempting to 'civilise' what they see as spirit worship, the secular imaginings of the *parha*, such as those being promoted by various activists and NGOs, are significantly different and at odds with the intimate sacral-polity link that is the basis of *parha* legitimacy in villages like Tapu.

Other visions of the Jharkhandi regional community being proposed by the *adivasi* activists are more obviously different from the social experiences of many Munda in Tapu. For instance, the Mundas are very aware that people around them speak several different languages and often more than one at the same time. And though they have learnt to identify themselves strategically as *adivasi* to NGO *wallahs* and state officials (cf. Mosse 2005), identity is of course processual as well as relative and Mundas are far more comfortable thinking of themselves in relation to different contexts. For example, as villagers of Tapu rather than Bero; as tenants in relation to *zamindars*; or as the members of certain kin groups and not others, or clans they can or cannot marry into; or groups such as Munda rather than Oraon or Maheli.

And still other visions of Jharkhandi regionalism more obviously further marginalise many of the villages like Tapu. In particular, I am concerned about the ecological nationalism, to use the term of Cederlof and Sivaramakrishnan (2005), that is being produced in Jharkhand by the activists who link up their cultural and political aspirations with the programme of *adivasis* as natural conservationists and environmental protectors through movements to save their forests. Cederlof and Sivaramakrishnan (2005) argue that such ethnic movements espoused around ideas of the environment are seen not just as reaffirming cultural identity but also as claims to territory and resources. On the one hand, this ecological nationalism incarcerates the poorest *adivasis* to the margins of idea of the Jharkhand state as a result of their alleged ties to their land and their need to protect these claims, and on the other hand it makes them suffer the violent consequences of the romantic ideas of their love for and worship of nature.

When *adivasis* are produced as 'sons of the soil', as morally and spiritually rooted in their land, their migration out of Jharkhand, even seasonally in search of work, becomes a problem that has taken the shape of anti-migration campaigns by Jharkhandi activists (Munda 2000a). For the activists such migration is a threat to the region as an imagined community of the same people living in the same place, and indicative of the history of displacement that affects marginal *adivasis* throughout India. However, back in Tapu this migration can represent, amongst other things, a space of escape from village constraints, a space in which the poorest feel they are to a certain extent free (Shah 2006).

Moreover, the other side of this ecological immobility, in the imagery of the *adivasi* worship of and love for nature, is costing lives in Jharkhand. Activists reinvent nature worshipping festivals such as Sarhul (flower festival) to mark Jharkhandi religion and regional culture, while in the rural areas these festivals are about pleasing and thanking malevolent and benevolent spirits by sacrificing animals, not coconuts, and with plenty of rice beer (Shah 2010). And most worryingly, the activists are significantly absent when the rural poor spend night after night chasing elephants that are killing people, destroying their homes and crops. The rural poor's voices remain unheard when they contradict the activists' nature loving ideas, when they want to chop down the forests that may have attracted wild elephants to the area (Shah 2010).

Conclusion

Whose imagined community, to draw on Benedict Anderson's (1983) phrase, is Jharkhand?[10] Recent discussions have drawn attention to the fact that nationalism is a political programme that is unquestionably modern – that the very notion of a nation with a fixed, 'given' cultural identity is a sign of success of a whole array of practices in naturalising that identity. They remind us to be sceptical of the claims for a separate Jharkhand State being underpinned by the idea that the region is characterised by a bounded and distinct indigenous cultural identity, which is almost an 'archaic survival' from a remote age. Promoting a focus on the regional, as an alternative and more flexible analytical category to the national, local or global, Sivaramakrishnan and Agrawal (2003) importantly see the national as a variant or as a species of the regional genus. They draw attention to the performative discourses that constitute the region, whether at the subnational, the national or supranational levels. In some contexts, such as Jharkhand, the region in and of itself is a performative discourse. I would contend that the Jharkhandi material shows the importance of tracing the continuities between the performative discourses of the region and those of the nation. The region is as much a historical construction as the nation.

In this chapter I have sought to examine the multiple ways in which different people have engaged, or not, in the imagination of the Jharkhand State. The inspiration for this endeavour came from the lack of concern with the formation of Jharkhand amongst some *adivasis* I lived with in Tapu. Ernest Gellner (1983) begins his thoughtful survey of nationalism with the idea that nationalism is the political principle which holds that the political and the national unit should be one.[11] For him it follows that,

> the problem of nationalism does not arise for stateless societies. If there is no state, one obviously cannot ask whether or not its boundaries are congruent with the limits of nations. ... The existence of politically centralised units *(the state)*, and of a moral-political climate in which such centralised units are taken for granted and are treated as normative, is a necessary though by no means a sufficient condition of nationalism.
>
> (Gellner 1983: 4)

Gellner thus points out that the problem of nationalism does not arise where there is no state. Gellner has been criticised on a number of fronts which include being too functionalist, failing to account for nationalism in non-industrial society and resurgences of nationalism in post-industrial societies, and not being helpful in explaining the passions generated by nationalism (cf. Hall 1998). While my purpose here is not to analyse Gellner's theories of nationalism, the Tapu Munda material does suggest an additional dimension to Gellner's contribution. Even in places where the state exists, the development of a nationalist or regionalist sentiment can be limited amongst people who do not embrace the idea of the state itself.

Baviskar has noted how, amongst some *adivasi* groups, the Indian nationalist struggle for independence received little attention.[12] But more generally, some scholars deemed unintelligible the western liberal ideas of the postcolonial state exported to India by its modernising bourgeoisie for its subaltern populations at the time of Independence. Kaviraj (1984, 1991, 1997) and Chatterjee (1986, 1993), following Gramsci, argue that social transformation was not driven from within society but was a function of domination through a state-bureaucratic agency and a 'passive revolution' that substituted planning for political reform. In this broader framework, the fight for Jharkhand and its particular symbols of ethno-regionalism could be seen, as has been argued by some (Damodaran 2006) as a struggle for hegemony in the political arena, a struggle which more truly represents the vernacular masses. Yet, as has been warned by Karlsson (2003) and Ghosh (2006), the arrival of new transnational discourses of indigeneity generates a set of political leaders from Jharkhand perceived by these anthropologists as distant from a grassroots base and grassroots concern, thereby locating authentic *adivasi* subjecthood at the local level. As I have argued here, if viewed from the perspective of some of the poorest populations in the rural areas, Jharkhand's ethno-regionalism remains a passive revolution of elite urban middle class activists that is little supported by the masses, figured here by my informants at Tapu. There remains a significant distance between middle class *adivasi* leaders and Jharkhand's subaltern classes.

In any region, there will of course be multiple and contested imaginings of that region which are intimately linked to each other. Munda imaginations coexist with that of a higher caste village elite who have indeed celebrated the formation of Jharkhand State, not least because of the hope that this decentralisation will bring the state closer to them and aid their ability to colonise it. This elite, I have suggested, reproduces Munda imaginations of the state. That many Mundas did not know or care about Jharkhand's independence is the result both of their historical experience of *sarkar,* and the way in which *sarkar* has been represented to them by village elites.

Munda imaginings of Jharkhand, however, have the potential for transformation through the work of Jharkandi activists who spearheaded the struggle for autonomy and who are prolifically reimagining the Jharkhandi regional community, through the re-invention of indigenous rituals, symbols and traditions. At one level it is possible that these activists may cause people in villages like Tapu to identify with a regional community and as a result transform their moral ideas of the state. However, I have suggested that some of the images of the Jharkhandi community being reproduced by these activists are starkly at odds with the social experiences of the villagers, even serve to marginalise them further and will continue their alienation from the state. As such, situated within the broader inequalities of the area, a widely shared imagination of Jharkhand will remain a subject of long-term contest that may well intensify.

Notes

1 I take this title from that of Sudipta Kaviraj's essay (1993).
2 Demands for a separate state were first made to the Simon Commission in 1928 and, after Independence, to the States Reorganisation Commission (SRC) in 1954.
3 The shift from the term 'tribe' to '*adivasi*' has a long history (cf. Shah 2010). The contested history of the term 'tribe' goes back to colonial times when 'race' and racial ideology were the norms of a broader political order and the anthropological construction of the country's aboriginals as 'primitive' tribes. Colonial policies of subordination, domination and protection united a wide variety of communities living in India's forests and hills. In the late 1920s this shared history became the grounds for a political movement, with its centre in what is now Jharkhand, to better protect the rights of the people concerned through the demand for a separate state in the Jharkhand region. In this struggle, the term *adivasi* as a more positive political identity replaced the more pejorative 'tribal' or 'primitive' peoples.
4 All names are pseudonyms.
5 When I spent three months in the corridors of the Block Development Office in Bero, the attitude amongst the staff towards the *adivasis* of Jharkhand was that they were beyond development because they were *jangli,* literally people of the jungle with a wild and savage character.
6 Not everybody from such a background (landlord, revenue collecting or educated) became the brokers of state development resources, though people from this background generally did. In a study of local elites in Orissa and Gujarat, S.K. Mitra draws attention to the social heterogeneity of local elites, arguing that adivasis and *harijans* were a significant proportion of these elite. However, Mitra does note a significant

difference between the two states, arguing that in Orissa, *adivasis* and harijans were not dominant amongst the local elites. In the part of rural Jharkhand, the older analysis of Frankel applies and the state has been colonised by and extended itself through existing local elites, and has been the means of their continued domination (see Frankel 1978; Mitra 1991).

7 In 1910, the Dacca Students Union, which later became the *Chota Nagpur Unnati Samaj* (Chotanagpur Improvement Society), was formed by missionaries from the Gossner Evangelical Lutheran (GEL) Church in order to demand better educational facilities and job opportunities for tribal students. Following this, the more popular Roman Catholics formed the *Chota Nagpur Catholic Sabha,* which won two seats in the 1937 pre-Independence elections. In 1938, these Christian *sabhas* merged to form the *Chota Nagpur Adivasi Mahsabha.* By 1950, realising that it needed support from non-tribals, the *Adivasi Mahasabha* renamed itself the Jharkhand Party and extended its membership to non-tribals. In the first State Assembly Elections in 1952, the Jharkhand Party, as the main opposition to Congress in the Bihar Legislative Council, secured over 70 per cent of the 34 assembly seats reserved for Scheduled Tribes in Bihar. In 1954, it put forward the proposal for a separate Jharkhand State in to the States Reorganisation Commission.

8 As Corbridge (2002: 57) argues, the break-up of Bihar hardly signalled a success of India's democracy; the reasons had far more to do with political bargains between a restricted number of elite actors than with pressures from below. The BJP and National Democratic Alliance (NDA) government in New Delhi, that granted Jharkhand independence, had the intention of weakening Laloo Yadav and the *Rashtriya Janata Dal* (RJD) in Bihar, as the separation of Jharkhand from Bihar would deprive the latter of substantial sales and excise revenues.

9 See Amita Baviskar (2005a) and Nandini Sundar (2005).

10 Until the 1980s, ideas of nationhood had rarely been subjected to sustained intellectual scrutiny. However, recent works, particularly those by Anderson and Gellner, have pointed out that nations are not natural entities but social constructions. Anthropologists have since fruitfully discussed Anderson's problems of imagining the national community in terms of rites and symbols (see McDonald 1990; Verdery 1991). They have concentrated on the way in which intellectuals and cultural producers have made the rituals and symbols of nationalism – pursuing a line of inquiry also opened up by Hobsbawm and Ranger (1983).

11 Anthropology has been slow to take on Gellner's theory of nationalism. For Gellner, nationalism is the result of a process of a transition to industrial society. Cognitive and economic growth of industrial society requires a shared system of communication, a necessary cultural homogeneity. This is an argument for the political pre-eminence of culturally homogenous units that is the basis of nationalism. The cultural homogeneity of nationalism is established through mass schooling by the state.

12 Baviskar (2005b) quotes Aurora (1972: 210) as having said, 'in 1942, when all of British India was rocked by the struggles of the nationalists, only a few people in Alirajpur knew about it. The tribals were not even remotely aware of the nationalist movement'.

References

Anderson, B. (1983) *Imagined Communities*, New York: Verso.

Baviskar, A. (2005a) 'Adivasi Encounters with Hindu Nationalism in Madhya Pradesh', *Economic and Political Weekly*, 40(48): 5105–13.

—— (2005b) *In the Belly of the River: tribal conflicts over development in the Narmada Valley*, New Delhi: Oxford University Press.

Bosu Mullick, S. (2003) 'Introduction', in R.D. Munda and S. Bosu Mullick (eds) *The*

Jharkhand Movement: Indigenous Peoples' Struggle for Autonomy in Jharkhand, Copenhagen: International Work Group for Indigenous Affairs and New Delhi: Uppal Publishing House, iv–xvii.

Cederlof, G. and Sivaramakrishnan, K. (eds) (2005) *Ecological Nationalisms: nation, livelihoods and identities in South Asia*, New Delhi: Permanent Black.

Chatterjee, P. (1986) *Nationalist Thought and the Colonial World: a derivative discourse*, 2nd edn, London: Zed Books.

—— (1993) *The Nation and its Fragments: colonial and postcolonial histories*, Princeton: Princeton University Press.

Corbridge, S. (2002) 'The Continuing Struggle for India's Jharkhand: democracy, decentralisation and the politics of names and numbers', *Commonwealth and Comparative Politics*, 40(3): 55–71.

Damodaran, V. (2006) 'Indigenous Forests: rights, discourses, and resistance in Chotanagpur, 1860–2002', in G. Cederlof and K. Sivaramakrishnan (eds) *Ecological Nationalisms: nature, livelihoods, and identities in South Asia*, Seattle and London: University of Washington Press.

Das, V. (1992) *Jharkhand: caste over the graves*, New Delhi: Inter-India Publications.

Frankel, F. (1978) *India's Political Economy, 1947–1977: the gradual revolution*, New Delhi: Oxford University Press.

Gellner, E. (1983) *Nations and Nationalisms*, London: Blackwell.

Ghosh, K. (2006) 'Between Global Flows and Local Dams: indigenousness, locality and the transnational sphere in Jharkhand, India', *Cultural Anthropology*, 21(4): 501–34.

Hall, J. (1998) *The State of the Nation: Ernest Gellner and the theory of nationalism*, Cambridge: Cambridge University Press.

Hardiman, D. (1987) *The Coming of the Devi: Adivasi assertion in Western India*, New Delhi: Oxford University Press.

Hobsbawm, E. and Ranger, T. (1983) *The Invention of Tradition*, Cambridge: Cambridge University Press.

Jha, J.C. (1990) *History of the Freedom Movement in Chotanagpur (1885–1947)*, Patna: Kashi Prasad Jayaswal Research Institute.

Karlsson, B. (2003) 'Anthropology and the 'Indigenous Slot': claims to and debates about indigenous people's status in India', *Critique of Anthropology*, 23(4): 402–23.

Kaviraj, S. (1984) 'On the Crisis of Political Institutions in India', *Contributions to Indian Sociology (n.s.)*, 18(2): 223–43.

—— (1991) 'On State, Society and Discourse in India', in J. Manor (ed.) *Rethinking Third World Politics*, Harlow: Longman, 72–99.

—— (1993) 'The Imaginary Institution of India', *Subaltern Studies: Volume 7*, 1–39.

—— (1997) 'The Modern State in India', in M. Doornbos and S. Kaviraj (eds) *Dynamics of State Formation: India and Europe Compared*, New Delhi: Sage Publications, 225–50.

McDonald, M. (1990) *We are not French! language, culture and identity in Brittany*, London: Routledge.

Mitra, S.K. (1991) 'Room to Manoeuvre in the Middle: local elites, political action and the state in India', *World Politics*, 43(3): 390–413.

Mosse, D. (2005) *Cultivating Development: an ethnography of aid policy and practice*, London: Pluto Press.

Munda, R.D. (2000a) *Autonomy Movements in Tribal India*, Ranchi: Department of Tribal and Regional Languages, Ranchi University.

—— (2000b) *Adi-Dharam, Religious Beliefs of the Adivasis of India: An outline of religious reconstruction with special reference to the Jharkhand region*, Chaibasa: Sarini and BIRSA.

Prakash, A. (2001) *Jharkhand: politics of development and identity*, Hydrebad: Orient Longman.

Shah, A. (2006) 'The Labour of Love: seasonal migration from Jharkhand to the brick kilns of other states in India', *Contributions to Indian Sociology (n.s.)*, 40(1): 91–118.

—— (2007) 'Keeping the State Away: democracy, politics and the state in India's Jharkhand', *Journal of the Royal Anthropological Institute*, 13(1): 129–45.

—— (2009) 'Morality, Corruption and the State: insights from Jharkhand, Eastern India', *Journal of Development Studies*, 45(3): 295–313.

—— (2010) *In the Shadows of the State: Indigenous Politics, Environmentalism and Insurgency in Jharkhand, India*, Durham, NC: Duke University Press.

Sivaramakrishnan, K. and Agrawal, A. (eds) (2003) *Regional Modernities: the cultural politics of development in India*, New Delhi: Oxford University Press.

Skaria, A. (1997) 'Shades of Wildness Tribe, Caste, and Gender in Western India', *The Journal of Asian Studies*, 56(3): 726–45.

Sundar, N. (2005) 'Teaching to Hate: RSS pedagogical programme', *Economic and Political Weekly*, 38(16): 1605–12.

Verdery, K. (1991) *National Ideology Under Socialism: Identity and Cultural Politics in Ceausescu's Romania*, Berkeley: University of California Press.

Weiner, M. (1988) *Sons of the Soil: migration and ethnic conflict in India*, New Delhi: Oxford University Press.

Index